# TOURISM INTEGRATES THE WORLD
# 旅游整合世界

伍 飞 著

图书在版编目（CIP）数据

旅游整合世界/伍飞著．—北京：北京大学出版社，2008.1
ISBN 978-7-301-12622-6

Ⅰ.①旅…　Ⅱ.①伍…　Ⅲ.①旅游业—经济史—世界　Ⅳ.①F591.9

中国版本图书馆 CIP 数据核字（2007）第 126476 号

| | |
|---|---|
| 书　　　　名： | 旅游整合世界 |
| 著作责任者： | 伍　飞　著 |
| 策 划 编 辑： | 李　玥 |
| 责 任 编 辑： | 李　玥 |
| 标 准 书 号： | ISBN 978-7-301-12622-6/G·2150 |
| 出　版　者： | 北京大学出版社 |
| 地　　　　址： | 北京市海淀区成府路 205 号　100871 |
| 电　　　　话： | 邮购部 62752015　发行部 62750672 |
| | 编辑部 62765126　出版部 62754962 |
| 网　　　　址： | http://www.pup.cn |
| 电 子 信 箱： | zyjy@pup.cn　新浪官方微博：@北京大学出版社 |
| 印　刷　者： | 三河市博文印刷有限公司 |
| 发　行　者： | 北京大学出版社 |
| 经　销　者： | 新华书店 |
| | 787 毫米×1092 毫米　16 开本　25.25 印张　602 千字 |
| | 2008 年 1 月第 1 版　2015 年 9 月第 4 次印刷 |
| 定　　　　价： | 52.00 元 |

未经许可，不得以任何方式复制或抄袭本书之部分或全部内容。
**版权所有，侵权必究**
举报电话：(010) 62752024　电子信箱：fd@pup.pku.edu.cn

全世界旅游者，联合起来！

——作者

*Tourists all over the world，unite！*

*—author*

# 再版代序一

## 为人类的共同利益而祈祷！
——读伍飞《旅游整合世界》

智 圣

人类究竟有没有共同利益？成立于1968年的罗马俱乐部在1972年出版的《增长的极限》一书中提出，物质生产的无节制增长正在造成环境危机和资源危机，从而对整个人类的生存构成威胁。显然这一思想已经包含了对全人类共同利益的存在的肯定。在此之前于1955年发表的《罗素—爱因斯坦宣言》，也对全人类共同利益的存在以及人类改变思维方式的必要性做过更为突出而又简明的强调。

世界进入新时期以来，人类核武库问题、生态问题、资源问题等日益凸显，特别是随着经济全球化步伐的加快，人们对全人类共同利益的关注与日俱增，相关研究逐渐成为学术讨论的热点。只是在我国，到了20世纪90年代才大规模地投入到全球化的历史潮流之中。

随着中国改革开放的日益深入，发达国家早已遇到的一些问题也一一出现在我们面前，不论是自身的经济发展，还是所面临的各种冲突，使我们对人类历史正在经历的这场深刻变革有了越来越清楚的认识。全人类共同利益已经成为我们在处理国内外各种问题时，不能不加以考虑的重要因素。

也就是在这样的历史大背景中，我有幸捧读了我国青年思想家伍飞先生的再版著作《旅游整合世界》。这本被誉为旅游界"圣经"的论著，围绕"旅游整合世界 人类共享文明"的核心理念所构建的理论体系，旨在为维护人类的整体利益而提供国际政经新秩序建设的必然通道及指示方向。

在全球化浪潮迅速而深入发展的今天，中国理应对人类的未来给予更多的关注。作者的这个思想迄今得到了世界60余个国家驻华大使的赞同和解读，《旅游整合世界》的和平理念在整个世界呼声越来越高。我相信，本书的再版一定能够引起人们对人类共同利益的重视，促进对它更系统更深入的研究，并对我国的全球化问题研究起到重要的推进作用。

亨廷顿的《文明的冲突》曾引发了全球学界、政界的滔天巨澜，在世纪之交以及新世纪不断的冲突中，人们隐隐约约看到了"文化"的影子。在众多的诘问面前，亨廷顿不解地问："如果不是文明，那是什么？"

一位外交家说："我们需要解释'为什么各种文化都有自己一套不同的价值观以及这些价值观的含义，世界必须摆脱那种对各种文化和各种宗教的肤浅解释'。我们要做的'不是消除不同的价值观，而是提倡更好地理解、更好地尊重别的文化'"。

西方中左翼政党吉登斯说，全球化时代的世界，是一个"失控的世界"，"我们从来不能成为我们自己的主人，但是我们能够而且必须找到驯服这个失控世界的方法"。在某种意义上来说，《旅游整合世界》理论就是当代西方中左翼政党"驯服这个失控世界"的方法。

作为经济全球化时代人类文明发展的主要方式，"旅游整合世界"具有其独特的性质和特征。正如伍飞先生在《旅游整合世界》中所表述：政治的力量常常产生地域的壁垒，宗教的力量又往往导致心灵的隔阂，只有旅游，才能使不同种族、不同信仰、不同文化的人们走到一起，共同分享人类文明的成果。

像人类文化的发展永远不会停止自己的脚步一样，"旅游整合世界"所体现的人类文化本身所包含的矛盾运动也不会停止。人类社会只要向前发展，就不可能抛弃这种文化的整合过程。文化冲突的互不相让和文化融合的美好向往，在旅游整合世界的长河中不断纠合交错，形成了人类文化发展史上一道真实而靓丽的风景。

在人类"旅游整合世界"的不同阶段、不同层次，人类文化的冲突与融合具有不同的表现。在科技高度发达的今天，如果人类还要生存下去，我们就需要一种全新的思考。人们必须根本地改变对待他人的态度以及未来的观点。武力必须不再作为政治的手段！

在科技革命日新月异的岁月里，世界诸多有识之士早已心知肚明：今天，留给人类的时间已经不多了；从过去到现在，我们一直在进行着不同的思考，如果我们失败，人类将面临文明的消失。

历史上唯一不变的是变化。在人类事务中，非暴力的力量定会加强，而暴力的力量则会削弱。建立在民族国家基础上的世界体系可能会让位于建立在文明认同基础上的世界体系，就好像对核武器的依赖会被对核武器广泛厌恶所取代。

有许多人相信，如今的世界正处在重大转型的边缘。对于《旅游整合世界》中关于利益"共享"的新认识可能预示着一个无法预料的激动人心的未来。之如互联网的出现,这是科技史上的里程碑,为人们带来了廉价分享信息的前所未有的机遇。在这样一个相互交流、交往达到史无前例的新阶段,谁敢说其他里程碑式的成就不可能实现?!

人类的每一次转化抑或升级都建立在新的理论和意识形态基础上,或者说建立在重新描绘宇宙和人的本性的基础上。在历史长河中,人类对新事物的认知不断地提高和升华,新发明与新发现正推动着社会前进和科技发展。人类对这个世界的探索是无穷无尽的,发现和发明也永无终止。

正如爱迪生所言:一项发明创造会带来更多的发明创造。《旅游整合世界》是一本旨在引领读者探索改变人类命运、发现人类文明的奥秘与规律,并在此基础上有所发明创造的思想著作。读《旅游整合世界》能让读者树立正确的思想观,增强创新能力,激发读者关注人类社会发展的重大问题,培养创新思维,产生创造文明的浓烈兴趣。

最后,让我们在为人类的共同目标作祈祷之时,也衷心祈愿伍飞先生——一位为人类的和平运动摇旗呐喊的思想家,在推动人类和平与进步的道路上百尺竿头更进一步,再创辉煌!

是为序。

智圣辛卯年秋于北京香山

(此文原载于 2012 年 5 月 18 日《世界报》,此处有删改。智圣,又名乐后圣,亚太地区著名安全战略思想家,近年著作有《国家和平发展战略》《医道——身国共治的人本文明》《资本的整合》《文化产业浪潮》《文化军事战略》《祈祷太空和平》等近千万字作品。)

# 再版代序二

## 改变世界的文明征程
### ——读《旅游整合世界》

**曾 曦**

  在人类发展史上，改变世界格局或历史进程的，往往是某种思想或理念。这些思想出现和形成在特定的社会形态里，当它以看似平凡的方式出现时，一些人可能将它作为物质世界的一阵异响。但是，在一些智者看来，这声异响，却成为高悬在世界上空的黄钟大吕。这声异响成为改变世界的先声。伍飞的《旅游整合世界》给我们传递的正是这样一种声音。

  近些年来，随着全球经济一体化进程的加快，旅游业高度迅猛的发展备受瞩目。在世界范围内，旅游作为一项越来越多人参与的人类共同行为，正在以它独特的方式实现不同地域、民族、国家在经济、社会、文化等不同领域的多重对话；而旅游业的繁荣也在促进现代文明的蓬勃发展。从物质、政治、精神的立体层面不断催熟着现代文明更加丰硕的成果，在时间与空间的纵横里完成有效的整合，达到人类共享文明的愿望。伍飞先生正是在这样一个全球化视野之下，在宏观上，提出了"旅游整合世界，人类共享文明"的新定位。

  在多种行为方式当中，旅游永远具有源源不断的生命力，随着时间的推进，旅游也被不断解读，并让研究者和参与者重新寻找其在社会进程中的新坐标。在本书中，作者对旅游给予了一个全新的定义。他认为：旅游是为满足人的多种多样的审美需求和好奇心而向目的地运动所产生的各种关系的总和。这一定位，从核心上诠释了旅游的本质。

  古代的人们从来没有两手空空周游列国，现代人虽然已经抛开一切繁杂事务出行，但他们也背起了沉沉的行囊穿越在千山万水之间，没有人是为了完成纯粹的行走，他们的脚步都承载着文明的使命。当然，前后两者的旅行实际上并非一个范畴，前者附带明显的功利性，在时间的长河里进行了华丽的转身而成为后者，这也是一种进程。正如该书所言，形式多样的帝王巡游是为了维护统治，弘扬功绩，炫耀威力，震慑臣民；功利明显的士人游说是为了完成自我价值提升；艰苦探索的地理考察是为了采集地理样本，执着顽强的宗教远足传播各种宗教意识；只有少数的文人漫游才仅为了逍遥在山水之间。在当前多元背景之下，大多数人被新型的文化环境冲洗之后，旅游，在聚合了更多的元素后，正在渐淡功利为主体的远足方式，以一种更加自然、有效的旅游方式完善旅游本身的纯粹性。这种纯粹，成为文化融合和文明交流的最为有效的方式。这正是伍飞的《旅游整合世界》的一个未来指向。

回顾人类发展历史，当那些帝王的手指顽强地划过大块大块的疆土的时候，政治的手段常常让后人看到孤悬的地域更加狼烟四起。譬如春秋战国政治"整合"。而后来大秦帝国实现对六国统一，也仅仅是在历史环境促使下完成的历史使命，虽然起到了整合的作用，但我情愿相信这只是一种被动的局部整合，而不是有效的。有时候甚至会适得其反，导致地域的壁垒也越垒越高。始皇帝修的长城不就是一个壁垒的象征吗？所以伍飞说，"政治的力量常常产生地域的壁垒，宗教的力量，又往往导致心灵的隔阂，只有旅游，才能使不同种族、不同文化、不同信仰的人们走到一起，共同分享人类文明的成果。"宗教试图通过教化人心的方式天下播种，浸淫在"自我完美"的意识形态之下，传教士周游列国走南闯北，试图用思想的教化去整合人类，然而，人心的隔阂却又使得这种"神圣"的使命寸步难行。那么，人类的未来在哪里？现代文明催生的社会，已经开始翘首企盼一种能够真正统合资源的社会行为和思想，来为人类的未来找到一条融合之路。

在不断的选择与摒弃当中，历史和真理的面纱正一层层抽去，我们看见了一张叫做"旅游"的面颊，这时候，我们才发现，不管是在古代还是现代，无论是东方还是西方，这种"脸"都格外有"亲和力"，正是它，在人类历史的发展中，以一种隐形的方式和历史随行，并传递着人类的文明。玄奘的行走达成了中西文化交流的重要成果，郑和七下西洋成就了半个世界的经济、文化等诸多方面的交流与合作，还有无数个马可·波罗的足音，都在不断地证明旅游是一种有效的整合世界的方式。从这点上来看，成吉思汗的铁蹄抵不上一对穿布鞋的脚，拿破仑的军刀还不如旅游者的一根扶杖。

伍飞是一个智者，他的"旅游整合世界"的理念已经得到60个国家的大使的认同和解读。一个理念能引发世界范围内的共鸣，这是他对社会的一个重大贡献。沿着他的思想，我们再去旅游，就会发现，无论是古代带有强烈功利性的旅行，还是现在超脱于物质之上的精神行走，它始终包容了地域内涵和文化交融，旅游的过程就是一个资源整合、文明共享的过程。从这点上，我们有更多的理由相信，人类的脚步能够走出地域的壁垒和心灵的隔阂，历史最终选择旅游去完成整合世界的使命。

（此文原载于2008年1月23日《中国旅游报》，此处有删改。作者系新华社高级记者。）

# 再版代序三

## 深化旅游的文化思考
——读《旅游整合世界》有感

**朱昌勤**

近日读到北京大学出版社出版的《旅游整合世界》一书。仅看书名，我就读而快之，眼睛为之一亮，感觉为之一新。这是妙语，这是"妙计"。很有思想力，很有创造力，很有张扬力。"旅游整合世界"这个提法，很新奇很大胆。

旅游能整合世界？粗读生疑，细想有理。其实这是一个新而不奇的问题。这个问题的无疑答案，早已被现实所证实。何谓旅游？今古有别。古时旅游，舟马天下，足履山水。今时旅游，时空旷广，益利博长，且旅且游，且闻且见，且乐且健，且学且思。可谓是无所不可及、无所不可有、无所不可为的特大业体。现在，旅游业已是世界通业，各个国家都在打旅游牌。旅游早已冲破时空局限，不再是有权者、有钱者、有闲者的专利享受，不再是"知者乐水，仁者乐山"的高雅话题。到处都在发掘旅游资源，到处都在发展旅游产业。面之广，速之快，难于估考。而正是这个特大业体的拉动和驱动，使相关相应的多种产业一俱腾飞。全球游业突起，实当刮目相看。专家张广瑞有文说：不到30年的时间，人们对旅游的理解有了许多重大变化，它从"民间外交"变成"创汇产业"、"无烟工业"、"无形贸易"，后来又被称作"先导产业"、"强势产业"、"支柱产业"，近来人们又开始把它叫做"环保产业"、"学习产业"、"文化产业"和"动力产业"……另有专家称，旅游业的不断快速发展，在一定程度上会使世界经济出现结构性变化。

"旅游整合世界"是一个既有现实性又有前瞻性的观点。旅游不但对于世界的经济发展有促动、调节和整合作用，更值得注重的是，在人类文明舞台上，它具有力不可遏、势不可断、功不可没的整合功力，即软整合力。世界上没有哪一种产业，具有旅游业那样大的包容性、运动性和多元性，它使多种文化、多种信息、多种信仰在自身演进的过程中，得到或有形或无形或实际或理性的交流、融汇、整合和升华。它没有国界。它不问肤色。它不择语种。它使人们在观赏世界的同时，广泛地、自由地交流、沟通、感受智慧和文明成果，从而又去创造更美好的世界。旅游是人类生活中最文明、最和谐、最美好的方式，也就是人类构建大同理念的"最优方法"。这就是旅游使世界变成有充分自由度和满足感的"地球村"的伟力所在。这是一种长久的永恒的潜在力量，作用于现在更作用于未来。"旅游整合世界"这一思想的前瞻性正在于此。

（此文原载于2008年4月10日《人民日报》，作者系中国著名作家、高级记者）

# Article one used as a perpace for the second edition

## Pray for the common interests of humanity!

——Review of *Tourism Integrates the World* Written by Wu Fei

Zhisheng

Are there any common interests for humanity? The Club of Rome, inaugurated in 1968, argued in the *Limits to Growth* published in 1972 that the immoderate growth of material production was resulting in crises to environment and resources, thereby threatening all humanity. Apparently, this standpoint confirmed the existence of common interests of humanity. *The Russell-Einstein Manifesto*, issued in 1955, more explicitly and concisely stressed the existence of common interests of humanity and the urgency for humanity to change its mode of thinking.

New era of the world has witnessed the emergence of many increasingly acute problems such as nuclear arsenals, ecological damage as well as the lack of resources. As the people throughout the world are paying more and more attention to the common interests of humanity, related issues have also become hotspots for scholarly argument. In China, however, the participation in the globalization trend just began in the 1990s.

With the reform and opening up continuously going forward, China is gradually faced up to problems that have entangled those developed countries. Through its own economic development and a variety of emerging conflicts, we gain a more thorough understanding of this profound revolution in the course of human history. The common interests of humanity have become an important element we must weigh when coping with various problems both at home and abroad.

Under such a historical background, I am fortunate enough to read a book named

*Tourism Integrates the World* (the 2$^{nd}$ Edition), written by Wu Fei, a young Chinese ideologist. This book, eulogized as "the Bible of tourism", centers on the core concept, "Tourism integrates the world and humans share civilization", to fabricate its theoretical system, aiming to direct the way for reconstructing the international political and economic order and therefore safeguarding the common interests of humanity.

Today, as globalization rapidly progresses around the world, China ought to pay more attention to the future of humanity. The author's proposal has been endorsed and read up so far by more than 60 foreign ambassadors in China, and the peace concept contained in "Tourism Integrates the World" gains more and more advocacy throughout the world. I believe the reprint of this book will surely arouse the worldwide concern about the common interests of humanity, boost more systematic and profound studies on related issues, and also fuel the globalization researches in China.

*The Clash of Civilizations and the Remaking of World Order*, the works of Huntington, once astounded both the academic and political circles on a world basis. Behind ceaseless conflicts at the turn of the century and in the new century, "culture" has been partly hidden and partly visible. Faced with so much criticism, Huntington responded by asking "If not civilization, what"?

A diplomatist stressed that "we need to figure out the reason why every culture has its own value as well as the significance of such value and the world must ward off any superficial interpretation on one culture or religion". What we should do is to more thoroughly understand and revere other cultures, rather than eliminate any alien values.

Anthony Giddens, a well-known scholar from western center-left parties, argues that the world in the globalization era is a "runaway world". "Although we can never manipulate our own fates, but we can and also have to find the ways to tame this runaway world." To some extent, the theory in "Tourism Integrates the World" can lend aid to modern western center-left parties in their practice to "tame this runaway world".

As the principle development way of human civilization is in an era of economic globalization, *Tourism Integrates the World* has its unique characteristics. Just as Mr. Wu Fei has described, "while political power leads to regional barriers and religious power results in spiritual estrangement, only tourism is capable to congregate together the people from different races, religions and cultures, hereby impelling them to share the fruits of human civilization."

Just as human culture will never stop taking big strides forward, the cultural contradiction implied in "Tourism Integrates the World" will never suspend as well. The human society cannot shake off the endeavor of cultural integration at all during its development. The intensity of cultural conflict and the prospect of cultural integration are interlaced during the process when tourism unifies the world, forming an authentic and beautiful landscape in the history of human culture.

Relying on the stage or level that the process of Tourism Integrates The World has reached, the conflict and integration of cultures usually take on different appearances correspondingly. Nowadays, with highly advanced science and technology, mankind need adopt a brand-new thinking mode to live on and must ultimately transform the way to get along with others or the future. Force should not be used as the political approach any more...

Incessant scientific and technological revolution has awakened wise men all over the world to the reality that the situation is rather urgent for humanity now. We have been keeping thinking in a variety of ways in the past course of history. Once we failed, human civilization will be endangered.

The only eternal thing in history is change. As for mankind, the strength of non-violent effort will go up, while violent force will be gradually crippled. The world system grounded on national states will possibly change into the one based on mergence of civilization, just as the dependence upon nuclear weapons will finally be replaced by the extensive repulsion.

It is widely believed that the world is edging to a tremendous transformation. The viewpoint of "sharing" in *Tourism Integrates the World* may predict an unexpected and dramatic future. The emergence of such as space travel and internent is a milestone in the scientific and technological history, which creates unprecedented opportunities to share information at rather low cost. In such an era with historically peaking mutual communication and exchange, who can arbitrarily exclude any potential milestone achievements in the future?

Each transformation or advancement of humanity has been triggered by relevant new theories and ideologies, or the reinterpretation of universe and human nature. In the course of history, mankind continues to enhance and sublimate its recognition about newborn things, while up-to-date inventions and discoveries constantly push the society and technology forward. As mankind keeps probing into the world, more inventions and discoveries will spring up one after another.

Edison once said that one invention could stir up more inventions. "Tourism Integrates the World" is designed to inspire readers to grope for the secrets and principles on the fortune of humanity as well as human civilization, thereby making some inventions. This book is able to shape the ideas of readers, elevate their abilities of innovation, arouse them to concern those important issues related the development of human society, and become keenly interested in creating civilization.

Finally, while praying for the common objectives of humanity, I also sincerely hope Mr. Wu Fei, an ideologist persistently advocating the peace activities of mankind, could harvest more eminent fruits in his efforts to push forward the world peace and human progress.

The preface is hereby written.

By

zhisheng

The Fragrant Hill, Beijing 2011

(This article was first published in *World Journal* on May 18, 2012 and here has been revised. Zhisheng, also known as Le Housheng, is a famous security strategist and thinker in the Asia-Pacific region. He wrote many books, totaling more than 10 million words and his latest works including *Peaceful Development Strategy of a Country*, *Medical Doctrines*, *The Integration of Capitals*, *Cultural Industry*, *Cultural and Military Strategies* and *Wish the Space Peaceful*, etc. )

# Article two used as a preface for the second edition

## The Civilization Journey to Change the World

Zeng Xi

Usually, it is certain idea or concept that changed the world pattern or historical progress in the history of humanity. Such idea came into being in correspondingly specific social formations. When it turned up in a seemingly ordinary appearance, some might simply treat it as an abnormal sound in the material world, but those wise men would regard it as a prodigious blare resounding in the air throughout the world. That blare heralded the transformation of the world. Mr. Wu Fei's *Tourism Integrates the World* has sent forth such blare.

In recent years, as the global economic integration speed up, tourism has undergone swift and dazzling development. Nowadays, tourism has developed into a worldwide common human activity attracting more and more participants, promoting in a particular way the economic, social and cultural interactions of various regions, nations and states. Through the space-time integration, the prosperity of tourism also fertilizes modern civilization to develop by leaps and bounds and bear plentiful fruits, thereby realizing the dream to share the civilization by all mankind. Based on such a global vision, Mr. Wu Fei macroscopically advances his new viewpoint, i. e. "Tourism integrates the world and humans share civilization."

Among a variety of act ways, tourism has been endowed with the constant flow of vitality. Over time, tourism will continue to be interpreted and also relocated in the social advancement by researchers and participants. In this book, the author redefines tourism as "the sum total of various relationships created when tourists flock to the destinations to satisfy their authentic demands". This definition provides an essential illumination on tourism.

Traveling in the ancient times was rarely simply for the sake of sightseeing. In spite of the fact that modern men have left behind all the multifarious affairs out of their minds, they also shoulder the heavy "packages" on the journeys. Because objectively speaking, the purpose of traveling can not be confined to the simple sightseeing of an individual; each footstep taken in fact carries on the mission of the responsibility of civilization transmission. Certainly, the tours of above two sorts of tourists belong to different categories. The former is somehow utilitarian and narrowly able to develop into the latter through time. As the book indicates, multiform imperial ceremonial journeys aimed to reinforce the sovereignty and display sheer merits; those obviously utilitarian canvassing tours by scholars were meant to heighten their self-values; the laborious geographical surveys were to collect geographical samples; the unremitting religious hikes were conducted to disseminate various religious principles; and only few of literary men wonder about to enjoy the beauties of nature. Under a diversified background at present and as the majority of people are bathed in the new-style cultural environment, tourism has gathered more and more elements and gradually leaves behind the utilitarianism to be more natural, effective and unadulterated. Such pureness becomes the most effective way of cultural integration and exchange. This is rightly the expectation contained in Mr. Wu Fei's *Tourism Integrates the World*.

Reviewing the history of mankind, when those emperors wantonly swept their fingers over massive isolated territories on the map, people would see the warfare burst out there induced by political measures. Take the political integration occurring in Spring and Autumn Period for instance, although Qin Dynasty occupied other six kingdoms and met its historical mission, I'd rather say that it was some sort of passive and partial integration, not effective at all. Sometimes, such integration even has an exactly negative effect, heightening the regional barriers. Wasn't the Great Wall, constructed by the First Emperor of Qin, a symbol of such barriers? Consequently, Wu Fei argued that "while political power leads to regional barriers and religious power results in spiritual estrangement, only tourism is capable to congregate together the people from different races, religions and cultures, hereby impelling them to share the fruits of human civilization". Religion tries to popularize itself through moralizing people's hearts, so those missionaries, intoxicated with self-perfection, travel around different nations and endeavor futilely to integrate mankind through moralization. However, the people's estrangement frustrated their "sacred" efforts. Then, where is the future of humanity? The society born in modern civilization is looking forward to some social act and idea that is really capable to unify various resources and find the reasonable integration way for the future of humanity.

Article two used as a preface for the second edition

During repeated selection processes, history and truth have uncovered their veils layer by layer until the face of "tourism" emerges. Then we suddenly find that no matter in ancient times or today, in the East or the West, this gracious "face" has been quietly following the pace of human history and passing human civilization on from generation to generation. The journey of Xuanzang gave birth to the important fruits of Sino-Western cultural exchange; Zheng He's seven expeditions to the "Western Ocean" facilitate the economic and cultural communication and cooperation across half of the world; and there have been many foreigners coming to China as well, like Marco Polo. Above examples strongly prove that tourism is an extremely effective approach to integrate the world. Considering this, the iron heels of Genghis Khan's forces have been inferior by comparison to the feet wearing a pair of cloth shoes, and the saber of Napoleon has been shamed by a crutch of the tourist.

Wu Fei is a wise man and his concept of "Tourism Integrates the World" has gained widely supports from more than 60 foreign ambassadors in China, which is undoubtedly a remarkable contribution to the society. Following his idea, we will find in our future travels that both utilitarian tours in old ages and today's unadulterated tours are embedded with regional significance and cultural interaction. Therefore, the travel is actually a process of resource integration and civilization sharing. Due to this, we have more reasons to believe that mankind will break through the regional barriers and spiritual estrangement, and history will finally endue tourism with the mission to integrate the world.

(This article was first published in *China Tourism News* on January 23, 2008. The author is a senior reporter of Xinhua News Agency)

# Article three used as a preface for the second edition

## Deepen Cultural Reflection on Tourism

Zhu Changqin

I have read *Tourism Integrates the World* newly published by Peking University Press Recently. Before perusing its content, I have been deeply attracted by the title, which is both a witticism and good idea. The viewpoint of "tourism unifying the world" is really newfangled and audacious.

Is tourism capable to unify the world? It seems suspicious at first sight but turns out to be valid. As a fresh but not surprising question, its incontrovertible answer has been authenticated long ago. What is tourism? Its present definition is distinct from the past. In ancient ages, tourism referred to travel around the world by boats and horses and trudge over hills and rivers on foot. In contrast, today's tourism becomes an outsized activity, more extensive, easy and relaxed than ever before. Nowadays, all nations attach much importance to tourism as it has grown to be a worldwide industry. Meanwhile, tourism has broken through the space and time restriction. It is no longer the privilege of the authorized, wealthy, and leisure classes, or one of those especially elegant issues. At this stage, tourism resources are being explored nearly everywhere at an inestimable speed. It is such an oversized industry that propels forward a variety of related industries. The springing up of tourism industry is really stunning. "Within less than 30 years, the significance of tourism has severely changed. It has been labeled as 'nongovernmental diplomacy' at the first beginning, then 'export-oriented industry', 'smokeless industry', 'invisible trade', 'leading industry', 'strong industry' and 'pillar industry', until 'eco-friendly industry', 'learning industry', 'cultural industry' and 'dynamic industry' in recent days", written

Zhang Guangrui, an expert. Another expert argued that to some extent, the rapid and continuous development of tourism may reconstruct the world economy.

"Tourism Integrates the World" is a realistic and forward-looking standpoint. Tourism not only boosts, adjusts and integrates the world economy, but also plays an important role in integrating human civilization, namely "the soft integration power". No other industries can be more inclusive, sportive and diversified than tourism, which enables various sorts of cultures, information and beliefs to communicate with each other and converge together at last. Without any limitations on nations, races or languages, tourism helps tourists to freely exchange and experience the achievements of wisdom and civilization, thereby encouraging them to work hard to make the world better. Tourism is the most civilized, unisonous and efficient way to harmonize the world. As some sort of eternal and potential strength, it is powerful enough to convert the world into a "global village" full of freedom and satisfaction. This is why the idea of "Tourism Integrates the World" is forward-looking.

(This article was first published in *Peoples' Daily* on April 10, 2008 and here has been revised. The author is a famous writer and senior reporter in China)

# 目 录
## CONTENTS

第一章 总　　论 　　　　　　　　　　　　　　　　　　　　　(1)
　　第一节　旅游是人类本能属性和社会属性相结合的产物　　　(3)
　　第二节　古代旅游是有权有钱有闲人的活动　　　　　　　　(12)

第二章　科学技术的发展开启了人类旅游的新纪元　　　　　　(47)
　　第一节　影响人类旅游活动的几项重大发明　　　　　　　　(49)
　　第二节　旅游范围和旅游人数发生质的飞跃　　　　　　　　(53)
　　第三节　近代中国旅游　　　　　　　　　　　　　　　　　(55)

第三章　旅游的过程是人类文明传递的过程　　　　　　　　　(57)
　　第一节　旅游是不同文明之间的桥梁　　　　　　　　　　　(59)
　　第二节　没有传播就没有文明　　　　　　　　　　　　　　(61)

第四章　旅游的整合力是人类文明发展的加速器　　　　　　　(73)
　　第一节　旅游有着包容广泛的硬整合力　　　　　　　　　　(75)
　　第二节　旅游有着不可估量的软整合力　　　　　　　　　　(79)

第五章　人类文明的发展促动旅游价值的提升　　　　　　　　(87)
　　第一节　战争是古代人类文明传播的主渠道　　　　　　　　(89)

第二节 战争传播文明更摧毁文明 (95)

第三节 人类文明未来发展趋势 (98)

# 第六章 人类文明"整合"的最终选择——旅游 (103)

第一节 和平发展逐渐成为人类共识 (105)

第二节 现代旅游发展与日俱进 (114)

第三节 现实发展所预示的乐观前景 (126)

# Chapter 1  General Introduction (145)

Section 1  Tourism is a result which combines human beings' instinctive attribute and social attribute (147)

Section 2  Tourism in ancient times is an activity belonging to the rich, the powerful and the carefree (161)

# Chapter 2  A new epoch of tourism opened for humans amid scientific and technological development (213)

Section 1  Several important inventions affecting mankind's tourism activities (215)

Section 2  A qualitative leap in tourism spheres and number of tourists (221)

Section 3  Tourism in modern China (223)

# Chapter 3 Tourism is a process transmitting human civilizations (227)

Section 1  Tourism is a bridge linking different civilizations (229)

Section 2  No dissemination, no civilization (231)

# Chapter 4  The unifying force of tourism is an accelerator on developing human civilizations (249)

Section 1  Tourism has a "hard" unifying force with widespread intensions (251)

Section 2  Tourism has an immeasurable "soft" unifying force (257)

## Chapter 5　Development of Human Civilization Increases the Value of Tourism　(265)

　　Section 1　War is the Main Channel for the Transmission of Human Civilization in Ancient Times　(267)
　　Section 2　War Can Disseminate Civilization and Also Can Damage civilization　(276)
　　Section 3　Developing Trend of Human Civilization in the Future　(280)

## Chapter 6　Tourism, the Last Choice of Unifying Human Civilization　(287)

　　Section 1　Peaceful Development is Gradually Becoming a Common Understanding among Human Beings　(289)
　　Section 2　Modern tourism develops swiftly and actively　(300)
　　Section 3　The Existing Development Indicates an Optimistic Outlook　(317)

附录一:驻华大使解读"旅游整合世界"　(341)
Appendix Ⅰ: Comment on "*Tourism Integrates the World*" by China-based Ambassadors　(341)

附录二:在2012联合国记者颁奖大会上的书面演讲——
　　旅游整合世界　人类共享文明　(364)
Appendix Ⅱ: Writen speech to the General Assembly of the United Nations Correspondents in 2012——
　　Tourism Integrates the World and Shares Civilization　(368)

附录三:初版自序　(372)
Appendix Ⅲ: The first edition preface　(374)

参考文献　(377)

# 第一章 总 论

# The Great Wall
万里长城

## 第一节 旅游是人类本能属性和社会属性相结合的产物

### 一、中国古代旅游观

什么是旅游？旅游是什么时候产生的？旅游是人的本能还是社会发展的产物？旅游的内涵包括哪些内容？这些看起来简单的问题，却是一直以来困扰国内外专家学者的学术难题。其实，这也并不值得奇怪。旅游作为一种活动或现象虽然在地球上已存在了成千上万年，但旅游学研究不过是近几十年的事。

据考证，中国最古老的旅游概念，可能出自于《周易》中的"观卦"和"旅卦"。"观卦"中有这样的表示："观国之光，利用宾于王"，"观国之光，尚宾也"。意思是说，观乎国家之盛态，既有利于成为君王的贵宾，也说明国家正礼尚宾贤。虽然，此处的"观光"与现代意义上的"观光"有相当大的距离，但其为"观光"一词的出典。

"旅游"一词在中国的出现，则为南朝时期的梁代诗人沈约的《悲哉行》诗中所写："旅游媚年春，年春媚游人，徐光旦垂彩，和露晓凝津，时嚶起稚叶，蕙气动初蘋。一朝阻旧国，万里隔良辰。"诗中所言之"旅游"，与我们今天的理解，有颇为相近之处，含有愉悦性情、享受美景之内涵。

在南朝之前，汉语中在较长时间内"旅"和"游"是两个独立的字。《礼记·学记》中有"息焉游焉"的字句，古人称"谓闲暇无事之为游"，说明古人所描述的旅游，也是在人的闲暇时候的一种行为，已有旅游活动必须在业余时间的观念；唐朝孔颖达在其《周易正义》中对"旅"作出解释道："旅者，客寄之名，羁旅之称；失其本居而寄他方，谓之为旅"，强调了"旅"是从一个空间到另一个空间的活动。

在中国古代浩繁的典籍中，通过"旅"和"游"的记载，展示了中国古人多方面的生活画卷。如《诗经》："驾言出游，以忘我忧"；《尚书》："罔游于逸"；《楚辞·远游》："悲时俗之迫厄兮，愿轻举而远游"；《庄子·逍遥游》："乘天地之正，而御六气之辩，以游无穷"。其中，《庄子》是古人旅游思想的第一次高峰，在中国旅游文化史上有着划时代的意义。

庄子是我国古代道家的代表人物，像《论语》记载了孔子的言行一样，《庄子》也记载了其一生漫游、远游的丰富经历。《庄子》既是一本哲学著作，也是一本旅游著作。庄子提倡"天地与我并生，而万物与我为一"，实际上是希望达到"物与神游"、"物我两忘"的超然境界。

庄子的"道"，通过旅游，表现得玄之又玄，而其旅游，又通过虚无之"道"，描写得更加超脱和逍遥。历史上著名的"濠梁之辩"，把庄子"神与物游"、"天地与我并生，而万物与我为一"游乐观表现得淋漓尽致。

濠水位于今安徽凤阳县境内。惠施是战国时期的一位政治家、辩客和哲学家。庄子与惠施出游濠水时，来到一座小桥上，庄子对惠施说："小鱼悠闲地游出来，多么快乐啊！"惠子问："你不是鱼，怎么知道鱼是快乐的?"庄子回说："你不是我，怎么知道我不晓得鱼的快乐。"惠子辩说："我不是你，固然不知道你；以此而推，你不是鱼，你便不知道鱼的快乐，这是很明显的啊。"庄子又回说："请把话题从头说起吧！你刚才说：'你怎么知道鱼是快乐的'云云，就说明你知道了我的意思而问我，那么我在濠水的桥上也就能知道鱼的快乐了。"

庄子在这场"知鱼之乐"的争辩中向世人表明，观赏山水，要将身心同大自然融为一体，以达到心旷神怡、物我两忘的美好境界。他的这种"乘物以游心"的心态，启发了后人对山水的纯粹审美态度和古代的隐逸文化。

可见，古代中国人对"旅"和"游"或者"旅游"的理解，虽然因时代的不同，具体的含义也有所不同，但都至少反映了三个方面的共同特征，即异地性、暂时性和审美性。

在现代，专家学者对旅游的理解一直存在差异，有关旅游以及旅游者的定义在学术上至今未有明确的统一。并且随着社会经济和文化的发展，旅游的本质、定义和外延在描述上的纷乱状态，丝毫没有减轻的现象。

但这也说明，旅游总在不断地丰富和发展，人们对旅游的认识也在不断地加深。虽然有关说法五花八门，各种解释侧重有异，但透过中外专家学者的观点，也可进一步揭示旅游的科学含义。

沈祖祥在《观乎人文以化天下——旅游与中国文化论纲》中谈道："旅游是一种文化现象，一个系统，是人类物质文化生活和精神的一个最基本的组成部分，是旅游者这一旅游主体借助旅游媒介等外部条件，通过对旅游客体的能动活动，为实现自身某种需要而作的非定居的旅行的一个动态过程的复合体"，他认为，"旅游属于文化范畴，是文化的一个内容"。

冯乃康先生则在其《中国旅游文学论稿》中说："旅游的基本出发点、整个过程和最终效应都是以获取精神享受为指向"，"旅游不是一种经济活动而是一种精神活动,这种精神生活是通过美感享受来获得的,因此旅游又是一种审美活动,一种综合性的审美活动"。

2001年出版的《基础旅游学》作者谢彦君先生的观点近年来在中国颇具代表性。他认为:"旅游是个人以前往异地寻求审美和愉悦为主要目的而度过的一种具有社会、休闲和消费属性的短暂经历。"

在田里所编著的《旅游学概论》中,他对旅游的定义为:"旅游是人们离开常驻地到异国他乡访问的旅行和暂时停留所引起的各种现象和关系的总和。"

## 二、西方旅游观

在西方,有关旅游的概念也是说法不一,从无定论。

"旅游"一词出现在英文中,最早是在19世纪。在《韦伯斯特大字典》中,对"旅游"的注释是:"一个人回到其出发地所经历的历程;是一次出自商务、娱乐或教育的目的所作的旅行,旅行期间通常计划访问不同的地方。"

1927年,德国出版的《国家科学词典》给旅游下的定义是:"狭义的理解是那些暂时离开自己的住地,为了满足生活和文化的需要,或个人各种各样的愿望,而作为经济和文化商品的消费者逗留在异地的人的交往。"

奥地利经济学家赫曼翁斯奎勒德的观点,颇具代表性。他是西方较早用经济的眼光来审视旅游的学者之一。在他看来,"旅游是外国或外地人口进入非定居地并在其中逗留和移动所引起的经济活动的总和。"

法国学者吉恩·梅特森的说法在西方也颇有市场,他说:"旅游是一种休闲的活动,它包括旅行或在离开定居地点较远的地方逗留。其目的在于消遣、休息或为了丰富他的经历和文化教育。"道格拉斯·皮尔斯也表达了类似的观点:"从一个更为技术性的意义上来说,可以把旅游看作是人们出自休闲和娱乐的目的而旅行以及暂时逗留而引起的关系与现象。"

谈到西方有关旅游定义的发展,不可不提到瑞士学者汉泽克尔和克拉普夫。他俩在20世纪40年代合写了一本旅游学专著,名字叫《普通旅游学纲要》。此书中给旅游下的定义是:"旅游是非定居者的旅行和暂时居留所引起的现象和关系的总和。这些人不会导致永久定居,并且不会从事任何赚钱的活动。"这个定义对后来学者影响很大,并成为孵化"关系论"和"综合论"定义的窠臼。

1972年,英国学者伯卡特和梅特利克认为:"旅游发生于人们前往和逗留在各种旅游地的流动,是人们离开他平时工作和居住的地方,短期前往一个旅游目的地的运动和逗留在该地的各种活动。"

1973年,美国国家旅游资源评审委员会有关旅游者的说法是:"旅游者是指为了出差、消遣、个人事务，或者出于工作上下班之外的其他任何原因而离家外出旅行至少 50 英里（单程）的人，而不管其在外过夜还是当日往返。"加拿大也有类似定义："旅游者指到离开其所居社区边界至少 50 英里以外的地方去旅行的人。"

联合国"官方旅行机构国际联合会"对旅游下的定义是："到一个国家访问、停留超过了 24 小时的短期旅客，其访问目的属于下列两项之一：（1）休闲（包括娱乐、度假、保健、研究、宗教或体育运动）；（2）业务、家庭、出使、开会，谓之旅游。"

1979 年，英国旅游协会（BTS）认为："旅游是指与人们离开其日常生活和工作地点向目的地作暂时的移动以及在这些目的地作短期逗留有关的任何活动。"1981 年，"旅游专家国际联合会"也推出了一个后来非常出名的 ALEST 定义，该联合会专家认为："旅游是由人们向既非永久定居地亦非工作地旅行并在该处逗留所引起的相互关系和现象的总和。"

## 三、中外旅游观的差异

从以上给出的旅游的定义，我们不难发现中外专家学者在旅游定义的理解上的差别：中国的专家学者多数对旅游的认识比较偏重审美和愉悦，而西方的专家学者虽然也认识到旅游的消遣和休闲特性，但更多看重其经济和教育功能；在对旅游外延的界定上，中国的一些专家学者似乎更乐意"缩小化"，将旅游的概念锁定在"吃、住、行、游、娱、购"的范畴，而西方的专家学者恰恰相反，往往将旅游外延"扩大化"，在他们眼里，旅游是集休闲、商务、教育、文化和阅历等方面为一体的"综合"活动，所谓各种"关系总和"。

从中外旅游观的比较中，我们还可以发现，中国的一些专家学者往往把旅游看作是一种"单向"的消费行为，这从谢彦君先生给出的定义可见一斑。在这个定义中，他把旅游的基本属性定为三种，即消费属性、休闲属性和社会属性。他认为："旅游在其全过程中不向社会也不为旅游者个人创造任何外在的可供消费的资料，相反，却吞噬着旅游者以往的积蓄和他人的劳动成果"、"旅游的目的表现为借助各种可以娱情悦性的活动到审美体验……在旅游的全过程中，总是自然的天放的随意性和畅意自娱的目的性占据着主导地位，表现出与一切休闲行为相一致的品性。"

谢彦君先生在提及旅游的社会属性时说："旅游的社会属性的存在不仅因为审美意识作为旅游的前提条件而社会性地存在，而且，在不同的社会条件下，人们的旅游需求还表现在受时代的强烈影响所具有的特征。"

谢先生还引用了沈祖祥在《观乎人文以化天下——旅游与中国文化论纲》中所说："中国古代的旅游就好像是中国文化的一面折光镜，在这面镜子里，或隐或现反映出时代文化的影子，或强或弱地袒露着中国文化的灵魂。先秦的朦胧，魏晋的颓废，隋唐的高昂，明清的恬静……"从这里我们可以看到，谢的所谓旅游社会性的观点，并不是从旅游是社会"关系总和"的视野来审视，而是从不同时代具有不同"审美意识"的角度来反映，仍未脱离"消费观"的樊篱。

在西方论者中，从"旅游"一词在西方最早出现所作的解释："是一次出自商务、娱乐或教育的目的所作的旅行"，到现代"旅游是由人们向既非永久定居地亦非工作地旅行并在该处逗留所引起的相互关系和现象的总和"，似乎都没有把旅游看作是一种纯粹的"休闲"、"愉悦"的单向消费行为，而认为是"相互关系和现象的总和"，即旅游不单单是一种"吞噬着旅游者以往的积蓄和他人的劳动成果"的"消费"行为，也是一种吸收知识、丰富阅历、增加财富的双向的"投资"行为。

其实，西方论者的观点与中国古代先贤在对待旅游的理解上有颇多相通之处。在中国古代先贤们最早对旅游的认识中，并不认为旅游仅仅是娱乐性情、满足审美心理的一种休闲行为，而认为旅游还是一个增长见识、扩展视野的学习过程。中国古代大思想家、教育家孔子便是这种观点的典型代表。

孔子有关旅游的话，著名的有涉及山水之言，他说："智者乐水，仁者乐山"。孔子十分欣赏大自然的井然有序，并希望社稷和人事也能像大自然一样保持一种自然和谐的秩序。这种把自然和社会和谐统一的思想就是儒家"天人合一"价值观的核心所在。"读万卷书，行万里路"是宋代著名学者刘彝有关旅游的另一家喻户晓的论断，他把"读书"和"旅游"放在同等地位加以考察，认为二者在塑造心智、成长人生的过程中相辅相成，缺一不可。

## 四、旅游的新定义

面对古今中外对旅游理解的千差万别，"求同存异"是一种现实的状态，探究本真则是科学的必然。笔者以为，虽然人类发展到今天，还未能对旅游的本质、内涵和外延有一个清晰的定论，但在现有框架下去追溯旅游的起源、去考察人类本能和社会对旅游所起的作用，仍不失为站在巨人肩膀上的一种格致之为。

把旅游看成是社会发展的产物，谢彦君先生的观点颇具典型性。他在《基础旅游学》中说："旅游在根本上是一种主要以获得心理快感为目的的审美过程和自娱过程，是人类社会发展到一定阶段时人类最基本的活动之一"。

这个定义突出了旅游作为"人类最基本的活动之一"，是"人类社会发展到一定阶段时"的产物。不过，在许多中外论者看来，如果这种说法果真科学，那么人类发展到什么阶段，才有旅游这样一个"产物"？这恐怕是一个在时间上难以划定的不确定值。

谢彦君先生认为中国完整意义上的"旅游"一词的南北朝时期，因为它正值"旅游实践蓬勃发展时代、对自然美的审美意识迅速分化独立的时期"，"此时的旅游行为及其背景，存在着与今天的旅游几乎统一的性质，有限的差异仅仅表现在形式上和方式上"，所以，他认为"在此前发生的个别的旅行行为以及此后发生的出自非休闲、娱乐和审美目的的旅行，都不是旅游"。

对于这样一个命题，我们不要轻易作出判断，我们可以从历史中寻找答案。

在中国秦汉时代，关于旅游出现了一个新词"游观"。李斯在《上秦二世书》中说："治驰道，兴游观，以见主之得意"。意思是说，治理车道，大兴游览之风，而体现皇帝的大恩大德。秦汉人认为，旅游活动有四种功能，其一可观风察政，《礼记·王制》说："天子五年一巡狩"，"命大师陈诗以观民风"；其二可修身养性，枚乘《七发》所言七种"灵丹妙药"中，竟有三种"浮游观览"，具"共乐忘死"功效；其三可格物致知，西汉王褒在《圣主得贤臣颂》中说："今臣辟在西蜀，生于穷巷之中，长于蓬茨之下，无有游观广览之知"，表明自己因为无法从事旅游而孤陋寡闻，这说明远古时期的人们已知旅游是知识、智慧和才能的来源；第四种也是秦汉旅游观最了不起的进步，那就是和今人相同的看法：可愉悦人生。

秦汉时期老百姓的旅游活动，以春游、秋游最为盛行。如三月三的上巳节，本为一种传统的消灾纳祥的祭祀活动，后发展到去流水中沐浴，到后来又出现"曲水流觞"之景象。所谓的"曲水流觞"，就是游乐的人们，引水环曲成渠，曰"曲水"，然后将盛酒的"觞"浮于水面，使之顺流漂下。觞杯飘至曲折拐弯处，当杯子缓缓经过宾客面前时，宾客即可取过一饮而尽，然后吟诗作赋，以为娱乐，此即曲水流觞。

历史上曾有一段记载，说的就是大书法家王羲之传承古俗，流觞赋诗的佳话：永和九年（前353）三月初三上巳日，晋代有名的大书法家、会稽内史王羲之偕亲朋谢安、孙绰等四十二人，在兰亭举行的修禊活动。王羲之在《兰亭集序》中曾记载："又有清流激湍，映带左右，引以为流觞曲水。列坐其次，虽无丝竹管弦之盛，一觞一咏，亦足以畅叙幽情。"

汉朝人存在广泛的春游活动。张衡在其名作《南都赋》中说："斯乃游观之好，耳目之娱"，并对汉朝上巳节群众的游观盛况作了生动的描述："暮春之禊，元巳之辰，方轨齐轸，被于阳滨。"在这一天，官民都去水边洗濯，不仅民间风行，连帝王后妃也去临水除垢，祓除不祥。不仅如此，到了秋天，汉朝人还有秋游活动，九九重阳，饮酒登高。对汉朝人来说，春游秋游是他们一年两次最为普遍的旅游活动。

明朝谢肇淛所著《五杂组》中提道："此是魏晋以后相沿，汉犹有巳，不以三日也"，说明汉开此类风气之先。

远古士人旅游，早期多以游说、取仕、讲学为目的，功利性较强。而秦汉时人们以愉悦为目的的旅游，使得旅游的娱乐功能得到突出，这在中国旅游发展史上具有里程碑式的意义。随着社会的发展，旅游的这一功能在各个朝代，均有长足发展，得到越来越多的游人尤其是文人雅士的推崇，以至于有时人们对旅游的认识，因"一叶障目"而几乎忽略了旅游的其他功能。

从秦汉时期的旅游发展可见，把中国"完整意义"的"旅游"的分水岭放在南北朝时期，显然不是一个很有说服力的命题。尤其是"个别的旅行行为"本身就是一个十分模糊的概念，无法在时间上对其始终、空间上对其规模进行一个较为明晰的界定。

罗伯特·朗卡尔在《旅游及旅行社会学》中说："自有人类就有旅行"。中国学者范能船先生在给章必功所著《中国旅游史》所作序言中也有相同观点："旅游的历史与人类的历史相始终"。这些观点，毋庸置疑，是建立在对旅游是人类生命中的不可分割的一部分的认识基础之上。确立此类观点，我们还可从人类生理学和心理学出发来分析。

中国有句俗话：花有五颜六色，人有七情六欲。何谓七情？中国古代著名经典《礼记·礼运》中说："喜、怒、哀、惧、爱、恶、欲七者弗学而能。"可见，情是喜怒哀乐的情感表现或心理活动，而欲是七情之一。

那么，什么是六欲呢？东汉哲人高诱对此作了注释："六欲，生、死、耳、目、口、鼻也。"可见六欲泛指人的生理需求或欲望。人要生存，而且要活得有滋有味，有声有色，于是嘴要吃，舌要尝，眼要观，耳要听，鼻要闻，这些欲望与生俱来，不用人教就会。

按照马斯洛有关人的需要层次的解释，人的需要由低到高可分五个层次：生理需要、安全需要、社交需要、受尊重需要和自我实现的需要。从这个理论我们可以推知，人所能体会到的快感有两种，一种是生理快感，另一种是心理快感。生理快感为动物界所共有，心理快感则为人类所独有。

试想，最原始的人群会不会对山外的世界产生好奇心？在狩猎的过程中，当他们发现有好吃的、好看的、好听的境况时，日后会不会有再次光顾的念头？回答是肯定的。正如谢彦君先生在《基础旅游学》中所说："事实上，远古时代人们在很大程度上怀有远方崇拜心理，这种对异地的憧憬，会成为驱动人们跨出旅游的第一步的巨大动力"。

古人的这种满足，如果仅仅从生理快感上来看，恐怕不是一种容易解释的行为，只有生理快感和心理快感的统一，才是具有说服力的理解。

但是，发生在远古时代的这种主要是在人的本能驱使下的"零星"的旅游活动，还不能算得上是真正的旅游。只有随着生产力的发展，人们有了闲暇时间，有了审美倾向，社会有了"旅游现象"的产生，真正意义上的旅游才得以出现。

原始社会末期，随着金属工具的问世，农业和畜牧业有了较快的发展，促使手工业成为专门性行业。人类历史由此出现第二次大分工，即手工业和农业畜牧业的分离。人们的闲暇时间自然越来越多，审美意识也越来越丰富，审美需求也逐渐强烈。

何谓"审美意识"？审美意识是人类有别于普通动物的一种独有的思维活动。简而言之，是人类在社会化的过程中对美的一种思维定式或思维活动。亚里士多德在其《伦理学》中对超功利性的审美体验，作出了比较详细的特征描述："这是一种在观看和倾听中获得的极其愉快的体验"，"这种愉快的经验是人所独有的。虽然其他生物也有自己的快乐，但那些快乐来自于气味的嗅觉或味觉。而人的审美快乐则源自于视觉和听觉感受到的和谐……"由亚里士多德的这种描述，我们可以了解到，人通过审美所获得的心理享受和一般生理快感是有本质区别的。

由于这种区别，"审美意识"便会随着人类文明的发展而发展，随着社会的进步而进步。

马克思说："劳动创造一切"。格罗塞在《艺术的起源》中写道："生产事业真是所谓一切文化形式的命根"，"与生产方式这种最基本的文化现象比较起来，一切其他文化现象都是派生的、次要的"。所以，"审美意识"与劳动相伴始终，劳动内容越丰富，审美对象和审美意识也越丰富。

从以上内容可以推断，旅游作为"人类最基本的活动之一"，既有本能的自然属性，又有客观的社会属性。从古今中外的旅游史我们可以看到，旅游会随着社会的发展而发展，旅游观也会随着社会的发展而改变。

在当今"全球化"的时代，面对众说纷纭的学术见解，我们是以狭隘的、单纯从"愉情悦性"的角度来看待旅游，还是以超视野的、"关系总和"的标尺去考量，这不仅是摆在中国的专家学者面前，也是摆在各国的专家学者面前的一个亟待解决的课题。

黑格尔说过："存在的就是合理的"。古今中外论者从不同的角度对旅游的仁智之见，丰富了人们对旅游的认识和理解。纵观古今中外的这些见解，笔者尝试着给旅游以新的定义：**旅游是为满足人的多种多样的审美需求和好奇心而向目的地运动所产生的各种关系的总和。**

这个定义与传统定义的最大不同是突出了"多种多样"的"审美需求"。它强调了人的"审美需求"是多种多样的，旅游不仅仅只体现在游山玩水、愉情雅性上，还体现在知识追求、政治满足、信仰崇拜、商贸往来等多方面。如中国古代春秋战国时期出现的士阶层，他们四处奔波，或为卿相披星或为名利戴月，虽然他们周游列国的政治目的性很强，但长期的旅行实践，不可能不从中获得一些审美满足，而加强对旅游的审美思考。

正如中国社科院旅游研究中心副主任刘德谦教授在谈到旅游的本质时所说："旅游的本质是什么？我的主张是：人类旅游活动的共同本质，应该是人类的交流。这种交流，既包括人与自然的交流、人与历史的交流，也包括人与人之间的交流。虽然旅游常常是指为了休闲、娱乐和度假而进行的旅行活动……但随着人们个性化需求的强化，形式多样的旅游形式就必然越来越盛行，逐渐成为主导。"

随着人类的进步，社会日益变得多姿多彩，人们的"审美需求"也变得日益丰富，有时即使是在同一次旅游过程中，游客的"审美需求"也存在多样性。人们不仅仅在自然山水之中寻找"乐趣"，与现代文明有关的各种文化、体育、科技、商务、宗教、探险、修学、保健等多方面的旅游活动，都从不同角度满足当今人类的"审美需求"。

虽然这个定义的外延相对我国一部分学者的定义有所"放大"，但旅游是为满足"审美需求"的本质没有改变，这与一些西方学者将旅游看成是什么都可装进去的大麻布袋式的"关系总和论"有了明确的区别。它揭示了旅游的核心价值——人们之所以喜欢旅游，就是因为旅游能满足人们对自然美、艺术美、科技美和生活美的欣赏和享受。

有一些看似人们仅仅是为满足好奇心而从事的旅游活动，"审美"特征不是那么显著，但是从游客的心理活动来和精神活动来看，这种因满足而带来的快感，不能不说是一种"美"的享受。

所以，中国社科院旅游研究中心刘德谦教授在撰文中说："人类的审美同样也是'交流'，只是在这种交流中审美者表现为动态和主动，而审美对象常常表现为静态（也不完全是这样）和被动罢了。"

《旅游学概论》中写道："旅游是一项综合性的审美活动，它集自然美、社会生活美和艺术美于一体，熔文物、古迹、建筑、雕刻、绘画、书法、音乐、舞蹈、戏剧、风情、美食等为一炉，不仅能最大限度满足人们各方面的审美需求，还能满足人的生理、认识等方面的需求与欲望。"

不仅如此，该定义由于强调了旅游的审美特性，就将旅游与旅行、迁徙等形式相同或相似的人类活动进行了区别。

在早期人类社会，生产力十分低下，人类祖先在与恶劣的生存环境的搏斗中，被迫作出一次又一次离开原驻地的决定，迁往另一个地方。即使到了新石器时代中期，人类频繁"挪窝"的状况都没有改变。像这种人类在客观上无物质基础，在主观上又无"审美"愿望的图"生存权"的迁徙活动，与后来出现旅行活动，有本质区别，更与今天意义上的旅游差之甚远。

迁徙虽然也是离开定居点，但它不是一种"短暂经历"，并且它不计划再回来。它的目的是求取好的生存环境。旅行和旅游则在形式上完全相同，都有"异地性"

和"暂时性"的特点，在内容上它们之间有时难以划分。如古代皇帝巡行，虽主要出自政治目的，但谁能说其中不包括"审美"和"休闲"的成分呢？当然，也有可以明显划分的事例，如我国历史上广为流传的大禹治水的故事，就是一次为图生存而进行的艰辛的旅行活动。

大禹为了找到治水方法，在外十三年，三过家门而不入，足迹几乎遍及黄河、长江两大流域，后来终于实现了"四海会同"、"九州攸同"的目的。大禹治水所进行的旅行活动，是我国原始人类为征服自然、改造自然而进行的旅行活动的高峰。显然，它没有脱离生活的被迫性，所以，不属于真正意义上的旅游。

任何目的都有可能导致旅行，但旅游的目的是同满足快乐联系在一起的。旅行与旅游虽然不能画上等号，但随着社会的发展，因为人类"审美需求"越来越多，"审美"的内涵也随之发生变化，变得越来越丰富，旅行和旅游的概念有时变得越来越模糊。不过，从理论上来讲，旅游必须通过旅行来实现，"不是所有的旅行都是旅游"的观点现在仍被普遍的认可。

旅游和旅游业也是现代人容易混淆的两个概念。二者其实可以明显划分：旅游是旅游者的一种个人行为，而旅游业是旅游企业的集合行为。旅游业可以从广义和狭义两方面进行理解：广义认为是指一切与旅游者的消费行为有关，为旅游活动创造方便条件并提供旅游产品和旅游服务的综合性产业；狭义理解是指为旅游者提供能够满足其审美和愉悦的产品和服务的部门企业。

## 第二节 古代旅游是有权有钱有闲人的活动

### 一、中国古代旅游

从前面我们可以了解到，旅游是人类的一项重要活动，自有人类文字记载以来，就存在有关旅游活动的记载。

旅游作为人类的一项特殊的社会活动，它的消费、审美及社会的综合特性，使得旅游与其他社会活动有着本质的不同。《旅游学概论》一书在概括旅游的本质时指出："旅游是一种高层次的消费活动"，"旅游是一种以审美为特征的消闲活动"，

"旅游是人类的一种社会交往活动"。

旅游有这样的特性，决定了在远古生产力极不发达的条件下，旅游只是少数人的专利，准确地说，只是少数有权有钱有闲人的活动。旅游的发展，无论是从质量上还是从数量上来看，都是由低级到高级的一个转化过程。

中国是世界文明古国，也是旅游发生最早的国家之一，旅游活动初期可以追溯到公元前 2250 年以前。

由于生产力十分低下，在原始社会早期，全体社员几乎都在为满足生存需求，而与大自然作艰苦的搏斗。随着人类两次大分工的完成，生产力得到长足发展，阶级开始出现，财富和余暇时光也渐渐积累到少数人的身上，使得真正意义上的旅游得以实现。在古代中国，旅游主要是以帝王巡游、士人游说、文人漫游、宗教远足、地理考察、外交旅行等形式出现。

（1）形式多样的帝王巡游

帝王巡游是指历代最高统治者对自己所管辖的国家或领土所作的巡视游览活动。通过巡游，帝王一则可以炫耀自己至高无上的权威，威加四海，观察政情民风，以稳固统治；二则可以饱览风光，享受美景，祭祀封禅，以娱乐身心。

先秦时期，以天子、诸侯为代表的少数奴隶主旅游活动，主要有巡游、封禅、会盟、游猎、娱游等。如《楚辞·离骚》记录夏太康"娱以自纵，不顾难以图后"，《说苑·正谏》记载齐景公"游于海上而乐之。六月不归"，成为中国海上旅游史的最早记录。

中国有史记载最早的天子巡游，是周穆王西行漫游。据说，有一天穆王做了个梦，梦中名叫"化人"的人邀请他去化人国旅行。于是，穆王选了一个吉祥的日子，从成周（今洛阳市东南）启程，任用善于养马、驾马的造父为车夫，由七队勇士护卫，沿太行山西侧北进，经过今青海省东南的积历山脉，到达昆仑山，拜见西王母，并把带去的礼品珍珠宝石奉献给西王母，宾主欢聚一堂。之后，穆王又北上到达巴基斯坦的瓦罕，最后回到喀什东归。

穆王西行，在时间上耗费两年有余，行程三万多里，经过了河南、山西、河北、内蒙古、青海、甘肃、新疆等地，一直到达今天的中亚地区。其所走的路线，与后来张骞出使西域的路线基本相同，所以他不愧是中国历史上的大旅行家。

秦始皇是中国封建社会中帝王巡游的第一个重要代表。其在位 11 年，远途巡游就达 5 次。巡游期间，秦始皇一路下令立碑刻石，颂扬秦皇大功大德，国家统一，如著名的泰山勒石、会稽勒石、碣石勒石等等，均记载了当时巡游雄风。在巡游过程中，秦始皇不忘游览各地山水风光，封禅祭祀是其主要内容之一。在泰山，他封救命松为"五大夫松"。他在洞庭湖行船时，因波涛汹涌，险些翻船，所以他一气之下，命令侍从到君山上，把娥皇、女英两个神庙烧个精光，并刻下"永封"二字，意为永世不得翻身。

由于劳累过度，秦始皇在作最后一次巡游时，在北上咸阳途中，客死他乡，终年50岁。

汉武帝刘彻，其游踪与秦始皇相仿，但巡游次数超过秦始皇，一生中远近巡游不下十余次。据《所志》上记载，汉武帝登泰山后的感觉是"高矣，极矣，大矣，符其，壮美，特矣，驻矣，惑矣……"。在泰山，刘彻立并下了著名的无字碑，意思为自己功德无法用文字来记载。在河南嵩山，据传他在登山时，忽然松涛阵阵，四周响起"万岁"之声，刘彻认为这乃神之旨意，即命此峰为"万岁峰"。汉武帝在位时，国家强盛，开边未已。刘彻派大将卫青、霍去病不断出击，打通了漠北交通线，苏武出使匈奴，张骞出使西域，都是中国旅游史上光彩夺目的旅游故事。

在帝王巡游中，要数隋炀帝的规模最大，也最为奢华。据《大业杂记》记载，隋炀帝南巡江都时，他自己所乘坐的龙船高45尺，宽50尺，长200尺，上下共有四层楼。皇后和妃子也分别单独乘舟。除此之外，还有供宫廷美人乘坐的船36条，供宫女乘坐的船100余条。排在这些船之后，才是王公大臣、僧人以及外国宾客和五品以下官员的楼船。其中王公大臣所乘五层楼船有52条，僧人的三层楼船有120条。整个巡游队伍，连同侍卫人员、船夫等在内，有数十万之多。巡游开动，大运河中首尾相连，迤逦200多里。隋炀帝所到之处，方圆500里地要进贡美食珠宝，吃不掉就扔到河里，谁送的财物多，谁就能被擢升高官。

隋炀帝一生中巡游江都三次，劳民伤财，哀鸿遍野。当他第三次巡游时，虽全国遍燃农民起义的烽火，他却依然饮酒作乐，荒淫无道，直至被起义军摘了脑袋。

狩猎历来被封建帝王及其臣们视作为一项综合的军事训练和娱乐消遣活动。明初时，皇帝多在北京西郊大兴地区的南苑狩猎。这里地势低洼，沼泽密布，水草丰茂，繁衍着无数飞禽走兽，风景十分优美。每当冬去春来之时，皇帝来此打猎。永乐皇帝还在这里设上林苑监，修建行宫。明中叶以后，皇帝们大多由于生活荒淫，体质虚弱，无力狩猎。

到了清朝，狩猎活动又兴起。从顺治起，清朝就规定"令禁旅行围"，并订立"大狩扈从例"作为狩猎条例。康熙时期，规定一年两次狩猎。康熙本人也是狩猎能手，每年秋冬都要外出打猎，传说他一生中到承德地区狩猎四十八次。乾隆也因打猎勇敢得到康熙的赏识，登上王位。做了皇帝后，乾隆更加迷恋狩猎生活，直至八十岁才停止打猎活动。

祭祖谒陵是封建皇帝倡导以孝治天下，祈求先祖保社稷的诸多活动之一。清朝的祭祖谒陵十分频繁，超过历史上任何一个朝代，每年几乎多达三十次以上。每次皇帝祭祖几乎成了春游、秋游活动，边谒陵边行围狩猎。还以祭山为名，登长白山观景，或泛舟于松花江上。据《临榆县志》记载，康熙、乾隆、嘉庆和道光，去关外谒陵途经山海关达九次之多，在那儿，他们北登角山寺，南游澄海轴，赐宴赋诗，欣赏山水相连的大自然美景。

明清皇帝利用外出巡游，一方面查看民情，整饬边防；另一方面借机寻仙访贤，游览名山大川，体验"小桥流水人家"的乡间生活风趣和野味，一饱眼福和口福。康熙自1684年至1707年二十二年中，先后六次亲临黄河沿岸视察，并设计指点治河方案，最后得以"河工已经告成"自慰。同时，他借南巡"省方察吏"，了解民情以及笼络争取南方知识分子。这些举动都对18世纪中国社会安定和经济繁荣起着不可磨灭的促进作用。

乾隆在位六十年中，也曾仿效康熙六次巡视江南，并把南巡当作自己用兵之外的另一重要活动。所不同的是，与康熙节俭简朴相比，乾隆这六次南巡，兴师动众，耗尽大量人力物力。每届南巡前一年就进行准备，筑桥铺路，修建行宫，随同南巡人数达两千五百人之多，一千多只船首尾相接，岸上有官员骑马沿河行走，以备随时差遣。沿河三十里以内，地方官员皆穿朝服前来接驾，男女老少夹道欢迎。每天的膳食极尽铺张扬厉，豪华奢靡。

但不同于荒淫的昏君隋炀帝，乾隆毕竟是有作为的君主。他的文功武略，在我国统一多民族的历史发展中有一定的贡献。第六次南巡结束时，乾隆已经是七十五岁的老人，他写了一首诗："六度南巡止，他年梦寐游。"缅怀其巡游江南往事，字里行间充满眷恋之情。

（2）功利明显的士人游说

在中国春秋战国时期，正值奴隶社会瓦解、封建社会逐步建立之际，代表不同阶级利益的"士"或著书立说、争鸣论战，或率领门徒周游列国，宣传政见，弘扬主张，以求受到赏识，风光仕途。在这种别具风格的政治游说活动中，孔子、苏秦、张仪等就是这样一群游历各国、游说诸侯，谋求高官显爵士人的代表人物。

孔子（前551—前479），名丘，字仲尼，鲁国陬邑（今山东曲阜东南）人，春秋末期思想家、政治家、教育家，儒家学派的创始人。孔子其思想核心是"仁"，"仁"即"爱人"。他把"仁"作为行仁的规范和目的，使"仁"和"礼"相互为用，主张统治者对人民"道之以德，齐之以礼"，进而实现他一心向往的"大同"理想。

据《韩待外传》解释："天山者，万物之所据仰也，草木生焉，万物植焉，飞鸟集焉，走兽休焉，四方益取与焉。出云导民异乎天地之间。天地以成，国家以宁、此仁者所以乐山也"，这和孔子"仁者乐山，智者乐水"的旅游观如出一辙。这种比德伦的山水观已具有人性的内容，它开始摆脱对山水直接的物质性功利，而代之以超然的精神性功利了。

孔子在外十四年，游历宋、卫、陈、蔡、齐、楚等国，广泛宣传儒家思想。在周游列国中，面对老百姓的颠沛流离，孔子斥责暴君"苛政猛于虎"；在日常游历中，他看到江水汩汩而去，慨叹"逝者如斯夫！不舍昼夜"，以此激励后人把握时光，奋发向上。长期的旅游经历，形成了孔子和谐自然与和谐社会相统一的"天人合一"的儒家思想。

孔子还提出"父母在，不远游"的近游观。这里的"游"既包括"旅游"的含义，也有现代意义上的"外出打工"的意思。这种观点反映了生产力低下时的时代特点。孔子近游观的目的是实现"老者安之，少者怀之"的仁政思想。所以，纵览孔子的旅游观，孔子从未把"旅游"看作是一种纯粹的游乐行为，而处处与儒家的仁礼思想、义利观、尚古意识和"与民偕乐"观相融合，给后世相当影响。

孟子和孔子一样，为弘扬儒家仁本思想，也曾周游列国，他曾对宋勾践说过："你喜欢游说各国君主吗？我告诉你怎样游说：别人理解也安详自得，别人不理解也安详自得。"问："怎样才能安详自得呢？"孟子答道："尊崇道德，喜爱仁义，就可以安详自得了。所以士人穷困失意时不离开仁宅义路，显达得意时不背离道德。穷困时不失仁义，士人就能安详自得；显达时不背离王道，民众就不会失其所望。古代的士人，得志时恩惠施于百姓，不得志时修养自身以显现于世。穷困就独善其身，显达就兼善天下。"

另一些看起来并不起眼的士人，在关键时刻，也往往起着不可或缺的作用。他们或为主子解一时之难，或在强手面前保卫国家尊严。如魏国人范雎，欲周行天下，游说诸侯，一展平生所学，却因家境贫寒，既无钱作旅途之资，也没有托人引见之费。只好先在魏国中大夫须贾门下奔走效力。一次，他随须贾前往齐国，见须贾被齐襄王数落得嚅嚅无言以对，挺身而出，仗义执言，让齐襄王自讨没趣。

齐襄王退朝以后，对在庭上仗义执言的范雎的胆识念念不忘。当晚，他派人劝说范雎留在齐国，以客卿相处。范雎义正词严地拒绝道："臣与使者同出，而不与同入，不信无义，何以为人？"齐襄王闻知，心中甚为敬重，特赐予范雎黄金十斤以及牛、酒诸物。

"毛遂自荐"这个成语在中国流传两千多年，毛遂这个名字也成为自我推荐的代名词。这位战国时代在赵国平原君门下原本默默无闻的宾客，随着这一成语的流行而名垂不朽。

公元前260年，秦国大将白起率大军攻打赵国，长平一役，斩杀赵军45万人，赵国元气大损，闻秦丧胆。赵胜决定精选二十名文武兼备的门客，前往楚国，向楚国求救。

但他门下虽有数千宾客，真到用时，却凑不齐二十人。这时有个叫做毛遂的人，自我推荐。赵胜以其呆三年而不被发现为由拒绝选拔，毛遂据理力争才得以成行。

赵胜一行人到了楚国，游说工作颇不顺利，从旭日初升到日正当中，向楚王阐述联合抗秦的重要，楚王仍然犹豫不决。

毛遂十分不满，按着佩剑走上台阶，对赵胜说："合纵抗秦一事，利害得失一句话就说得清楚，哪需谈这么久？"

楚王见之怒斥道："我和你主人讲话，你来干什么？"

毛遂于是向前说："大王斥责我，是仗着楚国人多势众。但现在咱们相距不到十步，人多势众没有用，你的性命操在我手上。"

毛遂语带威胁，接着话锋一转，指出楚国兵多将广，地大人多，却臣服于秦。毛遂说："白起，只是一个小角色，却率数万之众攻打楚国，夺去鄢、郢两座城，并火烧夷陵，毁去楚国宗庙，羞辱楚国祖先，连我赵国都为你羞愧，大王却不以为耻。现在提倡联合抗秦，其实是为楚国啊！"

毛遂一席话，说得楚王哑口无言，于是下令联合共同对抗秦国。赵胜回国后叹息说："我再也不敢自称能辨识人才了。"毛遂从此被奉为上宾。

在春秋战国时期士人中，最为知名的莫过于苏秦、张仪两人。"战国七雄"是中国历史上七个诸侯国争霸的动荡时代，在"七国"的较量中，秦国异军突起，对其他六国构成了威胁。当时的政治家有两种完全不同的政治方案，一种是以苏秦为代表的合纵抗秦方案，另一种是以张仪为代表的连横亲秦方案。双方往来六国，凭"三寸不烂之舌"，极力劝说六国国君接受自己的主张。

苏秦一生坐车骑马，行遍天下，在宫廷游说各国诸侯，使国君左右之人缄口不言，天下无人能敌。

其实，苏秦的游说并非一帆风顺。他早年出身于穷门陋巷，为一介贫寒困苦之士。他曾向秦王上书十次，但他的主张一直未被采纳，最后黑貂皮袍破了，带的钱花光了，只得离开秦国回到老家。

他裹着腿，穿草鞋，担着行囊，形容憔悴，脸色黑黄，面带羞愧，回到家里。妻子见到他，依然织布不睬，嫂子不为他做饭，父母也不与他说话。苏秦见此情状，长叹道："妻子不把我当丈夫，嫂子不把我当小叔，父母不把我当儿子，这都是我的不好啊！"

于是他连夜翻检书籍，把几十个书箱打开，找到一部姜太公的兵书《阴符经》，伏案诵读，反复研习揣摩，深入领会。读书读得昏昏欲睡，他就取过铁锥，照着自己的大腿刺去，以至血流到脚跟。他发狠说："哪有游说君主而不能使其拿出金玉锦缎，并以卿相之尊位给我的呢？"

一年以后，他捉摸已经学成，便道："这次真可用所学去游说当今的君主了。"于是他出发了，来到赵国，在华丽的殿堂见到赵肃侯，两人谈得十分投机。赵王很高兴，封苏秦为武安君，任命他为赵国的相国，并相国给兵车百辆，锦缎千匹，白璧百双，黄金万镒，让他带着这些财物去游说各国诸侯，推行合纵的计谋，以打击强大的秦国。

　　当苏秦得意显耀之时,黄金万千为其所用,随从车骑络绎不绝,光耀于道路;山东六国,如草从风,倒伏于前;从而使赵国在诸侯中的地位大大提高。苏秦往南游说楚王,途经洛阳时,他父母闻讯,连忙张罗打扫住处,清洁道路;并且设置音乐,筹办酒席,在郊外三十里地迎接。苏秦来到后,他妻子不敢正视,只是偷偷地察言观色,恭敬地听他讲话。他嫂嫂如蛇伏地,匍匐而行,四次跪拜谢罪。苏秦说:"嫂嫂,为什么你以前那么傲慢,现在又如此卑下呢?"嫂嫂答道:"因为您现在地位显贵而且金钱很多啊!"苏秦叹道:"唉!一个人在贫穷时,连父母也不把他当儿子看待;等到他富贵了,就是亲戚也都害怕他。看来人生在世,对于权势富贵,怎么能够忽视呢?"

　　张仪是魏国人,在魏国穷困潦倒,跑到楚国去游说,楚王没接见他。楚国的令尹把他留在家里作门客。有一次,令尹家里丢失了一块名贵的璧。令尹家看张仪穷,怀疑璧是被张仪偷去的,把张仪抓起来打个半死。

　　张仪垂头丧气回到家里,他妻子抚摸着张仪满身伤痕,心疼地说:"你要是不读书,不出去谋官做,哪会受这样的委屈!"

　　张仪张开嘴,问妻子说:"我的舌头还在吗?"妻子说:"舌头当然还长着。"张仪说:"只要舌头在,就不愁没有出路。"

　　后来,张仪到了秦国,凭他的口才,果然得到秦惠文王的信任,当上了秦国的相国。这时候,六国正在组织合纵。公元前318年,楚、赵、魏、韩、燕五国组成一支联军,攻打秦国的函谷关。其实,五国之间内部也有矛盾,不肯齐心协力。经不起秦军一反击,五国联军就失败了。

　　在六国之中,齐、楚两国是大国。张仪认为要实行"连横",非把齐国和楚国的联盟拆散不可。于是他跑去楚国游说,与屈原结下冤仇,致使屈原被流放乡野,最后悲愤之至投汨罗江而死。

　　这些士人便是在这样频繁的周游列国中,企望实现自己的政治抱负,从而得到人生的满足感。他们满怀理想,长年车旅在外,与山水为伴,经受大自然的风吹雨打,但他们不以为苦,反以为乐,表现出一种特有的审美境界。到西汉时,诸侯聚养宾客,犹有游说余风。

　　(3) 色彩斑斓的文人漫游

　　秦汉时期,随着社会经济的发展,一些文人雅士生活优裕,他们有文化,有闲暇,从繁华都市回到山水的怀抱,往往激发对大自然的热爱,产生无限感慨。"驾言出游,日夕忘归","非必丝与竹,山水有清音"……

　　到了东汉时期,一些隐士有感官场的污浊和黑暗,"仕不得志"纵情山水,将旅游看作是遁世避俗、排忧解愁、洁身自好的人生途径,庄子逍遥游的基本态度重新得到重视，放志于自然山水成为文人隐士的一种生活情趣。有诗云："生年不满百，长怀千岁忧。昼短苦夜长，何不秉烛游？为乐当及时，何能待来兹。"

魏晋年代，文人雅士因政治失意而走上寄情山水、啸傲风月的道路者更是空前绝后，他们行其所行，得其所得，乐其所乐，或登山临水，畅然游览；或结庐而居，隐疲终倦；或行吟于山水，评棋品画，时俗世伪，皆之于脑后，成为中国历史上文人旅游的第一座高峰。

先秦以前的文学作品，也有对山对水对自然的描写，但他们的目的不是认识自然美，而真正以审美之情感去盛赞山水的，当首推文武兼备的曹孟德。其代表作为《观沧海》一诗。诗曰："东临碣石，以观沧海。水何澹澹，山岛竦峙。树木丛生，百草丰茂。秋风萧瑟，洪波涌起。日月之行，若出其中；星汉灿烂，若出其里。幸甚至哉，歌以咏志。"在这首诗中，诗人对碣石山和沧海的赞美，实际上表达了英雄豪杰借景抒情的自我溢美。

据《世说新语》中记载，被称为"竹林七贤"的阮籍、嵇康、刘伶、阮咸、王戎、山涛、向秀等七人，因不满曹魏时期司马氏家族党同伐异的政治暗局，常常联袂出游，聚会山野。据《晋书》记载，阮籍好游山玩水，常常数日不归。驾车行进时，他不走大道，专门在狭窄山道上随意奔驰，有时无路可进时，他便坐在车上痛哭一场。另记载，孙绰"居于会稽，游山放水，十有余年"，其兄孙统"家于会稽，性好山水……纵意游肆，名山胜川，靡不穷究"。

谢灵运当属魏晋南北朝时期最著名的大漫游家。他出身官宦世家，兼负才华，但仕途坎坷。为了摆脱自己的政治烦恼，谢灵运常常放浪山水，探奇览胜。在朝廷做官时，他出去旅游，常常十几天不回家，既不事先请假，又不请人代替公干，结果被朝廷免职。从此，"壮志郁不用"的谢灵运愤然遨游于山水，与大自然相亲相伴。

为登山方便，谢灵运还专门设计了一双带齿的木屐，人称"谢公屐"，这或为中国最早的登山旅游鞋。据说，谢灵运登山时，将前齿取下；下山时，又将后齿解除，穿上这双鞋，上山下山，如履平川，其乐融融。

谢灵运每次出游时，身后总跟着一支庞大的队伍。这其中有其好友，也有为其挑担铺路的仆人。有时这支浩大的队伍在行进途中伐木掘石，声势动众，引起众多百姓的观望。

见多识广的旅游生涯，使谢灵运的文学创作成绩斐然。他的《游名山志》是中国古代游记文学的诞生标志之一。尤其是他的山水诗，意境幽静，画面清丽，极大地丰富和开拓了诗的境界，从而扭转了东晋以来的玄言诗风，确立了山水诗的地位。从此山水诗成为中国诗歌发展史上的一个流派。谢灵运被誉为我国山水诗人的鼻祖。

与谢灵运同时代的大诗人是陶渊明。他因不愿"为五斗米折腰"而毅然"解绶去职",回到老家浔阳(今九江),在悠然南山(今庐山)之下,常与其他文人一起,于大自然的怀抱中唱和诗歌。陶渊明的《桃花源记》大约作于南朝宋初年。文中通过记叙自己"旅游"到桃花源,描绘了一个乌托邦式的理想社会,表现了诗人对当时社会制度的彻底否定与对理想世界的无限追慕之情。陶渊明是田园诗的开创者。它以纯朴自然的语言、高远拔俗的意境,为中国诗坛开辟了新天地,并直接影响到唐代田园诗派,所以,陶渊明有"田园诗人"之称。

唐朝是中国封建社会的鼎盛时期,因科举制度的实行,中下层知识分子的从政热情得到了极大的提高。魏晋以来知识分子远离官场,一味寄情山水的颓废精神状态有了根本改观。

在唐朝,"游宦"(为谋取仕途的旅游)与"游学"(考察旅游)十分盛行。"他们一方面欣赏山水,验证史书的正误;另一方面广交朋友,切磋诗艺,以求学问的提高。"(《旅游学概论》)在这些文人雅士之中,虽有自负才智而不愿科举者,但他们与魏晋时代的消极遁世行为有着天壤之别,他们常胸怀济世之志而远游,其中"托物言志"就是较高层次的旅游活动形式。李白、杜甫、柳宗元、欧阳修、苏轼等是杰出的代表人物。

李白(701—762),字太白,号青莲居士,祖籍陇西成纪(今甘肃秦安县)是我国历史上最伟大的浪漫主义诗人。李白于武后长安元年(701)出生在安西都护府碎叶城(今吉尔吉斯斯坦托克马克城),约五岁时,随父迁居蜀中绵州昌隆县(今四川江油县)青莲乡。李白少年时期受到很好的家庭教育,10岁诵诗书,观百家,作诗赋,学剑术,爱好十分广泛;15岁左右就写得一手出色的好文章;20岁以后,在蜀中漫游,饱览了四川的壮丽景色。

开元十四年(726),26岁的李白"仗剑去国",辞亲远游,开始了以安陆(今属湖北)为中心的十六年的大漫游,历经两湖、江浙、河南、山西等地区,足迹踏遍近半个中国。

天宝元年(742),42岁的李白由友人推荐,应诏赴京,供奉翰林。被召之初,李白异常兴奋,写下了"仰天大笑出门去,我辈岂是蓬蒿人"(《南陵别儿童入京》)这样的诗句。但不久他就发现,当时的唐玄宗昏庸腐朽,纵情声色,不理朝政。李白怀着理想幻灭的痛苦,开始了以梁园(开封)为中心的第二次漫游,历时11年,"浪迹天下,以诗酒自适"(刘全白《唐故翰林学士李君碣记》)。天宝三年秋,李白在洛阳和汴州分别遇见了杜甫和高适,三人便结伴同行,畅游了梁园和济南等地,李杜从此便结下了深厚的情谊:"醉眠秋共被,携手日同行"(杜甫《与李十二同寻范十隐居》)。这一段游历时期,是诗人诗歌创作最丰富的时期,代表作品有:《梦游天姥吟留别》《将进酒》《北风行》《梁园吟》等。

李白在政治上虽然没能实现自己的理想,但在诗歌创作中却取得了伟大的成就。

尤其是他一生酷爱旅游，动辄"人生在世不称意，明朝散发弄扁舟""五岳寻仙不辞远，一生好入名山游"，足迹遍布中国大江南北。他用大量的诗篇，歌咏山河的壮美，寄托爱国的深情。在诗人的笔下，险峻的山道，奇伟的群峰，奔腾的江河，飞泻的瀑布，都显得壮美动人。如他描写庐山瀑布："飞流直下三千尺，疑是银河落九天"；他慨叹蜀道坎坷："噫吁嚱，危乎高哉！蜀道之难，难于上青天！"

杜甫与李白一向被视为唐诗世界中两大巨擘，他们构成了唐诗的两大风格流派。杜甫原是河南巩县人，生长在一个没落的官僚家庭，从小就下苦功读书，也游历了许多名山大川。他曾经描写唐朝盛景："稻米流脂粟米白，公私仓廪俱丰实。九州道路无豺虎，远行不劳吉日出。"他在20岁时，南下漫游江南吴越等地，四年后回到东都洛阳，及试不举。但这次失败并没有挫折他的信心，次年他又东游齐赵，过着青春年少的"裘马"生活。他在游历泰山时写道："会当凌绝顶，一览众山小"，少年豪气，跃然纸上；在旅游途中，他与李白相遇，在《赠李白》诗中写道："亦有梁宋游，方期拾瑶草"，表达诗人对未来的美好愿望。

杜甫写过许多有关旅游活动的诗歌，他的一些咏物、写景的诗，往往渗透着对国家和人民的深厚感情。例如在著名的春游诗《丽人行》中，"三月三日天气新，长安水边多丽人"，诗人并没有直接去斥责杨氏兄妹的荒淫，而是通过对他们服饰、饮食等方面的描述，显露诗人的爱憎态度。杜甫被后人尊称为"诗圣"，与"诗仙"李白齐名。

由于经济的发达和文化的昌盛，唐代没有哪个诗人不爱山水，没有哪个文士不爱旅游。他们读书时，有"游学"；走上仕途时，有"游宦"；一旦官场失意，便归宿自然，寄情山水。"唐宋八大家"之一的柳宗元，就是这样一个典型代表。

柳宗元是唐代文坛改革家，可他在政治上却一直不如意，早期被贬永州（今湖南醴陵）。在永州十余年间，柳宗元因看不惯官场的丑恶，便把目光投向永州秀丽的山水。他钟情于山水，寓意于诗文，写下了不少山水名篇。游记代表了他散文的最高成就，其中《永州八记》，在中国文学宝库中闪烁着耀眼的光芒。

如今游客到湖南醴陵，还可以参观为纪念柳宗元而建的柳子庙。公元前810年，柳宗元定居冉溪，将它更名为愚溪，并写下《八愚诗》纪其事。《愚溪诗序》便是为这八首诗所作的诗序。愚溪何"愚"之有呢？柳宗元认为溪之愚有三点，一是它的水流低下，不能用来灌溉田地；二是它的水流湍急，到处是露出水面的石头，大船开不进；三是河道隐蔽偏僻，河床浅窄，蛟龙不屑一顾，不能兴云作雨。他揶揄自己时逢清明时代，言行却常常违背事理，岂止是愚，除这条小溪外，简直没有哪一个比他更愚蠢了。以溪之愚，衬己之愚，这种大智若愚，这种愤世嫉俗，足以说明柳宗元在永州徜徉山水，并非为山水而山水，而是在寻胜访幽中抒发心中的不平，寄托一种执着的理想。

宋元时代的大旅行家很多，他们当中不仅有在中国国内旅游的旅行家，而且还有一些去他国旅行的国际旅行家。

苏东坡名轼，在中国古代文人中，他是一位"全人"，在文学艺术领域，诗、词、赋、文、画、音乐都有极高的造诣。在旅游方面，苏东坡也显示出他那特有的潇洒豪迈，游域之广、游绩之丰，为别人所难匹及。

苏东坡出生于四川一个官僚家庭，长大后，随父苏洵进京考进士。他曾二十六次在十一个省十六下州任职，从而使他借每次赴任或离任的机会，到处游览各地的名胜古迹，写出大量赞颂大自然的豪放诗词。

苏东坡非常爱西湖，他曾两次到杭州做官。在杭州，他被西湖的湖光山色所陶醉，几乎天天前往西湖观景。《杭州府志》这样描述苏东坡的杭州生活："东坡镇余杭，遇游西湖……从出钱塘门，坡则自涌金门从一二老兵泛舟绝湖而来，饭于普安院，徜徉灵隐、地竺间，以吏牍自随，至冷泉亭，据案剖决，落笔如风雨，纷争辩讼，谈笑而办。已，乃与僚吏剧饮。薄晚，则乘马以归。"据统计，他写的有关西湖的诗词达三百以上。

苏东坡第二次去杭州做官时，由于年久失修，西湖已草盛水浅，湖面减少近一半。为治理西湖，苏东坡发动20万民工疏浚西湖，用挖出来的淤泥修筑长堤，连接湖的南北两岸，并建桥畅通湖水，使西湖恢复了其烟波浩瀚的景色，"苏堤春晓"也成为自古以来西湖有名的旖旎景点。为感谢苏东坡，杭州百姓送来他爱吃的猪肉以表心意。他让家人将肉切成块，连酒一起送给民工。民工烧肉时，因误把"连酒一起送"听为"连酒一起烧"，结果加酒后烧出来的肉味更鲜美浓郁。"东坡肉"随之传开，成为苏杭一带的历史名菜。

在湖北黄冈县黄州镇时，虽然正值他被贬官，"亲戚故人皆惊散"之时，他依然或泛舟于长江，或立醉于江亭，并写下了"大江东去，浪淘尽，千古风流人物……"的《念奴娇·赤壁怀古》这首千古绝唱。

晚年苏东坡再次被贬官至海南儋州。即使在"食无肉，病无药，居无室，出无友，冬无炭，夏无泉"的困苦劳顿、孤独寂寞的流放生活中，苏东坡仍还是一如既往地到处游览，乐而忘返。将自己的身心全部沉浸在山水自然之中，达到"圆融极至"、"无往不适"的人生境界。二年后，苏东坡遇赦，回归途中不幸患病，在常州逝世。

与苏东坡相似，同样爱好旅游，并在旅游文学、史学、艺术方面有所作为的宋元大旅游家，还有《岳阳楼记》的作者范仲淹、《游山西村》的陆游、《资治通鉴》的司马光、因游生文的王安石、有游有记的欧阳修、妙景自游的张可久以及朱熹、范大成、辛弃疾等，可谓游文相生，游人璀璨。

(4) 艰苦探索的地理考察

顾名思义,考察旅行是指后人对前人的遗著的正误进行考证或探索世界奥秘而形成的治学和旅游相结合的实践活动。这是自古以来"读万卷书,行万里路"的中国优秀文化传统之一。一些文人学者或矢志求学之士,通过长期艰苦的实地考察旅行,在学术上和科学上取得巨大成就的同时,也成为著名的旅行家。

司马迁是西汉伟大的史学家、文学家。字子长,夏阳(今陕西韩城)人。他出生于史官世家,渊源久长的家学对司马迁治学道路有深刻的影响。20岁时,他随博士褚太等六人"循行天下",开始了他的游历生活。

据《史记·太史公自序》《汉书·司马迁传》记载,他"南游江、淮,上会稽,探禹穴,窥九疑,浮于沅、湘,北涉汶、泗,讲业齐、鲁之都,观孔子之遗风,乡射邹、峄,困鄱、薛、彭城,过梁、楚以归。"于此,后人可以得知,司马迁的足迹到过会稽(今浙江绍兴),到过姑苏,到过淮阴,到过丰沛,到过楚……在薛地,他考察了孟尝君的封邑;在邹鲁,他拜祭了孔孟的家乡,了解儒家思想。此外,他还北过涿鹿,登长城,南游沅湘,西至崆峒。壮游使他开阔了眼界,增长了知识。

公元前99年,司马迁因李陵事件而受到"腐刑",精神受到极大刺激,但他以古人孔子、屈原、左丘明、孙膑、韩非等在逆境中发愤有为鼓励自己,终于以惊人的意志忍辱负重地活了下来,"人固有一死,死有重于泰山,或轻于鸿毛",终于完成了"究天人之际,通古今之变,成一家之言"的巨著——《史记》。

《史记》是中国史学上第一部纪传体通史,开创了纪传体通史的恢宏先河。《史记》被鲁迅誉为"史家之绝唱,无韵之离骚",是当之无愧的。司马迁是中国古代学术考查旅行的最早和最杰出的代表。

郦道元,字善长,范阳涿鹿(今河北涿州市)人。郦道元出生于官宦世家,少年时随父旅居山东,游遍境内山川。成年后,经常随魏孝文帝出巡至今山西、河南等地,对那儿的江河水系和地理风貌进行考查。

郦道元从少年时代起,就有志于地理学的研究,尤其喜欢研究各地的水文地理、自然风貌。他充分利用在各地做官的机会进行实地考察,足迹遍及今河北、河南、山东、山西、安徽、江苏、内蒙等广大地区,每到一个地方,他都要游览名胜古迹、山川河流,悉心勘察水流地势,并访问当地长者,了解古今水道的变迁情况及河流的渊源所在、流经地区等等,掌握了大量的第一手资料。同时,他还阅读了大量古代地理学著作,如《山海经》《禹贡》《禹本纪》《周礼职方》《汉书·地理志》《水经》等,为他进行地理学研究和著述打下了扎实的基础。

《水经》是三国时代桑钦所著的一部地理学著作,此书简要记述了137条全国主要河流的水道情况。原文仅1万多字,记载相当简略,缺乏系统性,对水道的来龙去脉及流经地区的地理情况记载不够详细、具体。为此郦道元利用自己掌握的丰富的第一手资料。在《水经》的基础上，郦道元终于完成了《水经注》这一地理学名著。

郦道元为了写《水经注》，先后两次随北魏孝文帝出游，历时两年，行程万里。他学习司马迁写《史记》前的准备工作，所到之处，拜访许多耆老宿绅，参观许多历史遗迹，使他得到了大量前所未闻的新鲜材料。

由于书中引用转录了大量书籍和碑刻资料，文笔绚丽，具有较高的史学价值和文学价值。郦道元因此被后世公认为山水游记文学的鼻祖。

沈括是北宋著名科学家、政治家。他出生于钱塘一个仕官之家。年轻时便随父游历大江南北，据史书记载，他"凡所到之处，莫不询究，或医师，或里巷，或小人，以至士大夫之家，山林隐士，无不求访"。

在考察了风景秀丽、诸峰峭拔险怪的雁荡山后，沈括断定雁荡奇峰的形成"当时为谷中大水冲激，沙土尽云，唯巨石岿然挺立耳"。在奉命出使途经太行山麓时，沈括发现"山崖之间，往往衔螺蚌壳及石子如鸟卵者，横亘石壁如带"，由此他推测说："此乃昔之海滨，泥沙淤积而成陆地。"这些判断已被今日科学所证实，沈括也就成为科学解释我国华北地质形成的第一人。

在出使契丹期间，沈括实地了解当地山川形势、人情风俗，返回朝廷后。精心制作完成了我国第一幅立体地图《使契丹图钞》。在西北边境任职时，他发现当地有一种谓之"脂水"、"泥油"的物质，并断言"此物后必大行于世"。这一物质就是我们现代生活不可缺少的自然能源——石油。

晚年的沈括花了八年时间，潜心整理自己的笔记，因其宅前泉水溪名曰梦溪，所以起名为《梦溪笔谈》。笔记中，分别对当时科学发展和生产技术的情况，如指南针、活字印刷术、炼钢、炼铜的方法等，无不详细记录，"使之流传后世"。

《徐霞客游记》以日记体裁详细地记录了中国明代著名旅行家和地理学家徐霞客（1586—1641）一生旅行生涯中的所见所闻，包括山川河流、气候植被、风俗人情等，既富有文学色彩，又具有重要科学价值，是世界上较早的一本关于岩溶地貌的论著。

徐霞客生活在缙绅富贵之家，自幼受到良好的家庭教育，从小就特别喜爱看历史、地理和游记一类的书籍。成年后因不满明末政治黑暗而无意"科举取士"，立志游遍九州五岳，"问奇于名山大川"。

22岁那年，是徐霞客迈向旅游生涯的开端，他头戴母亲亲手为他编织的"远游冠"，告别了家人，开始了其一生先后达34年的探险游历生活。他北历燕冀，南涉闽粤，西北直攀太华之巅，西南远达云贵边陲，足迹遍及江苏、浙江、山东、山西、陕西、河南、河北、安徽、江西、福建、广东、广西、湖南、湖北、贵州、云南等16个省。

徐霞客出外旅游考察，得到了母亲的大力支持。母亲激励他说："志在四方，男子事也。"徐霞客的母亲甚至不顾70岁高龄，还满怀豪情陪同徐霞客游览了勾曲（今江苏宜兴一带）等地。

旅行中，徐霞客勤写笔记，每到一处必审视山脉来去，山脉分合，考查奇山异水成因。有时为了"索其源，探其脉"，有些地方还一游再游，"三误三返"。

他根据自己多年的旅游实践，总结出了一套系统观察与综合描述地理环境、表现地理特征的区域比较法等解释地理现象和成因的方法，这种近代地理学研究方法，比西方地理学家早了200年。他对中国西南石灰岩地貌的记载，比欧洲人也早了200年。因此，徐霞客被认为是近代地理学的先驱。

1636年，徐霞客母亲去世，他已51岁。徐霞客少了一种人间骨肉的牵挂，他从家乡出发，途经江苏、浙江、江西、湖南、广西、贵州，到了此次旅游和考察最远的地方——云南，历时5个春秋，成为徐霞客一生中最后一次和为期最长的一次。

为考察地理，徐霞客长年累月奔波在荒山野林，不仅接受着大自然的考验，而且还受到各种人为因素的挑战。他脚穿布鞋，肩背行装，粗茶素食，夜宿寺院，在最后一次考察旅行途中，他三次遇盗，四次绝粮，到了"身无寸丝"、饥肠辘辘的境地。在极度困难的情况下，一些好心人劝他不要再冒风险进行考察了，徐霞客则说："我如果遇到困难就结束考察返回故乡，以后若想重新出来进行考察，妻子和儿女必定不会同意。我继续考察的意志不能改变。"他说道："我已背着挖土的工具，什么地方不能埋我的骨头？"

为了探寻自然界的奥秘，徐霞客猎奇而从，见险而行，登山必登最高之巅，下洞必到最深之地。一次他在湖南茶陵时，欲考察当地传说中的"妖洞"——麻叶洞。消息传出，轰动了周围的乡亲，他们从四面八方赶来，十分惊奇地把徐霞客包围起来。有人说"洞中有神龙"，有人说"洞中有精怪"……然而徐霞客却毫不畏惧，从容地脱下衣服，拿着火把下洞进行探察。在洞中，他不仅没有遇到人们传说的各种神龙精怪，却感受了"石幻异形，肤理顿换，片窍俱灵"的大千世界。

徐霞客一生，足迹南抵滇粤，北至燕冀，历经19个省市，成为我国历史上第一位不肩负政府使命，没有朝廷资助，既不同于宗教旅游的求神拜佛，也不同于士大夫漫游的风花雪月，而是纯粹出自个人爱好的，以崇尚山水、崇尚实学为目的而进行考察旅行的伟大旅行家。《徐霞客游记》也成为我国第一部野外考察记录和优秀地理著作，因其文笔生动，内容精详，所以被誉为"世间真文字、大文字、奇文字"和"古今记游第一"。

中国明清时期，本土资本主义处于萌芽时期，逐渐衰落的封建社会面临一场新的变革。许多怀有抱负的知识分子，纷纷走出书斋，在大自然中游历和思考，寻找济世利民的良方。《本草纲目》作者李时珍，便是这样一位大有作为的历史人物。

李时珍，字东璧，号濒湖，湖北蕲（今湖北省蕲春县）人，生于明武宗正德十三年（1518）的一个世医家庭。李时珍自14岁中了秀才后的九年中，其三次到武昌考举人均名落孙山。于是，他放弃了科举做官的打算，专心学医，向父亲求说并表明决心："身如逆流船，心比铁石坚。望父全儿志，至死不怕难。"

李时珍行医的十几年中，不但熟读了八百余种万余卷的医书，还看过不少历史、地理和文学名著。

在编写《本草纲目》的过程中，最使李时珍头痛的就是由于药名的混杂，莫衷一是。在他父亲的启示下，李时珍认识到，"读万卷书"固然需要，但"行万里路"更不可少。于是，他远涉深山旷野，遍访名医宿儒，搜求民间验方，观察和收集药物标本。他首先在家乡蕲州一带采访。后来，他多次出外采访。除湖广外，还到过江西、江苏、安徽好多地方。盛产药材的江西庐山和南京的摄山、茅山、牛首山，都有他的足迹。

李时珍了解药物，并不满足于走马看花式的调查，而是一一采视。当时，太和山五龙宫产的"榔梅"，被道士们说成是吃了"可以长生不老的仙果"。他们每年采摘回来，进贡皇帝，官府严禁其他人采摘。李时珍不信道士们的鬼话，于是，他不顾道士们的反对，竟冒险采了一个。经研究，发现它的功效跟普通的桃子、杏子一样，能生津止渴而已，是一种变了形的榆树的果实，并没有什么特殊功效。

李时珍经过长期的实地调查，于1578年完成了《本草纲目》编写工作。全书约有200万字，52卷，载药1892种，新增药物374种，载方10000多个，附图1000多幅，成了我国药物学的空前巨著，在动植物分类学等许多方面有突出成就，还涉及天文、地理、科技等方面，达尔文称赞它是"中国古代的百科全书"。

（5）执着顽强的宗教远足

宗教的产生是人类精神活动的产物。早期人类对风雨雷电、江河湖海、高山巨川、日月星辰等理解不深，从而产生敬畏，继而开始膜拜、祈祷活动。人类自从脱离动物界变成理性动物后，就开始了对自然界、人类社会和人的自身的来龙去脉的思考。宗教远足是以取经拜佛、寻仙求福、布道施法为目的的一种古老的旅行方式。它历史久远，即使是今天，也是一种影响深广的旅游方式。

魏晋南北朝时期，由于朝廷的提倡，佛教逐渐兴盛起来。例如在南北朝，仅建康一带就有寺庙500余所。唐代诗人杜牧有一首《江南春》云："千里莺啼绿映红，水村山郭酒旗风。南朝四百八十寺，多少楼台烟雨中。"诗中所记，便是当时时尚的真实写照。当时曾把官赐者称为"寺"，私造的叫"招提"。后来通称佛寺为"刹"，故寺院也有梵刹、禅刹、古刹之称。刹是梵文音译，意为土田、国。

佛教寺庙大多建在名山之中，故有"天下名山僧占多"之说。葛洪在《抱朴子·金丹篇》中所描述的道教中的"仙境"：华山、泰山、霍山、恒山、嵩山、少室山、长山、太白山、终南山、女儿山、地肺山、王屋山、抱犊山、安丘山、潜山、青城山、峨眉山、经山、天台山、罗浮山等等，也大多为中国的风景胜地。

为求风调雨顺，免受灾祸袭扰，古人很早就开始了祭祀山神的活动。据史籍记载，当时，有451座山被奉为山神祭祀，贫民和统治者都不例外。据《史记·封禅书》载："天子祭天下名川大山，五岳视三公，四渎视诸侯，诸侯祭其疆内名山大川。"

各种寺庙古刹依附于名山，形成"天下名山僧占多"的客观现象。反过来，名山之所以有名，则大多因为其拥有众多的古刹名寺。自古民众游览名山，大多也是因为他们要朝山进香。即使到了如今，情况依然如此。这也应验了古人之言：山不在高，有仙则名。

魏晋时期，庙主和寺庙拥有许多特权，如土地、薪俸、商贸、高利贷等。一时间，寺院经济发展迅速，这样就为宗教旅游提供了经济和物质条件。取经、传经和修行活动日益频繁，许多僧人和信徒都加入到求法修行的旅行者队伍中来。

魏晋时期佛教旅行活动，大致可以分成两类：一类是为传经、取经而从事的旅行活动。这个时期，因为海陆路比较发达，所以不少国外僧人来华传经。最早从陆路来华传经的是大月氏（今阿富汗）使者伊存，他于西汉末年到达中国。随后竺法兰、摄摩腾两人由敦煌东游长安、洛阳，他们死后安葬在今河南白马寺。三国孙权时代，陆续有僧人从越南等南亚地区漂泊而来。其中天竺（今印度）人菩提达摩，来到中国后，对中国文化影响较深。史书记载，他先后到过广州，建康（今南京）等地的寺庙，最后落脚河南嵩山。在嵩山，他开创了静坐修行的佛教禅宗派，并创立了享誉世界的少林武术。

这一时期的外来传经者，促进和繁荣了我国佛教文化，同时也推动了我国僧人西行求法旅行的步伐。据考证，中国佛教史上第一位西行求法者是曹魏时代的朱士行。他是颖川（今河南）人，平日在诵经念法中深感有些读本上下缺乏连贯，每每看到外来传经者的身影，便动了出国求法、寻本溯源的念头。继他之后，又有康法郎等数十位僧人分别去了西域、印度等地求法，其中最为著名的是山西平远郡武阳名僧法显，他根据自己所见所闻撰写的《佛国记》，对当今研究南亚古代史都有十分重要的作用。

魏晋时期外来僧人传经和中国僧人西行求法，标志着中国首具规模的国际旅游是从宗教开始的。为促进中国佛教的发展和中外文化的交流开了先河。

除了僧人的西行，佛教旅行的另一种形式就是本土僧人在自然山水中修身养性、清谈佛理的旅游。当时有名的僧人旅游家分别有于法兰、支道林、释道安、慧远等人。他们认为，"山水可以休闲"，可以养性，在自然中品味山水，切磋禅理，是高僧的一种风度。

慧远是释道安的高徒，45岁时，为弘扬佛理，他告别师傅只身南下。慧远路过庐山时，"见庐山间旷，可以息心"，于是就在西林寺筑龙泉精舍，后又迁东林寺。在长达36年时间里，慧远"迹不入俗，影不出山"，阐扬佛理，遂成远近闻名的南方佛教中一重要派别的代表人物。

　　道教是中国本土教。在秦汉时期，为求长生不老，秦始皇、汉武帝就曾派高士走访奇山异水，人们将这些高士的活动称为仙游。魏晋时期，随着道教的兴盛，参加者不仅有道士，文人墨客、宦海官吏、普通百姓都加入到这一行列中来。

　　葛洪是东晋时期著名的道教领袖，擅丹道，习医术，研精道儒，学贯百家，思想渊深，著作弘富。他不仅对道教理论的发展卓有建树，而且于治术、医学、音乐、文学等方面亦多成就。

　　为了搜集道教的神术仙方，葛洪"不远数千里崎岖冒涉"，广游天下名山，广结天下朋友，终于得到不少仙养典籍。据说，在他81岁高龄去世时，众人仍观"其颜色如生，体亦柔软"。

　　由于宗教的兴盛，各地寺庙、道观不断涌现，普通信徒也日渐众多。这些信徒虽然不能像教长方师那样去云游四方，但一旦农闲之时，尤其是节假祭祀之日，去宗教圣地参观朝拜甚众，使得宗教旅行的规模日渐扩大。但宗教旅游真正盛行起来，还是经济文化都兴旺发达的隋唐时期。

　　到了唐代，禅宗开始兴盛，禅僧寻师访道之风蔓延。行脚成为当时的一种特殊的修行方式。禅僧的行脚不同于一般意义上的游山玩水，他们四处游历，往来于各宗师名派之间，切磋佛理，增长见识，开阔心智。

　　禅宗行脚的这一独特的修行方式，是禅宗根本思想的体现。禅宗强调"无住者人之本性"，所以在修行上"贵自求不贵他求"、"贵行解不贵知解"、"贵超圣不贵住圣"。

　　所谓"住"即意念定住在某一点上。禅宗认为，人若拥有什么，"心"就会被什么所缚住，人所拥有的东西越多，"心"被系绊的东西也越多，只有把所拥有的东西减少到最低点，人的心才会无过多杂念，才能真正做到六根清净。因此，行脚僧通常是通过云游方式，去体验那种闲云野鹤、无牵无挂的禅的境界。因禅僧的此一行为没有任何功利目的，所以他们得以与山水做伴，与大自然融为一体。

　　禅僧们日日漫游于山山水水之间，日长月久，吸取大地精华，炼就非凡修养，对山水草木的感受自然与普通人不一样。这种不同，反映在他们所写的诗歌当中，能看到与传统的文人山水诗歌的区别，为中国古代诗坛增添了新的内涵。

　　他们往往以佛寺为题，选择的意象点总是幽谷深山、荒寺白云、月夜寒松之类，以从中体会到禅悦和禅趣。如常建有一首《题破山寺后禅院》，诗曰："清晨入古寺，初日照高林。曲径通幽处，禅房花木深。山光悦鸟性，潭影空人心。万籁此俱寂，唯闻钟磬声。"此诗极言山寺之寂、之静、以突出禅机禅味，实为写山寺的名篇。其他还有：《赠琴僧》"太古清音发指端，月当松顶夜堂寒，悲风流水多呜咽，不听希声不用弹"；《忘惶》"方春不觉来朱夏，秋色蝉鸣翠影斜。夜来风急柴扉破，满地霜铺落叶花"；《半窗松影半窗月》"半窗松影半窗月，一个蒲团一个僧，盘膝坐来中夜后，飞蛾扑灭佛前灯"等，都是描绘虚灵缥缈禅的意境之佳作。

因经济的发展和文化的发达，唐朝佛教僧人西行求法出现新的高潮。一批佛教旅行家将自己的游迹延伸得更远，行脚行到国外。这类旅游当中，往往因路途遥远艰险，使其披上一层神奇色彩。中国四大名著《西游记》唐僧的原型玄奘，就是这种旅行的首倡者。

玄奘（600—645），俗姓陈，名袆，洛州缑氏（今河南偃师缑氏镇）人，生于儒学家庭，自幼聪慧过人。据说他八岁时，父亲给他讲《孝经》时，讲到"曾子避席"，玄奘忽然整理好衣服，站起来立在一边。父亲问他怎么啦？玄奘说："曾子闻师命避席，吾今奉慈训，岂敢安坐？"

玄奘遍学了传入中国的各家经论，看到其间诸多相异之处、不同之说，便立志要解决这些分歧。他选择西行求法的道路，希望在印度能找到统一国内佛教异说的经典。

公元前629年，玄奘离京西进，在高昌王和西突厥可汗等西域首领的协助下，穿越西域16国，越大雪山，又历十余国，进入北印度的滥波国。公元前633年，玄奘到达印度当时的佛学的中心那烂陀寺，该寺常住僧就有数万人。玄奘在该寺学习哲学、佛学、逻辑、医学、工艺、音韵等多方面知识，过了5年，成为精通50部经论的十大德之一。继而，玄奘离开那烂陀寺，先后去东印度、南印度和西印度游历，最后又回到烂陀寺。在那烂陀寺内，他有机会跟主持戒贤学习了《瑜伽师地论》和其他大小乘经，实现了玄奘在国内时的愿望。

经过这一番学习，玄奘对瑜伽和中观达到融会贯通的地步，并著有《会宗论》。由此，玄奘在印度的名声很大。后又写了《制恶见论》，被戒贤赞叹为"天下无人能敌。"玄奘在印度时，曾经有一位外道顺世论者将40条论点挂在寺门口，邀人辩论，称若辩不赢，将以斩首相谢。一般人都不敢去应对，只有玄奘去了。几番来回，顺世论者败北，要求履约斩首，玄奘不允许，只要求他禀事佛法就行了。

玄奘回国之前，戒日王为他在曲女城举行告别大会。会上，玄奘提出了他在《会宗论》和《制恶见论》中的观点，18天内，没有一人提出疑问，大家便一致推荐并授予他"大乘天"、"解脱天"的荣誉称号。

公元前645年中国农历正月24日，玄奘到达京师西郊，相迎者数十万，人群拥挤，道路阻塞，玄奘等几乎进不了城。当时唐太宗在洛阳，与太宗见面后，唐太宗要其把西域所见所闻写出来，又劝他还俗从政，玄奘只答应了太宗提出的前一条。

玄奘回国时，带回657部梵本经。玄奘回国后的近20年内，共译经75部，1350卷，另外还著有《大唐西域记》等作品，一些表、启、书等则收入《大慈恩寺三藏法师传》中。

玄奘的事迹，在唐代僧人中引起了很大反响，此后以玄奘为榜样西去求法者前赴后继，至死不渝。仅《大唐西域求法高僧传》就记载有此类高僧60人。他们面对艰难险阻，不畏惧，不退缩，不听天命，以一种不达目的绝不罢休的虔诚胸怀，一步一个脚印走下去，成为后世代代相传的历史佳话。

中国土生土长的道教在唐代也得到前所未有的大发展。因道教创始人为李耳，与唐皇同姓，所以道教在唐朝享有与佛教同等的特权。全国各地兴建了许多道教祠院，尤其是"三官（天官、地官和水官）"庙遍布全国。"送子张仙"、"钟馗捉鬼"、"八仙过海"等在今天都有影响的民间故事，都是起源于唐朝。受"道在山林"影响，许多著名道人如元丹丘、李治、皇甫松等人，或隐居山中或遨游江湖，陶醉在大自然的神韵之中。从某种程度来说，与佛家相比，道家更领会山水之精华，更贴近旅游之本真。

（6）智勇开拓的外交旅行

所谓外交旅行，是指为了达到某种政治或经济目的，肩负国家使命的而进行的一种旅行方式。这种旅行在中国最早起始于先秦时代，突出表现在烽烟四起的争霸年代，各诸侯国之间，士人频繁的外交游说。苏秦、张仪就是这样的典型代表。到了西汉时期，著名外交家张骞两次出使西域，则是中国旅行史上浓墨重彩的一页。

在汉代以前，西域对几乎所有中原人而言都是十分陌生的神秘地方。西汉初年的时候，虽然人们逐渐从东西往来的商人的描述中了解到西域的一些情况，引起了汉朝人的好奇心，但由于交通不便，西汉人对西域的了解，总是一鳞半爪，很难有新的突破。

汉武帝时期，汉朝北部边境经常受到匈奴族的袭扰。公元前138年，为了抗击匈奴，汉武帝派张骞出使西域，联合大月氏人，一起夹击匈奴。

张骞是汉中人，《三国志》作者陈寿说是"汉中成固（今陕西城固县）人"。当时，随行的人有100多人。公元前139年，张骞一行人途经匈奴时，被匈奴抓获，被扣留达10年之久。他采取韬光养晦之计，使匈奴人放松警惕。后来，张骞抓住一个机会和少数随从逃跑，张骞在东归返回的途中，再次被匈奴抓获，后又趁匈奴内乱逃回长安。张骞前后用了13年时间，出发时带的随从100人，返回时，只剩下一人同行。

张骞这次出使，是中国历史上第一次以汉朝使者的身份，与西域的一些国家交往，沟通了汉朝与西域各国之间的联系。这次出使虽然没有达到汉武帝要求的政治目的,但是通过他的旅行观察,却获得了有关西域各国极为丰富的地理知识和民情风物,使生活在中原内地的人们了解到西域的实况,并激发了汉武帝"拓边"的雄心,以后发动了一系列抗击匈奴的战争。

公元前119年,汉王朝为了进一步联络乌孙国,断"匈奴右臂",便派张骞再次出使西域。这次与上次出使西域不同,不用再担心匈奴袭扰,张骞带了300多人,顺利地到达了乌孙。但由于乌孙内乱,未能实现结盟目的。乌孙使者和张骞一起回到长安,之后他们把在中原王朝看到的繁荣在乌孙广为传颂。其后汉朝与乌孙之间农牧产品的交流蓬勃开展起来,最终还确立了和亲关系。

张骞不畏艰险,两次出使西域的经历,加强了西汉政府与西域少数民族的关系。他两次出使西域,不仅丰富了中国人的地理知识,扩大了中国人的地理视野,而且直接促进了中国和西方物质文化交流。中国精美的手工艺品,特别是丝绸、漆器、玉器、铜器传到西方,而西域的土产如苜蓿、葡萄、胡桃(核桃)、石榴、胡麻(芝麻)、胡豆(蚕豆)、胡瓜(黄瓜)、大蒜、胡萝卜,各种毛织品、毛皮、良马、骆驼、狮子、鸵鸟等陆续传入中国。西方的音乐、舞蹈、绘画、雕塑、杂技也传入中国,对中国古代文化艺术产生了积极的影响。张骞西行,沟通了亚洲内陆交通要道,与西欧诸国正式开始了友好往来,促进了东西经济文化的广泛交流,开拓了从我国甘肃、新疆到今阿富汗、伊朗等地的陆路交通,即著名的"丝绸之路",因而他完全可称之为中国走向世界的第一人。

畅通了140余年的丝绸之路,在西汉末年、东汉初年又因匈奴的干扰而几近中断。朝廷于是选派班超再度出使西域。

班超是咸阳人,他从小勤奋好学,一心想像张骞那样立功异邦。东汉建立后,经过50年的"休养生息",经济逐步恢复,国力渐渐强大。公元前73年,班超带领随从到了鄯善国后,了解到了由于匈奴人的监视,鄯善国王不敢和他们亲近的真相,他们就纵火焚烧了匈奴人的营舍。鄯善国王见到汉朝使臣如此机智骁勇,立即打消了顾虑,归附汉朝。西域其他国家见此备受震动,纷纷改怀亲汉之心。从此,西域各国恢复了同汉朝的关系,纷纷派遣使者悦服汉朝,阻塞了五六十年的丝绸之路又得以重新开通。在西域南道上,还出现了"大漠无兵阻,穷边有游客"的和平景象。

其时,班超还派甘英出使西罗马,由于各种原因,甘英虽然仅到达波斯湾就中途返回了,但是,他的这次旅行了解了许多有关中亚各国的宝贵资料。班超在西域前后呆了30余年,使50多个国家与东汉通好。

元代著名航海家汪大渊,字焕章,是江西南昌人,西方学者称他为"东方的马可波罗"。还在他少年时,就跟随长辈游历了当时中国最大的商港,也是世界最大商港之一的福建泉州。泉州港内各种肤色和操各种语言的人们摩肩接踵,各种中外物品堆积如山，让他煞是兴奋。尤其是那些中外商人、水手所讲的异国风情，深深地激起了汪大渊的好奇心。

1330年，年仅20岁的汪大渊来到泉州，搭乘泉州远洋商船，开始了他的第一次远行。这次海上旅游，从泉州港出海，1334年夏秋间返回泉州，前后有数年时间。他从泉州经海南岛、占城、马六甲、爪哇、苏门答腊、缅甸、印度、波斯、阿拉伯、埃及，再横渡地中海到西北非洲的摩洛哥，然后回到埃及，继而出红海到索马里，往南直到莫桑比克，横渡印度洋回到斯里兰卡、苏门答腊、爪哇，再到澳洲，又从澳洲到加里曼丹岛，经菲律宾群岛，最后返回泉州。

这次远航，不仅让汪大渊满足了其由来已久的好奇心，而且使汪大渊打开眼界。1337年，汪大渊第二次又从泉州出发，游历南洋群岛，印度洋西面的阿拉伯海、波斯湾、红海、地中海、莫桑比克海峡及澳洲各地，两年后返回泉州。

汪大渊回国后，便着手编写《岛夷志》的工作。他要把两次航海所亲眼看见的所到各国社会经济、奇风异俗记录成章，作为资料保存下来。后来，汪大渊回到他的故乡南昌，又将《岛夷志》节录成《岛夷志略》，并且在家乡刊印发行。此书便在群众中得以流传开来。

汪大渊在撰写《岛夷志》时，态度是十分严肃的。他曾说书中所记"皆身所游焉，耳目所亲见，传说之事则不载焉"。明朝永乐年间，随郑和七下西洋的马欢说："随其（郑和）所至，……历涉诸邦，……目击而身履之，然后知《岛夷志》所著者不诬。"证实了其所言皆是实。

删略后的《岛夷志略》比其前身虽然文字上有所减少，但仍涉及二百二十多个国家与地区。《岛夷志略》一书中有关台湾、澎湖也有记录，书中记载当时的台湾属澎湖、澎湖属泉州晋江县，盐课、税收均为晋江县所辖办。书中还多处记载了华侨在海外的情况，如泉州吴宅商人居住于古里地闷（今帝汶岛）；元朝出征爪哇部队有一部分官兵仍留在勾栏山（今格兰岛）；在沙里八丹（今印度东岸的讷加帕塔姆），有中国人在1267年建的中国式砖塔，上刻汉字"咸淳三年八月华工"；真腊国（今柬埔寨）有唐人；龙牙门（今新加坡）"男女兼中国人居之"，甚至马鲁涧（今伊朗西北部的马腊格）的首长，是中国临漳人等。

《岛夷志略》也有颇多篇幅记载澳洲。当时中国称澳洲为罗娑斯，把达尔文港一带称为"麻那里"。那时候泉州商人、水手认为澳洲是地球最末之岛，所以称之为"绝岛"。汪大渊描写当时澳洲人的形象时写到，有的"男女异形，不织不衣，以鸟羽掩身，食无烟火，唯有茹毛饮血，巢居穴处而已"；有的"穿五色绡短衫，以朋加剌布为独幅裙系之"。除了一些少见之物，汪大渊还说澳洲北部某地"周围皆水"，实际说的是今天澳洲达尔文港以东一大片沼泽地。在其所记载的澳洲北部海岸的安亨半岛和高达八百米的基培利台地"奇峰磊磊，如天马奔驰，形势临海"。

后来都被证明是真实无误的。

《岛夷志略》因其记载翔实，文字精当，在历史地理的研究上有重要史料价值，因此很早就引起国外史学家的重视。自 1867 年以来，西方学者中陆续有人研究该书，并将该书翻译成多国文字。例如《岛夷志略》中有多处详细记载的澳洲的风土、物产，这应该是至今为止有关澳洲发现的最早的文字记载。但是众多西方学者，他们似乎都不敢或不愿承认汪大渊到过澳洲，因为在汪大渊到澳洲后近 200 年，欧洲人才知道世界上有这样一个大陆。

## 二、世界古代旅游

从国外来看，旅行和旅游活动也是最早产生于埃及、巴比伦和印度等文明古国，还有经济、政治和文化比较发达的古希腊和罗马。

（1）埃及、巴比伦、印度等文明古国的旅游活动

早在公元前 1000 多年前，埃及就是远近闻名的旅游胜地，每年都有众多游客从陆路和水路赶来参观。贵族们有时乘着小船，沿尼罗河顺流而下，一边欣赏两岸风光，一边享用美味佳肴，欢度休闲时光；从陆路而来的贵族们或坐着轿子或赶着四轮马车，云集金字塔旁，目睹金字塔这一神圣奇观。

在金字塔时代，埃及商业异常繁荣，农产品和手工制品都有盈余了，所以贵族们不得不去国外从事商务活动。他们或乘船，或走陆路，到达目的地后，或以物换物，或以金钱在国外采购，以满足他们的金钱欲望和奢侈生活的需求。公元前 2700 余年的时候，埃及同克里特岛、腓尼基、巴勒斯坦、叙利亚等国的海外贸易就十分盛行。

埃及的宗教旅行也很发达。每年要举行几次宗教节日集会活动，其中规模最大的是"布巴提斯市的阿尔铁米司祭"。每到这时，前往参加盛会的男男女女，便乘坐大型游艇，妇女打着手板，男子吹着笛子，歌之舞之，沿途经过临河的镇、市，都要靠岸表演。到达目的地布巴提斯时，便供上丰盛的祭品，进行各种热闹的仪式，男女老幼，白天黑夜，场面甚是壮观。公元前 1501—前 1480 年，埃及皇后 Hatshepsut 还前往 punt（红海地区）旅行，被称为是世界上最早的游程。

美索不达米亚文明产生于幼发拉底河和底格里斯河形成的两河流域，也就是今天的伊拉克、伊朗等中东地区。该地区不仅土地肥沃，物产丰饶，两河、地中海、波斯湾、红海等的存在为其繁茂的商业贸易提供了便利的交通条件。

2100 年前的汉谟拉比时代，巴比伦社会经济文化空前繁荣，庞大的骆驼商队不再限于来往各大城市之间，发达的内河航运和海上航运使得巴比伦商人能与外国商人进行频繁的贸易活动。由于国内外商人众多，当时有一个名叫哈兰城的商业中心，

被称为"商旅城"。游客至今仍可从石头上绳索刻勒的痕迹和砖制楔形文字，想见当时的繁盛。美索不达米亚人所创造的工业、法律、政治、文化、天文、历算等文明，随着人数众多的旅游者如商人、水手和征服者的活动，传播四方。

美国学者威尔·杜兰在《世界文明史——东方的遗产》中这样写道："今天的西方文明，也可说是欧美文明，与其说系起源于克里特、希腊、罗马，不如说系起源于近东。因为事实上，'雅利安人'并没有创造什么文明，他们的文明系自埃及和巴比伦。希腊文明，世所称羡，然究其实际，其文明之绝大部分来自近东各城市。……近东才真正是西方文明的创造者。"

在希腊人之前，腓力基水手和商人就控制着地中海的大部分航权。公元前3000年时，被称为"海上民族"的腓力基，有着发达的商业和手工业，造船工业也高居世界榜首，这为商业旅行提供了条件。由于多年的航海经验，腓力基人认识了北斗星，希腊人将之称为"腓力基星"。他们西越直布罗陀海峡，北至北欧波罗地海各地，东达波斯湾、印度。腓力基人对世界的贡献，突出的一点是将埃及的字母，通过他们的旅行活动传到西方世界。

波斯帝国也是较早有商务旅游活动的国家。它处在东亚和南亚通往西方的交通要道上，自古在东西方文化交流中扮演着重要的角色，因而在各种文明的融合过程中，也发展了丰富多彩的旅游文化。美索不达米亚文明和埃及文明的一部分就被波斯帝国所继承。

波斯强盛时期，为了控制各地分散的总督，加快政治、军事、商务信息的传达，波斯王大兴修路之风。在公元前6世纪中叶，波斯帝国兴建了两条"御道"，第一条东起帝国首都苏萨（今伊朗胡齐斯坦省油兹富尔城西南），直抵地中海的以弗所，全长约2400千米。另一条道起自巴比伦城，东达巴克特里西（大夏）和印度边境。这路后来成为"丝绸之路"西段的基础。

在古代，印度是西方人知道的最远的国家。他们认为，印度民族居住在日出的东方，从印度再往东走，就是荒无人烟的沙漠了。尽管地理遥远和文化不同，但印度与西方的交往很早开始就从未间断过。公元前975年，推罗王希兰的船队就有可能带着象牙、猿猴和孔雀来到印度，以换取香料。据说，印度有些有知识的旅游者有可能到达过雅典，并与当时的大哲学家探讨过哲学问题。印度人问苏格拉底的研究哲学的目的何在，苏格拉底回答："探究人世之事"，而印度人笑着说道："人不首先精通神明，又怎么能了解人世之事呢？"如果此记载属实，那么印度和西方之间的旅游交往的历史就要重写。

希腊人也很早与印度有来往。伏尔泰曾写道："在毕达哥拉斯以前，希腊人就远游印度求学。"据记载，当亚历山大到达印度北部时，他发现印度的道路系统和波斯的一样发达。道路两旁和今天一样，种植了树木，开凿了水井，并设有治安场所和客栈。

(2) 古希腊旅游

克里特岛是一个海岛，处于意大利、埃及和希腊的战略要冲。公元前 2500 年左右，贵族们住入城市搞贸易，为了与埃及、叙利亚等国通商，他们在小岛上建立了不少港口。从公元前 2000 年到公元前 15 世纪，克里特凭借着一支强大的船队建立了海上霸权。《荷马史诗》中提到当时的克里特有 90 个城市，其繁荣和强盛足傲今人。克里特岛便是早期希腊文明的发源地。

公元前 8 世纪，希腊人与地中海的其他民族如腓尼基人、埃及人、叙利亚人和伊特鲁立亚人，就开始了大规模的贸易往来。希腊人用他们的酒、油、毛、矿物、陶器、武器、奢侈品、书等物品，去换回腓尼基的水果和肉类、黑海的鱼、小亚细亚的坚果和塞浦路斯的铜、英格兰的锡等等。为了鼓励外国商人的到来，希腊人还出台了一系列优惠措施，如雅典的优良港口一律对外开放，外国商人可以带走他们所赚的真金白银等。一时间，地中海成了历史上第一个庞大的"共同市场"。

古希腊有一个时期，人们盛行乘着小船作短程航海。到了伊阿宋和传说中的亚尔古英雄时期，人们认为旅游要比正常生活更有趣味。在希腊各城邦，尤其是在雅典，好客是一种普遍的美德。未经介绍的陌生游人也会受到欢迎，一位被邀请的客人永远可以带一位陌生朋友同来。城邦里的许多旅馆都是由富人捐助的，游客即使未经熟人介绍，也照样受到欢迎。

古希腊哲学家泰勒斯、毕达哥拉斯、柏拉图和亚里士多德都是有名的大旅行家。在他们看来，旅游是观察社会、思考人生、享受生活的一个过程。在航海和旅行中不断增长的对客观世界的认识，直接催动了古希腊的自然科学和哲学的产生。

泰勒斯的自然哲学是有关地球的一种玄想物理学。据说他出生在有多种文化汇集的小亚细亚的米利都。因为他早期经商，所以有了不少去各地旅游机会。他在埃及旅游时，去测量金字塔的高度，他认为，当人的影子等于人的实际高度时，就可测量金字塔的高度。他将在外边学到的数学、天文学和几何学带回希腊，并提出世界的本原是水，从而为希腊哲学的发端打下了基础，开始了希腊哲学的"始基时代"。

毕达哥拉斯生于希腊商业城市萨摩斯，少年好学，曾游览各地达 30 余年。他到过阿拉伯、叙利亚、腓尼基、迦勒底、印度和高卢。他在总结自己漫游一生的体会时，给旅游者提出忠告："到外邦去旅行时不要带着本国的成见。"这与中国人提到的"入乡随俗"有着异曲同工之妙。

柏拉图曾经游历埃及和小亚细亚，访问意大利，拜访过毕达哥拉斯的信徒；亚里士多德 17 岁时入柏拉图的学园学习，在那里学习和教书度过了 20 余年。柏拉图死后，他旅行到梅西阿的阿索斯，从那里又到米替棱奈。柏拉图和亚里士多德可谓世界最早的旅游客座教授。因为亚里士多德有在散步时教学的习惯，他的学派被称为逍遥派。逍遥派最有名的学生就是后来征服世界的亚历山大。

不过，古希腊最著名的旅行家非希罗多德莫属。希罗多德将文化人类学家、地理学家、自然学家和历史学家的角色结合到了一起，他的旅游足迹遍布地中海世界。他被罗马著名的政治家西塞罗称为"历史学家之父"。他在其游历作品中虽然集中叙述希波战争，但同时也是对近东和希腊各种文化的记叙。希罗多德的亲身经历和在旅游中收集的大量口头素材使得他的叙述十分生动。希罗多德喜欢把希腊和非希腊的文化作比较，并对各地的风俗进行分析，得出了这样的结论："风俗，天地之王，既主宰着众生，也引导着神灵。"

从有关希罗多德史料和他本人的作品，我们还可以知道他到过许多地方：除小亚细亚诸城市外，还可以举出希腊本土、马其顿、埃及、腓尼基、叙利亚、黑海沿岸、意大利南部和西西里等地。就当时的条件而论，他见闻之广应当说是罕见的，所以后来人们称他为"旅行家之父"。

宗教旅行最鼎盛的时期是在古希腊时代。古希腊的提洛岛、特尔斐和奥林匹斯山是当时著名的宗教圣地。在建有宙斯神庙的奥林匹亚，奥林匹亚节是最负盛名的盛典，宙斯神大祭之日，前来参加者不绝于道。节庆期间，举行赛马、赛车、赛跑、角斗等体育活动。早在《荷马史诗》记载的年代里，希腊人就开始进行各种体育运动，人们从四面八方赶来，一睹心目中偶像的风采。

古代奥运会自公元前776年开始，到394年被罗马人废除，每四年一次，共持续了一千多年。奥运会对于希腊人来说是一个真正的欢乐的节目，它无疑刺激了希腊人的各种旅游活动。为举办地带来了勃勃生机。这种活动一直延续至今，发展成了现代的奥林匹克运动会。当时的奥林匹亚庆典，纯属一种宗教活动，但它却促进了周围剧院的建立和宗教旅游的发展。后来，宗教旅行逐渐遍及全球，成为一种世界性的旅游活动。

（3）古罗马旅游

罗马时代曾是世界旅行的全盛时期。古罗马著名历史学家、文学家塞涅卡在文章中写道："很多的人都不惜长途跋涉，一睹遥远的景物。"在罗马时代，以罗马为中心，修建了许多公路，它们和现代各国的管理有些相似，例如由相关地区分段管理，各负其责。

由于适合旅游的条件越来越完备，一部分有钱有权有闲的罗马人，便开始了以寻求乐趣为目的的闲暇旅行。此时旅行与早期人类旅游有所不同，它超越了商务、宗教信仰等的局限，出现了以鉴赏艺术、疗养、徒步行走、庙宇观赏、建筑游览等各种各样目的的旅行。

罗马著名作家瓦罗（前116—前27）曾写道："你也许漫游过许多地方，你是否看过比意大利更美丽的地方？这么多的地方，人们如何能够把它统统都列举出来？而且，每个地方的名气都如此之大。"在假日的时候，罗马人去观看奥林匹克运动会，同时也去泡温泉和看戏剧等。这一时期还出现了最早的自然观光旅行。例如，英国北部的湖泊、希腊北部的河谷，以及作为文化标志的尼罗河、莱茵河和小亚细亚蜿蜒曲折的河流，都成了极富魅力的旅游吸引地。另外，埃及的金字塔、希腊的神庙、西班牙和高卢的独特民俗、北非的新兴城市都成了吸引旅游者的因素。普鲁塔施说："世界的涉足者将他们一生中最宝贵的时间都花在旅馆和船上了。"据史书记载，古罗马甚至在去那不勒斯沿途还建起了豪华别致的别墅，供旅游者享用。

由于大规模航海旅行的缘故，罗马时期的地理学得到了很大的发展，地理学家们知道了欧洲、东南亚、南亚和北亚等地区，对这些地区的方位和风土人情都有了一定程度的掌握。波赛都尼奥斯（前135—前51）是古代世界一位著名的综合哲学家、地理学家和长跑健将。他旅行过罗马帝国的许多地方并写下了许多旅行报告和游记。他在当时预言，一个航海家自西班牙航行8000英里（12874.4千米）将可以到达印度。

斯特拉波（约前58—前25）是罗马最著名的旅行家和地理学家，他受过很好的教育，在年轻时期，就游历过欧亚和非洲的广大地区，他强调用自然和人文相结合的方法研究地理学。在他所完成的《地理学》和《历史》的两部著作里，大凡山川形势、气候土质、万物生息、矿泉土产、民族风俗、城郭交通以及历史沿革等均包含其中，因而内容详尽，对后世的继承有着积极的作用。他的《地理学》成为现代地理学的非常重要的源泉。

斯特拉波既擅长在旅游中观察各种自然和人文现象，又强调尊重前人的研究成果。他写道："我本人曾经由亚美尼亚起程向西方旅行，到过埃特鲁里亚的与撒丁岛遥遥相对的地方；另外又从攸克辛海向南旅行到埃塞俄比亚边界。至于其他的地理学家，没有任何一人所走的区域比我走过的区域为大。因为那些曾深入西方比我走得更远的人，就没有到达过如此遥远的东方地点；其他在东方比我走得更远的人，却在西方比我落后了。讲到南方和北方的区域，也可以同样地断言。但是关于各地方的报道，其中总有大部分来自别人的口述，所以我们所阐述和与别人的报道，总有相似的地方。……有的人只认为亲眼见过的才算是知识，而不相信从口述中获得的报道。殊不知就学识方面来说，耳闻比目见重要多了。"

斯特拉波还把世界划分为三部分：欧洲、亚洲、和利比亚（非洲）。他并断言，有人居住的全部世界仅占温带陆地的三分之一，在这个空间外，还有另一个或几个有人居住的世界。因此，现代人文地理学家 Lebon 认为："有了斯特拉波，古代地理学达到了它的顶点。"

老普林尼（23—79）是一位多产的博物学家，长达37卷的《自然史》是他的鸿篇巨制，同时，老普林尼也是一位地理学家、旅行家、律师和军人，他曾经担任过日耳曼骑兵队首长和西罗马舰队的司令。由于职务的关系，他的旅行足迹几乎到达了罗马帝国的任何地方。

《自然史》的内容包括数理学、宇宙学、地理学、人类学、动物学、植物学、医药学、矿物学及其应用术，他参考了 400 多位作家的著作，并在自己的书中标明观点和文献的出处。在亚里士多德和斯特拉波等人之后，老普林尼也强调地球是球形的。在他的著作里，当然也有不少谬误，如他认为欧洲是地球最大的洲，占地球面积的 5/12；印度占有人居住的陆地的 1/3，并向东西方扩展等。老普林尼在审美观上，强调"应当临摹自然本身，不应当临摹艺术家。"他认为自然才是美的源泉。老普林尼几乎一生都在旅行途中，在公元前 79 年他奔赴维苏威火山研究时，在火山爆发时遇难身亡。

古代世界对地球最详尽的论述，是古希腊时期的地理学家托勒密（90—168）所著的《地理学导论》。不仅对地球有一个较为详细的论述，同时，书中还记载了一位提尔的旅行家和地理学家马林的旅游和他对地理学的贡献。另外，这一时期，还出现了一本著名的旅游著作《寰球游记》，由罗马诗人阿维恩所译，它的第一卷中有关地中海、黑海以及里海沿岸的游记被保留了下来。

（4）阿拉伯帝国的旅游

公元前七八世纪，地跨亚非欧三洲的阿拉伯帝国，空前繁荣。帝国驿道四通八达，交通运输空前发展。驿站不仅备有马、骡和骆驼，还有客舍等为过往旅人服务的机构。由于伊斯兰教已取得合法地位，并对教徒规定了朝觐制度，使得每一个穆斯林者平生都有欲望作一次长途旅行。朝觐期间，来自各地的哈只旅行团纷纷云集麦加，商人、艺术家也趁机而来，或做生意或献艺，驿传局还编写了许多旅行指南，对哈只、旅客、商贾等均有实用价值。

阿拉伯人是寻求知识而爱好旅行的突出代表。阿拉伯帝国时期，以求知求学为主的旅行盛行。穆罕默德曾教导哈只们："学问虽远在中国，亦当求之。"例如，阿拉伯的旅行家和历史学家马苏第，被称为阿拉伯的希罗多德，他曾经游历过埃及、巴勒斯坦、印度、锡兰（今斯里兰卡）、中国等地。在其所著《金色的草原》中，有多处提到中国，他十分推崇中国人的手工技巧，说他们特别长于塑像及其他技艺，并认为中国人是世界上最聪明的民族。

阿拉伯帝国时期另一位旅行家白图特约，在 1345 年至 1346 年间到过中国，他在外旅行长达 28 年之久，他的著名的《亚洲非洲旅行记》记载了中国的城市、商埠、物产和风俗。

意大利旅行家马可·波罗（1254—1324）随其经商的父亲经两河流域，越过伊朗高原和帕米尔高原来到中国。1275 年到达元朝大都（今内蒙古自治区多化县西北），并得到元世祖忽必烈信任。马可·波罗在中国为官多年，并游历各地。1292年，马可·波罗从海路经苏门答腊、印度等地返国。《马可·波罗游记》一书记述了中亚、西亚、东南亚等地区许多国家的情况，特别叙述了中国的富庶和繁荣。

（5）欧洲中世纪旅游

中世纪早期的欧洲旅行，大多是出于传教目的而进行的旅行活动。由于中世纪早期，人们主要生活在以城堡为中心的庄园里，严酷的劳作和宗教的禁锢，使得人们很难有钱有闲从世俗的生活中得到快乐。但随着贸易的开展，特别是十字军东征后文明的交流和整合，欧洲的文化氛围渐渐放松，人们开始带着好奇和梦幻，寻找知识和乐趣。中世纪后期，一系列的文化复兴运动，重新开启了欧洲旅游曙光。

与马可波罗同时代的文化巨匠但丁（1265—1321）是欧洲文艺复兴的奠基人。为了追寻古典文学和艺术，但丁去那不勒斯和罗马等地旅游，并于1348年写出了后来闻名世界的《十日谈》。由于该书对罗马教会提出了质疑，从而激励了人们对基督教教义的寻本求真，并导致了16世纪以马丁·路德为首的宗教改革，动摇了罗马教会的基础。

文艺复兴的根本目的就是使禁锢已久的古代罗马希腊的人文主义精神得到复活，使得在宗教重压下的任命得以解放。不过，真正开启文艺复兴大门的还是彼特拉克（1304—1374）。他出生在阿雷佐，年轻时就游历比萨、热那亚、博洛尼亚、米兰等文化底蕴深厚的城市。在罗马，他发出了"全部历史除了赞美罗马以外，还有什么"的呼喊，号召人们学习古典文化。他1331年又到巴黎、法兰德斯、科隆等地旅游。1336年，他在伏格罗斯附近购买了一座别墅，并在那里开始过起日日垂钓溪畔的隐居生活，潜心写作成为他生活的追求。

彼特拉克以其作品激发了人们对古典文化的激情，以其简洁有力的文辞表达了人们关心和享受生活的愿望，以其特有魅力刺激着人们人文精神和鉴赏力的复活，不仅可称为名副其实的"文艺复兴之父"，而且是人文主义时代真正的旅行家。

文艺复兴运动自14世纪意大利起源扩展到欧洲各地，其影响一直持续到16世纪。在欧洲各地出现的人性解放的文化和艺术的复兴活动，促使文化旅游蓬勃开展。

著名的文艺复兴研究学者布克哈特有一句名言，它概括意大利文艺复兴是"发现世界和发现人"：前者指的是探索外部世界，是客观的；后者探索人的个性，是主观的。"回归自然"与"回归古人"是当时普遍使用的话语。

意大利著名文学家写道："人们到外边，欣赏高山、大海、汹涌的河流和广阔的重洋，以及日月星辰的运行，这时他们会忘了自己。"

"像在对于自然的科学叙述上一样，伊尼亚斯·希尔维优斯仍是他那个时代的最重要的作家之一……这里，他引起我们注意的是：他不仅是第一个领略了意大利风景的雄伟壮丽的人，而且也是第一个热情地对它描写入微的人……因为他的爱好主要是在领略自然之美、访求古迹和欣赏朴素而宏伟的建筑上。在以优美而流畅的拉丁文所写的《回忆录》中。他坦率地谈到他的乐趣。他似乎有可以和任何现代游览者媲美的敏锐而熟练的观察力。他以狂喜的心情从阿尔本山的最高峰——卡弗山上眺望周围壮丽的景色，从那里他能够看到腊契纳港和契尔切奥海岬那边圣彼得湾的海岸，远及于阿尔金达罗山峰和周围的广阔的田野，那里有古代城市的废墟和对面的中部意大利的山脉。然后，他的目光转向于它们下边洼地上的苍翠的森林和在树林中间的清澈的湖水。他觉得托第山峰姿势很美丽，它高踞在布满葡萄园和橄榄树的山坡上边，俯瞰远处的森林和台伯河的溪谷，那里在弯弯曲曲的河流的两旁建立起许多市镇和城堡。锡耶纳附近可爱的山峦，高高低低地到处点缀着别墅和修道院，那是他自己的家乡；他以一种特殊的感情作了描写。"（《西方旅游史》）

文艺复兴的巨匠达·芬奇强调艺术家应师法自然，同时又要发挥自己的想象力，并强调画家要与自然竞赛并胜过自然。他在其所著《达·芬奇论绘画》中写道："绘画科学的神圣性质，将画家的心灵变得和神灵的心相仿佛。画家自由地思考着多种多样事物的产生，例如动物、植物、果实、风景、田园、山坡以及使人见了害怕的可怖可惊的地方；还有那些可喜的、柔美而悦目的场所，那里有不遭风雨而又微风吹拂的、开遍各色鲜花的草地；还有从高山倾泻而下的河流，势如洪水，挟着连根拔起的树木、岩石、树根、泥土和泡沫，卷走一切不愿自身破灭而拼命挣扎的东西。同样（画家的心）能创造暴风雨的海洋，在那里，海水和狂风激战，跃起傲慢的巨浪，它落下时就击毁那些正在浪底作恶的风，把风包围、囚禁、击碎和分裂它，把它与污浊的浪沫混合起来。这样，怒海方才平息，但有时它被风击败，逃离海洋，向邻近海角的高岸突进，翻过山巅，落入另一侧的溪谷里。这时，海水一部分化成飞沫，变成风暴的战利品；一部分逃脱风的掌握，化为阵雨落归海中；一部分却落在高高的海角上，大肆破坏，冲走一切抗拒自己灭亡的东西，时时遇到另一股迎面而来的巨浪，互相搏击，飞入天空，将大气充满混乱的、泡沫的雾气，这雾又被风击碎在海岬边缘，产生了被风追踪的乌云。"

文艺复兴运动不仅是以古典文学和艺术为主要内容的人文精神上的复活，在其"300年"间，自然科学也得到了飞跃的发展。具有"百科全书式博物学家"之称的罗吉尔·培根通过实验，预想人类可以生产出自动舟船、潜水艇、飞机等机械。这些预言被逐步实现，从而使人类旅行范围越来越大。

（6）哥伦布和麦哲伦

15世纪西方产业革命兴起，《马可波罗游记》对东方的描述，吸引了欧洲的商人、航海家和封建主从事旅游的欲望。哥伦布（1451—1506）是西班牙著名航海家，是地理大发现的先驱者。

哥伦布是个意大利人，自幼热爱航海冒险。他读过《马可·波罗游记》，十分向往印度和中国。当时，地圆说已很盛行。他先后向葡萄牙、西班牙、英国、法国等国的国王请求资助，以实现他向西航行到达东方国家的计划，但均遭拒绝。当时，西方国家对东方物质财富需求除传统的丝绸、瓷器、茶叶外，最重要还有香料和黄金。其中香料是欧洲人起居生活和饮食烹调必不可少的材料，需求量很大，这些商品主要经传统的海、陆联运运输。哥伦布为了实现自己的计划，四处游说。十几年后，直到1492年，西班牙王后说服了国王，甚至要拿出自己的私房钱资助哥伦布。

1492年8月3日，哥伦布受西班牙国王派遣，带着给印度君主和中国皇帝的国书，率领三艘百十来吨的帆船，从西班牙巴罗斯港扬帆出发，直向正西航去。经过七十昼夜的艰苦航行，1492年10月12日凌晨，终于发现了陆地。哥伦布以为到达了印度。1493年3月15日，哥伦布回到西班牙。此后他又三次重复他的向西航行，又登上了美洲的许多海岸。直到1506年逝世，他一直认为他到达的是印度。后来，一个叫做亚美利哥的意大利学者，经过更多的考察，才知道哥伦布到达的地方不是印度，而是一个原来不为人知的新的大陆。

哥伦布的远航是大航海时代的开端。1498年，又有葡萄牙人达·迦马发现了绕过非洲南端的好望角通向印度的新航线。新航路的开辟，改变了世界历史的进程。它使得海外贸易的路线由地中海转移到了大西洋沿岸。从那起，西方终于走出了中世纪的黑暗，开始以不可阻挡之势崛起于世界，并在之后的几个世纪中，成就海上霸业。一种全新的工业文明成为世界经济发展的主流。

麦哲伦的远征是人类航海旅游事业中的一部伟大史诗。他于1519年至1522年间进行的绕地球一周航行，是人类历史的首次。

那时哥伦布已经发现了美洲新大陆，达·伽马也从印度返航并带回了巨大的东方财富。1505年，麦哲伦参加了海外远征队，从此开始了远洋探航的生涯。在这次远征印度、马六甲、马来群岛的过程中，为了与阿拉伯人争夺贸易地盘，远征队与阿拉伯商人和当地居民打过几仗，麦哲伦也因此三度负伤。

在返回葡萄牙的途中，远征队船只触礁，正当大家心灰意冷之时，麦哲伦挺身而出，带领大家与困难搏斗。由于这次事件，麦哲伦被提升为船长，被留在了印度。此后，麦哲伦在印度和东南亚一带参加了殖民战争，并在这一带进行了探索和游历。

1513年麦哲伦回到葡萄牙。他一再请求国王允许他组织船队进行环球探险，却没有得到支持。绝望的麦哲伦投奔西班牙塞维利亚城的要塞司令，要塞司令非常欣赏他的才能和魄力，不仅把女儿嫁给他，还向西班牙国王举荐了他。麦哲伦的环球航行的计划得到西班牙国王的批准，与他签署了远洋探航协定。

1519年9月，麦哲伦率领一支由200多人、5艘船只组成的浩浩荡荡的船队，从西班牙塞维利亚城的港口出发，开始了环球远洋探航。

经过两个多月的海洋漂泊船队，在第二年1月份到了一个宽阔的大海湾。海员们以为已到达了美洲的南端。然而随着船队在海湾中的前进，发现海水变成了淡水，原来此处只是一个河口，就是今天乌拉圭的拉普拉塔河的出口处。

两个月后，船队在南纬52°处又发现了个海口。这个海峡异常弯曲，窄宽多变，港汊交错，波涛汹涌。麦哲伦派出一艘船去探航，然而这艘船却调转船头逃回了西班牙。麦哲伦只好率领剩下的3条船像钻迷宫似的在海峡中前进。在这个海峡迂回航行1个月后，他们终于走出海峡西口，见到了浩瀚的大海。为了纪念麦哲伦这次探航的功绩，后人把这条海峡命名为"麦哲伦海峡"。

麦哲伦的船队在这片大洋中航行了3个多月，海面一直风平浪静。因此，他们就为它取了个名字叫"太平洋"。

1521年3月初，在水尽粮绝、人人疲乏虚弱之际，航队来到了富饶的马里亚那群岛，受到当地居民的热情款待。3月底船队来到了菲律宾群岛，当麦哲伦原来从马六甲带走的仆人用马来语与当地土人对话时，表明他从西方向西航行终于到达了东方。

然而在一次与当地部族的冲突中，麦哲伦被杀害了。最后，麦哲伦的助手带领仅存的两条船，载满香料越过马六甲海峡，经印度洋、过好望角，辗转一年多，终于在1522年9月回到了西班牙。整个船队仅剩下一条船与18名船员了。麦哲伦和他的船员们，花了整整3年的时间，终于完成人类的第一次绕地球一周的航行。

（7）"大旅游"时代

17世纪到18世纪是科学文化在欧洲迅速传播的年代，国际间的交流十分密切。旅游活动呈现出丰富多彩的文化特性。规模波及全欧洲的"大旅游"不但成为当时的一种时尚，同时也为文化和思想在全欧洲的传播奠定了基础。

"欧洲受过教育的阶级从来没有形成过比这更加世界主义化的社会，他们以法语为通用语言，经常出国游历——这是一个伟大的旅行时代——特别是在18世纪上半叶战争不甚频繁期间"（《西方旅游史》）。

1713年的《乌得勒支条约》开始了欧洲相对平静的时期，大陆重新对旅游者开放。许许多多年轻人开始在全欧洲旅游并且发现它的奇迹：阿姆斯特丹、凡尔赛、佛罗伦萨，尤其是罗马。这个时期，欧洲各个国家的贵族青年，带着一位仆人或指导他们行为和学业的家族教师，到国外去旅游一两年，成为一种时尚。

"大旅行是年轻贵族教育中的重要内容，因此全体欧洲贵族才分享同一文化。让·雅克卢梭在谈到必须结束国际冲突时说：'都是欧洲人，都有同样的趣味、同样的热情、同样的生活方式。'不管是法国国籍，还是德国国籍，还是其他国籍，政治家和哲学家，科学家和艺术家都意识到自己是欧洲人。"（《西方旅游史》）

卢梭也是"大旅游"的倡导者，他认为回到自然是最好的教育方法，他自己也经常去欧洲其他国家徒步旅行。从17世纪到19世纪中叶大众旅游兴起之前，大旅游作为教育年轻人的一种重要方式，在欧洲就非常受欢迎。欧洲人素有"旅游育人"和"旅游培养下一代"的说法，所以年轻人去旅游的目的是学习新语言，发现新习俗，抑或熟悉美术和礼节。

十八十九世纪，大旅游在欧洲各地都非常普遍，其中尤以英、德、俄、北欧国家等地的人出游最为常见。这种旅游活动并且成为当时培育未来行政人才及政治领袖的一个重要方式。旅游者们大都怀着一颗对古典文明和现代文化的崇敬之心，踏上"大旅游"之路。他们一边游历大川、名山、古城，一边学习语言、文化、艺术、社交礼仪和风俗人情，日来夜往，走走停停，从一地到另一地，视野不断地开阔，思想不断地丰富。

英国科学家、哲学家弗朗西斯·培根的《论旅行》是当时脍炙人口的作品。我们不妨看看其全文：

对于年轻人，旅游是一种教育的方式。而对于老年人。旅游则构成一种经验。

当你不懂一国语言时，就可以旅行到那里去学习。假如一个年轻人在旅行中。身边有一个了解别国语言和风情的向导，那对他将是大有助益的。否则，他就可能像只蒙着头的鹰，很难说会看到什么了。

在海上旅行时，尽管除了天就是海，航海家却总要写航行日记。而在陆地上，尽管有许多层出不穷够新奇的事物，人们却常常忘了写日记。这是很奇怪的，难道一览无余的东西倒比应该认真观察的东西更值得记录吗？所以在旅行中，日记是应该坚持写的。

在一个地方旅行时，要注意观察下列事物：政治与外交，法律与实施情况，宗教、教堂与寺庙，城堡、港口与交通，文物与古迹，文化情况，如图书馆、学校、会议、演说（如果碰上的话），船舶与海军，雄伟的建筑与优美的公园；军事、兵工厂，经济设施，体育，例如骑术、剑术、体操等等，以及剧院、艺术品和工艺品之类。留心观察一切值得长久记忆的事物，并且访问一切能在这些方面给你以新知识的老师或人们。相对而言，有些典礼、闹剧、宴会、红白喜事等热闹一时的场面，倒不必过于认真，当然也不应忽略不顾。如果一个年轻人想通过一次短促的旅行迅速得到一些知识的话，以上所谈的方法是可以借鉴的。

为了达致这一目的，他就必须通晓所去国的语言，还要找一个熟悉国情的向导，带上介绍该国情况的书籍、地图，坚持写日记。在每一地逗留时间的长短，要根据提供知识的价值来决定。但最好不要逗留过久。在一地住下时，如果可能，最好能经常换换住所，以便更广泛地接触社会。

在交际方面，不要只找熟识的同乡，要设法接触当地的上流社会和人士，以便在必要时能获得他们的帮助。如果能设法得到各国使节之秘书的交往和友谊，那就还能得到许多不同国家的知识。

在旅行时还可以去拜访一下当地有名望的贤达人士，以便观察一下他们的实际与所负的名望是否相称。但千万要注意避免卷入纠纷和决斗。这种决斗的原因无非是由于争夺情人、位置、荣誉或语言冒犯而引起的。为了避免发生纠葛，在待人接物上就必须谨慎，尤其是在和那种性情鲁莽之徒来往时更要小心，因为他们总是乐于招惹是非的。

旅行者回国以后，不要把已游历过的国家全然抛在脑后，而应当继续与那些新认识而有价值的人保持联系。再者，他的游历应表现在他的言谈中，而不要过分表现在异国装束和仪态上。在人们问及旅行情况时，最好只作为一个答问者而不要作为一个夸耀者。而且应该做到在别人看来，他并不是在用外国的风俗改变本国的风俗，而只不过是把他在国外所学到的精华移植到本国的习俗中而已。

18世纪中叶，由于西方科学技术的迅猛发展，在欧洲还出现了科学考察旅行和带有掠夺性目的的探险旅行。如英国就曾为掠夺殖民地，组织了多次探险旅行队，其中包括自然科学工作者，对航海路线、动物、植物和地质进行研究。以库克船长为首的探险队，曾进行了3次环球航行。达尔文在航行过程中通过在南美的实地考察，找到了物种起源的解释，创立了伟大的进化论学说。这一时期具有科学意义的旅行，对人类社会的进步起到了重要影响。

## 三、古人旅游的范围和方式均有限

旅游是人的基本需求之一。随着人类文明的发展，人们对旅游的认识越来越丰富，越来越深刻。在中国古代多种多样的旅游活动中，"旅游"一词也被历代文人墨客用诗文记录下来，分门别类，多姿多彩。

如周游，含有四处游说的意思，《管子》中"使出周游于四方，明号召收天下贤士"即指此；优游，指悠然自得地游览，东汉史学家班固曰："莫不优游自得，玉润而金声"；神游，泛指精神或梦魂的出游，南朝文学家沈约有"迹屈岩廊下，神游江海中"的描述；漫游，则有无拘无束、随意游览的含义，唐代文学家元结在其诗中说："漫游无远近，漫东无早晏"；胜游，为惬意游览之意，唐代文学家刘禹锡诗曰："管弦度上留高韵，山水途中作胜游"；壮游，顾名思义，乃胸怀壮志的游历，元代学者袁桷诗曰："壮游诗句豁，古戍角声悲"；卧游，是指以欣赏山水画代替游览，元代画家倪瓒有诗云："一畦杞菊为供具，满壁江山作卧游"；宸游，专指帝王出游，明代文学家归有光在诗中写道："御苑清风上麦秋，金舆晚出事宸游"等等，都说明我国古人对旅游的理解和认识达到了一个很高的水平。

但由于生产工具的落后和生产力的低下，古人活动的范围十分有限。尤其是早先人类，即使是那些"有权"、"有钱"人，也因受科技水平局限，很难在从事旅游活动时"走得好"、"走得远"。就是到了欧洲"大旅游"时期，科技有了长足进步，游客们也要面对道路艰险、旅店简陋、食物怪异、病疫传染、强盗扒手出没的困难。有些富家子弟常常携一帮仆从打理旅途生活，以保证主子在旅游过程中的舒适和安全。

古人在出行方式的选择上，除了徒步，不外乎车、马和木船，所以古人旅游，很大一部分时间要花在跋涉之中，不仅浪费了到达目的地的时间，也对人的体力是一个无谓的消耗。

中国是最早使用车的国家之一。相传在中国黄帝时代就已经会造车。夏禹时代有一个专门以造车闻名的部落叫薛部落，其部落中，有一个名叫奚仲的人曾任夏朝"车正"，主管夏朝车辆的制作、保管和使用。为便于橇、车通行，人们还意识到必须平整路面，拓宽路幅，改原来仅适应步行的羊肠小道为大道。

人类最早的水上交通工具是独木舟。据《易·系辞》中说，古人"刳木为舟，剡木为楫"。也就是说，古人掏空巨型树干制成独木舟，砍削树干成扁平作桨。人类自从有了舟，人们便可以跨越水域，开拓旅游活动的新空间。

古人旅游，不仅因生产力的落后而受限制，还因政治动荡、社会变化而影响旅游者的出行。据史书记载，在中国远古西周时代，周王在边境设立多达十二道关卡，被史学家认为可能是中国出现的最早的关卡。

到了春秋战国时期，因列强争霸，狼烟四起，各国设卡立哨就十分普遍了。由于哨卡功能特殊，地位重要，关系到各国的军事、经济和社会要枢，所以普通人要通过这些关卡不是件容易的事。有时即使是一些社会"名流"，要想蒙混过关也有马失前蹄之时。如秦国的商鞅因没有闯过关口而被抓捕车裂；伍子胥逃往楚国的途中，因无法出韶关，而急得一夜白发。

史书还记载西周有一种叫"符传"的东西，作用和今天的身份证有点相似，但只有临时性。国人要迁徙或旅行时，必须先申领"符传"。一旦出行，不仅旅途当中随时有人查，每当过城关，城门或遇到宵禁、戒严时，均要出示"符传"。而且，这种"符传"按规定一般只能使用一次，使用完后必须按时上交，否则，就要受到惩处。

在古时，游客无论是在旅途，还是暂居旅舍，都要冒极大的生命危险，即便是君王出游，有时也是如此。如周昭王在外出巡游时，突遭遇风浪，不幸死于沉船；徐霞客在旅行途中，曾三次遭匪徒的洗劫，四次彻底断粮，55岁在云南又染上重疾，回家后的次年就去世了……正因为古人在旅游中要面临许多危险，所以那时候的人在旅游途中也显得特别的迷信，在考虑出行之前，一般都要占卦、算命。前面说到的《周易》中的"旅卦",便是专门用来占卜旅行吉凶的。

《山海经》记载了 60 多种"见则死""能食人""见则大水"等旅行途中可能遇及的自然凶险,都是当时的旅行者必须提防和躲避的。而书中记载的 130 多种"食之不饥""服之不夭""服之不寒冷"的食物,则常常成为古人旅途中保命的法宝。

为了方便民众的旅游,古代的官吏制度中,早在公元前 10 世纪便设有主管有关事务的官员,并制定了相关的迎宾制度和旅游法规。据《逸周书》记载,当时的官府已经明文要求地方必须为商旅者开辟道路,每隔 10 千米处设井,每隔 20 千米设旅舍,守城的人还得为旅行者提供兑换零钱的服务。

春秋战国时期,由于路途往来商旅很多,私营旅店也越来越多。"逆旅"就是中国最早的私营旅店,为此,秦、魏等国还专门下发命令,对这类旅店进行管理。而《周礼·地官司徒》中记载:"凡国野之道,十里有庐,庐有炊食。三十里有宿,宿有路室,路室有委。五十里有市,市有候馆,候馆有积。"这种建设在都城、交通干线及边境线上的旅店,应该是我国最早的官办招待所。

总之,古代旅游主要是帝王、贵族、官僚、地主等人及其附庸士大夫阶层的少数人的活动,平民百姓仅在佳庆节日到近地出游,如踏青、赶庙会等;国内旅行家多以学术考察旅行为主,是在古代"读万卷书,行万里路"的思想影响下进行的;古代旅游活动都和当时的社会政治、经济、文化、科技的发展密切相关,是社会文明进步的晴雨表。当社会处于安定、强盛的时候,旅游活动就特别活跃;反之,便一蹶不振。因此,旅游会随着人类的发展而打上时代的烙印,内容和形式都会有不同的特点。

古时的国际旅游以政治交往(如互派使者)、宗教求法和经商贸易等形式为主,因科技水平相对落后,无论是远洋还是陆地旅游,每次游程都充满坎坷,花费时间也多以年月甚至数十年来计算,因而,与近现代旅游相比,古代旅游不是一件轻松的事。

第二章

# 科学技术的发展
# 开启了人类旅游的新纪元

# Pyramid

金字塔

## 第一节
## 影响人类旅游活动的几项重大发明

18世纪中叶到19世纪的一百年间，欧洲进入工业革命时期，人类文明由于科学技术的飞跃发展而得到突飞猛进。在这时期，大部分劳工已从乡村农业转投小镇或工厂，过起城市生活。中产阶级工作时数缩短，休假日期增加，无论在财富、教育、休闲时间以至休闲旅游活动方面的需求都有大幅增长。

（1）蒸汽机

人类对蒸汽的认识和利用，经历了一个漫长的历史过程。公元前2世纪，古希腊人就制造过一种利用蒸汽喷射产生反作用的发动机。

1698年，法国物理学家巴本创造性地设计了汽缸—活塞装置。这个装置的原理是高压锅上压力阀所受的重力（自身重量）由锅内蒸汽的压力（作用在阀上）来平衡而产生机械运动。

在巴本之后，英国工程师托马斯·塞维利修改了巴本的设想，于1698年设计发明了第一台实际应用于矿井抽水的蒸汽机，第一次真正把蒸汽变成了工业动力。但是这种机器由于热损失极大，效率很低，使其工作受到限制，而且也很不安全。

1705年英国锻工托马斯·纽可门在另一位工人考利的帮助下，发明了一种更加适用的大气活塞式蒸汽机，他将从矿井里抽水的工作机和为它提供动力的蒸汽装置完全分开，这样便保证了蒸汽机的安全运行。

詹姆斯·瓦特1736年1月19日出生于英国格拉斯哥市附近的一个小镇，祖父和叔父都是机械工匠，父亲早年也是个造船技术工人。由于耳濡目染，瓦特从幼年起就随父亲学习各种手艺，并养成了一种独立思考和探索奥秘的兴趣和习惯。

由于体弱多病，瓦特没有受过完整的正规教育。但是，他在父母的教导下，一直坚持自学。1753年，瓦特到格拉斯哥市当学徒工，第二年又转到伦敦的一家仪表修理厂继续当学徒。凭借着自己的勤奋好学，他很快学会了制造那些难度较高的仪器。

1756年，瓦特的才能引起了格拉斯哥大学教授台克的重视。在他的介绍下，瓦特进入格拉斯哥大学当了修理教学仪器的工人。

1763年，格拉斯哥大学请瓦特修理一台纽可门蒸汽机。他通过大量实验和分析，对旧式蒸汽机进行深入研究，找出了旧式机器效率低的主要原因。

1765年的春天，瓦特在一次散步时突发灵感，既然纽可门蒸汽机的热效率低是蒸汽在缸内冷凝造成的，那么为什么不能让蒸汽在缸外冷凝呢？

从1766年开始，在三年多的时间里，瓦特克服了材料和工艺等各方面的困难，终于在1769年制出了第一台样机。同年，瓦特因发明冷凝器而获得他在革新纽可门蒸汽机过程中的第一项专利。虽然第一台带有冷凝器的蒸汽机试制成功了，但它同纽可门蒸汽机相比，除了热效率有显著提高外，在动力机械方面仍未取得实质性进展。

1781年，瓦特从行星绕日的圆周运动受到启发，想到了把活塞往返的直线运动变为旋转的圆周运动就可以使动力传给任何工作机。同年，他研制出了一套被称为"太阳和行星"的齿轮联动装置，终于把活塞的往返的直线运动转变为齿轮的旋转运动。1781年年底，瓦特以发明带有齿轮和拉杆的机械联动装置获得第二个专利。

由于这种蒸汽机加上了轮轴和飞轮，在把活塞的往返直线运动转变为轮轴的旋转运动时，多消耗了不少能量。这样，蒸汽机的效率不是很高，动力不是很大。1782年，瓦特根据这一设想，试制出了一种带有双向装置的新汽缸。由此瓦特获得了他的第三项专利。把原来的单向汽缸装置改装成双向汽缸，并首次把引入汽缸的蒸汽由低压蒸汽变为高压蒸汽，这是瓦特在改进纽可门蒸汽机的过程中的第三次飞跃。通过这三次技术飞跃，纽可门蒸汽机完全演变为了瓦特蒸汽机。

由于瓦特把蒸汽机的往复直线运动变成为连续而均匀的圆周运动，从而可以经过传动装置带动一切机器运转，成为能普遍用于工业和交通运输业的"万能动力机"。

英国人瓦特发明了蒸汽机，从此，揭开了人类工业革命的序幕。蒸汽机以其科学的构造，产生出人类前所未有的动力，远远大于人类此前采用的兽力。但蒸汽机最初只是被用于煤矿抽水。到19世纪初期，好几百台蒸汽机广泛用于煤矿开采中。

如何将这个"大力士"更多的为人类造福，一直是科学家们在思考的问题。1769年，法国工程师库纳研制成功第一辆蒸汽机车，这辆车装有3个轮子，前面一个，后面两个。当车子载着4个人，以每小时4.5千米的速度在大街上做行使表演时，人们除了新奇以外，实在搞不懂它有什么实用价值。这说明任何重大发明都要经历"幼稚阶段"。

1801年，英国煤矿工程师特里维克研制成功第一辆能在铁轨上行使的蒸汽机车。这是一辆单缸蒸汽车，拖着5节车厢的煤，在煤矿的铁路上行使。虽然速度很慢，但基本具备了火车的性质和功能。使得煤矿运输煤炭不再靠马作为动力。

英国人海德利继续对蒸汽机车进行完善，他将车速提升到了每小时8千米，并拖挂8节货车厢。海德利的改进，为真正火车的诞生奠定了基础。

（2）火车的发明

斯蒂芬逊是英国人。他从小失学，进入煤矿后，当了一名锅炉工。通过自学和钻研，他掌握了蒸汽机车的结构和性能。斯劳芬逊负责苏格兰北部的世界第一条商业铁路的设计时，创造性地将原来用生铁制造的铁轨改为钢轨，并设计在钢轨下铺设枕木，从而解决了过去铁轨因震动而常常发生的断裂问题，使火车提速和加大运输量成为可能。

1825年9月27日，由斯蒂芬逊设计制造并亲自驾驶的名为"旅行号"的火车头，拖曳着12节货运车厢和20节客运车厢，以每小时24千米的速度前进。当车上400多名旅客安全抵达终点时，人们热情欢呼。这就是世界上第一次火车通车典礼。从这一天起，世界上有了能用于交通、运输的机动车——火车，从而开辟了世界车辆史和交通史的新纪元。

19世纪的英国，制造火车的并非斯蒂芬逊一人。一些财团看到了其前景，也纷纷投资研究制造火车。他们不甘示弱，互不服气。如何才能达到优胜劣汰的目的呢？英国政府通过用"比赛"的方式，达到机车选型的目的。

1829年10月6日，在利物浦至曼彻斯特的铁路线上，举行了有3辆火车参加的"比赛"。参赛机车必须牵引一列满载石子的车辆，货物的重量必须是机车重量的3倍，要求在2.4千米的线路上来回行驶20次。胜者可获500英镑的奖金。

当参赛机车"新奇"号挂上沉重的装满石子的车厢后，行驶不久只听一声巨响，锅炉炸裂了。参赛机车"桑士·巴里"号，挂上装满石子的车厢后，虽然勉强开动，却慢慢吞吞走不快，最后瘫在铁轨上。

轮到由斯蒂芬逊和他儿子的"火箭"号机车开始时，这辆呼着粗气的"铁牛"拖着沉重的车厢以平均每小时28千米的速度，平稳地来回行驶。最后，更以每小时46千米的高速度冲过了终点。最后，斯蒂芬逊的成就和贡献得到了社会的公认，他被誉为火车的发明人。

1825年，英国享有"铁路之父"之称的乔治·史蒂文森建造的斯托克顿至达林顿的铁路正式投入运营。此后，各地的铁路也开始建设起来。被公认为第一个真正的旅行代理商的英国人托马斯·库克，第一次组织旅行所采用的交通工具就是火车。

1841年7月，英国人托马斯·库克凭他的语言艺术和满腔热情，说服了540名主张戒酒的人，从雷斯特乘火车到拉夫巴罗参加戒酒大会。这是第一次集体打折扣的包租列车旅行。后来，委托他筹备旅行的人增多，他成了短途旅游的组织者。1846年他又成功地设置了旅游向导，这是历史上最早的导游。1851年，库克组织了16万多人参加在"伦敦水晶宫"举行的第一次"世界博览会"。1872年，库克组织了一次9人团体的环球航行，历时220天。因此，托马斯·库克被誉为近代旅游业的创始者。

1879年，德国西门子电气公司研制了第一台电力机车，重约954公斤，只在柏林贸易展览会上做了一次表演。1903年10月27日，西门子与通用电气公司研制的第一台实用电力机车投入使用，时速达到200千米。

1894 年，德国研制成功了第一台汽油内燃机车，并将它应用于铁路运输，开创了内燃机车的新纪元。但这种机车因以汽油为燃料，耗费太高，不容易推广，所以工程师们一直在研究新的产品。

1924 年，德、美、法等国成功研制了柴油内燃机车，并在世界上得到广泛使用。1941 年，瑞士研制成功新型的燃油汽轮机车，以柴油为燃料，且结构简单、震动小、运行性能好，因而在工业国家普遍采用。

(3) 汽车和飞机的问世

19 世纪开始，蒸汽动力的轮船得到了迅速的普及和发展。1807 年，美国"克莱蒙特"号轮船已在哈德逊河上开始了定期航班载人运货。1838 年，英国蒸汽轮船"西留斯"号首次横渡大西洋的成功，大大缩短了旅客来往欧美之间的时间和距离。

汽车的出现应归功于内燃机的发明。由于瓦特发明的蒸汽机体积笨拙、效率低下，科学家和工程师们一直都在寻找一种高能量转换机器。

1862 年，法国工程师德罗夏提出了四冲程内燃机理论，10 年后年德国工程师奥托制造出了世界第一台煤气内燃机。19 世纪中叶，由于燃料工业领域的进步、石油工业的发展以及柴油、汽油、煤油的出现，使得内燃机的改造发生了新的革命。

1883 年，德国发明家戴姆莱制造出了第一台石油内燃机，大大优于传统煤气内燃机。1892 年，德国另一位工程师又发明了以柴油为燃料的自动点火内燃机，性能进一步得到提高。

1885 年汽车内燃机发明者戴姆莱和自己的同胞本茨各自发明了以汽油内燃机为引擎的三轮汽车，几年后本茨又制造出了四轮汽车。1892 年，美国人福特也发明了美国第一辆汽车。并且，本茨和福特也都开办了自己的汽车公司，批量生产汽车，形成了后来经济的支柱产业：汽车工业。1908 年，福特公司还建成了世界第一条汽车生产线，给汽车工业的发展插上了腾飞的翅膀。

内燃机的问世也将人类翱翔蓝天的梦想变成了现实。莱特兄弟是这个行业的先行者。1900 年 10 月，莱特兄弟制成了他们第一架滑翔机。第二年，兄弟俩经过多次改进，又制成了一架滑翔机，飞行高度一下子达 180 米之高。有一天，他们看到门口停了一辆汽车，兄弟俩灵机一动，想到用汽车的发动机来推动飞行。

经过无数次的试验，1903 年 9 月，莱特兄弟带着他们新做的飞机再次来到吉蒂霍克海边试飞。虽然这次试飞失败了，但他们从中吸取了很多经验。那时候，有一位名叫兰莱的发明家，受美国政府的委托，也制造了一架带有汽油发动机的飞机。但不幸的是，这架飞机在试飞中坠入大海。

消息传到莱特兄弟那里，他们便前去调查，希望从兰莱的失败中吸取教训，获得经验。这一次调查收获很大。后来，他们对飞机的每一部件作了严格的检查，制定了严格的操作规定，于 1903 年 12 月 14 日，又来到吉蒂霍克海滩，进行试飞试验。

这天下午，兄弟俩先把他们制造的飞机放在铁轨上面。飞机在斜坡上刚滑行3米，就挣脱了结在后面的铁丝，呼啸着升到空中。但飞机很快减慢速度，掉落在地上。整个飞行时间不到4分钟。

兄弟俩左思右想，逐一检查。弟弟奥维尔终于发现了原因。他说道："咱们是利用斜坡滑行的，距离只有3米飞机就起飞了。而这时螺旋桨的转动还没有达到高速，所以一会儿就栽了下来。"

1903年12月17日上午10点钟，天空低云密布，寒风刺骨。只见奥维尔爬上飞机，端坐在驾驶位上。一会儿，发动机开始轰鸣，螺旋桨也开始转动。飞机滑动起来，起飞并一下子升到3米多高，随即便水平地向前飞去。

在旁边应邀来观看试验的几个农民高兴地呼唤起来，在飞机后面追赶着。飞机飞行了30米后，稳稳地着陆了。威尔伯激动地扑到刚从飞机里爬出来的弟弟身上，热泪盈眶地喊道："我们成功了！我们成功了！"消息传开后，人们奔走相告，美国政府非常重视，决定让莱特做一次试飞表演。1908年9月10日这天，天气晴朗，飞机飞行的场地上围满了观看的人们。人们兴致勃勃，等待着莱特兄弟的飞行。

10点左右，弟弟奥维尔驾驶着他们的飞机，在一片欢呼声中，自由自在地飞向天空，在人们视野里，恰似一只展翅飞翔的雄鹰。飞机在76米的高度飞行了1小时14分，并且运载了一名勇敢的乘客。当它着陆之后，人们从四面八方围了过来。之后不久，莱特兄弟在政府的支持下，创办了一家飞行公司，同时开办了飞行学校。从这以后，飞机成了人们又一项先进的运输工具。

在1914年之前，人们还不知道汽车和飞机的发明会给人类的生活带来哪些变化，而进入20世纪以后，人们不断发生的旅游方式的改进，都与这些发明息息相关。

## 第二节
### 旅游范围和旅游人数发生质的飞跃

由于资本主义工业革命，企业生产率得到大幅度提高，资本家和员工的财富都得到了前所未有的增长，因而不仅扩大了旅行和旅游的人数，也使得旅游的范围越来越广。少数正在成长着的中产阶层要求到就近的山地风景区和海滨胜地作短暂的旅游，而那些中上层人物，有比较多的金钱和时间到异国去旅游，如到地中海游览，

或是欧洲人到北美洲旅游等。还有部分人伴随着对外殖民侵略和扩张到国外去。

尽管在20世纪初，汽车和飞机的出现只是人类新型交通工具的雏形阶段，但它意味着人类工作和休闲方式都发生着空前的改变。自从有了汽车和飞机，人类的旅游活动范围得到了空前的扩张，人类的旅游过程在便利性、舒适度和时效性方面均发生了天翻地覆的变化。19世纪中叶，世界各国无论是国内旅游还是国际旅游都有了突破性的发展。

铁路因其迅捷、快速、安全、全天候的特点，成为了主要的旅游交通工具。铁路不仅能运送更多的人，让人而且可以花少量的钱到更远的地方去旅行。在马车时代，一个人从纽约到芝加哥需要三个星期时间，1857年之后，乘火车只要三天。因为铁路既节省时间，又节约开支，越来越多的中下层人士加入到旅游的行业中来。托马斯·库克开始的旅行代理业逐渐确立地位，成为旅游事业的重要环节，旅行和旅游这项古老的社会活动，开始变成一项经济活动。

产业革命加速了城市化的进程，并且使人们工作和生活的重心从农村转移到了工业城市。原先那种随农时变化而忙闲有序的多样性农业劳动开始为枯燥、重复的单一性大机器工业劳动所取代。这一变化这既为工人创造了休假条件又促使人们产生了强烈的休假需求，以便获得喘息和调整的机会。人们需要适时逃避节奏紧张的城市生活和拥挤嘈杂的环境压力，因而无论是客观上还是主观上都产生了对返回自由、宁静的大自然环境中去的追求。工人阶级要求带薪假日的斗争经历了一个多世纪，直到本世纪终于在社会立法上真正获得胜利。

19世纪下半叶，许多类似的旅游组织在欧洲大陆上纷纷成立。1857年，英国成立了登山俱乐部，1885年又成立了帐篷俱乐部；1890年，法国、德国也成立了观光俱乐部。1938年，被公认为第一个真正的旅行代理商的托马斯·库克创办的通济隆旅行社在世界各地设立了350余处分社。1872年创办的旅行支票，可在世界各大城市通行。通济隆还编印了世界最早的旅行杂志《Travel Gazette》，曾被译成七国文字，再版达17次之多。到20世纪初，美国"运通公司"和以比利时为主的"铁路卧车公司"成了与托马斯·库克公司齐名的三大旅行代理公司。

由于科学技术促进旅游方式的大发展，旅游景点和旅游设施的建设也得到了迅速发展。例如铁路沿线的餐馆、商店多起来了，紧靠城市的山地风景区海滨，逐渐建设起具有先进娱乐设备和宜人环境的综合企业，那些原有的专供上层社会享受的游玩风景区、海滨浴场，变成了常年开放的旅游景点。

不过近代旅行、旅游活动虽然已有很大发展，但还未发展到能称之为独立的经济行业——旅游业的地步。从整个时代来看，它只是一种局部地区个别人经营的旅游代理业。

## 第三节
## 近代中国旅游

1840年鸦片战争以后，中国由独立的封建国家逐渐沦为半殖民地半封建国家。国家性质的变化使得社会各个领域都逐渐发生深刻的变化，旅游也不例外。外国人来华的旅行和旅游，与西方列强对中国殖民化过程，是密不可分的。

王晓云先生在其《中国旅游史话》中说，这时期旅游的变化具有的特点是："一是由于西方文化的入侵，使中国人的旅游观念发生了深刻的变化，平民阶层步入旅游队伍。二是随着现代化交通的发展，旅游的空间形式也得到进一步拓展，参加的人数越来越多，去的地方越来越远，国际旅游交往频繁。三是为适应这种旅游形势的发展，为旅客服务的民间旅游组织逐渐形成一个独立的行业。"

1840年以后，帝国主义用坚船利炮打开了中国封建锁国的大门，西方的商人、传教士、学者和一些冒险家，纷纷到中国来，有的还在中国的名胜地区，例如北戴河海滨、庐山等地建造房舍，作为居住区，中国几乎成了外国冒险家的乐园。

与此同时，中国人出国旅行的人数也大大增加，其中有的是出国考察游历的旅行者，有的是出国求学的留学生。如洪秀全、康有为、严复和孙中山等，就是最早向西方寻找真理的人物。

鸦片战争后，清朝官员林则徐、魏源等，提出"师夷之长以制夷"的主张。魏源的《海国图志》是一部使锁国闭门、坐井观天的中国，开始知道世界之大的启蒙著作，使"先进的中国人"产生了走向世界的要求。从19世纪40年代开始，有不少人到欧美、日本去游学，如1866年张德彝等游历欧洲，把自己的观感写成游记，介绍了西方的经济、政治、科学技术等，对于打开中国人的眼界，解放思想，做出了一定贡献。

中国革命先行者孙中山，见到外国"轮船之奇"，感到"沧海之阔"，产生了向西方学习之心。他从12岁起出国，一生来往于美、英、日及南洋各国。19世纪70年代洋务时期，清政府为了培养办"洋务"的人才，先后派了许多12岁到14岁的留学生到美国和欧洲国家去学习西方科技。中国第一个铁路工程师詹天佑就是第一批去美国的小留学生。

19世纪末20世纪初的"戊戌变法"时，又派出大量留学生，其中以去日本者最多。至 1906 年官费、自费留学生增至 8000 多人。他们大多数勤奋学习，"师夷之长"，经受资产阶级民主思想的洗礼，所以，留学生中不少人如黄兴、陈天华等，成为资产阶级民主革命的积极宣传者和实践者。

虽然旅行和旅游在中国自古有之，但作为一项经济事业的旅游业，从 20 世纪 20 年代才开始。1923 年，运行多时的上海商业储蓄银行的旅行部改名为"中国旅行社"，成为中国第一家专业旅行社，开始作为企业，承担旅行代理业务。该旅行部成立前，出国者多托外国在华的旅行机关，如英国通济隆旅行社、美国运通银行旅行部办理，外国来华的旅游者也由他们接待，由于他们不精通中国情况，不能正确的引导和介绍，使得来华旅游者对中国的名胜、古迹、历史、风尚、物产、文化艺术，不能有深入的接触，并产生误解，影响中国的旅游事业。因此，旅行部的成立，很受国内外人士欢迎，发展很快。

第三章

# 旅游的过程是人类文明传递的过程

# Cape of Good Hope

好望角

## 第一节
## 旅游是不同文明之间的桥梁

从前面的论述我们知道，虽然古今中外对旅游的理解不尽相同，但从一个地方到另一个地方的旅游的移动性的特点，是迄今为止众人的共识。旅游的本质属性决定了旅游活动既是文明的传播者又是文明的接收者。

要深入了解旅游在人类文明传递过程中所起的不可或缺的作用，我们首先必须从哲学上对人类"文明"有一个清晰的了解。

像诸多学科一样，中外学者对"文明"的理解也是五花八门，多种多样的。中国最早出现"文明"一词的书籍是《周易》，《周易·乾·文言》中说："见龙在田，天下文明。"大概意思是说，龙出现在田野上，天下因此充满文采而显光明。《尚书·舜典》中说："睿哲文明，温恭永塞。"意思为：开化、光明和富有文才。从中我们可以领会到，古代中国人对"文明"的理解，与文化有关。

中国近代知名人士梁启超在其所著《文明之精神》中说："文明者，有形质焉，有精神焉，求形质之文明易，求精神之文明难。"大概意思为，文明既是有形的也是无形的，得到物质的容易，得到精神的就难了。

孙中山是中国民主革命的先驱者，他在《孙文学说》中提到："实际则物质文明与心性文明相持，而后能进步。"把文明看做是物质和精神共同的产物。

梁启超和孙中山的观点更看重文明精神的一面，而中国"五四"时期思想家胡适则把物质文明和精神文明放到同等重要的地位。他认为，一种文明的构成，必须是两部分，一是物质的，一是精神的，物质的包括自然界的势力和质料，精神的包括一个民族的聪明才智，性情理想。他指出，没有单一的物质文明，也没有单一的精神文明。

《中国大百科全书·哲学》对文明的解释是："人类改造世界的物质和精神成果的总和；社会进步和人类开化状态的标志。"

法国年鉴学派巨匠、著名史学家布罗代尔认为，文明是"一个空间、一个'文化领域'，是文化特征和现象的一个集合"。

美国学者亨廷顿认为，文明和文化涉及一个民族的全面的生活方式，它们包括："价值、规则、体制和在一个既定社会中历代人赋予了头等重要性的思维模式。"

沃勒斯坦把文明定义为："世界观、习俗、结构的文化（物质文化和高层文化）的特殊连接。它形成了某种历史总和，并与这一现象的其他变种（即使不总是同时）共存。"

汤因比认为，文明是"文化不可避免的命运——是一种发达的人类能够达到的一些外部的和人为状态——是一个从形成到成熟的结局"。

梅尔科认为，"文明具有一定程度的整合。文明各个部分之间的关系和它们同整体之间的关系规定了它们的各个部分"。

恩格斯说："文明是个历史概念，文明是和蒙昧、野蛮相对立的，是人类历史发展到一定阶段的进步状态。"

从以上学者大同小异的说法，我们可以得知，文明既包括人类物质成果，也包括人类精神成果，是人类改造世界适应世界的进步形式，它往往以价值观、劳动规则、文化习俗、社会体制等状态表现出来，是一个国家和民族在物质领域和思想领域的综合反映。

我们考察人类文明的发展可以得知，创新是人类进步的不竭动力，很多时候创新就是人类文明进步的代名词。我们看一种文明是否有朝气、有生命力和前途，就是要考察这种文明是否有创新精神。

段亚兵先生在《文明纵横谈》中写道："文化创新是整体的创新，具体分为思想创新、科技生产创新和制度创新等几个方面。它们之间的关系为，理论创新是文明创新的核心和前提，科技生产的创新是文明创新的不竭源泉和动力，体制和机制的改革是文明创新的中心环节。"

德国哲学家、精神病学家雅斯贝尔斯（1883—1969）把从公元前1世纪上溯1000年共10个世纪的时代称为"轴心时代"，因为人类几大文明基本上都在这个时期定型的。他在著作《历史的起源与目标》中写到：

"在公元前800到公元前200年间所发生的精神过程，似乎建立了这样一个轴心。在这个时候，我们今日的人开始出现。让我们把这个时期称为'轴心时代'。在这一时期充满了不平常的事件。在中国诞生了孔子与老子，中国哲学的各种派别的兴起，这是墨子、老庄子以及无数其他人时代。在印度，这是优波泥沙和佛陀的世道，如在中国一样，所有哲学派别，包括怀疑主义、唯物主义、诡辩派和虚无主义都得到了发展。在伊朗，祆教提出挑战式的论断，认为宇宙的过程属于善与恶之间的斗争。在巴勒斯坦，先知们奋起：以利亚、以赛亚、耶利米、第二以赛亚。希腊产生了荷马，哲学家如巴门尼德、赫拉克利特、柏拉图，悲剧诗人，修昔底德和阿基米德。这些名字仅仅说明这个巨大的发展而已，这都是在几个世纪以内单独也差不多同时在中国、印度和西方出现的。"

由于受到早期人类生产力的限制，不同区域的文化都是独立萌生和成长起来的。

它们基本没有产生相互影响。经过2000余年的发展,至今仍为人类文明的重要组成部分。

## 第二节 没有传播就没有文明

没有创新,就没有文明,同样,没有传播,也无文明。创新是文明的源泉,传播是文明的生命。文明的传播、交流、互动,构成了当今人类文明发展的壮丽图画。

美国历史学家塔夫里阿诺斯在《全球通史》中指出,人类文明诞生于开放的环境,因为开放的环境有利于文明的传播和流动。他以公元前1500年为界限将世界历史分为两段:1500以前的各人类社会均处于不同程度的彼此隔离的状态之中,而1500年以后,整个世界连成了一片。人类后期的历史在很大程度上也就是人类的活动范围如何从当地扩展到地区、扩展到各地区之间,进而扩展到全球的过程。

人类社会早期,陆地交通是主要的交通方式。由于欧亚大陆交通方便,因而成为世界历史的心脏地区。欧亚大陆占地球陆地总表面的情况2/5,其人口为世界人口的9/10。两河文明和古埃及文明是人类最早的文明,原因就在于中东地区地处欧亚非大陆的交接处,这里地势平坦,交通方便,车马往来,舟楫通行,商贸活动发达,很早就成为经济发达地区。

欧亚大陆之外的世界由非洲、南北美洲和澳大利亚这三块大陆组成,彼此之间没有建立起任何联系。而北非与欧亚大陆相连出现了埃及文明,南部非洲因被沙漠阻隔,则没有出现什么著名的文明。澳大利亚的土著居民生活在海岛上,与大陆完全隔绝达30000年之久,因此发展受到严重阻碍,全部停留在食物采集阶段。

著名人类学家弗朗兹·博厄斯说:"人类的历史证明,一个社会集团,其文化的进步往往取决于它是否有机会吸取邻近社会集团的经验。一个社会集团所获得的种种发现可以传给其他社会集团;彼此之间的交流多样化,相互学习的机会也就越多。大体上,文化最原始的部落也就是那些长期与世隔绝的部落,因而,它们不能从邻近部落所取得的文化成就中获得好处——换句话说,如果其他地理因素相同,那么,人类取得进步的关键就在于各民族之间的可接近性和相互影响。只有那些最易接近、最有机会与其他民族相互影响的民族,才最有可能得到突飞猛进的发展;而那些与世隔绝、缺乏外界刺激的民族,多半停滞不前。"

某个地区与世隔绝的时候，文明的发展主要靠创造；当世界逐渐连成一片时，文明的发展主要靠传播。传播与创新相比较，要简单容易得多。研究一项新技术、新发明，需要花费大量的人力物力，而向别的民族学习、购买是会节省大量的人力物力。例如，中国的"四大发明"，这样的东西一经发明，传播出去就会成为全人类的共同财富。

新技术、新发明被创造出来，有时候有许多偶然因素起作用。许多发明创造具有独创性，其他人只向发明者学习和移植，不可能重新发明一次。例如，英国工业革命的发生就是具有独创性的一个例子，而欧洲其他国家的工业革命都是属于"输入"，是向英国学习的结果。一些国家所具备的工业化条件比英国还要优越，却没有成功实现工业化。因此，这不是一个地区或一个民族自觉选择的结果。发生工业革命，远比学习工业革命的成果要艰难得多。我们观察历史可以发现，地球上一些较大、较重要的文明区，都不是在与外界没有丝毫交往的情况下独立发展的。

各文明体之间存在着竞争，它是推动文明传播的力量。由于竞争产生了压力和威胁，人们就不得不向别人学习，把其他民族先进的经验变成自己的东西，保持大家一致前进的步伐。随着文明的进步，世界逐渐地连成为一片，文明之间的联系紧密了，竞争就变得更加紧张、更加激烈。

由于1500年以前的世界基本上是分散的、相互隔绝的，竞争没有那么激烈，落后的文明体还可以生存；1500年以后的世界逐渐连成一片，尤其是到了知识经济来临的今天，世界经济逐渐一体化，随着通信技术的发展，信息交流越来越容易，地球变得越来越小，成为一个地球村。在这种情况下，不管愿不愿意，所有的文明体都被迫进入竞技场。由于世界的联系越来越紧密，文明进步的步伐越来越快，文明体之间的竞争从自发转向自觉，从被动转向主动，而且越来越紧张和激烈。所以，文明传播的速度就越来越快，辐射的面积越来越大。

开放的环境有利于文明发展，环境封闭的文明不但不会进步而且会倒退。中国清朝闭关锁国造成中华文明的严重衰退就是典型的反面事例。

17—18世纪，世界发生了巨变，欧洲先后出现了哥白尼、伽利略和牛顿等大科学家。科学成为推动生产力发展的强大动力。但是，同一时期的中国，却完全是另一种情况。

康熙时期四口通商，全国允许四个口岸可以和外国通商。乾隆时期一口通商，只允许广州一个地方通商。康熙时期允许传教士到中国来，带来了自然科学知识，如天文、数学、历法、地理、物理、化学、医学等。雍正时期则把传教士通通驱逐出去。

由于自我封闭，自我满足，当时的中国人，就算是最先进的知识分子，也不了解世界的情况，不知道英国、法国有多大，位置在哪儿。

1792年，英国特使马戛尔尼带领英国使团来到中国，使团规模庞大，有好几艘大船，700多名成员，带来了600多箱礼物。其中有最先进的科学仪器如天文仪、地球仪，大型的仪器安装起来装满了圆明园的一间大屋子。此外还有西洋船模型和西瓜大炮、自来火焰等先进武器。

这次英国使团访华，本来是中国一个接触外国先进文化、放眼世界的极好机会，但因乾隆皇帝的傲慢无知而失之交臂。

英国人马戛尔尼向英皇汇报时说："清帝国好比是一艘破烂不堪的头等战船，它之所以在过去150年中没有沉没，仅仅是由于一班幸运的、能干而警觉的军官们的支撑。"

乾隆末年，中国经济总量占世界第一位，人口占世界1/3，对外贸易长期出超。但只过了短短100年，中国就陷入落后挨打的境地。马克思曾经予以评价说："一个人口几乎占人类1/3的大帝国，不顾时势，安于现状，人为地隔绝于世并因此以天朝尽善尽美的幻想自欺。这样一个帝国注定最后要在一场殊死的决斗中被打垮。在这场决斗中，陈腐世界的代表是激于道义，而最现代的代表却是为了获得贱买贵卖的特权——这真是一种任何诗人想也不敢想的一种奇异的对联式悲歌。"

中国与日本的近代化起步时间差不多，日本明治维新跟中国洋务运动时间是相同的。但日本因为无所顾虑，大踏步向前，国力迅速提升，反过来侵略中国。

中国台湾地区曾经请来了美国哈佛大学的一位著名教授演讲，谈到美国为何全球竞争力一直排名世界第一时，这位外国教授回答说，哪个社会最开放，它的竞争力就最高。全球的资金、科技、资讯、物美价廉的货物和优秀的人才都会流向这个国家。日本的例子恰好相反。从20世纪70年代后期到80年代初期，日本的全球竞争力排名世界第一，但从1990年开始到现在的十年里，日本不再第一了，原因何在？人们说有两个日本，一个是大家所熟悉的、先进的电器、汽车等工业品行销全球的日本；另一个就是不开放的、保守的日本。

（1）中华文明的传播

黄帝是中华民族的始祖。据说黄帝经常出外旅行，不仅自己游历了中国五大名山，还带着妻子到各地旅行。旅行归来，黄帝一行便将沿途所见所闻告诉自己的部落，如造车、造兵器和养蚕织布等技术，大大提高了部落民众认识自然、征服自然的能力，从而推动了人类社会的发展。旅游使皇帝见多识广，因而更受人尊重，使自己在部落里一直处于领先地位。

黄帝时代，嫘祖就已教人养蚕缫丝。丝绸之路开辟后，大大便利了中国丝绸向外传播。公元前1世纪，罗马贵族恺撒身着中国丝绸制的袍子看戏，曾经引起剧场的轰动。养蚕法7世纪传到阿拉伯和埃及，10世纪传到西班牙，11世纪传到意大利，15世纪传到法国。现在世界各国的家蚕、柞蚕，都来自于中国。

通过远古旅游,冶铁和水利技术也从中国传到中亚以至欧洲。大宛自中国学会凿井技术,中亚以及欧洲的冶铁技术是在通西域以后从中国学得的。

造纸术从中国传播出去以前,朝鲜、日本也用简和帛写字,印度用白树皮和棕榈树叶(中国通称贝叶)写字,埃及用纸草的内皮压成"纸草纸"写字,欧洲用羊皮作纸写字。这些书写材料,有的笨重,有的很脆,有的很贵。

据说欧洲写一部《圣经》,要用300张羊皮。因此,这些材料也都不适于大量使用。中国造纸术传播出去以后,大大促进了文化教育的普及,推动了世界科学文化的传播和交流,深刻影响着世界文明的进程。

正如英国科学家培根在评价包括造纸术在内的中国四大发明的时候所说的:"它们改变了世界上事物的全部面貌和状态,又从而产生了无数的变化;看来没有一个帝国,没有一个宗教,没有一个显赫人物,对人类事业曾经比这些机械的发现施展过更大的威力和影响。"

"丝绸之路"曾是东西方文明联系的纽带。395年,罗马帝国正式分裂为东西两部分,东罗马帝国拥有从巴尔干半岛直到两河流域与埃及的广大疆土,在相当一段时间里,成为中西交通与交流的主角。为了打破波斯中介贸易的垄断,它甚至两次派遣使节前往当时地跨红海两岸的强国阿克苏姆,企图联合阿克苏姆,对波斯展开一场抢购中国丝货的贸易战。

隋唐时期,隋炀帝一方面派大臣裴矩动员西域商人来内地经商做买卖,另一方面,在都城洛阳建造新的商贸工程。竣工后,下令每一年的正月,洛阳城内要整顿市容,张灯结彩,并将端门外、建国门内八九里长的天津街开辟为戏场,欢迎各国来华使节、商贾及游人。同时又将洛阳丰都市辟为国际商场,商人穿上华丽的衣服,备足百货奇珍,迎接各国来宾与客商。政府还建造四方馆,外交外贸事务一并办理,"以待四方使客,各掌其方国及市事"。外交外贸事务一并办理,有点像现代社会的"一条龙"服务,保证了国际商贸活动的开展。

唐帝国出于对外政治威望与经济交流的考虑,十分重视陆路丝道的经营。唐代的陆上丝绸之路最为繁荣。在汉代以来的南、北、中三道以外,又开辟了两条新的路线。

唐太宗初年,府军击败了连年侵扰的东突厥。然而,活跃在阿尔泰山以西的西突厥仍很强大。639年,唐太宗决心收复西域,出兵高昌,次年在该地设都护府,后又迁至龟兹,统领龟兹、碎叶、于阗、疏勒四镇,史称"安西四镇",保证了丝绸之路的安全与繁荣。沿着这条丝绸之路,中国和西方各国的商旅、使团络绎不绝。

人员的交往,是两种文明或文化之间交流的一个重要前提。唐帝国首都长安居住着大量来自欧、亚各地的侨民。当时长安人的服饰受到西方人的影响,妇女身披印度的披肩,头戴波斯的耳环,男子头顶胡帽,都为当时司空见惯的现象。从唐太宗贞观之治起，每年正月初一，各国及少数民族的使节前往长安参加唐朝朝会，各种的肤色相貌、不同的服饰和语言及舞蹈汇聚一堂，将长安变得异常热闹，盛况空前，一时成为世界性的大都会。

由于国际交往旅行活动日益活跃，长安逐渐成为亚洲各国经济文化交流的中心。不仅各种文化争相辉映，许多国家还派学者、留学生（包括僧侣）来中国深造学习。长安的国子监（中国封建社会的最高学府）里的外国留学生数达八千之多，其中尤以朝鲜和日本为最多。

朝鲜多时一次就派遣留学生 105 名。他们受到唐政府的特别优待，被称为"宾贡进士"，并被允许参加科举考试。朝鲜留学生回国时，不仅带走他们所学的知识，而且还带走大量中国典籍。佛教、佛经连同中国的雕版印刷术，于唐末也一起传入朝鲜。据记载，朝鲜京都平壤，是模仿唐朝长安和洛阳的风格建造起来的；朝鲜文武官职的设置也与唐朝相仿；甚至连其国家的历法、年号及百姓的服装也跟大唐一致。以至于唐玄宗称朝鲜是懂诗文的君子国，知情达理，和中华同类。他往朝鲜派使臣时，也一定经过精心挑选，有文学修养者才能入选。另一方面，朝鲜的音乐、特产等也传入中国，丰富了我国人民生活。

中日文化交流在隋唐时期也达到了高潮。史书记载，841 年至 903 年间的 62 年中，中国去日本的使节与商舶有 32 次之多。而日本来华学习的遣唐使、留学生则更多，有的一批就有五百多人。

学成而归的日本留学生，对日本国的发展起了积极的推动作用。在他们的鼓励及协助下，日本孝德天皇进行了大化革新，即从中央到地方，政治、经济、文化、教育、医学及其他技术，一切学习唐朝。719 年，天皇还下诏书，令全国仿照唐服，和服从此成为日本人的国服。

唐朝与南亚、中亚、西亚和欧洲的往来也非常频繁。在相互交流的过程中，印度的天文学、医学传入中国，中国的中医药，如人参、麻黄传入印度，养蚕植桑技术则流入波斯。波斯人不仅学会了养蚕缫丝，还吸收中国丝织品的工艺特点，研究创造出波斯锦花缎。

此时，国际商贸旅行更为活跃，长着高鼻子、留着络腮胡子的波斯（今伊朗）商人，或牵着骆驼，或骑着大象、毛驴，满载着商品，来来往往，一片繁忙的景象。地处欧亚非三洲的大食帝国（阿拉伯帝国）商人，用他们的香料来换取中国的茶、瓷器及纺织品。阿拉伯大商人、旅行家苏莱曼，851 年前后来中国经商游历，回国后将其在东方的所见所闻由一位不知名作家写成《苏莱曼东游记》。

在古代中外文明的交流中，郑和七下西洋更是一项壮举。郑和本姓马，名三宝，是我国明代著名的航海家。朱棣称帝后，为向外界宣传大明王朝，开展国际贸易，命郑和组织大型经济文化使团远洋航行。当时，人们习惯将今天苏门答腊与马来半岛以西的水域称为西洋。1407年7月11日，郑和率领包括翻译、水手、工匠、医生、文书、算术家在内的27800百人，分别乘坐满载丝绸、瓷器、茶叶、黄金等物品的62艘宝船，从苏州刘家港出发，经东海、南海扬帆到爪哇、马六甲、印尼等地，最远抵达印度西海岸，然后返回南京，共历时27个月。

郑和于1431年至1433年间第七次下西洋。每次——拜访前六次访问过的大多数国家和地区，又走访新的国家。在麦加城，郑和虔诚地在先知穆罕默德的墓上行圣礼，实现了他有生之年要前往圣地朝拜的愿望。最后一次远航后回南京不久就病逝。郑和以后，虽然明朝海上贸易与海外交往依然丰富多彩，但再也没有出现过大规模的航海活动。

郑和下西洋，纵横驰骋于太平洋、印度洋，涉海十万余里，历时28年，足迹到达30多个国家和地区，最远到达了非洲东海岸，这不仅是中国航海史上的先例，也是世界航海史上罕见的壮举。郑和的船队所到之处，带去了中华文明的硕果，受到了当地人民的欢迎。至今爪哇、泰国等地的三宝垄、三宝庙和三宝塔，就是这种友好关系的见证。郑和的航海记录《郑和航海图》和其所著《针位篇》，以及随从马欢所著的《瀛涯胜览》、费信所著的《星槎胜览》、巩珍所著的《西洋番国志》，都是远航的宝贵资料。所以，郑和不仅是中国航海史和世界航海史上杰出的航海家，也是中华文明海外传播的"文明使者"。

若论及谁是中西文化交流第一人，那非意大利旅行家马可波罗莫属。他是自丝绸之路开通以来，从海路和陆路完成从欧洲的威尼斯到达中国再回到欧洲旅游的第一人，他的足迹遍及欧亚大陆。

1271年，马可·波罗和他的父亲及伯父开始前往东方旅行。他们沿着塔克拉玛干沙漠南部的道路，经和阗、罗布泊，到达敦煌地区，最后抵达中国元代上都，于1275年完成了横贯欧亚的艰苦旅行。由于马可·波罗聪明睿智，而且通晓多国语言，便被忽必烈留在朝廷里担任职务。直到1291年回国，他在中国共生活和旅游了17年。

大汗曾几次派他到甘州等地去检查税收，还派他去过东南亚和印度。横跨北京郊区永定河的卢沟桥，被西方人称为"马可·波罗桥"，因为《马可·波罗游记》中写到这座桥："一座美丽的桥，显示了造桥技术的高超绝伦，造型手艺极其高明，精巧的雕刻，使整座桥气势如虹，蔚为壮观。"他还对元朝的宫殿和国都发出了由衷的赞赏："君等应知此宫之大，向所示见、宫上无楼，建于平地。惟台基高出地面十掌。宫顶甚高，宫墙与房壁满涂金银，并绘龙、兽、鸟、骑士形象及其他数物于其上……宫中有殿广大，其中贮藏守城之兵杖。街道基直，以此端可见彼端，盖其布置，使此门可由街道远望彼门也。城中有壮丽宫殿，复有美丽邸舍甚多。"

马可·波罗在中国的旅游路线是元代驿道所经之地，主要有两条，一条是大都到云南的驿道，另一条是大都至泉州的驿道。这一驿道系统是元帝国统治的重要的基础设施。他赞道："应知有不少道路从此汗八里城首途，通达不少州郡，由是各道即以所通某州之名为名，此事颇为合理。如从汗八里首途，经行其所取之道时，行25英里（40千米），使臣即见有一驿，其名曰站，一如吾人所称供给马匹之驿传也。每驿有一大而富丽之邸，使臣居宿于此，其房舍满布极富丽之卧榻，上陈绸被，凡使臣需要之物皆备。"

马可·波罗对杭州的社会生活做了较为详细的记述，特别提到了杭州当时的旅游业。他写道："既抵此处，请言极灿烂华丽之状，盖其状足言也，谓其为世界富丽名贵之城，良非伪语……此行在城甚大，周围广有百英里，内有一万二千石桥，桥甚高，一大舟可行其下。其桥之多，不足为异……此外湖上有大小船只甚众，以供游乐。每舟容10人、15人或20人以上。舟长15至20步，底平宽，常保持其位置平稳。凡欲携亲友游乐者，只需选择一舟右矣，舟中饶有桌椅及应接必需之一切器皿。舟顶用平板构成，操舟者在其上执篙撑舟湖底以行舟（盖湖深不过两步）。拟赴何处，随意所欲。舟顶以下，与夫四壁，悬挂各色画图。两旁有窗可随意启闭，由是舟中席上之人，可观四面种种风景。地上之赏心乐事，诚无有过于此游湖之事也。"（《马可·波罗》）

在中国多年后，马可·波罗等人开始思念故国，终于有一个机会，他们的愿望实现了。当时马可·波罗刚从印度回来，地中海东部鞑靼人派了3个使者向忽必烈求亲，请忽必烈送去一位公主阔阔真。马可·波罗建议由他们父子三人护送使者和公主从海路回程，忽必烈答应了他的要求。马可·波罗三人从陆路到土耳其黑海岸边，再乘船到君士坦丁堡，于1295年回到了威尼斯。

1298年在热那亚和威尼斯的海战中，马可·波罗成了俘虏，被带到了热那亚，在那里他见到了宫廷作家鲁思梯谦。于是，马可·波罗口述自己的经历，由鲁思梯谦写出了《马可·波罗游记》。鲁思梯谦在书的前言写道："欲知世界各地之真相，可取此书读之。君等将在其中得见所志大阿美尼亚、波斯、鞑靼、印度及其他不少州区之伟大奇迹，且其叙述秩次井然，明了易解；凡此诸事，皆是物掷齐亚（即威尼斯）贤而贵的市民马可·波罗所目睹，间有非彼目睹者，则闻之于确实可信之人。所以吾人之所征引，所见者著明所见，所闻者著明所闻，庶使本书确实，毫无虚伪。有聆是书或读是书教区牧师，应信其真。盖书中所记皆实，缘自上帝创造人始祖阿聃以来，历代之人探知世界各地及其伟大奇迹者，无有如马可·波罗君所知之广也。故彼以为，其事诚为不幸。余更有言者，凡此诸事，皆彼居留各国垂二十六年之见闻。迨其禁锢于吉那哇（即热那亚），乃求其同狱者皮撒城人鲁思梯谦诠次之，时在基督降生后之1298年云。"

《马可·波罗游记》出版后受到极其热烈的欢迎,被翻译成拉丁语和各种意大利方言。

(2) 西方文明的传播

13世纪的欧洲对于广大的亚洲的了解,多半停留在想象和道听途说的水平上,如有人描述:"探险家到遥远的地方旅行,面对的是陌生的新世界,那里住着半人半兽的魔鬼、神奇的动物和风俗奇异的种族……当地的女人具有人形,而男人则长得像狗……根据可靠的资料,那里住着人形的魔鬼,两脚成牛蹄状,头部和人一样,面孔却像狗,这种怪人能说两种人类的语言,又像狗一样吼出第三种语言……有人言之凿凿,说他们在穿过沙漠时,发现了一些人形的怪物,只有一只手,长在胸部中央,而且只有一条腿。两个怪物合用一张弓,跑得极快,连马匹都追不上。它们用一条腿跳跃,累了就以手着地跳,再用腿跳,身体像车轮一样转过来转过去。"(《马可·波罗游记》)

诸如此类的传说,一方面使西方提到东方时惊恐万分,另一方面也刺激他们的好奇心,增加了他们前去了解神秘东方的欲望。正是出于对好奇、贸易机会的渴望,促使一大批欧洲旅行家开创了欧亚大陆旅游的新篇章。

据说,马可·波罗回到威尼斯后,因讲述东方见闻,只被看做是一个在威尼斯舞厅和游乐场所,向观众讲些离奇故事,博观众一笑的小丑。以致当他临终的时候,他的亲戚朋友出于好心,劝他对神表示忏悔,承认撒谎的过失,以拯救灵魂。马可·波罗则声明,他不但没有撒谎,而且他所讲的故事,尚不足他所见的一半。

15世纪末,两股势力侵入了印度:一股从海路而来的是葡萄牙人,另一股是从陆路而来的在中亚地区征战的莫卧儿人。这两股势力的到来,给印度带来了巨大而持久的变化。到1526年,马布尔在德里建立印度的莫卧尔王朝,开始了穆斯林势力的统治。

西方最早进入印度的是葡萄牙人。《西方旅游史》写道:

"487年,葡萄牙国王派身为语言学家、士兵、间谍和外交家的佩罗达·科维利亚由陆路出使印度,以搜集有关这一国家的情报。科维利亚会说阿拉伯语,他沿传统的商人路线行进到开罗和亚丁,接着乘一条阿拉伯独桅帆船到印度的卡利库特。他侦察了印度西海岸即马拉巴尔海岸港口,然后搭一条阿拉伯船返回东非。在东非,他访问了许多阿拉伯城镇,再回到开罗,最后在阿比西尼亚结束全部行程……在离开开罗之前,他将自己的调查结果写成一份千金难买的报告,寄回里斯本。"

"在他之后是西方人引以为豪的新航线的开辟。达·伽马于1498年到达印度,在其后的50年里,葡萄牙人占领了果阿海岸长约96.5千米,纵深48千米的地区作为其贸易的据点。之后，又在南方占据了一连串的海港要塞，并与当时印度北方的莫卧儿王朝和南方的各土邦之间，互派了使者。"

"葡萄牙人利用在里斯本和果阿之间的贸易，发动了一场重要的商业革命，它使印度、甚至还有整个亚洲最终实际上加入单一的全球交换体系。葡萄牙船队从果阿返回里斯本，又驶向安特卫的皇家'商行'，比以往任何时候都更彻底地开发了正在发展的北欧贸易。而且印度经过里斯本，同全新的市场、葡萄牙人的巴西殖民地和在西非的拓居地也连接起来。"

该书还写道："必须承认是从印度向西到非洲和阿拉伯，向东到马六甲、香料群岛、中国和日本贸易的利润，特别是转口贸易的利润，支撑着葡属印度的整个大厦。贸易和以合法方式或贪污手段对贸易征收的税款，负担了军队和官吏的费用，又使传教的活动可能从阿比西尼亚扩展到北京。"

西方文明的传播，多半是从宗教开始的。因为随着商业和航海的繁荣，大大刺激了欧洲人向异教徒传播上帝福音的决心。甚至葡萄牙约翰二世还发誓要"将人类可居住的世界统一于基督教"。

罗马教皇很关心如何在海外实现教会的直接控制。西班牙和葡萄牙都是罗马教会的势力范围，伴随着海外殖民地运动的推进，天主教也传到了美洲和亚洲。当有人问达伽马是什么促使他去印度时，他毫不犹豫回答："是基督徒和香料。"

1500年，葡萄牙指挥官佩德罗·阿尔瓦雷斯·卡布拉尔率领一队人马前往东方开拓贸易，同船的还有8名平信徒和8名方济各会会士，他们奉命去印度海岸传播基督教。但不幸的是，在两个月内，就有3个传教士被杀。不过，其余的传教士并没有退缩，一直留在那里传教。

当德·阿尔梅达于1505年成为葡萄牙第一任印度总督的时候，更多的传教士前往印度传教。在耶稣会士进入印度前的40年间，其活动范围主要集中在以果阿为中心的海岸附近，并在果阿建立了马德拉斯方济各大主教辖区，其传教活动一直持续到了19世纪。

1707年，莫卧尔王朝的最后一个统治者奥朗则布去世。在此之后，印度进入了英国的殖民地统治时期。印度从一个典型的非西方传统社会转变为一个深受西方影响的社会。

17世纪初期和中期，英国人、荷兰人、法国人就陆续在印度坎贝湾的苏拉特开设商行。1665年以后，苏拉特的经济发展十分迅速。在船舶云集的港口，有大批的简易棚屋供欧洲或其他地区的水手暂住。据记载，苏拉特常住人口达百万，可与里昂相比。除繁荣的商业景象外，世界各国的种族和宗教也都汇集于此，形成另一大景观。

由于各地的产品都很丰富，印度次大陆的贸易旅游十分兴旺，在靠近港口和河流的地方，陆路的商队把货物源源不断运到内陆的广大地区。

16—17世纪，天主教各教团的传教活动继续发展。许多葡萄牙的耶稣会教士也把印度作为向其他地区传教的基地。如方济各会士在锡兰的一些地区传教，做礼拜，接受有身份人士的造访。每个较大的村镇都建有教会学校，在教会建的学院里，学生们经常排练神迹剧。在一些大的基督教社区，经常可听到用拉丁语和泰米尔语吟唱的圣乐。一些传教士也留下了关于17世纪印度的游记。如著名的《旅行记》就叙述了西班牙传教士曼里克1612年在孟加拉的经历，该书描写了恒河的富饶，棉织品的华丽，人们对牛和恒河的尊敬以及一些地区自我牺牲以祭神的稀奇做法。

到了16—17世纪，随着商贸的繁荣和发展，越来越多的西方旅游者进入印度。尼古拉康蒂和德拉·瓦勒分别于15世纪和17世纪在印度旅游时携带家眷，表明了当时印度的旅游文化也很发达。

耶稣会教士是近代基督教在世界范围内传播最为成功的例子。1541年，罗耀拉成为耶稣会的领袖，并宣布所有的教徒皆为基督教兄弟。通过耶稣会教士努力，在欧洲的天主教部分地区形成了一个具有吸引力的宗教团体。耶稣会教士的志向并不仅限于欧洲，他们要把主的福音传播到世界其他的地区。

为了确保耶稣会在海外传教活动卓有成效，教会"派遣精选而更可靠的人士前往"，也就是我们今天所说的德才兼备的教士去往世界各地。

经过一系列的准备，从16世纪中叶开始，耶稣会士们就向印度、中国、日本及新大陆传教，他们的活动内容包括教育、布道、亲人救济以及其他各种传教活动。

早在隋唐时期，伴随着中外交流的发展，外国的宗教就不断传入中国。世界三大宗教中的伊斯兰教、基督教，继佛教之后，在唐朝初期纷纷传入中国。742年，长安城里兴建了我国第一座清真寺。此外，外国的乐器和娱乐活动也传入我国，如北方少数民族的胡旋舞、波斯乐器箜篌和唢呐及欧洲罗马帝国的杂技等。由于胡旋舞的流行，胡服也成为当时流行的时髦服装。一时间，长安、洛阳城两城内，"胡化"严重。今人在敦煌、西安及盐池三处发现的雕刻和壁画中，可以看到胡旋舞的图案，足见胡旋舞当时的盛况。

由于明清两朝推行闭关禁海的政策，导致外国来华游客稀少。据历史记载，明永乐21年，到南京的海外游客只有1200人，国际旅游处于停滞状态。但毕竟世界潮流浩浩荡荡，科学技术日益发达，交通往来更加便利，西方来华的传教士客观上也迅速增加。传教士在传播宗教的同时，也成为中西文化科技交流的文明使者。罗明坚和利玛窦是明清来华传教的奠基者。

1578年3月29日，罗明坚、利玛窦和巴范济，以及同行的另外13名耶稣会士，离开里斯本，开始了到东方的航程。1578年9月13日，他们到达果阿。1579年4月，罗明坚动身，搭上前往中国的航船，于同年7月到达澳门。36岁的罗明坚通过两年的学习，便"认识15000个中国字，逐渐可以看中国书籍"，还试着翻译中文的小册子。他最终写成了一部系统介绍基督教义的书，称之为《新编天主实录》或《天主圣教实录》，这"是欧罗巴人最初用华语写成之教义纲领，于1584年11月抄刻于广州"（沈定平，2001）。

从1580年12月起，罗明坚曾多次随同被允许到广州做生意的葡萄牙商人进入这座富庶的城市，并开始了在广东的传教活动。

为了尽快赢得中国官员的信任，罗明坚在澳门卡内罗主教的协助下，排演了一个旨在增强传教士声望及率领西方商人学习中国礼仪，如长跪、磕头、谦恭、礼让等颇具戏剧性的场面。长期以来，一些葡商因对中国烦琐礼节不以为然，遂招致中国官员的反感，视之为蛮夷。由于神职人员在西方宗教和社会生活中具有重要的地位，他们的言论带有一定的威慑作用。经过罗明坚的一番开导和教化之后，葡萄牙商人过去那种粗陋的行为不再有了。并且因为罗司铎的"明智、温和、又不携带武器"，官方在每次公共拜谒的时候，必定要有他在场作证，罗明坚慢慢受到官方的重视。

他还与广州的官员建立了个人的友谊，并获得了暂时居住的权利，从而开始小规模的传教活动。1583年9月，罗明坚和利玛窦一起到达了当时广东总督府所在地肇庆，得到了肇庆知府王泮的首肯，开始在肇庆修建教堂和传教，并逐步扩展到中国其他一些地区。罗明坚于1588年离开澳门，返回欧洲，他再也没有作为教皇的特使回到中国，而于1607年5月11日在等待中去世。

利玛窦是明清来华传教士中最有影响的一位。利玛窦出生于意大利，毕业于罗马神学院。由于中国人长期以来很少接触西洋教会，所以利玛窦和罗明坚一样，在传教初期并不顺利。为了吸引中国人的好奇，他在教堂陈列室展出西方制造的时钟等科技产品，并在墙上悬挂一幅自制的世界地图。他故意把中国的位置画在地图的中间，用汉字标出，以求得中国人的好感。在取得一些地方官员的信任后，利玛窦先后在南京、南昌、苏州等地传教，并一路游览名胜。后经人推荐进入北京，受到万历皇帝的召见。皇帝赐给他一所邸宅，并允许其在北京宣武门建立天主教堂，所需经费皆由朝廷供给。

利玛窦在中国居住了29年，除传教讲经，大多数时间还是用于介绍西方文化、翻译书籍。西方测绘技术就是由他引入中国，所以他被称为"引进西方测绘技术的第一人"。他先后测出中国南部海岸、北部边缘和北京、广州等地的经纬度，并绘制出多种世界地图，使得中国人有了东西半球的概念。他还翻译了《几何原理》《测量法义》《万国典图》等自然科学书籍，对丰富中国人的自然科学知识，开启中国人科技智慧不无裨益。

第四章

# 旅游的整合力
## 是人类文明发展的加速器

奇琴伊察古城 Pre-Hispanic City of Chichen-Itza

# 第一节
## 旅游有着包容广泛的硬整合力

### 一、旅游业是世界上最大的混合产业

美国著名学者丹尼尔·贝尔在他 1973 年出版的《后工业社会的来临》一书中把旅游产业说成是世界上最大的混合产业,其所包含或涉及的内容是其他任何产业都无法相比的。他指出,旅游业的关联行业不仅相互影响,而且相互制约。

也有专家研究统计,旅游有 180 多个"绰号",如"旅游是和平的使者","旅游是通向全球的护照","旅游是推动经济发展的润滑剂"……这种现象恐怕是任何产业所没有的。

笔者以为,之所以社会对旅游的认识会存在如此多的说法,至少说明两种情况:一是至今为止,大家对旅游的认识还不够全面深入,以至于有点像"瞎子摸象",摸到哪里说哪里;二是从反方面论证了旅游的包容性确实大,牵涉面确实广。

"整合"的概念源自于欧洲理论界,牛津现代高级英汉双解词典中指出,"整合"即为"Integrate",指连接各部分使其成为一个整体,使成完整之物,结合成一体。

从静态的角度看,旅游整合是指产业通过结构调整和组织改造,在市场经济条件下,进行资源优化配置,从而达到产业组合和产业竞争的最佳结果与状态,它是旅游产业发展的终极目标;从动态的角度来看,旅游整合是指达到上述结果和状态的一个过程。

而从旅游的经济和文化属性出发,从表现方式来看,旅游又可分为硬整合力和软整合力。旅游的硬整合力是指形成旅游产业链条或产业集群所表现出来的物质性力量。何谓旅游业的产业链条?从经济的角度来观察,旅游的发展不仅刺激了直接为之提供服务的产业,如交通、住宿、餐饮、娱乐、商业、景区等行业,而且会带动相关产业的发展。

就拿饭店业来说,宾馆的增加必定刺激建筑、建材、家具、装潢业等相关产业的发展;餐饮服务业要求农业、牧业、水产、林业等扩大加工能力,增加产品供应。

作为一个综合性的产业，旅游产业与众多的要素、产业、系统发生关联。一是要素关联：旅游活动的食、住、行、游、购、娱"六要素"之间彼此关联互动，相互依赖，互为依存，形成一个完整的要素体系；二是产业关联：除了属于第三产业外，它还涉及众多的行业和部门，如为旅游业提供物质支撑的农业、林业、畜牧业和渔业等部门属于第一产业；轻工业、重工业和建筑业等部门属于第二产业；邮电通信业、金融业、保险业、公共服务业、卫生体育业、文化艺术业、教育事业、信息咨询服务业等部门，以及旅游行政管理部门、海关、边检等属于第三产业。据澳大利亚有关方面统计，旅游产品的提供涉及29个经济部门共109个行业。旅游业的发展带动这些部门和行业的发展，而这些部门和行业又为旅游业的发展提供了强大的物质基础；三是系统关联：旅游产业主要由旅游吸引力系统、服务系统、交通运输系统、市场营销系统和信息提供系统五个部分组成。五部分之间的有机联合、协调互动，是旅游产业持续发展的必然要求。

所谓"硬整合力"的产业集群，简单地说，就是相同的企业或相配套的企业，在一定的范围内，高密度地聚集在一起。

产业集群已经成为一个世界性的经济现象，并得到许多国家和地区政府的重视。地域化、专业化和社会化分工的产业集群模式，吸引越来越多的旅游企业朝着产业化区域或目标靠拢。例如，中国苏沪杭、珠三角和京津冀三大城市群落，被誉为中国经济"三驾马车"，而活跃在三大都市经济圈内的热点产业——旅游业，如今也积极表现出不同程度的一体化发展态势。

以上海为龙头的长三角旅游协作区，率先实现了旅游资源的整合和旅游功能要素的配套，成为中国旅游业最大的经济产出区域。2001年，上海、江苏和浙江三省以建立"大上海"旅游集散中心的方式，主动进行上海与江苏、浙江14个沿江城市的150多个景点的联合，集中包装和推出36条跨区域旅游线路，3年即实现旅游收入2300亿元的业绩；广东省则利用珠三角的城市集群品牌优势和港澳市场的辐射优势，积极做"大旅游圈"的文章，也获得了1260.83亿元的回报，显现了大区域旅游的独特作用。

## 二、旅游的整合力无可替代

可以这么说，没有旅游就没有人类经济的发展，没有旅游就没有人类文明的进步。观古察今，旅游随着人类生产力的发展而发展，也随着自身的不断强大和活跃而推进人类生产力的进步。

朱昌勤先生在2006年10月16日的《环球游报》上撰文说："旅游发展到今天，可谓是无所不可及、无所不可有、无所不可为的特大业体，旅游业已是世界通业,各个国家都在打旅游牌。旅游早已冲破时空局限,不再是有权者、有钱者、有闲者的专利享受,不再是'智者乐水,仁者乐山'的高雅话题。到处都在发掘旅游资源,到处都在发展旅游产业。面之广,速之快,难于估考。而正是这个特大业体的拉动和驱动,使相关相应的多种产业一俱腾飞。全球游业突起,实当刮目相看。"

中国社会科学院旅游研究中心主任张广瑞先生说得更加具体:"不到30年的时间,人们对旅游的理解有了许多重大变化,它从'民间外交'变成'创汇产业'、'无烟工业'、'无形贸易',后来又被称作'先导产业'、'强势产业'、'支柱产业',近来人们又开始把它叫做'环保产业'、'学习产业'、'文化产业'和'动力产业'。"张先生的这段概述,十分清楚地说明了旅游业与各行各业的连带关系和对世界经济的发展、人类文明进步所做出的重大贡献。

旅游业是世界公认的新兴产业,有些国家把旅游作为他们的立国之本,甚至有些国家或地区仅仅只有旅游这样一个产业,如马尔代夫、夏威夷、雅典就是如此。雅典是一个有400万人口的城市,只有两个产业,最大的产业还是旅游业,其次是纺织业。纺织业全行业一共只有18万人,其余全靠旅游业养活。还比如意大利的威尼斯,是一个水城,也只有两个产业,一个是旅游业,一个是海运业,海运业也是为旅游业服务的。一个只有160万人口的城市,每年来的游客数量是6千万人次。

有关研究认为,每1美元的直接旅游收入可带动2.5美元的间接旅游收入。2005年,世界旅游总收入突破6万亿美元,占世界生产总值的10%,从业人员达2.21亿。按此推算,则相应带动国民生产总值增加了15万亿美元,两项合计实现旅游总效益达到21万亿美元。

在中国,旅游业的带动效应更强,据有关研究测算,旅游业每收入1美元,可使国民生产总值增加3.12美元;旅游收入每增加1元人民币,可带动第三产业相应增加10.7元人民币;旅游外汇收入每增加1美元,利用外资金额则相应增加5.9美元。2005年中国国内旅游收入为760亿美元,国际旅游收入为293亿美元,相应带动国民生产总值分别为2300多亿美元和1700亿美元。

世界旅游理事会(WTTC)2005年的一份名为《播下增长种子》的关于中国旅游发展研究报告称,中国旅游业的直接增加值达445亿美元,相当于GDP的比重为2.8%,旅游经济的总增加值达2178亿美元,相当于全国GDP的11.7%;旅游的直接就业人数为1429.56万,占全国总就业人数的1.9%,而旅游经济一共创造就业岗位6462.51万个,占全国总就业的8.6%;旅游服务的总出口收入为581亿美元,占服务与货物总出口收入的7.7%;旅游资本投资为1003亿美元,占总资本投资的9.9%;其中政府旅游支出83亿美元,占政府总支出的3.8%。

中国老教授协会旅游研究所所长于英士在撰文中说:"一个产业要有一大堆产业群支持它的生产,这对旅游产业来讲非常复杂,因为别的产业是可以独立的,例如炼钢的,从采矿到炼出钢材都可以自己独立搞。旅游产业则没有自己的产业群。旅游产业的产业群都属于别的部门,它是借助于社会的产业群来实现自己的产业目的的,这是旅游产业的特点。"

旅游产业的发展促进了区域内资源配置、经济增长、基础设施、生态环境、劳动就业、社会文化、对外开放等方面的整合互动。同时,区域经济发展可以快速拉动旅游消费规模增长与消费水平的提高,区域基础设施和供给水平的增强、生态环境的改善则为旅游业的发展提供充足的保障。

旅游业对资源的整合是其他任何一个产业、一个行业无法相比的。传统产业和行业对资源只能选择适合的产品生产需要的资源。但旅游产业不一样,它可以把几千年甚至上万年的东西和现代社会连接在一块;它还可以把经济的、文化的、民俗的、社会的甚至于包括心理学的资源结合在一起;它可以把物质的、精神的融合在一块;它还可以把历史的、地理的、建筑的,包括水文的、地质的、生物学的、植物学的、动物学的、微生物学的东西都结合在一块,为我所用,做成产品,销售给游客。

迟国维先生在《也谈"旅游整合世界"》一文中说:"人们正在逐步改变对旅游行为的看法,学术研究也在改变对旅游行为的看法,现在也渐渐加入到研究的行列。学者们已经不像过去那样,把旅游视为一种通过旅客与东道主'临时性'接触和交流所表现出来的表面化的、近似的、不能准确认识现实的一种活动和行为,而是把旅游置于促进不同民族和族群的相互理解、平等对待、文化交流等的层面来认识。这样的认识又建立在对社会和文化的历史深度和广度的传统认知和理性理解的基础之上。所以,旅游也自然地对许多学科进行重新整合,许多学科也把旅游纳入到自己的研究领域。

如,农业——主要涉及乡村旅游;人类学主要研究'游客和东道主'的关系;商业——主要涉及酒店投资等;生态学——研究旅游与自然相关的因素;经济学——研究旅游经济;教育学——有关旅游教育问题;地理学——旅游地理学;历史学——主要关注与旅游历史相关的问题;酒店管理——主要涉及酒店管理与服务相关的问题;法律——主要探讨和研究与旅游相关的法律问题;休闲与再生——关于休闲与游客再生产的关系;市场交易——有关旅游市场的交易事宜;政治科学——世界无边界的宏观研究;心理学——主要涉及旅游动机方面的研究;宗教学——朝圣旅行以及所涉及的宗教礼仪问题;社会学——旅游社会学;交通——与旅游交通有关的事务,如航空等;城市与区域规划——旅游发展问题。"

迟国维在文中还谈道:"现在,旅游不仅成为世界上一个最大的、发展最快的产业,它对全世界的经济、政治、环境、资源、就业、文化交流、管理、全球化等问题都提出了一系列崭新的课题,同时也意味着巨大的挑战。"

在现实中我们体验到,旅游业作为现代服务业的龙头产业,其整合能力非常之强,辐射范围非常之广。现代旅游业几乎包括了第三产业的所有内容,在这些众多的产业中,有些搞了几十年的老产业,一直都没有发展起来,但是随着旅游业的发展,就迅速发展起来了。如中国邮电业的发展就是非常典型的例子,根据中国电信部门的测算,近几年流动人口和游客每年为他们提供的收入占其总收入的46%。

在众多的产业里,旅游业担当了龙头产业的角色,旅游业的发展决定了其他许多产业的发展。在2003年"非典"期间,突来的疫情一度使许多国家政府手足无措,为了避免通过旅游渠道传播,许多国家明令停止了一切旅游活动,虽然这期间其他行业没有停止,但这些行业因旅游的停止而停止了。不久,"非典"终止,这些行业又随着旅游业的恢复而恢复了。这个事例从反面又一次证明,旅游业可以起着"一业举百业举"、"一业兴百业兴"的"龙头"作用。

## 第二节
## 旅游有着不可估量的软整合力

### 一、什么是"软力量"

美国学者约瑟夫·奈在80年代后期创造了"软力量"一词,该词现在为世界各地的政治领袖、编辑和学者们频繁地使用。

什么是"软力量"?简而言之,就是一个国家通过"吸引"而非"命令"或者"强制"他国做某些事或采取某种选择的能力。约瑟夫·奈认为,美国之所以能在冷战中击败苏联,并取得最后胜利,依赖的就是"软力量",即美式民主和价值观念的广泛传播。作为一位曾经担任过美国国防部前助理部长的学者,约瑟夫·奈的"软力量"在美国政界深受重视,并为美国在新形势下"领导世界"提供了理论依据。

根据约瑟夫·奈的分析,软力量靠的是吸引和劝服的能力,而硬力量(即强迫的能力)来自一个国家的军事和经济实力。相对于以军事、科技、教育、经济力为基础的"硬力量"而言,软力量的资源主要包括三个方面:文化、意识形态(或者价值观念),以及国际规范与制度。

周庆安在《环球时报》上撰文指出，一个软力量资源大国，并非天生就是一个软力量大国。当20世纪60年代李小龙把中国武术搬上西方银屏，引发世界注目的时候，当时的跆拳道已经成为不少西方国家百姓日常练习的运动。他写道"近现代历史证明，在整个软力量的发展过程中，二者甚至没有必然的因果关系。在国际政治历史上，世界几个重要的传统文化中心地区，如东亚地区、爱琴海地区、两河流域和南亚大陆，都没有形成能够影响国际政治话语体系的软力量中心。这有两方面的原因：一是这些地方的发展中国家居多，长期的落后影响了这些国家的形象；另一方面，文化并非软力量，能否产生'力'的效应，取决于这些文化的传播和应用效果。"

周庆安认为，一个软力量资源大国，要成为软力量大国，其软力量产品必须经历三个阶段：

"首先，一种文化产品从存在到成为国家软力量的重要手段，需要良好的包装。软力量之所以成为软力量，不但是因为其内容能够产生认同，更是因为它的形式容易为人接受。

"其次，一个国家的文化产品能否成为软力量的有效手段，取决于其产品的国际化程度。跆拳道正是这样的一个典型软力量的使用。文化产品的展示和文化手段的输出，是软力量。

"再次，软力量需要资源的充分整合。软力量发挥作用是一个长期的过程，任何一种软力量资源，都已经不可能独当一面了。在跆拳道的推广过程中，韩国政府、商业机构和民间组织运用了包括影视、音像制品、网站这些大众传媒手段，以及跆拳道俱乐部等人际推广模式在内的多种手段。这些渠道的整合，使跆拳道从客观上成为一个综合的文化载体，同时也是韩国国家文化资源品牌的一个立体符号。这也是软力量之所以成为'力量'的一个原因，毕竟'力量'的来源是整体和全方位的。"

按照约瑟夫·奈的软力量模型，软力量有文化吸引力、意识形态或政治价值观念感召力、塑造国际规则和决定政治议题的能力等多个层面。

旅游性概念产品是名副其实的软力量。主题鲜明、特色显著、文化感强且又朗朗上口的概念性产品，既是城市旅游实物性产品的理论升华，更对实物性产品有着锦上添花、如虎添翼之功效。如中国著名旅游城市大连注册城市商标"浪漫之都"就是一个典型例子。

大连位于中国辽东半岛最南端，东濒黄海，西临渤海，冬无严寒，夏无酷暑，年平均温度10℃。大连是中国的优秀旅游城市、卫生城市、园林化城市，2001年6月5日联合国授予大连为中国第一个、亚洲第二个"世界环境500佳"城市。

大连的旅游特点是以大海为背景，以绿色为依托，以漂亮的城市环境为品牌，以大型旅游活动为载体，以特色旅游项目加之时装城、足球城、田径之乡、夜光城等元素来打造深具个性的城市品位。围绕将大连建成"东北亚重要的国际城市"这个目标，该市旅游业全力实施"浪漫之都"旅游品牌战略。经过多年努力，2003年，中国国家工商行政总局商标局同意受理大连市关于"浪漫之都"为城市形象称谓的注册申请。一个城市以整体旅游形象申请商标，这在全世界都是没有先例的。

与此同时，大连又提出把"浪漫之都"作为商标，对该市相关的43个系列产品领域进行全面注册。而它注册中国'浪漫之都'的旅游品牌的这一举动，使得它成为一座将城市变成风景，将风景变成资本的城市。世界旅游组织专家评价："浪漫之都"旅游城市品牌无形资产价值1000亿人民币。

当今世界，美国不仅在世界范围内迅速推广其实物性产品，而且也在世界范围内扩散其文化精神产品，并使其社会价值观、日常生活方式与商业管理模式的影响力日长夜大。其文化传播业2006年已达到26400亿美元的年产值，占GDP的20%左右，349家上市公司也已拥有3800亿美元的资本市场价值，而十大传媒公司中的时代—华纳2001年员工人数十万，营业收入已达370亿美元。

迄今为止，西方社会所拥有的巨大话语权，使它们有效地包装了西方主流价值、意识形态甚至文化潮流。这些软力量的发展，甚至超出了西方学者自己的估计。

## 二、旅游是"软力量"实现的最佳途径

由于旅游活动的本质特点，决定其对人们的思想、观念所带来的冲击和导向是非常巨大的。世界上没有任何一种活动能像旅游那样，将世界各国的距离拉得如此之近，使不同民族之间的交流变得如此之广。它是一个多形式、多层次、多渠道、大范围或全方位的接触和互动。

我们还可从旅游产业来看。旅游产业具有文化和经济的双重属性，文化与经济的融合是旅游产业的显著特征。旅游的本质是文化，没有文化就没有旅游。虽然在旅游产业发展的初级阶段，需要大量的资金投入和建设，往往经济性质在旅游产业中占主导地位，但当旅游产业进入发达阶段以后，由于旅游者文化消费的日益增强，文化性质便逐渐占据了主导地位。

毫无疑问，文化是旅游业的灵魂，也是对大众最具吸引力的重要因素。而这些文化大多是通过特定的物质和建筑遗产而承载的。一谈到埃及，人们便会想到金字塔；一谈到中国，人们便想到万里长城、北京故宫。正是这些有形和无形的东方文化和建筑，在给世人带来强烈视觉冲击的同时，彰显了一个国家或民族的历史文明，也正是这些文化遗产所承载的精神，具有穿越时空和地域的魅力，让人们趋之若鹜。

当今世界已是一个不断推进和实现一体化的时代，无论政治改革、经济规则还

是文化活动，都在不断地促进国际间的沟通与交流，由此才形成了生机勃勃的现代文明。然而，我们越来越清楚地看到，任何一项活动都没有比旅游在整合世界、促进交流、共享文明中发挥的作用更大更广泛。

朱昌勤在《很有思想力的报头格言》一文指出："整合有有形整合也有无形整合；有物质整合也有精神整合。旅游不但对于世界的经济发展有促动、调节和整合作用，更值得注重的是，在多元化的人类文明舞台上，它具有力不可遏、势不可断、功不可没的整合功力，即软整合力。世界上没有哪一种产业，具有旅游业那样大的包容性、运动性和多元性，它使多种文化、多种信息、多种信仰在自身演进的过程中，得到或有形或无形或实际或理性的交流、融会、整合和升华。它没有国界，它不问肤色，它不择语种。它使人们在观赏世界的同时，广泛地、自由地交流、沟通、受应一切信息、智慧和文明成果，从而又去创造更美好的世界。人们只有在旅游的时空中，才远离战争、远离灾难。所以，旅游是人类生活中最文明、最和谐、最美好的和通方式，也就是人类构建大同理念的'最优方法'。这就是旅游使世界变成有充分自由度和满足感的'地球村'的威力所在。这是一种长久的永恒的潜在力量，作用于现在更作用于未来。"

甘肃省旅游局局长邓志涛曾在文中说："旅游业是推动整个社会文明进步的产业。旅游活动不仅带动经济的发展，旅游活动也是人民精神文化生活的重要内容。生产力的发展和经济指标的增长并不是社会核心价值的代表，重要的是以社会文明进步为表现形式只有交流才能使一个与世隔绝封闭的小山村看到社会文明进步的曙光，享受到世界精神文明的成果和物质文明的成果。所以可以说旅游业是物质文明、精神文明、政治文明三大文明结合在一起的产物，单纯的政治运动是绝对达不到这种效果的，而是综合文化的结果。"

在这里，要进一步了解旅游的软整合力，我们不妨也对"文化侵略"进行一些探讨。因为长期以来，文化或文明的传播一向是与反"文化侵略"相伴随的。

我们知道，侵略是一个国家或种族有计划、有目的对他国的征服行为，以获取物质和精神财富为目的。那么，当一个国家和政府向外宣扬它的价值观、政治理念、生活方式、文化理念时，这是否就是"侵略"？

在中国历史上，佛教传入后一度成为国教，它的文化征服至今没有人认为它是一种侵略。而中国的文字也已深深嵌入到日本文字之中，成为日本文化的有机组成部分，日本人也没有为这种"侵略"而坐卧不宁。在今天，非英语国家的白领时不时夹杂着英语单词聊天，非但没有被看着是一种伤害民族尊严的"侵略"，反而被看成是一种时髦。

吴祚来先生在《"文化侵略"辨析》一文中说道："'文化'并不存在主权问题，只存在：这种文化是不是更先进的、更丰富多元的、更适合人性的。文化说到底是一种'方式',是可以交流、传播、融合、学习、使用、复制的……文化与战争不一样,文化是一种符号化,不具有攻击性,它是在一个人、一个群体、一个民族自愿接受的情况下'征服'人的心灵、思想意识形态,从而改变人的人生观、世界观以及生产生活方式。"

文化传播是一个矛盾运动的过程,包括文化冲突与文化适应。如果没有新文化的输入,本民族只在一个有限度的范围内存在和发展,自然不会有文化冲突,然而也不会有冲突所带来的张力,本地文明就不会有发展和进步。所以,文化既没有主权,也就无所谓侵略,文化只有落后与先进之区分。落后文化通过非暴力方式"心甘情愿"接受先进文化,这是人类文明的发展规律。

20世纪80年代,日本的动画和美国的卡通曾充斥中国国内电视荧屏,有人便以中国动画片走下坡路为由,疾呼反"文化侵略"。但实际上,中国动画片当时在国际评比中连连败北,主要原因是因循守旧,题材老化并缺乏市场意识。后认识到自己的要害所在,并吸收外来文化的一些新思维,终于又东山再起。

2005年9月20日,《湖南日报》有一篇新闻报道,题目叫《好!中国终于也可以"文化侵略"美国了》,说的是中国最大的卡通艺术制作基地湖南三辰公司与美国美中贸易发展协会签约,由该公司创作的卡通系列片"蓝猫"远涉重洋,进入美国。我们看看以下报道:

温柔可爱的"蓝猫"将远涉重洋,进入美国,伴美国孩子一起成长。这是在今天开幕的广博会上,由湖南三辰公司与美国美中贸易发展协会正式签约敲定的。美国驻广州总领事馆领事、国家广电总局有关领导与长沙市市长谭仲池等出席了签约仪式。

湖南三辰公司是中国最大的卡通艺术制作基地,该公司创作的"蓝猫淘气3000问"深受中国儿童喜爱,年销售过亿元。该公司通过台湾子公司全新包装的国际版蓝猫卡通,一问世便大受青睐。曾经担任过尼克松总统远东经济顾问的美国美中贸易发展协会主席罗伯特先生热心牵线搭桥,使"蓝猫"出口美国正式签约。

据悉,第一次出口美国的"蓝猫"为900集,4个月后将在全美播出,让一代美国儿童熟悉了解中国。这是中国卡通第一次出口美国。签约仪式上,罗伯特先生说:"美国孩子是看'米老鼠'长大的,这些卡通大都是打打闹闹的逗乐,而'蓝猫'温柔可爱又聪明,美国的孩子可以通过这些动画片了解中国。"长沙市市长谭仲池说:"中国儿童对美国了解较多,这在某种程度上还得益于美国的卡通,既创作了'米老鼠'喜剧式的经典,也创造了白雪公主悲剧式的经典,我们的卡通制作还需好好学习。"

这个事例说明，如果对待外来文化，采取顺其自然，"有朋自远方来，不亦乐乎"的态度，并对其认真加以甄别、吸收、消化，与本民族文化中优秀的成分相结合，或有对"先进"文化进行"反攻"的可能。

我们很容易发现，在现实世界里，所谓反"文化侵略"叫得最响的往往是文化相对落后的国家或地区。他们往往打着保护"民族文化"的旗号，抵御、扭曲外来文化，但结果于事无补，该来的还是来了，"大喊大叫"敌不过"随风潜入夜"的进攻。而旅游活动就是包裹这种"进攻"的纷繁具象。

人类文明历史的发展证明，文化的互动不仅能够产生新的文化，而且能够产生巨大的经济效益，到一定时候，"软"力量可以转化为实实在在的"硬"力量。如前面提到的大连注册中国"浪漫之都"的旅游品牌，一旦其进一步开发"浪漫之都"旅游品牌的商业价值，43个系列产品商标使用所产生的经济效益，将无法估量。

一些产业虽然并非与旅游者直接消费有关，但是，旅游业的发展，不仅能提高一个城市或地区的知名度，也能提高旅游目的地产品的知名度，从而创造出新的商业机会。旅游业甚至还有"化腐朽为神奇"的特殊功能，将一些看似没有价值的地方或物质，打造成身价百倍、人们趋之若鹜的旅游场所。

迪斯尼乐园原本就是建在荒漠的旅游目的地；一次奥运会的举办使澳大利亚悉尼市的发展加快了十年；韩国的一次世界杯足球赛，不仅使韩国的形象令世人刮目相看，韩国泡菜也成为该国最为重要的出口产品之一。因此说，看待旅游业，要从广泛的意义上去理解，不要只看到旅游带动相关产业发展的物质的一面，而要从它的物质性和精神性的双重内容去理解。尤其是旅游所产生的精神力量，有时会产生意想不到的爆发力，这种力量将推动一个地区或一个城市的政治、经济、文化等各领域全面发展。

中国山西省临汾市是4700多年前中国古代皇帝尧的建都之地。史书记载"中国之初始于尧"，因此尧都临汾被誉为"华夏第一古都"。元朝建立后，忽必烈曾降旨拨地大修，规模空前。但由于战乱地震等的毁坏，尧都在历史的风尘中渐渐被埋没。直到2000年，尧都人决定全面修复尧都，并于三年时间内，建造了一座纪念帝尧建都临汾，展示华夏五千年文明的大型文化建筑——中国华门。这个旅游景点不同于传统，而有极强的创新精神。法国旅游部长贝特朗在与华门总设计师和创建者宿青平的对话中如是说："我很敬佩你的创造，华门在现在看来是新的，若干年后就会成为历史遗产，更加显现它的魅力和价值。"

几年前，当华门的总设计和创建者尧都区区长宿青平提出这一构想并实施时，非议就没有停止过，有人说这是"形象工程""打肿脸充胖子"；有人说为古人建庙，还不如为现代人盖房……但宿青平顶着各种压力，用三年时间将这一文化创新之作呈现在世人面前。

　　建成之后的华门不仅是目前世界上最高的门建筑，而且以其独特的文化内涵展现出巨大的文化影响力。它被媒体报道为"中国第一座华夏文明纪念碑"、"中国首座文化旅游景观"。短短一年时间，华门所在的尧庙景区门票"硬收入"比以往增加百倍，当地交通、餐饮、酒店、商贸、信息等第三产业得到前所未有的快速发展。

　　数字所能反映的或许只是物质效果，而精神效果却要比这大出几十倍，甚至几百倍。如今，华门已经成为临汾的标志，已经成为华夏文明起源的象征，临汾人重新找回了失去已久的自豪。一位从香港来到临汾的商人，本来不打算在临汾投资，但他看过华门后一改态度，连连赞不绝口。据悉，华门建立后，临汾的外商投资次年就有明显的上升。一位当地干部对笔者说："因为有了华门，临汾人的底气足了，开口就说自己是临汾人，就好像过去的上海人，开口就说'阿拉（我）是上海人'。"

　　从诸多事例中，我们可以看到，旅游产业的发展，对人们的思想、观念所带来的冲击和导向是非常大的。由于旅游业的发展和旅游活动的开展，一个国家和其他国家的距离拉得很近，通过旅游业这样一个多形式、多层次、多渠道、大范围，甚至于全方位的广泛接触和交流渠道，人们固守了上千年的思维模式和生活习俗都有可能改变。

第五章

# 人类文明的发展
# 促动旅游价值的提升

秦始皇兵马俑（Qin Terra-Cotta Warriors and Horses Figurines）

第五章　人类文明的发展促动旅游价值的提升

## 第一节
## 战争是古代人类文明传播的主渠道

　　我们在前面的论述中知道，旅游是传播人类文明的一座流动的桥梁。但古代的旅游活动因受低下的生产力影响，人数太少，规模太小，还不足以在社会中产生巨大影响。所以历史上的文明传播的主渠道，并不是旅游，而是战争。

　　战争对文明的发展和交流起到了十分重要的作用，战争在毁灭一种文明时往往孕育着另一种文明。马克思曾指出："暴力是每个孕育着新社会的旧社会的助产婆。"

　　当亚历山大决定性地战胜埃及法老时，不仅摧毁了法老文明，也同时将先进的希腊罗马文明带到了埃及。亚历山大的战争也使不少希腊学者来到东方，研究东方的科学技术和文化艺术。埃及的亚历山大城就是当时希腊化文化的最大中心。

　　战争往往以摧枯拉朽的方式强行改变国家的疆域、政权的属性、民族的生活方式乃至宗教信仰，使一些政权、国家和民族灭亡，另一些政权、国家和民族取而代之。在战争过后甚至某一文明中断运行，迫使其走上另一条道路。另一方面，战争也因其独特的功能促进了科学技术的发展，加强了不同国家、民族之间的交流与互动，而这些又促进了人们生活方式的改变。

　　自古以来，部落与部落、国家与国家之间因土地、人口和信仰所发生的冲突比比皆是。不同文明的各国力量相当时，尚能保持和平状态，一旦一方力量增强，均势被打破，战争就可能随时爆发。一般而言，冲突是由强势文明一方挑起。

　　战争本身是文明集大成者。因其关系社稷安危、身家性命，所以最好的科技，最智勇的部民，都首先要用于战争。例如，在中国春秋战国时期，200多个诸侯国在反复的战争和兼并中，最后形成赵、燕、楚、秦、魏、韩、齐七国的争霸局面，中国历史上称为"战国七雄"。

　　诸侯混战、争霸图强，不仅要求各诸侯国硬实力如战车、长矛等要有先进性，也要求各诸侯国的软实力也要胜人一筹，即人才首当其冲。那时，作为拥有专业知识的人才——士，成为王侯公卿竞相招揽的对象，"蓄士""养士"蔚然成风。据史书记载，战国四公子孟尝君、平原君、信陵君、春申君，门下豢养食客数千，多为有一技之长的士人。秦国吕不韦门下的食客，也多达三千之众。

在先秦士人群体中，思想家如老聃、孔丘、墨翟、孟轲、庄周、邹衍、荀况、韩非；政治家如管仲、子产、晏婴、商鞅；军事家如吴起、孙武、孙膑；外交家如蔺相如、苏秦、张仪；史学家如左丘明；诗人如屈原、宋玉；论辩家如惠施、公孙龙；医学家如扁鹊；水利专家如李冰、郑国；天文家如甘德、石申等，可谓群星璀璨，蔚为大观，代表当时"文明水平"最高的士阶层成为战争年代中最为活跃的团体。

在世界范围内，古希腊的状况也是如此。公元前5世纪至前4世纪，东西方爆发了第一次大规模军事冲突——希波战争，战争最终以波斯人的失败而告终。战争期间，雅典民主政治进入全盛阶段，公民的经济和政治权利受到国家强有力的保护，国家鼓励贫民参加文化和政治活动。这一时期，希腊的诗歌、文学、戏剧、史学、建筑及造型艺术都获得辉煌的成果。

公元前4世纪初，希腊北方马其顿地区出现了君主制国家，其政治、经济、军事实力日益增强，并迅速控制了希腊各城邦，成为地中海上的强国。公元前336年，亚历山大即位，开始大规模东侵。

公元前334年亚历山大开始远征，引导他的军队穿过小亚细亚、叙利亚和埃及，进入波斯高原到达里海边，又向南进入锡斯坦地区，由此穿过阿富汗斯坦到巴克特利亚，越过兴都库什山脉，直到印度河口而达于海。

他用武力征服了地中海世界、波斯帝国和印度北部地区。马其顿人的武力征讨成为希腊文化传播的导体，军队打到哪里，希腊文化亦随之传到那里。对于公元前4世纪的欧亚大陆的诸文明来说，这是一次前所未有的交流和碰撞。

亚历山大打败了波斯国后，把印度河流域、埃及、中亚乃至希腊的全部地中海文明区联合在一个大帝国中，促进了该地区的文化发展，使希腊文化对西方文化的发展产生了重大影响。在希腊化时代，东西方文化交流与融合的规模和程度都是空前的。

亚历山大远征印度，直接的影响似乎很小，但这一伟大的远征，对于印度的历史却有不可磨灭的影响。东西隔阂的打破，东西交通线的贯通，为旅游活动的进行和文明的传播提供了优越的条件。印度的艺术，希腊对其影响很大，最为明显的便是乾陀罗的雕刻。印度佛教也因与希腊文化接触而大为改观，尤其佛教仪式中所采用的偶像，显然是希腊文明影响的结果。

在罗马的强大军事进攻下，希腊沦陷了。395年，希腊被并入拜占庭帝国（东罗马）版图。但是，罗马虽以武力征服了希腊人，古老的希腊文化却从一开始就征服着文化上相对落后的罗马人。罗马人从希腊人那里学习了先进的哲学、修辞学、诗歌、雕塑和科学技术，并将基督教升格为国教，希腊语被确定为官方语言。拜占庭（东罗马）帝国逐步演变为希腊化帝国。

恺撒是一位勤奋好学有远大抱负的罗马将领，一生充满冒险和传奇。据说恺撒在旅行途中被海盗俘获，海盗索要20泰伦黄金的赎金。恺撒斥责海盗低估了他的身价，自愿把赎金提高到50泰伦。仆人便回去四处借钱，当赎金凑足后，海盗将他释放，他迅速回到米利都，招募部下和船只，掉头追赶海盗，将海盗抓到后一一处死并追回了赎金。

恺撒以其雄辩的演讲术和灵活的政治手腕迅速获得政治势力。公元前58年，他开始了长达6年的对高卢的征战，并且留下了脍炙人口的《高卢战记》。在战记中不但记载了历次战斗的敌我军事行动，而且也对高卢全境的各个部落和各地的地理特征包括河流、山脉、森林分布，都作了记录。从某种意义上来看，它也是一部很有价值的游记。

在征服和统治的过程中，恺撒将罗马的政治制度和文化成果，带到了高卢。他给予了高卢人罗马公民的待遇，以至罗马当时的民谣有："恺撒在凯旋仪式上牵着高卢人，却牵进了元老院；高卢人脱掉戎装长裤，却穿上了罗马大袍。"

恺撒经常在他所征服的地区巡游，《高卢战记》中记载了他的一次旅游："所有的自治市和殖民地都以难以想象的荣誉和热爱来欢迎恺撒，因为这是他对全高卢联合作战取得胜利之后第一次到来。一切可以用来装饰城门、道路和恺撒经过的每一个地方的手段，都尽量用上了。"

罗马帝国后期，经历了一系列蛮族的入侵而走向灭亡。地中海统一体的结束，蛮族和基督教的相互影响以及罗马教会和希腊教会的分离，影响了中世纪欧洲文明的建立。

自11世纪开始，西欧基督教世界对西班牙南部伊斯兰世界发动了所谓"十字军东征"和"光复运动"。基督教和伊斯兰教这两大信仰，经过数世纪的争论，最后诉诸战争来解决。

十字军东征是中世纪欧洲和近东历史上最有影响的事件之一。这次战争长达200年，是一场为解救人类灵魂及获取商业利益的多种因素的战争混合体。宗教狂热，商业扩张，骑士精神，圣战热忱，所有文明间的冲突与交流，都在这一富有戏剧性的事件中达到了顶点。

从7世纪开始，到耶路撒冷朝圣早已成为教徒虔诚与赎罪的一种方式。在欧洲各地，遇到身戴交叉的巴勒斯坦记号的游客被称为"戴棕榈叶者"，表示已完成了朝圣的人。但自1070年开始，朝圣者开始带回基督徒被压迫和土耳其人亵渎神明的消息，这成为引发十字军东征的一个原因。

十字军东征的另一个原因是意大利的各个商业城市的扩张欲望。当基督徒从穆斯林手中夺回了西西里之后，西地中海的贸易便对基督徒开放了。意大利的一些商业城市如比萨、热那亚和威尼斯等因日益富裕和强大，它们企图夺取穆斯林在地中海东岸的商业霸权,以期打开通往东方的市场,因此,它们积极支持和参与十字军东征。

十字军实际上是一些厌倦了生活的无业游民、冒险家、尚武的骑士、狂热的教士、逃离领主土地的佃农、为其商品寻找新市场的商人和期望到东方去开拓新天地的年轻人以及随军妓女组成的"杂牌军"。他们各自的动机与他们的组成一样复杂。

第一次东征的十字军于1096年出发,经过混乱和艰苦的跋涉于1099年到达了耶路撒冷。耶城被攻陷后,十字军们对耶路撒冷城内的犹太人和穆斯林展开了疯狂的屠杀和劫掠。在朝拜了圣墓,留下圣墓的保卫者之后,便以胜利者的姿态回欧洲去了。在撤退的途中,他们在巴勒斯坦、叙利亚和土耳其建立了许多独立的基督教拉丁王国。在这以后的两个世纪里,西欧又发动了7次十字军东征。

基督教的扩张在穆斯林世界引起了强烈的反应,他们根据《古兰经》发动"圣战",抗击基督教的侵略。1148—1149年,第二次十字军东征,被努尔丁所领导的穆斯林打败,结束了"法兰克人不可战胜"的神话;1192年,穆斯林世界的英雄萨拉丁又击败了第三次东征的十字军,双方签订和约,耶路撒冷回到穆斯林的手中,但基督徒享有朝圣的自由;第四次十字军东征则在基督教的罗马和拜占庭之间进行,君士坦丁堡于1204年被攻破并遭洗劫;1291年,十字军在巴勒斯坦的据点阿克被穆斯林攻占,随后基督徒建立的拉丁国相继被穆斯林收复,十字军在欧洲终于销声匿迹。

不同文明间的战争促进了文明的交流,尽管这种交流是被迫的。基督教和穆斯林长达200年的拉锯战,使得东西方文明进行一次又一次的碰撞。许多西方的旅游者开始对更遥远的东方感兴趣,在以后的岁月里,西方人探究神秘东方的脚步从未停止。

"十字军东征"的一个直接后果就是大翻译运动——将保存在穆斯林和拜占庭的古代希腊和罗马的经典翻译成拉丁文的学术活动。

大翻译运动使得欧洲的文明传统与世界其他文明之间产生了联系。欧洲的知识分子自12世纪开始接触到由十字军从东方穆斯林和拜占庭带回的希腊和罗马著作。同时,阿拉伯人的文化传统和科学成就,以及他们所保存的世界其他地区的文化、科学与技术,通过他们的桥梁作用,进入了欧洲。这在很大程度上刺激了欧洲对自身文明传统和其他文明取得的成就的认真思考。

这种结果的深入,使得一种新的文明——现代科学在欧洲孕育和发展成为可能。因此,怀海特说:"现代科学诞生于欧洲,但它的家在整个世界。"欧洲中世纪留给现代世界的最大的财富是大学,而这也是"大翻译"运动所带来的必然结果。

现代全球范围内的文明间的冲突是自哥伦布开始的。当哥伦布进入美洲的时候,就在古巴和海地与当地的土著发生了冲突。就在麦哲伦离开塞维利亚作环球航行的

1519年，科尔特斯也离开了古巴，开始他对墨西哥阿兹特克帝国的远征，从而开启了血腥的征服时代。

1519年3月，科尔特斯率领只有数百人的部队进攻阿兹特克帝国。欧洲人的冷酷、勇气和优良的装备显示了巨大的优势，并利用了印第安人内部的不和，将印第安人逐个击破，于1521年8月攻破阿兹特克的都城，进行了疯狂的屠杀。

另一个在历史上臭名昭著的征服者是皮萨罗。他率领一支180人的远征队，越过安第斯山脉进入秘鲁。印加皇帝出于好奇，正式拜访了皮萨罗。皮萨罗效仿科尔特斯，将皇帝监禁起来，并处死了他的随从。他要印第安人用黄金和白银堆满一个房间，以赎回皇帝。皮萨罗取得金银后，却背信弃义，处死了印加皇帝，随后洗劫了印加首都库斯科。他们的成功鼓舞了后来者，也使得美洲的印第安人遭受更大规模的屠杀和奴役。

史学家们一般认为，哥伦布进入美洲以前，印第安人总共有2500万。至17世纪中叶，仅剩950万。西班牙在美洲首先是疯狂的屠杀，而后又是日益猖獗的贩奴和蓄奴，用武力和殖民文化建立了殖民统治。

为了使屠杀获得法理上的借口，西班牙国王卡洛斯五世的法律顾问胡安·希内斯·德苏伯尔维达还以论点证明对印第安进行战争的必要性：

"第一个论点：因为印第安，至少是在落入基督徒的控制之前，其风俗全部都是野蛮的，他们中的大部分人生性不识文字，不具备审慎的理性并沾染着各种野蛮人的邪恶。……"他们"仅仅被称作野蛮人——按照圣托马斯——是那些缺乏理性的人，或者是由于气候，使他们中的许多人发现自己发育不全；或者是由于使人几乎成为野兽的那些恶习。第二个论点：野蛮人的罪违背了自然法——这些野蛮人陷入了异常深重的违背了自然法的罪孽之中。"（《西方旅游史》）

庞大的帝国和全球性的贸易网络为西班牙积累了无数的财富，西班牙国力得到空前提升。西班牙史学家戈麦拉在其《印第安史》的尾声中写道："历史上没有一个国王和民族像我们这样在如此短的时间里占领和征服了如此大的地方，我们在传播神圣福音和使偶像崇拜者皈依方面的所作所为也是无与伦比的，为此，我们西班牙在世界的每个地方都值得赞美。"

战争传递文明不是单向的，而是双向的。也就是说，战争不仅输出文明，也输入文明。

前面我们谈到，罗马人击败希腊人后，古老的希腊文化却使相对落后的罗马人着迷。罗马人潜心学习希腊文化，并将基督教升为国教，希腊语为官方语言。拜占庭（东罗马）帝国逐步演变为希腊化帝国。

中国历史上，也有相同的例子。还处在游牧时代的蒙古族和满族，夺取了汉人的政权后，都自愿放弃了自己的"文化主权"，融入汉民族文化的河流之中。

元朝（1271—1368）是由蒙古族建立起来的庞大王朝。1271年，成吉思汗之孙忽必烈在大都（今北京）建立起元王朝。从此，北京逐渐成为中国此后近七百年的政治、经济、文化中心。元朝是中国历史上第一个在全国范围内建立起来的、以少数民族统治者为主的政权。蒙古族不仅征服了中原及长江以南地区，还将其控制范围扩张至整个西亚地区，成为中国有史以来疆域最大的王朝。

　　因为蒙古族以前的生活方式大多以游牧为主，生产力较低。进入中原后，元朝统治者采用汉族的经济模式和管理方式，以汉族农业代替了畜牧业，并大力发展商业、手工业，使得元朝的国内经济很快得到恢复。由于元朝的疆域扩展到了西亚地区，使得欧洲与中国的交往也更加频繁，技术交流也更加迅速。

　　由于大量采用汉族先进的物质和文化成果，物质的丰富使元朝的统治者生活逐渐奢华起来。尤其到了元朝后期，各皇帝都过起豪华的生活。为了满足他们贪婪的物质需求，统治者不断向人民收取各种赋税，于是汉族人民以各种形式起来反抗元朝暴虐的统治。1368年，朱元璋开始北伐，在大将徐达、常遇春等人的协助下，攻陷元大都，结束了元朝的统治，建立了明王朝。

　　清朝是中国封建社会最后一个朝代，由满族贵族建立。1644年，李自成农民军推翻明朝统治，明朝崇祯帝自杀，清军乘机入关打败农民军。同年，多尔衮迎顺治帝入关，定都北京。

　　清朝进入中原后，对待汉文化的态度比元朝更为激进，在生产模式和经济管理等方面几乎全盘吸收，甚至生活方式也向汉人靠拢。到18世纪中叶，封建经济发展到一个新的高峰，史称"康乾盛世"。18世纪后期，清人口就已达到三亿左右。清朝版图最大时达1200多万平方千米。

　　虽然明清以来中国手工业都有发展，但始终没能发展到资本主义。尤其是清朝晚年愚蠢的闭关锁国政策，破坏了沿海当时已相当发达的造船业、航海业及对外贸易，也将先进的西方科技文化推至门外。

　　康熙五十九年（1720），从欧洲来华的29条船只运来西方的自鸣钟、呢绒、玻璃等机械工业品，而英国则从中国进口茶叶、瓷器、丝绸等物品。可惜，这一本来可以与西方文明碰撞的历史机遇只是昙花一现。乾隆年间，原先负责对外通商的四个海关，只剩下广州一个，直至清朝末年。

　　著名学者顾准在《顾准文集》中指出："认为任何国家都会必然产生出资本主义是荒谬的。特别在中国，这个自大的天朝，鸦片战争和英法联军敲不醒，1884年的中法战争还敲不醒，一直要到1894年的中日战争猛敲一下，才打个欠身。到庚子、辛丑才醒过来的中国，说会自发地产生出资本主义，真是梦呓！"

　　可见，中国近代文明的起点，也是从战争开始的。1840年鸦片战争爆发之后，随着帝国主义的入侵，使清朝与侵略者缔结了一系列不平等条约，中国逐步沦为半封建半殖民地社会。但同时，西方列强的入侵，使得长期闭关自守的中国，终于打开了观察世界的门窗，呼吸到了海外吹来的新鲜空气。1911年，辛亥革命爆发，清朝被推翻，从此结束了中国两千多年来的封建帝制。

裴勇先生在其《文明的整合：开启地球文明的新纪元》文章中写道："16世纪以来，西方基督教文明逐渐发展壮大，在整个世界居于主导地位，这个文明创造了于今流行于世的社会政治体制、经济发展模式。特别是从这种文明生发出来的科学技术，使西方世界自信基督教文明是世界上最优越、最先进的文明。他们要把他们的文明带到世界每一个角落。随着科技的高度发展、经济和军事能力的强大，西方开始了将其文明强加于人的进程。其文明，特别是宗教的传播就是伴随着其在全球的殖民扩张而全面展开……300多年来在西方列强的殖民扩张过程中，由于对殖民地的争夺，西方国家之间的利益冲突，扩散和延伸到非西方文明国家，几乎到达世界每一个角落。"

## 第二节　战争传播文明更摧毁文明

战争虽然能够起到传递文明的作用，但战争打破了正常的社会秩序，破坏了环境，侵害了社会财富，更为严重的是，战争扼杀了创造财富和文明的最宝贵的东西：人！所以战争无疑是人类文明最大的破坏者和毁灭者。

中国古代皇帝刘邦建立汉朝以来，由于统治阶级意识到战争对社会的破坏给老百姓带来的痛苦，所以采取了"休养生息"的新政，汉朝国力渐渐恢复，一度出现了"太平盛世"的"文景之治"年代。但到了汉武帝时代，因"武帝外事四夷，内兴功利"，所以在完成辉煌事业的同时，也耗尽了文景以来库府的余财。这只是战争给文明带来的拖累。

玛雅人是中美洲的土著居民，居住在今天的墨西哥、危地马拉和洪都拉斯等地。他们拥有发达的古代文明，最早种植了玉米，天文和历法也相当精确。大约在公元前800年，玛雅文明到达顶峰。然而随之而来的是南部低地的玛雅人放弃了繁华的城市，神庙变成了野兽出没的废墟。直到16世纪，当欧洲殖民者登上美洲大陆大肆杀戮和掠夺时，玛雅文明终于完全衰落了。

考古学家认为，尽管目前不能判断交战的另一方是何许人，但可以肯定的是，玛雅人在这场战争中被打败了，城市中幸存的玛雅人不但被胜利一方斩尽杀绝，整个城市的文明也几乎全部被毁。随着战争的结束，坎祖恩也变成一个没有人烟的废弃之地。

但战争在人类历史上对文明的巨大摧毁，莫过于两次世界大战。第一次世界大战从1914年8月4日全面爆发到1918年11月11日结束，持续时间长达4年零3个月。在这次战争中，参加国家多达30多个，约15亿人口，占当时世界人口总数的67%。战争中双方共动员了7351万人上前线，有些国家如法国超过半数的男性公民走上前线。

据统计，整个第一次世界大战期间，有900万军人在战场上牺牲，受伤者更是达到2000多万，此外还有大约1000万平民在战争中饿死或病死；按当时的美元计算，参战国直接经济损失高达1805亿美元，间接经济损失也达1516亿美元。在战争主要发生地的欧洲，有人估计，工业生产水平至少倒退了8年。

第二次世界大战是人类历史上规模最大、损失最惨重的一次战争，是一场空前的浩劫。在这场决定人类命运的生死大搏斗中，先后有60多个国家和地区参战，波及20亿人口（占当时世界人口的80%），战火燃及欧、亚、非、大洋洲和太平洋、印度洋、大西洋、北冰洋。作战区域面积为2200万平方千米，交战双方动员兵力达1.1亿人，因战争死亡的军人和平民超过5500万，直接军费开支总计约1.3万亿美元，占交战国国民总收入的60%至70%，参战国物资总损失价值达4万亿美元。

据不完全统计，在日本侵略军的屠刀下，中国死伤人数达3500万，占二次大战参战国死亡总人数的42%。其中，死亡人数达2100万，仅南京大屠杀就死亡30万人以上。按1937年的比价计算，日本侵略者给中国造成的直接经济损失1000亿美元，间接经济损失5000亿美元。

二战参战国蒙受的全部损失中有41%是苏联的损失，因为苏联是抗击德国法西斯的主战场。据俄罗斯公布的材料，苏联在1941年到1945年的卫国战争期间，死亡2700万人，其中苏联红军牺牲866.84万人；物质损失按照1941年的价格计算达6790亿卢布。

美国和英国是世界反法西斯同盟的核心成员。据战史材料，美国共有40多万人在二战中丧生，英国有27万军人在战争中死亡。

德国、日本和意大利是发动第二次世界大战的元凶，遭到了反法西斯国家和人民的顽强抵抗和严厉惩罚。据统计，德国在战争中死亡和被俘人数为1360万人。仅在苏德战场，德军与其盟军死亡人数为600多万。日本在中国战场上损失150万人，有128万人向中国投降，在太平洋战场上损失124.7万人。意大利损失16万多人。

德、日、意发动的侵略战争也使这些国家国内的民众深受其害。在德国本土上，有400万平民死于战火，1400万人无家可归。1945年8月，日本广岛和长崎分别遭到美国原子弹轰炸，当时死伤20余万人，并且给当地居民留下了巨大的精神创伤。

二战后最惨烈的战争，是发生在20世纪的历经8年的两伊战争。两个所谓中东军事强国，动用了除原子弹以外的所有先进武器（化学武器都用上了），F14、F4、幻影战斗机、飞毛腿导弹，打了8年，死伤百万人。最后双方筋疲力尽，差点都经济崩溃，最后停战了事。这次战争被世界军界评论为"用先进武器打低水平战争"的最典型范例。

两伊战争伤亡总数相当于四次中东战争伤亡人数的12倍。直接经济损失相当于第一次世界大战全部经济损失的5倍。仅伊朗首都德黑兰就有20万妇女失去丈夫，有些地方鲜有完整的家庭。无数伊朗士兵中毒后失明、聋哑。伊拉克战前外汇储备有300多亿美元，战后外债高达1000亿美元。大量被炸油轮的原油流入海湾造成严重污染。

双方共损失飞机400余架，坦克3500辆，火炮2700门，舰艇31艘。双方被袭击的船只近500艘。由战争引起的直接经济损失高达9000亿美元。在伊朗，仅首都德黑兰在八年战争中，全市遭受导弹133枚，死1700人，伤8500人。

这些数据的罗列，也许还很难使人触及两伊战争给两伊人民乃至世界带来的灾难。伊朗一军方人士告诉记者：一个导弹，一个"化弹"（化学武器），成了战争给伊朗的致命伤。1988年初夏，伊拉克为迫使伊朗接受停火，在战场上大量使用化学武器，无数士兵中毒后失明、聋哑，就连死状也让人惨不忍睹。

在古代落后、封闭、交通不便的环境里，有些战争起到了沟通、交流的特殊作用，但多数战争是野蛮的屠杀和毁灭。而当人类历史进入近代，世界各国人民使用和平的方式，联络、沟通、商贸、往来已经没有什么困难时，战争更成为荒谬和愚蠢的人类自残自杀行为。这也是人们对至今发生在中东地区的没完没了的流血冲突，感到痛苦和厌烦的原因。

据统计，20世纪一百年间，全世界共发生了大大小小三百多次战争灾难。一次又一次的战争，一次接一次的灾难，人类拿着自己发明的枪炮屠杀自己，一部分人野性的勃发，将无数无辜的人们推入战火之中，生命在战争中枯萎了，人类文明被无情摧毁。人在战争灾难中的孱弱给人类再次敲响警钟，人类对战争的认识也达到了前所未有的深入。

## 第三节 人类文明未来发展趋势

上个世纪中后期，有识之士就对笼罩在核乌云之中的人类的前途表示了忧虑：文明是不是已走到了尽头，人类文明所遇到的各种问题是否能靠自己的力量解决，科学能不能给人类带来希望？

人类进入 21 世纪，随着交通、通讯技术的发展，"地球村"概念变得越来越清晰、实在。许多学者描绘出人类文明发展的现实图景：文明体的数量由多变少；人们的生活越来越多样化；文明体之间的互动越来越频繁和密切。

那么，人类文明究竟会朝哪个方向发展呢？人类社会会有一个什么样的前景呢？归纳起来，目前有以下三种观点具有代表性。

### 一、多元论

多元论的观点认为，文明的发展会越来越多样化。而且只有坚持多样化，文明才能更好地得到发展。多元文明的世界的发展既有各文明的发展历程，也有各文明之间的相互接触、交流和冲突、融合。

在农业文明时代，由于生产不发达、道路阻隔、交通不便，因此文明的交流特别缓慢。到了工业革命时代，生产力有了很大的发展，交通运输便利，电话、电报畅通，报纸、书籍这些传播媒介到处流通和发布，现在的互联网、大众媒体更使一个地方的信息瞬间传遍全世界，所以文明的交流更容易、更快速。

长期以来，伊斯兰文明、印度教文明、中华文明和日本文明对西欧工业文明一直都处在吸收和冲突之中。欧美工业文明的新变化、俄罗斯的新文明、拉丁美洲向工业文明的过渡、工业文明在南亚和东南亚的演进、东亚文明的演变、世界现代化进程中的中东伊斯兰世界、非洲争取文明复兴的努力等，都进一步说明各文明的交流形式和后果是多种多样的，它们相互排斥、冲撞，也相互吸收、融合。

文化的多元化，是迄今为止的基本事实。那么，文化的多元化是不是具有永恒性、普遍性？有人试图用《圣经》中的"造巴比伦塔"的故事来加以佐证：人们一开始语言相通，塔建得很快，后来上帝让人们之间语言不通，难以沟通，最终建塔工程失败。这个故事证明这样一个道理：人类文化无法融合为一体，因为那样会对上帝构成威胁。

虽然这种说法带有浓厚的宗教色彩，但现代电子网络技术的发展似乎支持了这种观点。比尔·盖茨描绘了未来网络社会中生活的情况：网络"是你进入一个新的、媒介生活方式的通行证——这种新的通信技术的一个最引人注目的特点就是它会消除距离——这一网络更像是由许多乡间小路构成的路网，人们可以在路上随心所欲地观看或做事。"

这说明，随着电子传播、网络技术的发展，人们的交往越来越个人化，每个人都可以在网站上发展自己的看法。"一个网络组织最重要的就是每一个人都是中心。"因特网正在变成未来地球村的街心广场。

奈斯比特认为，1976年美国建国200周年纪念的时候，是一个转折点。从这以后"非集中化潮流的力量不断增强，压倒了逐渐消亡的集中化倾向。他说："在日常生活当中，随着愈来愈互相依赖的全球经济发展，我认为语言和文化特点的复兴即将来临。简而言之，瑞典人会更瑞典化，中国人会更中国化，而法国人也会更法国化。"

托夫勒的看法也是一样。他说："事实上，向未来挺进，就必然要脱离标准化，脱离产品的划一化，脱离千人一面的艺术、一锅煮的教育和所谓的'大众化'文化。在社会技术的发展上，我们已经达到了辩证转变的关头了。技术绝不会限制我们的个性，却会大大增加我们的选择余地，也就是大大增加我们的自由。"

随着人类不断的发展，今天的社会表现出了越来越多的差异：民族的民族意识越来越强，"越是民族的东西越有世界性"；随着民主制度的改善，人们越来越关心自己生活的地区和社区；商品品种越来越多、越来越个性化，教育也在变得要满足人们不同的需要；传统的金字塔式的社会结构在弱化，新的网络式的社会结构正在形成。

"未来社会中，政治会越来越民主，社会形态越来越不同，人们的生活方式会越来越多样化，民族文化中会产生越来越多的亚文化人群"。（《文明纵横谈》）

## 二、趋同论

互联网的发明使人类在21世纪进入网络时代。比尔·盖茨认为，"信息高速公路将打破国界，并有可能推动一种世界文化的发展，或至少推动一种文化活动、文化价值观的共享。"

人类古老的"大同论"是"趋同论"的前身。中国古代圣人孔子提出的"人类大同"思想，其核心就是要实现天下文化的大同。但是，"大同"是指完全相同即同一、单一，还是"和而不同"、"大同小异"，是人们必须清醒认识的问题。

从中国文化典籍中，我们可以看到，中国古代哲学主张的"天下大同"，并非是一种排斥异己、完全相同的同一和单一，而是追求"和而不同"、"同中存异"的一种多样化之间的统一、和谐；不是那种单调的、清一色的"同"，而是一种丰富多彩、各种音符合拍的"同"。

1974年，85岁高龄的著名英国历史学家阿诺尔德·汤因比与日本著名政治家、公明党创建人池田大作，就人类历史的命运和前景问题在伦敦进行了长达10天的漫长讨论。两人共同的看法是世界文明最终会走向统一。

汤因比认为："按照我的设想，全人类发展到形成单一社会之时，可能就是世界实现统一之日。在原子能时代的今天，这种统一已经不可能再通过武力征服……这将由曾把地球上的广大部分统一起来的传统方法来完成。同时，我所预见的这种和平统一，一定是以地理和文化主轴为中心，不断结晶扩大起来的。世界统一是避免人类集体自杀之路。在这一点上，现在各民族中具有最充分准备的，是两千年来培育民族独特思维方法的中华民族。"

池田大作虽然同意汤因比人类的趋向走向统一的观点，但他认为实现统一的方式，不是以某个单一文明为主，而是多种文明的融合。他说："今后世界统一应走的方向，不是……采取中央集权的做法，可能是要采取各国以平等的立场和资格进行协商这种联合的方式。从这种意义上说，与其说哪里是中心，不如说哪里表现出先锋模范作用。我个人认为欧洲共同体的尝试，大概能成这样一个楷模。"

国际社会学会主席、"现代世界体系"创立者、美国著名学者伊曼纽尔·沃勒斯坦与汤因比有相近的看法。他分析了荷兰、英美等国家先后的历史经验，得出了"霸权是短暂的……的结论。"他认为，"由于资本主义世界体系始终充满压迫、剥削和不平等，由此引起复杂的阶级斗争和政治斗争，最终必导致资本主义世界体系的灭亡，一个效率更高、收入分配更合理的世界体系必将取而代之，那个体系可能建立一个"社会主义世界政府"。

## 三、全球文明论

所谓全球文明是指在全球范围内，建立一种人们能够普遍接受的文明和价值观。"全球文明"又称"普世文明"，有人认为最早是由西方学者提出来的。亨廷顿对普世文明也有论述。他说："总的来说，人类在文化上正在趋同，全世界各民族正在日益接受共同的价值、信仰、方向、实践和体制。"

实际上，普世文明或普世文化价值是一个古老的思想观念。中国以孔子为代表的儒家学派就提出过"天下大同"的政治理念；天主教的普世论主张四海之内皆兄弟。

许多学者认为,人类文明发展的趋势是世界上各种不同的文明,经过一个漫长的传播、交流、融会、综合的过程,最终成为共同的文明体系。不过,在具体操作上,却有两派观点泾渭分明。一些西方学者认为,所谓普世文明就是西方文明即西方文明的全球化;但另一派则认为,西方文明颓废的一面日益暴露,他们强调以"和而不同"为核心的中国文化更有可能成为未来全球文明的哲学基础。

西方很多严肃的学者也不同意"现代化是西方化"说法。例如,奈斯比特就说:"全球化是不是代表着美国化?从文化上讲,美国自身的变化远远大于美国对世界的改变,事实上,世界正在改变着美国。世界上的人们都在努力加强自己的文化特征,我为这种现象设立的反论是:我们越变得全球化,我们的行为就越是部落化。这就是文化特征。"

裴勇先生在《文明的整合》一书中说:"现实层面看,两次世界大战的发生是西方文明的耻辱,也是人类的悲哀。工业化导致的资源耗尽、生态危机、杀人武器的膨胀和扩散,都无不凸显了西方文明过度的消费主义、暴力倾向、对自然巨大的破坏力等反文明特性和暗藏的腾腾杀机。"

维多利亚瀑布(Victoria Falls)

他在该书中还写道:"在殖民时代,在西方眼里,非洲人是奴隶,印第安人、土著人是野蛮人,亚洲人是偶像崇拜者,他们要不就该被奴役、要不就该被灭绝、要不就该被控制。平等、民主、自由是不能被加诸其上的。在新帝国时代,在西方看来,他们需要输出平等、民主、自由,但是他们的目的却不是真正希望造福于其他文明国家的人民,而是要使他们西化,以西方文明统一天下,进而牢牢控制住他们,独占世界,独享单边利益。一旦其他国家真正因实现民主而变得强大,他们宁愿其退回到专制,只要独裁者对他唯命是从。一位美国总统的话是一个典型例子,'我知道他是个畜生,但他是我们的畜生'"。

中国艺术研究院中国文化研究所所长、研究员刘梦溪先生曾说过:"经济的全球化、现代文明的普世化是必然趋势,但各个国家的经济模式和文明的类型不必也不可能完全整齐划一。一个国家的现代化进程,不可能在与世隔绝的情况下单独完成,随时需要不同文化背景、民族与民族之间,是互为依存关系。东方离不开西方,西方也离不开东方。同和异,是就达到目的的途径而言。最终归宿,常常是相同的。《易经》上说:'天下同归而殊途,一致而百虑。'"

现代化与全球化的关系比较紧密,只有在现代化的条件下,经济才能扩充到全球。现代化是全球化的条件,而全球化是现代化的必然结果。《文明纵横谈》作者段亚兵先生认为,"作为人类伟大转变的现代化,是一个世界性的发展过程,它把各个民族、各个社会都纳入到统一的'世界社会',使世界成为一个有机的整体。"

全球化从1971年开始算起,已经超过30年。20世纪90年代新经济的开始,更为全球化火上添油。但是到了20世纪末期,许多国家已经看出全球化对弱小国家不利,甚至连进步的小国都深受威胁。国际上,出现了各种反全球化的理论。最著名反全球化的国家是马来西亚。总理马哈蒂尔在1997年亚洲金融危机时,片面宣布林吉特退出国际货币市场,大幅贬值,以利出口,并且冻结资金移往国外;中南美洲国家经历20多年的自由化、开放市场,大部分国家经济增长率还不如70年代。新上任的巴西总统卢拉提出的新经济计划中,仍然保有很多国营事业,市场也不完全开放。

面对经济全球化带来的越来越多的矛盾,其中最具说服力的名言是:"我们不能用经济理论(全球化)来决定文明的方向。"

当前,世界处于转型期,建立一种新的全球文明、建立一个新的世界无疑需要一种全球视野下的新思维。在这种新思维框架下培育出来的新文化,才能够代表世界未来发展的先进文化。而这个新文化既不是"全盘西化"、也不是"全盘东化",因为,到目前为止,世界上还没有任何一种文化可以独步天下,完全适应人类未来的发展,新的文化必然是一种博采众长的"混合"文化,这种新文化需要有一种包容的、生态的、合和的特点,它来自于全人类,又回归于全人类。在未来全球文明建立的过程中,这种新文化将是至关重要的基础。

第六章

# 人类文明"整合"的最终选择
## ——旅游

# Ancient Roman Colosseum

古罗马斗兽场遗址

## 第一节
## 和平发展逐渐成为人类共识

### 一、文明要共享

人类发展到今天,独领风骚数百年的西方文明弊病暴露无遗。两次世界大战以来,工业化导致的资源耗尽、生态危机、杀人武器……凸显了西方文明对自然和人类社会所带来的巨大的负面影响。

根据国际能源总署的预估,在公元前1997年到2020年间年之间,全球主要能源的需求将有57%的增长,而全球各种蕴藏的能源却存量有限。根据专家估计,全球的原油存量将在41年后枯竭殆尽,天然气是63年,煤矿也只有218年。如果人类找不到新的能源替代,人类也将无法继续生存。这个脆弱的世界将无法承受任何形式、特别是暴力的对抗和冲突。

德国前总理施密特在反对亨廷顿"文明冲突论"中的观点时认为:"在全球化时代,迫切需要树立一种对其他文明和宗教的有关学说持尊重和宽容态度的普遍意愿。这种宽容不是漠不关心的宽容,而是出于尊重和重视世界上所存在的、在历史上出现的其他基本信念而产生的宽容。"

中国国家主席胡锦涛在美国耶鲁大学演讲时也强调了"文明的多样性",他说:"一个音符无法表达出优美的旋律,一种颜色难以描绘出多彩的画卷","人类历史上各种文明都以各自的独特方式为人类进步做出了贡献,文明多样性是人类社会的客观现实,是当今世界的基本特征,也是人类进步的重要动力"。

但是,文明的多样性并不意味着冷战式的对立。胡锦涛在演讲中也提到:"历史经验表明,在人类文明交流的过程中,不仅需要克服自然的屏障和隔阂,而且需要超越思想的障碍和束缚,更需要克服形形色色的偏见和误解。意识形态、社会制度、发展模式的差异,不应成为人类文明交流的障碍,更不能成为相互对抗的理由"。

2006年2月,美国500多位科学家联合签名反对达尔文的进化论,起草者在文章中称:"我们对达尔文进化论中的自然选择理论表示怀疑。我们认为,作为科学家,我们有责任要求各领域科学界进行一系列更加深入的研究,以确定达尔文的理论是否合理"。

百余年来,达尔文的理论不仅影响自然科学领域的发展,而且几乎影响到人类社会的各个方面。有识之士不得不反复思考:在人类文明的发展过程中,"弱肉强食"的"丛林法则",到底是现象,还是规律?!

尤其是在科学技术日益暴露其"双刃剑"特质的今天,如果人类文明还要继续走下去,达尔文的"进化论"带给人类是一个什么样的未来,抑或还有没有未来?霍金曾说,按现有模式——"人类走不过千年",这是危言耸听还是科学臆断?

据2015年斯德哥尔摩国际和平研究所公布的数据,2014年全球军费总开支为1.8万亿美元,而以此同时,据世界银行统计数据,若以每人每天1.25美元消费数字计算,2014年全球贫困人口还有12亿。

也就是说,人类目前消灭贫困人口的总费用只需要5475亿美元。人们不禁要问:在人类经济全球化已经实现、文化全球化已经开始的今天,人类还在将有限的地球资源用于制造杀灭自己的武器,这还是不是"文明"?!

20世纪80年代,美国学者卡普拉出版了《转折点》(turning point)一书,他认为西方社会面临危机,同时,他又认为危机不是无法度过的,世界末日不会来临,人类还会继续进化,而要化险为夷的出路就在于实现西方整个文化的根本转变。

但卡普拉对西方文明和西方中心论的批判,绝不是鼓吹另一个世界中心的出现,例如去建立所谓中华文明中心论、印度文明中心论或阿拉伯文明中心论等形形色色的东方文明中心论。卡普拉认为,任何的中心论都会导致狂妄自大,走向衰败。如古代中国就曾经把自己看做世界的中心,以中央之国自居,结果在近代走向衰落。

尺有所短、寸有所长,各种文明都有长处、也有短处。所以需要各种文明扬长避短、优势互补,合作互利、协调一致。一个民间组织就曾经向全球推荐所谓"最优"生活方式,具体内容为:吃要推广美国模式,百万富翁和普通平民中午都吃快餐,不铺张,不浪费,节约时间;喝要推广中国模式,喝茶,既便宜,又健康;衣要推广英国模式,英国男人基本只有两套服装,但穿着很绅士;住要推广前苏联模式,集中住公寓,家家宽敞,又节约土地和能源;工作推广日本模式,员工很敬业;恋爱推广法国模式,讲究浪漫……

著名人类历史学家弗朗兹·博厄斯说:"人类的历史证明,一个社会集团,其文化的进步往往取决于它是否有机会吸取临近社会集团的经验。一个社会集团所获得的种种发现,可以传给其他社会集团;彼此之间的交流愈多样化,相互学习的机会也就越多。大体上,文化最原始的部落也就是那些长期与世隔绝的部落,因而,它们不能从临近部落所取得的文化成就中获得好处……换句话说,如果其他地理因素相同,那么,人类取得进步的关键就在于各民族之间的可接近性和相互影响。只有那些最易接近、最有机会与其他民族相互影响的民族,才有可能得到突飞猛进的发展；而那些与世隔绝、缺乏外界刺激的民族，多半停滞不前。"

人们必须了解到，人与自然、人与人是一体的，国家与国家，民族与民族也是一体的。人类发展应该坚持一种相互依赖、和谐共存的可持续原则。东西方各种文明互有短长，应该实现优势互补。只有建立新的世界观、文明观，实现全球的多样化、一体化，才能真正地结束各种冲突，实现人类真正的平等、民主、和平。

在这里特别要指出的是，尊重和维护"多元化"的世界，并不能否定人类普世价值的存在。当科学技术生产力发展到一定阶段，西方要进行工业革命，东方也要进行工业革命，因此工业革命及其成果就是文明的共性。同样，平等、民主、自由是人类的普遍追求，也是人类文明发展的共同成果，是每一个地球公民都享有的权力。科学与民主不是西方的专利，只是由于西方世界在科学与民主方面实行得较早，做得比较完善一些，没有理由将科学与民主同西方文明画上等号。

鉴于各个国家、各个地区的历史、经济、文化千差万别，所以人类还无法同步进入民主社会，这就要求已经进入民主社会的国家和地区尊重"落后"国家和地区的民主进程，不是强迫而是帮助他们加快民主的步伐；而那些尚未实现民主的国家和地区，必须以理性的眼光看待人类文明发展的规律，要充分认识到，"多元化"并不是落后体制和文化的保护伞。"多元化"应该是人类文明的一种积极的生存状态，是一种"优化"中的"多元化"。如果寄希望于"多元化"来对落后的甚至"反人类"行为予以延护，这无疑是与"多元化"的本质相违背的。

人类的发展已由大工业化时代进入自动化或信息时代，生产力水平达到前所未有的水平，历史上引发战争的各种因素大大减少。"先进"的与"落后"的国家和地区都要懂得，在一个或几个国家实现民主，不可能是真正的民主。只有民主在全球实现，才是真正的民主。

世界发展到今天，虽然目前战争的硝烟还未在地球绝迹，但人类的理性已将战争的形式唾弃。随着人类物质文明的发展和精神文明的提高，世界各国人民普遍增强了对话意识，以非暴力方式解决分歧已成为世界主流。

人类文明只有在人类发展的新阶段，通过旅游这种广泛而又具有特殊功能的交流互动，增进了解，相互尊重，相互欣赏，从而达到共同分享全人类文明成果的目的。

## 二、矛盾要缓和

人类历史上，国与国之间、民族与民族之间、部落与部落之间、党派与党派之间，通过"和平之旅"、"破冰之旅"化解矛盾，增进了解，消弭冲突的事件，恐怕不计其数，但发生在20世纪70年代的美国总统尼克松访华事件，则几乎使其他类似事件黯然失色。

让我们来看看《中国外交秘闻》一书的记载：

1972年2月21日，尼克松踏上中国内地的土地，开始了一次他称之为"谋求和平的旅行"。

11时30分，飞机平稳地停在候机楼前。机舱门打开了，穿着大衣的尼克松总统与夫人帕特两人走出舱门。尼克松看到，周恩来总理站在舷梯前，在寒风中没有戴帽子。旁边站着叶剑英副主席、李先念副总理、郭沫若副委员长、姬鹏飞外长等。

当尼克松走到舷梯快一半的地方时，周恩来带头开始鼓掌。尼克松略停一下，也按中国的习惯鼓掌相还。待离地面还有三四级台阶时，尼克松已经微笑着伸出他的手，周恩来那只手也迎上去，两双手紧紧地握在一起，足足有一分多钟。此时，尼克松感到，一个时代结束了，另一个时代开始了。

尼克松显得很激动，说道："总理先生，我感到很荣幸，终于来到了你们伟大的国家。"

周恩来说："总统先生，非常欢迎你到我们的国家访问。"

电视镜头一直对着这个历史性场面，并通过卫星将这一实况传到全世界……

接着，周恩来和尼克松一同进入一辆挂着帘子的防弹高级红旗轿车。在离开机场时，周恩来说："总统先生，你把手伸过了世界最辽阔的海洋来和我握手。25年没有交往了呵！"

当天晚上，周恩来在人民大会堂宴会厅举行宴会，欢迎尼克松一行。尼克松夫妇、基辛格等由周恩来陪同坐在主宾席的大圆桌旁。中国人民解放军军乐团为客人们演奏了美国名曲《美国的阿美利加》，这种热烈的场面通过卫星传递在美国早晨的电视节目中实况转播，在美国引起了很大反响。

周恩来在祝酒时说："尼克松总统应中国政府的邀请，前来我国访问，使两国领导人有机会直接会晤，谋求两国关系正常化，并就共同关心的问题交换意见，这是符合中美两国人民愿望的积极行动，这在中美两国关系史上是一个创举。"

"美国人民是伟大的人民。中国人民是伟大的人民。我们两国人民一向是友好的。由于大家都知道的原因，两国人民之间的来往中断了20多年。现在，经过中美双方的共同努力，友好来往的大门终于打开了……我们希望，通过双方坦率地交换意见，弄清楚彼此之间的分歧，努力寻找共同点，使我们两国的关系能够有一个新的开始。"

尼克松在祝酒时说："过去的一些时期我们曾是敌人。今天我们有巨大的分歧。使我们走到一起的，是我们有超过这些分歧的共同利益。在我们讨论我们的分歧的时候，我们哪一方都不会在我们的原则上妥协。但是，虽然我们不能弥合我们之间的鸿沟，我们却能够设法搭起一座桥，以便我们能够越过它进行会谈……"

2月28日，中美双方在上海发表了著名的中美联合公报。公报列举了双方对重大国际问题的不同观点，肯定了中美两国的社会制度和对外政策有着本质区别之后，强调指出了双方同意以和平共处五项原则来处理国与国之间的关系。双方同意，将通过不同渠道保持接触，包括不定期派遣美国高级代表前往北京，就促进两国关系正常化进行具体磋商并继续就共同关心的问题交换意见。双方希望，这次访问的成果将为两国关系开辟新的前景。双方相信，两国关系正常化不仅符合中美两国人民的利益，而且会对缓和亚洲及世界紧张局势做出贡献。

随着中美关系的改善，美中苏三角外交的态势开始形成，在很长一段时间里成为决定国际形势发展的重要因素之一。美中和解使苏联不得不加紧同美国和西欧实行缓和，迫使日本急切地要求同中国建立外交关系，并终于推动中日两国于1972年9月实现了中日邦交正常化。正如尼克松在离开中国前夕的宴会上祝酒时说的，他对中国的7天访问是"改变世界的一周"……

在这之前，因支持国民党打内战和朝鲜战争，中国和美国是不共戴天的宿敌。从以上生动的记录，我们可以再一次感受到旅游的力量。而这种力量一旦延续，其产生的效果更是无法估量。

2005年春，台湾主要在野党领袖先后访问内地，开始"破冰之旅"。共产党和国民党也曾经是死敌，国民党于1949年被赶到台湾，偏安一隅。时隔50余年，海峡两岸虽然还处在"非三通"之中，但国民党和亲民党通过旅游，跨海而来，尽释前嫌，实现了半个多世纪的突破。两党在内地的行程不仅受到两岸华人的瞩目，而且受到举世的关注。

2005年10月至11月间，中国国家旅游局局长邵琪伟率团访问台湾地区。这个考察团规模之大、规格之高、活动范围之广是前所未有的。这次旅行被媒体称作是一次台湾向中国内地旅游开放的"探路之旅"。

11月9日，邵琪伟离开台湾，在澳门逗留时他表示，中国内地将积极推动内地民众赴台旅游措施早日实行，建立包括香港、澳门在内的旅游圈。积极扩大两岸旅游交流与合作，推进内地居民赴台旅游早日实现，以更加有利于两岸的交流和往来，有利于两岸经济的繁荣与发展。

据统计，自1988年中国内地向台湾开放以来，台湾到内地的旅游者逐年增加，2004年达368万，2005年超过400万，已经成为内地最重要的客源市场之一。毫无疑问，旅游对台湾大众了解内地社会经济的发展、缓和台湾海峡两岸的政治矛盾，取到了十分重要的作用。

而人类历史上影响最大的政治和解、文化经济融合的事例，莫过于欧盟的成立。欧洲历史上战乱频仍，政治版图几经变化。特别是经受了两次世界大战的洗礼。

战后欧洲各国意识到，和则两益，斗则两败。二战结束后不久，欧洲的有识之士就一直在寻求通过政治联合避免欧洲重蹈战火之路的良策。欧洲联盟的诞生正是这一努力的结果。它使得欧洲众多不同文化传统的国家摆脱了历史的仇恨,走上了和睦相处、共同发展的道路。

2004年5月1日,初春的雅典风和日丽,欧盟历史上最大的一次扩大成员国的签字仪式,在古希腊遗址卫城脚下举行。该遗址曾经是古希腊许多著名的哲学家,宣扬民主自由的演讲场所,同时也是古雅典商业发展的摇篮。观察家分析说,签字地点设在这里体现了欧洲国家建立"大欧洲"的梦想。

扩大后的欧盟将从原来的15个成员国增加到25个,扩大后的欧盟人口将增加7500万,地域将扩大74万平方千米,即欧洲国家的大多数,整体国内生产总值将增加5%,经济总量将与美国不相上下。此前,欧盟先后在1973年、1981年、1986年和1995年4次扩员。

欧盟轮值国主席西米蒂斯在签字仪式上发表讲话说,吸收10个欧洲国家入盟是欧盟发展史上的"重大事件",它宣告了第二次世界大战后东西欧"分裂局面的终结",而且使欧洲一体化建设跨越了冷战时期遗留在欧洲大陆上的历史鸿沟。

欧盟的不断扩大,自然是各国在欧盟的发展过程中不断尝到"甜头"的结果。扩大后的欧盟将使欧洲更加和平、互助,在世界范围内,经济上变得更强,政治、外交和安全领域分量更重。例如在经济上,有关专家分析,将为经济注入新的发展活力。尽管经济增速被估计仅提高0.2%左右,但欧盟总产值将达10万亿欧元,所以超过了北美自由贸易区,成为世界第一大经济贸易实体。据欧盟预测,欧盟的扩大,中东欧地区丰富的历史文化遗产还将进一步刺激欧盟旅游业的发展。

诚然,正如欧盟一直走过来的道路一样,此次扩大后的欧盟未来之路也不会平坦和一帆风顺。随着新成员国的增加,欧盟内部的凝聚力势必面临空前的挑战。由于新老成员国之间存在着较大经济和社会差距,消极因素在短期内无法避免。

但实现欧盟扩大、最终实现"大欧洲"的梦想,是欧洲人消除分歧、避免战争、享受和平与繁荣的有效途径。正是着眼于此,欧洲的政治家才不遗余力地推动欧洲一体化建设向纵深发展。一个经济繁荣、社会安定、政治团结的欧盟既对欧洲有利,也为世界其他地区的和平与发展提供了借鉴。

## 三、宗教要对话

宗教的一个最显著的特点就是排他性。在一神教宗教中,他们宣扬在他们的教义中,只有一个真神。各教派都认为除了自己的真神,其他均为异端邪说。在历史上,为维护自己的信仰,往往刀剑相向。在我们这个地球上,60亿人口中有80%的人信仰各种宗教。"文明冲突论"实际上主要说的是宗教间的冲突。冲突的根源就是来自宗教的排他性。

　　当今世界，由于打着各种宗教旗号或者以宗教面貌出现的极端行为、暴力恐怖活动、种族冲突时有发生，在许多普通大众眼里，宗教似乎成为造成世界动荡不安的一个重要因素。

　　其实，宗教在本质上是不应该冲突的。伊斯兰教本意主张和平，基督教主张爱人如己，佛教讲究慈悲为怀，儒家传统讲仁义道德等，暴力、杀戮、掠夺、仇恨都不符合宗教的本怀。宗教之间之所以发生战争，其背后一定隐藏着政治或经济利益。

　　"9·11"之后，美国犹太州参议员哈奇在讲演中说过一句非常精辟的话："恐怖分子劫持了飞机，同时也劫持了宗教。"

　　事实上，很多穆斯林都认为，本·拉登的思想、言论和行为并不能代表真正的伊斯兰教。真正的伊斯兰教义，提倡仁慈、容忍和友爱，而不是提倡暴力、敌意和仇恨。在互联上，笔者看到一篇"博客"，似乎很有代表性。该文写道："伊斯兰崇尚进行圣战，要通过战争把非伊斯兰地区伊斯兰化，但在其征服了以后却并不强迫异教徒皈依，只要其交纳人丁税即可，而且还保护基督教和犹太教的发展，甚至在很多部门里都有异教徒担当要职。如果是在帝国征服初期为了稳定人心的话，似乎还可以理解，但这显然不是短期政策，唯一想到的可能就是伊斯兰教的宽容，真主安拉的宽容。与之相比的数次十字军东征却完全是一种占领和掠夺。"

　　宗教不仅仅是思想、信仰，而且是历史、文化、道德等。宗教与哲学、科学一样都是可以相互交流，相互学习和相互传播的。这说明，只要人们对宗教、对恐怖主义都有清醒的认识，并做出正确的区别，文明间的和解是可以实现的。

　　各国宗教界实际上也已经开始在这个问题上进行合作。1993年，来自世界各地的6500名宗教界领袖、神学家及其他人士汇聚芝加哥，参加世界宗教议会年会，会上发布了《走向全球伦理宣言》，并提出"没有新的全球伦理，便没有新的全球秩序"。还指出，"全球伦理"不是指超越一切现存各种宗教的一种新的单一宗教，也不是指用来支配所有的宗教，而是"对一些有约束性的价值观、一些不可取消的标准和人格态度的一种基本共识"。

　　2000年，联合国又召开了世界宗教和精神领袖千年和平会议，这是世界宗教之间对话与合作的有着非常重要意义的一次会议，它旨在团结宗教与精神界领袖，以通过联合国与宗教领袖的联合，达成全球性的共识与国际合作，从而获得和平。这次会议还发表了《世界和平宣言》，并建立宗教和精神领袖国际顾问会议，以成为联合国阻止冲突并试图加以解决这些冲突的一项不可或缺的新资源。

　　到目前为止，这些宗教间的对话还只是个别、临时性的，并没有形成一种常规的机制和实际可操作的办法。尤其是这次会议之后，在它结束不到一年的时间里，震惊全球的"9·11"恐怖袭击发生了。

但这并不等于宗教和解的希望面临绝望。事实上，宗教与宗教、宗教与俗民的和解的事例，并不鲜见，仍然能让人类看到曙光。电影《达·芬奇密码》的放映，就是一个很好的事例。

2006年5月9日，电影《达·芬奇密码》在全球上映，该影片以伪经为依据编造了早期教会历史，直接触动了基督教的根基。

其实，通俗文化作品给宗教带来的冲击，《达·芬奇密码》并非首次。过往，教会多采取抵制和对抗的方式来对待影片。例如，1988年，电影《基督的最后诱惑》以凡人的角度，编造耶稣在十字架上的经历，严重违背了《圣经》的本意，电影上映后掀起了全球性的抗议浪潮。在洛杉矶的环球影城，有25000人聚集抗议，电影制作人甚至接到了死亡威胁。

面对同样的现实，一位参与当年抗议活动的美南浸信会的基督徒领袖，总结了当年的经验，他认为，对基督教不友善的电影采取对抗行动得不偿失，因为这样做反而让世人更加深了对基督徒的偏见，认为他们心胸狭窄，目光短浅，无法接受外界的挑战。

因而，此次在对待电影《达·芬奇密码》上，美国的教会放弃了过去的对抗方法，他们既不抵制，也不忽略，而是用"文明对话"的方式，积极组织各种活动，讨论信仰问题。

例如，牧师们布置了会场，供应甜甜圈、三文治和咖啡，请人来大谈特谈《达·芬奇密码》。有些教会甚至还免费赠送iPod，以吸引非基督徒参加讨论会。当然，其宗旨只有一个：让人坚信《圣经》，相信耶稣的神性。许多教会干脆组织青少年前往观看电影，并在观片后组织讨论。

《达·芬奇密码》这部电影的制作者——索尼电影公司起先一直担心宗教界会采取激烈的对抗行动，因此他们也乐意看到教会放弃对抗的态度。制片商甚至还开设了"达·芬奇对话"网站，广邀基督徒、学者发表意见。

据媒体报道，教会以这种和平对话的方式解决矛盾，深得社会赞赏。群众感到基督徒心胸开阔、开明，且愿意聆听不同见解。因此，许多基督徒领袖认为，《达·芬奇密码》给教会一个建立基督徒新形象的绝好机遇。

据说，教会还发现，从前很难引人注意的《圣经》话题，如今成了热门话题。以往人们认为枯燥的教会历史，却成为吸引人的热点。一位经常在全美各地开《新约》历史讲座的神学院老师说，过去，他的班上能凑到15个学生就十分难得了，如今只要将讲座的名称改为"讨论《达·芬奇密码》"，讲同样内容，却有600多名听众要来听课。

出演《达·芬奇密码》的影星汤姆·汉克斯也说，如果教会贴出布告，说周三将有《圣经》课，那么只有12人出席，但如果说周三将讨论《达·芬奇密码》，那就有 800 人涌进教会。因此,《达·芬奇密码》为教会带来机遇。

教会的积极态度也促进了图书市场的兴旺。出版商们突然发现,几乎所有有关《圣经》的书都热销起来。因此教会态度的改变,让出版商不再成为抵制的对象,反而有了更多赚钱的机会。从社会各方面的反应看,教会在这次危机中的确找到了与社会对话的有效方式,化解了世俗文化所带来的冲击。

我们还可以看到另外一个事例,中东长期以来,一直是世界关注的焦点地区。在地中海沿岸的黎巴嫩国内,基督教和伊斯兰教的信徒的矛盾,由来已久,并且常常是该国发起内斗的根源。

2006 年 7 月,以色列打着消除真主党武装的旗号入侵黎巴嫩。在连续近一个月的轰炸中,生活在黎巴嫩首都贝鲁特的伊斯兰教信徒,为了躲避轰炸,搬到基督教信徒的生活区。两派的信徒,终于走到了一起。

据媒体报道,基督教的信徒不仅没有为难伊斯兰教信徒,相反,他们为伊斯兰教信徒提供食品和生活用品。双方在一种前所未有的和谐中祈祷战争尽快结束,和平尽快到来。

2006 年 9 月 12 日,梵蒂冈教宗本笃十六世引述中世纪拜占庭皇帝言论指圣战邪恶,触怒了伊斯兰教世界。请看当时的一则报道:

(伊斯兰堡综合电)罗马天主教教宗本笃十六世返乡牧灵,日前在德国雷根斯堡大学发表演说时,将伊斯兰教和暴力联系起来,引起许多伊斯兰教国家的不满,纷纷要求他公开做出道歉。

这位德国裔教宗,上周二在母校——德国雷根斯堡大学发表演说,引述中世纪拜占庭皇帝的言论指圣战邪恶,此举烧起了伊斯兰教世界的怒火,要求教宗道歉并撤回言论。一些地区的回教徒已经走上街头,对教宗的谈话表达他们的不满。

正当伊斯兰世界的怒火越烧越旺之际,事隔一周,教宗道歉,并派出特使前往伊斯兰教国家做出解释和进一步道歉。请看另一则报道:

教宗本笃十六世在 9 月 17 日的公开讲话中表示,为他于 9 月 12 日在里根斯堡大学(Regensburg University)向一群学者的讲话中,有些部分"在一些国家所引起的反应,深感抱歉"。他亦指出该言论"被认为冒犯了穆斯林(伊斯兰教徒)的感受"。

解决宗教矛盾不再需要历史上的兵戎相见;宗教矛盾的出现仍然是因为相互了解不够。各教派之间只要相互增加认识和理解,相互尊重和宽容,宗教就既可以找到与社会大众之间行之有效的对话方式,也一定能找到教派之间互通有无、和谐共存的生存方式。

虽然目前世界上还存在一些诸如拉登之类的宗教极端分子,但相对于热爱和平、渴望对话的广大教徒来说，他们只是极小的一部分。全球反恐力量迅速形成进一步证明，对话，只有对话，才是达到不同宗教、不同信仰之间双赢或多赢的唯一通道。

## 第二节
### 现代旅游发展与日俱进

### 一、科技的进步和"地球村"的加速融合

现代旅游业崛起于第二次世界大战后，在20世纪60年代开始加速，是"后工业化社会"发展最快的行业之一。第二次世界大战期间航空和雷达导航技术的突破，为战后民用航空业的发展奠定了基础，也对旅游业产生巨大的影响。1958年，波音707喷气机的问世标志着大众旅游时代的到来，航空旅游变得更加迅捷、安全、舒适。1950年，赖茨以"地平线假日"旅游公司的名义组织了一次航空包价旅游，目的地是科西嘉岛。他在这次实验性的旅游组织中采取了预订一些座位的办法，从而有效地降低了成本并以更低的价格将包价旅游线路推向大众。在随后的时间里，越来越多的旅游者接受了这种新的大众旅游方式。到1970年，第一架宽体客机波音747投入运营，每次运载的旅客数量超过了400人，更大的、更多的乘客数量使机票价格进一步降低。

随着欧美日等发达国家汽车工业的进一步发展和战后各国高速公路的大量兴建，自驾车旅游以惊人的速度取代了中短途的火车旅游和客车旅游。到了20世纪70年代，在美国平均每两个人拥有一部汽车。

英国，20世纪80年代，仅带住宿设备的家用旅行房车就有60万辆。每到七八月份的巴黎，城内的度假大军沿着巴黎通往法国度假的高速公路缓慢地行驶，巴黎这时成了外国旅游者的巴黎，几乎到处都是到巴黎的度假者。

西班牙于20世纪60年代开始一直位于世界旅游业发展的前三位，创造了一个旅游业的"西班牙奇迹"。到了2002年每年前往西班牙的外国旅游者达到了5170万，旅游业收入高达336亿美元，这两个指标均居世界第二位。

中国已成为亚洲最大的客源输出国，2005年，中国出境游人数达到3103万人次，较上年同比增加7.5%。2005年，中国总共接待入境游客1亿2000万人次，入境过夜游客 4681 万人次，分别比上年增加 10% 和 12%。外国游客为中国带来了 293 亿美元的旅游收入，比上年增长近 14%。

信息技术是 20 世纪下半叶最重要的革命，如喜来登集团，早在 1958 年就开始使用电子预订系统。60 年代则出现了计算机预定系统。进入 20 世纪 90 年代，旅游业普遍采用了计算机预定系统、旅行经销商视觉系统。而新的电子旅行中介是基于互联网技术的 3 种电子平台，即互联网、交互式数字电视以及移动装置。

根据世界旅游组织的统计，自 1950 年到 1998 年，国际旅游者人数从 2500 万增加到 6.35 亿，平均年增长率为 6.97%。按照国际货币基金会的统计，1998 年，旅游接待和旅客运输创造了高达 5040 亿美元的收入，位于所有国际贸易类别（包括汽车产品、化工产品、食品、汽油和其他燃料、计算机和办公设备、纺织品和服装、矿产品等）之首。

世界旅游组织在 1980 年的《马尼拉宣言》中明确指出："旅游是人类社会基本的需要之一。"许多国家也意识到将旅游纳入到国民经济的发展当中。在这种人类文明发展思潮的推动下，世界出现了"大众旅游"、"奖励旅游"、"社会旅游"等行为模式。

世界旅游组织成立于 1974 年 11 月，代表了当时的 89 个国家政府，其基本宗旨是："像那些已经存在的、其利益集团的呼声可以被关注的政府间国际组织一样，为旅游业争取其应有的地位。"该组织在促进世界旅游业发展方面发挥着巨大的作用，其成员包括政府组织和非政府组织。2003 年，该组织正式成为联合国的下属地机构。

美国社会学家罗兰·罗伯逊认为，"全球化"不是单纯的经济问题、政治问题、社会问题或国际关系问题，而首先是一个文化问题，因为"全球化"作为一个整体首先是一个社会文化"系统"。

马克思也说过："不断扩大产品销路的需要，驱使资产阶级奔走全球各地。它必须到处落户，到处开发，到处建立联系。资产阶级，由于开拓了市场，使一切国家的生产和消费成为世界性的了——过去那种地方的和民族的自给自足和闭关自守状态，被各个民族的各个方面的相互来往和各方面的相互依赖所代替了。物质的生产是如此，精神的生产也是如此"。

人类已经进入 21 世纪，随着科技的进步，交通工具和通信技术的发达，全球性范围内人们的交往日益广泛，文明体之间的交流，从以前主要通过战争、商贸、宗教等渠道，扩大到现在的旅游、传媒、文化、体育等多种领域。

随着大众传媒的影响，人们的文化爱好、生活方式越来越趋同，更容易对整个世界的现状和全球问题产生理性的认知并达成共识。并且，随着世界上的语言种类越来越少，英语、汉语、法语等语言成为几种流行语言，方便了人们的交流。

如今，人们在相同的名牌连锁店里购物，人们看着同样的电视节目和电影大片，关心的是明星们的趣闻轶事，甚至国界也不成问题。人们越来越喜欢旅游，熟悉不同国家和地区的风光，今天在东半球观光，明天到西半球度假，上午在北国雪山上滑雪，下午到南方海滩上游泳都已经变成现实。

资本的全球流动和以互联网为代表的信息化社会的出现，更使得文化产品及文化生产方式跨国界、跨民族的传播得到空前的发展。

而由于人类天生存在一些共同的文化心理、文化需求和基本价值观，以及一些共同的利益和问题，人类的文化行为和文化创造，便具有普遍性和共同性的一面，因而文化全球化是各民族文化交融的一种必然结果。

文化全球化迫使不同国家用一种新的眼光和视角来环顾世界，审视自己的文化，使得全球公民不再局限于一个国家或一个地区的狭小范围来考虑问题，它促进了不同文化的接触、对话和交流，使全人类能够分享世界文化的资源和人类文明的成果。

孙东民在2001年1月11日《人民日报海外版》上撰文称："环顾'地球村'，经济的全球化迅猛发展，跨国公司进出，对外投资扩大，各国经济中你中有我，我中有你。亚洲的金融危机危及世界，美联储降息瞬间使股市波动。'地球村'各个角落发生的事件，可以迅速传遍各地，世界从来没有像现在这样现实的上演或悲情或愉悦的现代剧"。

全球化资源流动的趋势无疑将在很大程度上推动旅游业的发展。人们掌握的外部资讯越多，就越渴望去体验异域的文明，而如今便捷的交通工具可以将旅游者迅速运送到世界几乎任何旅游目的地；人们日益开放的心态也克服了固有的排外、仇外心理或文化沙文主义的态度，促使人类更平等地交流。

2001年9月27日，在伊朗举行的庆祝世界旅游日的会议上，世界旅游组织提出了"旅游：作为文明间对话和和平的途径"口号。

## 二、旅游的力量触及人类各个领域

1992年，世界旅游总收入首次超过石油、汽车工业，成为世界上第一大产业。据有关资料显示，全世界的国际旅游人数从1950年的2500万人次，增加到了2000年的6.87亿人次，并且，全世界国际旅游者人次和国际旅游消费水平还在逐年增长。旅游业在全世界范围内迅速扩展，现已在170个左右的国家和地区基本形成了独立产业。1993年全世界的国际旅游人数达到5.13亿人，比1950年增长了19倍，年均递增了7.2%；国际旅游总收入达到3058亿美元，比1950年增长了115.5倍，年平均增长11.7%。世界旅游业的增长速度不仅超过了世界经济的平均增长速度，也超过了增长势头最好的工业的平均增长率（见表一）。

表一 世界旅游业增长水平比较表

| 年代 \ 项目 | 世界旅游业平均增长率% | 世界经济平均增长率% | 世界工业平均增长率% |
|---|---|---|---|
| 50 | 12.6 | 5.4 | 6.8 |
| 60 | 10.1 | 4.9 | 6.5 |
| 70 | 6.0 | 3.5 | 5.3 |
| 80 | 8.4 | 2.8 | 2.6 |
| 80~85 | 1.1 | 2.4 | 1.7 |
| 86~90 | 16.3 | 2.6 | 3.2 |

资料来源：《Intenational Tourism Quarterly》《世界经济年鉴》《中国旅游年鉴》。

进入80年代初期，由于世界经济危机的影响及国际形势的剧烈变化，一度使旅游业发展速度趋缓和下降，但整个80年代世界旅游业仍保持了8.4%的较高增长率。特别是80年代后期，年平均增长率高达16.3%，显示出其发展的良好势头，也预示着在迈向21世纪的过程中，世界旅游业将保持着光明的发展前景。

旅游业的迅猛发展，有力地推动了世界经济的持续健康发展。首先，旅游业对国民经济的贡献不断增大。1992年全世界国际国内旅游总收入达到35000亿美元，是当年世界商品和劳务总消费额的1/9。根据国际旅游与观光理事会（以下简称WTTC）的研究报告，1990年全世界旅游业新增值达到14490亿美元，占当年世界新增值总额的5.9%。世界旅游业提供的税收为2510亿美元，占当年全世界企业提供的直接税和间接税总额的5.6%。从WTTC对美、英、法、日、德五国旅游业同其他产业新增价值的比较看（见表二），五国旅游业新增值分别是五国农业的3.1倍，汽车工业的3.6倍，金属工业的4.3倍，纺织工业的5.7倍。这充分表明，旅游业的国民经济中的贡献份额在不断扩大。

表二 旅游业与其他产业增值、从业人数比较表

| 行业 \ 国家 | 美国 | 英国 | 日本 | 德国 | 法国 | 合计 |
|---|---|---|---|---|---|---|
| 旅游业从业人数（万人） | 3300 | 500 | 2300 | 1400 | 700 | 8200 |
| 农业从业人数（万人） | 900 | 300 | 650 | 200 | 190 | 2240 |
| 纺织业从业人数（万人） | 900 | 200 | 700 | 400 | 500 | 2700 |
| 金属业从业人数（万人） | 300 | 80 | 650 | 120 | 180 | 1330 |
| 汽车业从业人数（万人） | 500 | 200 | 250 | 250 | 250 | 1450 |
| 旅游业增值（亿美元） | 200 | 70 | 120 | 100 | 100 | 590 |

续表

| 行业 \ 国家 | 美国 | 英国 | 日本 | 德国 | 法国 | 合计 |
|---|---|---|---|---|---|---|
| 农业增值（亿美元） | 400 | 100 | 700 | 450 | 250 | 1900 |
| 纺织业增值（亿美元） | 100 | 20 | 100 | 110 | 30 | 360 |
| 金属业增值（亿美元） | 550 | 250 | 600 | 600 | 300 | 2300 |
| 汽车业增值（亿美元） | 100 | 30 | 110 | 120 | 110 | 470 |

资料来源：根据《中国旅游报》1992年6月1日"世界旅游与观光理事会1992年年度报告"数据整理。

随着交通技术的改进以及发达国家（后来是发展中国家）的生活水平的提高，旅行已经广为人们所接受并成为生活必需的一部分。后现代旅游是一个全球旅游、全民旅游的"大旅游"时代。

所谓"大旅游"是一种全新的旅游发展理念，反映了旅游业正向经济社会领域全方位、深层次发展的趋势。"大旅游"概念比传统的旅游定义层次更高，范畴更广，它是根据旅游业的产业性质，以及旅游业与其他相关产业间的密切关系，将旅游产业进行科学而又适度的延伸和扩展，进一步强化其综合性强、关联度大、产业链长和覆盖面广的产业功能。

"大旅游"的概念，被人们理解为是一种社会、经济和文化等多方面的互动关系，如旅游与商业设施的结合、旅游与高科技的结合、旅游与扶贫的结合、旅游与环境建设的结合、旅游与房地产的结合等，旅游不仅在规模上成为普及化商品，在质量上也日渐成为高度专业化的商品，并在传统的旅游体系如观光度假旅游、农业旅游的基础上推出了工业旅游、时尚旅游以及社会旅游等新项目。许多专业化的旅游产品纷纷出现，使得旅游的内涵更加丰富多彩，更加深入全面地触及人类发展的方方面面。

**商务旅游** 商务旅游自古有之，在历史上起着重要作用的"丝绸之路"就是人类发展史上最著名的商务旅游线路之一。人类历史上最早的旅游活动可能并非是从愉悦性情开始，而是从商务活动发端。但现代商务旅游活动无论从规模还是内涵来讲，古代商务旅游都不能同日而语。现代商务旅游是指商务人士在商务活动过程中产生的各种旅游消费行为，除了传统的商贸经营外，还包括参加行业会展、跨国公司的区域年会、调研与考察、跨区域的产品发布会以及近几年兴起的公司奖励旅游等。

以商务旅游为例，尽管在2003年，面对全球经济的激烈挑战，新加坡仍迎来125万名商务旅客，占抵境旅客总人数的两成。而新加坡的总人口，也不过是400万出头。从现实来看，"新加坡模式"的旅游事业，不仅仅表现在游览观光以及吃住方面，它的旅游业支柱包括商务旅行、会议、奖励旅游，以及大型会议和展览。

据有关资料显示，全球商务旅游市场将呈现高速增长，到 2007 年，世界旅游支出总额将增加到 8700 亿美元，其中 3500 亿美元来自商务旅行。还有，2005 年中国在商务旅行方面的支出约为 250 亿美元，鉴于中国企业家的日趋活跃和在中国开办的外国公司的增多，商务旅行市场将持续两位数增长，到 2020 年将达到 1150 亿美元。

**探险旅游** 随着旅游需求的多样化、个性化以及旅游的体验核心的凸显，人们对罕见目的地的向往和对探险旅游的选择，不仅会呈现出日益增多的趋势，而且将有可能成为未来的旅游潮流之一。探险旅游自主参与性强，科学内涵丰富，能最大限度满足游客猎奇和冒险心理。在喧嚣都市居住久了的都市人，到人迹罕至或险象环生的环境进行充满神秘性、危险性和刺激性的旅行考察活动，能获得一种特殊的快感和满足，如泰国的骑象探险旅游，丹麦的狗拉雪橇探险旅游等。

有一些以追求世界纪录为目的的冒险旅行，如乘气球环球旅行，驾脚踏飞机或滑行器飞渡海峡，驾游艇或小船周游世界，乘独木舟横渡大西洋等。而以科学考察为主要目的的探险旅游，种类繁多，如高山探险旅游、沙漠探险旅游、海洋探险旅游、森林探险旅游、洞穴探险旅游、极地探险旅游、追踪野生动物探险旅游、寻找人类原始部落探险旅游等。如 2004 年，美国退役海军上校阿尔弗雷德·麦克拉伦在巴哈马开办了一所"水下驾驶培训学校"，每位学员所需费用高达 9980 美元。麦克拉伦要手把手地训练每一位学员，使他们成为"深海巡航者"。新闻报道说："这无疑宣告了一场水下探险旅游的革命。"

**购物旅游** 以购物为主要目的的一种特殊旅游方式。购物是旅游的重要组成部分。不少国家和地区利用游客渴望购物的心理，大力发展具有民族特色的土特产品、手工艺品和精巧美观的各种纪念品以及迎合外国游客口味的名牌烟酒、化妆品和日用消费品，作为招徕游客创收外汇的重要手段。如新加坡专门建立了手工艺中心，多方罗致泰国、马来西亚、印尼、中国香港、日本及印度等地熟练艺人参加工作，此中心不仅制造、展出各种具有地方色彩的手工艺品，并让游客参观制作过程，购买产品留作纪念，从而使销售旅游商品的收入占旅游总收入的 60%；墨西哥新建旅游城阿卡普尔科旧市区的手工业品市场，每隔 20～30 米就有一个手工艺品销售点，商品琳琅满目，应有尽有；香港凭借自由港的地位被旅游者称为"购物天堂"，旅游者的购物支出高达 61%。

中国小商品城旅游购物中心坐落于义乌国际商贸城二期市场西大厅二、三楼，建筑面积 10000 余平方米，营业面积 5000 余平方米。按照打造"小商品海洋，购物者天堂"的理念，旅游购物中心集中了中国小商品城 34 个行业 1502 大类 32 万种商品中的精品于一堂，实行厂家源头价供应，价廉物美，品牌保证。据统计，2002 年义乌购物旅游者约 164 万人次，仅旅游购物收入就达 2 亿多元。

**生态旅游** 生态旅游是利用自然和人文生态资源开发旅游项目，吸引国内外关注生态者和其他居民前往游览、观赏、体验、考察。自然生态旅游既包括森林、草原等生态环境优良的区域开展的旅游活动，也包括沙漠、戈壁、荒漠等生态环境恶劣的区域开展的旅游活动，还包括为改善生态环境组织旅游者无偿进行植树、种草、认养树木等活动。

人文生态旅游目前主要是到人与自然及居民相互之间和谐、古朴的区域从事考察、交流、游览活动。民族生态旅游是其典型代表。如贵州六盘水市梭嘎布依族村寨、梨平县堂安侗族村寨和锦平县隆里等，依托中国和挪威联合建立的民族生态博物馆发展民族生态旅游，吸引了很多国外游客前往观光、考察、研究。高度关注生态环境是全人类根本利益所在。目前，国内外打生态旅游招牌、旗号的越来越多，通过发展生态旅游加强生态建设和环境保护已成为各国、各地区的重要选择。

**文体旅游** 文化体育旅游是利用文化体育项目、设施和比赛活动等开发旅游项目，吸引旅游者前往观赏、参与、体验等的旅游活动。根据世界旅游及旅行理事会（WTTC）2004年对旅游者的旅游动机进行的有关统计，在商务、度假、购物、探险以及文化体验五种旅游动机中，文化体验已居于首位。文化主要形式有艺术节、音乐节、电影节等，文化旅游就是在不同的文化领域进行探索和发现，文化旅游日益呈现出个性化的趋势。语言学习旅游是种非常典型的现代文化旅游方式。当前世界性旅游发展，回归文化成为旅游的核心内容，生态旅游与文化旅游交融是旅游业发展的新趋势。

体育和旅游是人们普遍比较喜爱的活动，将二者结合起来的体育旅游，使人的运动天赋和旅游时尚相统一，从而产生无穷的生命力和巨大的吸引力。体育旅游主要有奥运会和世界杯等重大国际国内体育赛事观赏，还有如自驾汽车、摩托车和自行车旅游，徒步、登山、探险，野外生存训练，峡谷漂流，滑冰、滑雪、滑草，网球、高尔夫球、乒乓球之旅等。由德国罗特旅行社组织、中国国际旅行社接待的丝绸之路自驾车旅游，特别是世界杯足球赛和奥运会旅游，都是规模非常大的体育旅游活动。

**科技旅游** 科技旅游是利用科学研究、教育教学活动过程、场景等资源开发旅游项目，主要吸引国内外学生、青少年、教师前往修学、参观、交流。科技旅游又被人们称为充满阳光的旅游，因其在旅游活动中可以学到科技知识，开阔科技视野，特别是一些旅游内容不但能看能听，还能动手实践，因此这种集知识性、趣味性、教育性和休闲为一体的旅游形式越来越受到人们特别是广大青少年的青睐。

目前主要形式有修学旅游（如中国北京和江苏开展的日本学生来华修学旅游）、书法美术旅游、名校参观（如北京大学和清华大学开展的"校园一日"）、参观航天中心及火箭和卫星发射、实验室和研究基地参观等。科教旅游性质上属于产业旅游，但其在普及科学知识、未成年人教育等方面显示明显优势，不但受到学校和家庭的重视，科研、教育、旅游部门积极性也比较高，甚至也受到成年人的欢迎，其发展前景非常广阔。

**保健旅游**　保健旅游包含两方面内容：一是指在旅游中倡导运动养生，安排和增加包括登山、垂钓、采摘、游泳、漂流、滑雪、滑草、野营及日光浴、空气浴、森林浴、外加用膳在内的健身化的旅游方式，通过旅游达到运动健身的效果；二是指那些年龄不很高、疾病不严重、有一定生活自理能力的老年人旅游并利用其中的便利条件进行治疗，从而达到保健和治疗的目的。

保健游中的森林浴，是由桑拿浴、日光浴等派生出来的一种时尚流行语，意即到树林中去沐浴那里特有的气息、氛围。据日本森林综合研究所对森林浴的一项最新研究成果表明，吸入杉树、柏树的香味，可降低血压，稳定情绪。在森林中散步时，血压和抑郁荷尔蒙的含量都会降低。除了树木发出的香气之外，林中小溪的流水声、触摸树皮时的感觉也会让人心旷神怡。享受森林浴并非为森林独有，城市里的公园、花房、林荫道都具有这种氛围。在越来越广泛的休闲生活中，与游乐场、健身房相比，森林浴可以给人以更多的放松和保健。保健旅游，把旅游和保健结合，让旅游者既能放松身心，又能增强身体免疫力，防病于未然，不失为受中老年游客欢迎的旅游形式。

**工业旅游**　对于一个行业中的人来说，也许一些工业生产过程、工艺和产品都是司空见惯的东西，而对一般公众来说，这些地方往往是陌生、神秘、具有吸引力的。例如，人们都认识煤，但真正知道煤是如何开采出来的则很少，地下的巷道、矿车、采掘机和在地下上千米的感受对许多人都是新鲜的。世界许多国家都开辟了大量的工业旅游项目。如德国鲁尔区，将工业遗址改造成工业遗址主题公园，获得成功；中国的海尔企业，把企业的旅游作为一项重要的日常活动，每天有主要负责人值班负责接待，带领游人游览一些生产过程，并请游人在游览过程中从陈列产品样品中选出自己最喜欢的产品。

一些有远见和实力的企业，将工业旅游作为公司的一项长期投资，有的还建立工业博物馆，既展示工业文物，也展示工艺发展过程。这样做，无异于一次次免费的市场调查，为市场营销战略的制定和产品的改进获得了重要的依据。

**会展旅游**　会展旅游以其兼容性强、辐射面广、消费档次和文化含量高等特性，成为一种新兴的旅游形态。目前，会展旅游对旅游业发展巨大的拉动作用及其创造出的经济和社会效益，已广为世界各地所重视。根据国际展览业权威人士估算，国际展览业的产值约占全世界各国GDP总和的1%，如果加上相关行业从展览中的获益，展览业对全球经济的贡献则达到8%的水平。国际会议同样是一个巨大的市场，根据国际会议协会（ICCA）统计，每年国际会议的产值约为2800亿美元。在中国香港、德国等会展业发达的国家和地区，会展业对经济的带动作用达到1:9的水平。

2008年北京将举办奥运会。据预测，从2002年起到奥运之年，我国旅游业每年会有50亿元的收入增量，旅游收入年增长率将达到18%。到举办当年，旅游收入会增加100亿美元，来华游客会增加100%，因奥运会直接增加的旅游收入将超过1500亿元人民币。据预测，2010年上海世博会将给上海带来7000万人次的游客。上海世博会的举办，将会和德国的慕尼黑、法兰克福、杜塞尔多夫和科隆等一样，成为亚洲最大的会展城市群。

**博彩旅游** 在世界旅游业发展过程中，的确有一些地方以赌场与博彩的形式发展旅游，甚至专门有类似博彩旅游或赌场旅游，出现了像美国的大西洋城、拉斯维加斯，欧洲的摩纳哥、蒙特卡罗和亚洲的中国澳门等以博彩业为特色的旅游目的地。对大众旅游者来说，到这些地方，主要是度假、放松，并非职业性的赌博或为了赚钱而豪赌。多数游客还是抱着一种好奇的心态见识一下。

中国的出境旅游和边境旅游使一些边陲城市的旅游业成为当地的经济支柱，而博彩则是"出境游"不可或缺的选择项目。在中国的周围边境沿线摆起了"赌场大战"，与黑龙江接壤的一个国家四个城市开设赌场60多个；云南边境外有三大赌场，而境外赌场达82个外；广西境外最大的赌场是"利来国际博彩俱乐部"及"越港国际娱乐俱乐部"；内蒙古边境也建起了赌场。据不完全统计，在中国边境线上，曾经有大大小小的境外赌场200个。

**特种旅游** 特种旅游的发展在全世界均属初创时期，其发展呈现出蓬勃的生命力。特种旅游是指为满足旅游者某方面的特殊兴趣与需要，定向开发组织的一种特色专题性旅游活动。由此而组成的旅游线路和项目，对旅游者具有新鲜感、刺激感和冒险性。参与特种旅游活动的旅游者，一般具有冒险精神和耐受艰苦条件的体魄，旅游队伍一般选择志同道合的人作为旅伴，旅游者在运动中感知外部世界，在冒险或面对全新的环境中得到精神上的满足。旅游者本身对行程的组织有较高的自主性和能动性，其内部有共同的文化准则。

与观光旅游、度假旅游相比，特种旅游除了具有为旅游者提供食、住、行、游服务的共性之外，最重要的一点就是要与旅游者共同参与旅行，以自己的专业知识指导旅游者实现其旅游目标。此种旅游活动面大，地区跨度广，往往涉及边远和人迹罕见的地域，自然环境和文化环境，具有浓烈的原始自然性。

就大多数国家来说，使用汽车、自行车、摩托车作为旅游交通工具的旅行和非赛事的滑雪、攀岩、漂流、热气球、滑翔等体育旅行，以及去高山、峡谷、沙漠、洞穴等目的地的探险旅行，还有以短期观赏、踏勘、参观为主要旅游形式的自然和人文景观的科考旅游等，均可列入特种旅游的范围。

根据世界旅游组织发表的《旅游报告精华2003版》对2002年世界旅游状况的分析，可以比较具体地看到世界旅游的一些具有代表性的国家旅游的发展特点。

**旅游接待人数和旅游收入前 10 位的国家（地区）**

| 国际旅游接待数/百万人 | | | | 国际旅游收入/百万 | | | |
|---|---|---|---|---|---|---|---|
| 名　次 | 2002 年 | 变化率% | 占有率% | 名　次 | 2002 年 | 变化率% | 占有率% |
| 1. 法国 | 77.0 | 2.4 | 11.0 | 1. 美国 | 665 | -7.4 | 14.0 |
| 2. 西班牙 | 51.7 | 3.3 | 7.4 | 2. 西班牙 | 336 | 2.2 | 7.1 |
| 3. 美国 | 41.9 | -6.7 | 6.0 | 3. 法国 | 323 | 7.8 | 6.8 |
| 4. 意大利 | 39.8 | 0.6 | 5.7 | 4. 意大利 | 269 | 4.3 | 5.7 |
| 5. 中国 | 36.8 | 11.0 | 5.2 | 5. 中国 | 204 | 14.6 | 4.3 |
| 6. 英国 | 24.2 | 5.9 | 3.4 | 6. 德国 | 192 | 4.0 | 4.0 |
| 7. 加拿大 | 20.1 | 1.9 | 2.9 | 7. 英国 | 178 | 9.5 | 3.8 |
| 8. 墨西哥 | 19.7 | -0.7 | 2.8 | 8. 奥地利 | 112 | 11.1 | 2.4 |
| 9. 奥地利 | 18.6 | 2.4 | 2.6 | 9. 中国香港 | 101 | 22.2 | 2.1 |
| 10. 德国 | 18.0 | 0.6 | 2.6 | 10. 希腊 | 97 | 3.1 | 2.1 |
| 世　界 | 703 | 2.7 | 100 | 世　界 | 4740 | 3.2 | 100 |

**国际旅游支出前 10 位的国家和地区**

| 国际旅游支出/亿美元 | | | |
|---|---|---|---|
| 名　次 | 2002 年 | 变化率% | 占有率% |
| 1. 美国 | 580 | -3.6 | 12.6 |
| 2. 德国 | 532 | 2.4 | 11.2 |
| 3. 英国 | 404 | 10.8 | 8.5 |
| 4. 日本 | 267 | 0.6 | 5.6 |
| 5. 法国 | 195 | 9.8 | 4.1 |
| 6. 意大利 | 169 | 14.4 | 3.6 |
| 7. 中国 | 154 | 10.7 | 3.2 |
| 8. 荷兰 | 129 | 7.5 | 2.7 |
| 9. 中国香港 | 124 | 0.8 | 2.6 |
| 10. 俄罗斯 | 120 | 20.5 | 2.5 |
| 世　界 | 4740 | 3.2 | 100 |

在以上表格中，我们看到西方国家在国际旅游业中仍然占据着统治的地位，但

随着东亚，特别是中国在国际旅游业中的突出表现，这种一花独放的局面被打破了。

尽管面对恐怖主义威胁、自然灾害、石油价格高涨、传染疾病和其他政治与经济不稳定因素的影响，但全球旅游的发展仍然势不可挡。全球旅客2005年达7.08亿人次，比上一年度的7.66亿人次增长5.5%。这个增长幅度比世界旅游组织（The World Tourism Organization）所定下的年均4.1%的长期增长目标还要高。

2005年的旅客人次增加4200万，其中到欧洲的旅客人次增加约1900万、亚洲及太平洋地区增加1100万、美洲增加700万、非洲大陆增加300万，中东地区则增加200万。按各区域的增长情况来看，2005年旅客人次增加最快的地区是非洲，取得10%增长，其次是亚洲及太平洋地区增长达7%、中东7%、美洲6%和欧洲4%。

传统上，欧洲和美洲是全球最热门的旅游目的地，不过据世界旅游组织指出，亚洲及太平洋区和中东将是2006年全球最具增长潜能的旅游区。它预测亚洲及太平洋区今年可取得9%的增长，中东地区则可取得8%的增长。

至于非洲、欧洲和美洲，世界旅游组织预测，非洲估计能取得6%的增长，欧洲和美洲各取得3%的增长。世界旅游组织认为2006年全球旅游业可取得4%至5%的增长。

从2002年至2005年，全球的旅客人次总共增加约1亿。并且，现在的中东各国，如卡塔尔和阿拉伯联合酋长国等都在大力改革经济，在国内投入庞大的资金，发展旅游产业。叙利亚大使向笔者介绍，叙利亚2006年头七个月，就向旅游产业投资超过100亿美元。

美国著名学者丹尼尔·贝尔在他1973年出版的《后工业社会的来临》一书中比较了前工业社会和工业社会的特征分别是农业和工业后指出："后工业社会是以服务业为基础的。随着人们生活的扩大和新的需要与爱好的发展，第三产业即个人服务部门开始发展：饭馆、旅社、汽车服务、旅游、娱乐、运动。"

在美国，服务及与服务相关的产业占GDP的比重在1980年为67.1%，1987年为71%，1993年为74.3%，到2000年已经超过了80%。

到20世纪90年代中期，世界上已经有120多个国家将旅游业收入列为支柱产业。世界旅游组织（WTO）称旅游业为"世界上最富有活力的经济增长点"。

据有关研究机构推算，"到2010年，国际旅游的总人数将达12亿多，约占全球总人口的1/5，国际旅游收入为9000亿美元；到2020年，全球旅游总人数将为1618亿，国际旅游收入超过2万亿美元。到此时，旅游已经成为社会经济的重要载体。2020年世界旅游目的地前5名为：中国、美国、法国、西班牙、中国香港，总共接待全球旅游人数的29%；客源地前5名为：德国、日本、美国、中国、英国，市场比例和为39%"。（《旅游概论》，2000年）

**2020 年世界十大旅游目的地预测表**

| 国家和地区 | 接待旅游者人数（万人次） | 占世界市场份额（％） | 1995—2020 年增长率（％） |
|---|---|---|---|
| 中国 | 13710 | 8.6 | 8.0 |
| 美国 | 10240 | 6.4 | 3.5 |
| 法国 | 9330 | 5.8 | 1.8 |
| 西班牙 | 7100 | 4.4 | 2.4 |
| 中国香港 | 5930 | 3.7 | 7.3 |
| 意大利 | 5290 | 3.3 | 2.2 |
| 英国 | 5280 | 3.3 | 3.0 |
| 墨西哥 | 4890 | 3.1 | 3.6 |
| 俄罗斯联邦 | 4710 | 2.9 | 6.7 |
| 捷克共和国 | 4400 | 2.7 | 4.0 |
| 总计 | 70880 | 44.2 | |

而北京航空航天大学经济管理学院院长、北京循环经济促进会会长吴季松教授在其出版的《新循环经济学》一书中预测，到 2050 年，旅游业将成为新经济十大产业之首。他在书中说："旅游业、再制造产业等将成为 2050 年世界经济的十大产业。这十大产业，还包括生态修复业、热核聚变发电业、生态农业、海水淡化业、信息产业、新材料产业、海洋产业和医药产业。"

吴季松说："到 2050 年，随着世界循环经济的发展和循环经济体系的建成，必然带来一批循环型产业的发展，成为循环经济体系的支柱。传统产业依然存在，但都是按照循环经济理念，以高技术改造的产业。"

吴季松认为，旅游业是以可循环利用的旅游资源为主、低资源消耗的产业，旅游产业同样有节约资源与循环利用的问题。目前西欧已开始利用因特网跨国联系，在异国游客之间互换住房资源的做法，就是一种尝试。随着旅游业收入的逐年递增，到 2050 年，将是世界最大的产业。旅游业在世界经济中所占的重要地位，使其在后工业社会中担任越来越重要的顶梁柱角色。

再举中国大连的例子，该城市在把"浪漫之都"的商标注册后，又受到可口可乐公司早年注册商标时，未对谐音、模仿产品注册，而导致其竞争对手百事可乐商标出现的启发，接着把"浪漫之都"作为商标，对该市相关的 43 个系列产品领域进行全面注册。

这个城市的所有"产品"均可使用"浪漫之都"的商标，也就是旅游商标。

这一切都说明，旅游业的发展，在后工业时代，已渗透到人类的各个领域。正如朱昌勤先生在《很有思想力的报纸格言》一文中所言："人不分男女老少，地不分天南地北，只要人类能够涉及的，几乎无所不及，无所不包。"

甚至旅游理所当然成为人权的组成部分。2010年4月19日，欧盟企业及工业事务专员塔亚尼（Antonio Tajani）宣布，旅游是人权，欧盟将以公帑资助区内退休人士、年轻人和穷人去旅行。英国《星期日泰晤士报》报道——

塔亚尼上周在西班牙出席欧盟部长会议时公布有关计划："今时今日旅游已是权利。如何度假是我们生活质素的重要指标。"这计划还有助增加欧洲人对欧洲文化的自豪感，拉近南欧和北欧之间的分歧，以及为度假村在旅游淡季开拓客源。

这计划会试行到2013年，之后全面实施。有条件获资助旅游的人，包括退休人士、65岁或以上的长者、18~25岁年轻人、"面对社会、财政和个人问题"的家庭，以及残障人士。

首阶段会鼓励南欧人去北欧，或北欧人去南欧，细节仍有待确定，但预料欧盟会资助30%旅费，每年会花上数以亿计欧元。

人类发展的历史证明，不同地区、不同民族间的文化交往越频繁、越深刻，人类文明作为一个整体的力量也就越大，因为这种交流符合人类共同的追求和利益。

## 第三节
## 现实发展所预示的乐观前景

### 一、人类的交流已完成两次大的飞跃

迄今为止，人类的旅游活动已进行了两次大的飞跃——

第一次出现在工业革命时期。由于蒸汽机的发明，生产力得到大大提高，人们不仅有了更多的休闲时间，而且因为轮船、火车的出现，使得人们第一次脱离了以动物体力为源动力的交通工具时代。人们的旅游范围和旅游过程中的舒适度、安全度都发生了革命性的变化。尤其重要的是，旅游不再是少数人的专利，普通白领、

蓝领也踏上了旅游的征途，人类开始进入"大众旅游"时代。

人类旅游活动的第二次飞跃始于20世纪八九十年代。以信息技术革命为中心的高新技术的迅猛发展，不仅冲破了国界，加快了信息的交流和分享，而且缩小了地球的距离，使世界经济越来越融为一体即"经济全球化"。

经济全球化主要表现为贸易自由化、生产国际化、金融全球化和科技全球化。目前，经济全球化已显示出强大的生命力，并对世界各国经济、政治、军事、社会、文化等所有方面，甚至包括思维方式等，都造成了巨大的冲击。这是一场深刻的革命，任何国家都无法回避。

经济全球化不仅促动了现阶段人类资源、资金、技术、产品、市场的大规模流动，而且促动了人类前所未有的大规模的交流，人类由此从"大众旅游"时代进入到"全球旅游"时代。

虽然人们还无法预期人类旅游活动第三次飞跃的准确时间，但人类"核心价值观的统一"将是旅游活动第三次飞跃的重要标志，也是人类"地球村"真正实现的前提。

因为只有全人类"核心价值观的统一"，传统的政治、宗教矛盾才能基本消除，人类交流的成本才能降到最低，人类才能最大限度地将地球资源用于创造财富、发展科技、保护民族文化、促进各国公民自由交流即提升人类的整体力量上来。

到那时，世界各国的政治、经济和文化的发展变得相对均衡，人类的旅游活动不再受政治——自由往来、经济——每个人都有足够的费用、交通工具——一天之内到达地球任何一点等几乎所有条件的束缚，只需要战胜自己。

而这美好愿景的实现是快是迟，很大程度上取决于全人类的"自觉"行为。经济全球化的发展，为人类旅游整合世界的进程提供了迫切的需要，也提供了实现这种需要的现实条件和物质基础。

可以说，经济全球化，既是旅游整合世界得以展开的舞台，又为旅游整合世界的表演提供了道具。正是在经济全球化的作用之下，旅游整合世界才有机会和可能充分展示人类文化发展的一幕幕悲喜剧。

所以，旅游整合世界的过程性决定了人类文化的整合过程是贯穿经济全球化的长期过程。信息科技的革命性进步，以网络空间为主要特征的信息时代的来临，使得社会文化形式以前所未有的加速度进行更新。旅游整合世界就是在这种更新当中发挥着自己潜移默化的作用。

在全球化时代，人类文化的发展也表现出许多新的特征。主要为：文化多样性成为全球文化发展的主要表现形式；文化帝国主义成为全球文化发展的新问题；追求文化发展的先进性成为各种不同文化共同的目标。

例如，随着中国经济的崛起，中华民族的文化软实力成为媒体越来越热议的话题。"争夺话语权是中国融入世界的前提"。香港凤凰卫视掌门人刘长乐在一次文化论坛上如是说。

文明的冲突和融合是旅游整合世界的主要表现形式。经济全球化的飞速发展，为地域文化的碰撞与互动提供了更多机会，也为文明的冲突和融合的深入化提供了新的空间。正是在这种不同地域文化形式之间的冲突和变化中，旅游整合世界才得以逐渐实现。

不同民族之间互相尊重对方的文化，增进相互理解，使不同的文化互补，使本民族文化得到发展。对于文化差异，如果漫不经心，就会造成误解，严重者造成冲突就不足为奇了。

文化差异虽然会造成不同民族之间交流的障碍，可正是地球上有了文化差异的存在，世界才变得丰富多彩，才有了以各种各样的旅游活动为表现形式的人类的交往，人类才有了共享文明的机会。

李小龙是国际著名的华人武打明星。位于欧洲中部的波斯尼亚的莫斯塔尔市市中心广场几年前竖起一座李小龙雕像。波斯尼亚作家加塔诺认为这有助于消除文化差异和种族隔阂。他说："一个人眼中的英雄可能是另一个人眼中的坏人，但李小龙是一个真正的国际英雄，并且是波斯尼亚所有种族的英雄"。

在哲学上，文化冲突与文化融合是对立统一的关系。文化的冲突是文化融合得以实现的前提条件。只有通过异质文化之间的相互竞争和对立，人类文化才能在相互冲突中找到各自的优势与缺点，并在相互之间的取长补短中实现自身的进步，为文化融合的实现奠定前提和基础。

旅游整合世界的过程，就是人类文化的相互冲突的表现形式与相互融合的发展趋势之间，建立起来的一种富有张力的文化发展过程。

在人类旅游整合世界的不同阶段、不同层次，人类文化的冲突与融合具有不同的表现，各自包含其特殊的含义。但是从人类文化发展的长河来看，这种对立统一是人类社会进步的主要方式。

经济全球化时代的文化冲突，虽然也强调不同文化主体之间的差异性，强调不同文化形式的存在价值，但是在其中都开始重视吸收和借鉴异质文化形式中的有用成分，改善和提高自己的适应性和生命力。

可以这么说，人类文化的求同存异思想，在经济全球化时代表现得比以往任何时候都更加强烈。因为在各种不同地域文化的发展中，大家都开始对一些具有"普世性"的问题诸如全球意识、全球伦理、网络文化、大众文化、消费文化、生态文化、可持续发展理念、现代性理念等等，予以更多关注。

人们都在试图寻找一种具有普遍价值的文化形式，以解决人类社会共同面临的问题，或以此寻找巨大的政治和商业利益。可以说，这种对共同价值目标的追求，是人类文化的融合所要追求的理想境界。

## 二、"民族意识"正向"人类意识"过渡

正是在人类文化的流变与整合之中，人类文化形态不断发出新的面貌，体现新的形式，作为文化主体的人的文化特质也在这种摒弃与吸收之中，逐渐展现其特有的魅力。

乔布斯去世后，美联社说，他"是一位CEO，一位科技奇才，一位未来学家，一位革新者，一位铸造者"；对于乔布斯的成就，《华尔街日报》同样也作了个人英雄主义的解读。

有人把乔布斯的成功归功于美国的"制度"，那么，为什么有着相似"制度"的日本、欧洲没有产生乔布斯？甚至一样生活在美国，能和乔布斯站在同样高度的创新者也凤毛麟角。

传统上把这一切归结为"天才"，而如今，人们更乐意把这一现象看作是成功者的个人经历、理念、个性对创新在起着决定性作用，其中有很多因素对企业家是有特殊意义的。

中国著名经济学家叶檀女士把乔布斯的成功归咎为"完美融合中西方文化精华"。她认为，强大的技术团队，快捷的物流链条，全球的营销网络，是苹果成功的技术基础，而支撑乔布斯内在的强大精神力量却来自东方。

她在《每日经济新闻》报上著文称："乔布斯有信仰，佛教禅宗不仅让乔布斯拥有精神支撑，更让乔布斯拥有了简洁的人生目标与审美趣味，所有的苹果产品设计都体现出简洁流畅之美。苹果设计以其日本枯山水式的凝练意境，俘获了万众用户之心。他既不盲从世俗之见，也不盲目遵从自己的内心，而是以强大的精神开拓新的道路。"她认为在中国很少有企业家、哲学家融合两者，而乔布斯做到了。

叶檀说，甚至乔布斯的座右铭都是东方式的——"Stay Hungry, Stay Foolish"即"求知若渴，处事若愚"。这一箴言既符合儒家的教诲，也符合道家的内核。一个美国的企业家居然能够如此精准地抓住东方文化的内核，贯穿在自己所有的行动中，实在让人感慨。

美国影片《2012》在该国上映首个周末，就称霸各地票房榜，并在全球狂揽2.25亿美元。它在中国的票房打破了9天吸金2.1亿的纪录。导演艾默里奇曾充满自信说："我决心让这部影片成为灾难片之冠。"

《2012》电影的主题其实并不复杂——"人类即将毁灭，全球共拯灾难"。影片把全人类的命运捆绑在一起，片中充满多元文化的要素，从而引起全球观众的兴趣，制作方赚个盆满钵满，自然而然。

如今，越来越多的"人类意识觉醒者"把这一对人类的整体关切，灌输到形式多样的文化产品中。他们不单是为追求全球化背景下的市场最大化，更多体现的是关注人类未来命运的责任感和使命感。

中国著名洲际战略学家乐后圣先生在其所著《文化军事战略》中写道："在人类文明发展史上，新文明的形成都是原有的文明形态、方向上的一次大转折……因此，新文明的产生都是一场文明革命。"

而在人类的每一次大变革中，新派政治家、宗教家们都是不可或缺的强力推手。

《世界是平的》一书中说，全球发展可以划分为三个阶段：第一个阶段的主体是国家，第二个阶段的主体是跨国公司，第三个阶段的主体是个人。

也就是说，随着人类文明的发展，"群众创造历史"的时代真正来临。这不是否定个人的作用，相反，未来的世界是一个表现自我的年代，是一个由无数个"自我"组合起来唱主角的时代。

传统政治家们或许对日本频繁更换首相有些厌倦，或对俄罗斯的普京、梅德韦杰夫唱政治"二人转"颇有怨言，但在选民控制的世界里，政治人物无论是"昙花一现"还是"基业长青"，本质上都显示出他们是多么的"微不足道"——因为决定国家方向的不再是"个体"而是"整体"。

纵观历史，人类的发展由蒙昧走向文明，由神秘走向开放，由专制走向民主，这是谁也无法改变的规律。从某种程度来说，整个人类历史其实就是统治者与被统治者的矛盾史。

在历史的长河中，每当被统治者发明了一个新的、更强大的控制统治者的手段，人类的文明就进了一大步。例如工业革命给世界带来的现代民主制度，它给选民一张选票，这张选票神奇般地控制了统治者的张狂。

统治者控制被统治者的最大武器是垄断信息。在古代，书籍和教育是皇宫贵族的专利，一般平民难以企及；在今天，世界上一些独裁政府仍然是靠杜绝国民的外界信息作为延长专制统治的重要手段。

二次世界大战期间，希特勒前期之所以能够成功，最重要的原因就是他的宣传部长戈培尔通过玩弄信息，从而控制公民的大脑。二战后人们不允许统治者利用控制舆论来玩弄群众的大脑。在独立媒体的监督下，统治者对被统治者的信息优势越来越小。

人类进入 21 世纪的第一个十年，互联网发明国的美国因"维基解密"事件而巩固了其作为世界信息科技最发达国家的地位。2010 年 7 月 26 日，"维基解密"在《纽约时报》《卫报》和《镜报》配合下，在网上公开了多达 9.2 万份的驻阿美军秘密文件，引起轩然大波。

2011 年出版的《维基解密：阿桑奇和他的解密王国》一书写道："刚刚过去的

一年，无疑是维基解密网站声名鹊起的一年，更是世界政治和外交陷入空前大混乱的一年。9万份机密文件，揭开阿富汗战争杀戮平民的真相；40万份秘密战地日记，让美国彻底背上伊拉克战争的罪恶；1000余封顶级科学家的往来邮件，戳穿全球变暖的惊天谎言；25万份外交电报，让各国首脑形象尽失……掀起这一切的，只是一个人和一个网站。"

"真相通常是战争的第一个受害者，所以美国或更广泛的国际社会的公众有权知道真相。"阿桑奇如是说。35岁的阿桑奇于2006年12月创建"维基解密"网站，他相信信息的透明和自由交流会有效地阻止非法治理，这样才能对抗靠隐瞒真相来维持统治的政府。

阿桑奇的做法自然引起美国政客们的恼羞成怒。总统奥巴马谴责"维基解密"的做法"糟糕、悲哀"；国务卿希拉里在华盛顿发表评论说，"维基解密"公开密件的行为不合法，是对美国和国际社会的攻击，严重损害了国际的互信；美国司法部长霍尔德说："美国将根据反间谍法等相关法律就解密事件进行刑事调查和起诉。"

但阿桑奇的支持者却认为，"我们不但不该追捕他，还应把今年的普利策新闻奖颁发给他，他应该获得2011年的诺贝尔和平奖。"请看一篇2010年12月14日，媒体刊发的《全球60万维基解密支持者网上签名请愿力挺阿桑奇》专稿：

据澳大利亚新闻网、法新社12月14日消息，"维基解密"网站创始人阿桑奇即将在伦敦二次出庭受审，日前，全球约60万维基解密网站支持者在网上签名请愿，希望伦敦法院不要打击阿桑奇及其合作者。

这项请愿行动是由全球采取行动组织Avaaz面向全球发起的，目的是向伦敦法院及有关方面请愿，"立即停止打击'维基解密'，不要惩罚阿桑奇及其合作者"，"尊重信息自由、新闻自由"。

截至格林尼治标准时间13日下午4时，已经有59.4万人在这份网上请愿书上签名，估计目前签名者人数早已突破60万。（国际在线）

与此同时，在美国《时代周刊》年度风云人物评选的网站上，阿桑奇得票位居所有候选人之首，得到28万票，领先第二名6万票，是第三名得票数的两倍多。

对于阿桑奇来说，他打的是"一个人的战争"——网络信息自由战。这场战争剑指三个方向：第一个方向是针对战争中虐杀民众的行径予以反对，第二个方向是反对政府在国际行为中隐瞒人民的黑暗行为，第三个方向是反对垄断银行对人民的剥夺行为。

阿桑奇认为，政府和大机构隐藏了太多秘密，使得传统报道难以平衡，因此他希望通过自己的努力来改变现实。他还批评传统媒体被政府所主导，不能将调查深入下去，因此自己的工作是为了自由而奋斗。

这就是"维基解密"的历史意义，它向传统政客们发起挑战，旨在要夺下他们在信息领域的最后优势。这场战斗的胜利果实有多大目前还不好预测，但国家之间政治走向更文明的时代来到了。

这是一个人类文明进步的转折点。"维基解密"标志着人类政治文明已经全速进入信息时代。统治者不得不忌惮他们的政治行为而最大程度置于民众的监督之下。正如阿桑奇自己所说的那样："此次行动将会改变世界历史"。

对于大众而言，通过"维基解密"，可以窥见国家机器、情报机构如何有恃无恐、肆无忌惮；窥见国际政治暗流涌动，八卦横行，从而消解统治者长期以来赖以依靠的神秘感和权威性。

"维基解密"就如同一个脆弱的鸡蛋，但鸡蛋能将石头——权力击倒，技术无疑起到了决定性的作用。在互联网时代，每一个人都能成为信息的发布者，"维基解密"正是借助了全球网民的力量，将信息发布到自己搭建的平台上，公开传播，才造成了异常轰动的效应。

"维基解密"只可能产生在互联网时代。作为传统媒体的报纸、杂志、电台、电视台都易于被强权操控，而互联网作为媒体被操纵的可能性就大大降低了，尤其是推特（Twitter）等自媒体的出现，使每个人可成为独立媒体，这时候政府想管理就力不从心了。

的确，经过无数个"个体"的推动，"维基解密"已经不仅仅是一个网站，它已然蜕变为一种"可怕"的政治力量。"潘多拉魔盒"已打开，一切才刚刚开始，好戏还在后面！

正当"维基解密"掀起的冲天大浪余波未平，美国又爆发了另一场影响全球的事件——"占领华尔街"运动。

2011年9月17日，上千名示威者聚集在美国纽约曼哈顿，试图占领华尔街。他们通过互联网组织起来，要把华尔街变成埃及的解放广场。示威者称，他们的意图是要反对美国政治的权钱交易、两党政争以及社会不公正。

示威者们最著名的口号是："我们都是99%"。他们强调，99%的美国人被金融危机剥夺了财产，剩下的1%的人却依然拥有一切；99%的人不能再忍受1%的人的贪婪。

不到三个星期里，星火燎原，"占领华尔街"运动爆发成一个全美性的大规模民众抗议活动。200多个美国城市积极呼应，纷纷举行了持久的抗议活动。

欧洲、亚洲、大洋洲、南美洲也爆发了民众响应的集会，"占领华盛顿"、"占领伦敦"、"占领墨尔本"，甚至"占领台北"等活动也开始露出了苗头。北京时间10月6日，中国河南郑州的几百名市民在文化宫门前打起横幅，声援地球另一侧的那场"伟大的华尔街革命"。

10月6日的白宫新闻发布会上，美国总统奥巴马第一次对"占领华尔街"运动做出了回应。"我理解公众对于国家金融系统工作的关心，示威者们表达的是自己沮丧的情绪。"他说，"美国人看到，作为金融行业的一个样本，华尔街并不总是能遵守规则。"

这位美国历史上第一位黑人总统最为示威者诟病的决定是，2008年金融危机时对银行展开了高达7870亿美元紧急救助。当时很多人以为，根据救市政策，自己会从这些流向华尔街的资金中获益。但随后，他们对此却没有明显的感受，华尔街却照样派发高额的红利。

美国经济学者奥尔森20多年前在其名著《国家的盛衰》中指出，在一个强盛的国家中，某些行业即特殊利益集团，会不断积蓄力量，用金钱等实力去影响政府，使政府的政策向该行业倾斜，从而获致更多金钱，再进一步用来影响政府决策。

美国的金融集团，正是这样一种在近年依靠其巨大实力为自己争得政策倾斜，以致过度发展的特殊利益集团。次贷危机后，美国会去年通过了加强金融规管的《多德弗兰克法案》。但华尔街以其强大游说力量施压国会和政府，长时间的博弈妥协，减弱了法案力量。

在欧洲，也有类似的不公。英国示威者珍妮·麦金太尔在接受路透社记者采访时说："我们不要一个建立在取悦大商贾、偏袒金融系统基础上的所谓民主，这不是民主。"

"这不是资本主义，不是市场经济，而是一个扭曲的经济。"哥伦比亚大学经济学教授、诺贝尔经济学奖得主约瑟夫·斯蒂格利茨支持示威者说，"如果这种形势继续下去，我们就无法实现增长，也无法成功创造一个公正的社会。"

日本《行政调查新闻》评论称，一小撮的富裕阶层统治着国家，很多人在贫困当中喘息，"资本主义国家的多数是这样的状态，由此产生的不满正在世界掀起波澜"。

中国现代国际关系研究院学者袁鹏认为："在21世纪，全球公民社会将经历又一轮觉醒，各国人民在这一过程中表达出共同的诉求，无论哪种体制都不能例外。"

出人意料的是，这场声势浩大、席卷全球的"占领华尔街"运动却是一场没有确定的领袖，没有系统的组织，没有惑人的口号，甚至没有明确的目标的"漫散"运动。

在示威活动的前两周，美国媒体对这次运动的报道寥寥无几。在10月5日，全美500份纸质报纸的首页上只有60份（也就是12%）报道了有关占领华尔街的游行。这让很多人猜测："大财团和华尔街大鳄的关系太好，屏蔽了新闻报道"。

而活动的"组织者"倒是对此充满理解——"对于媒体而言，很难报道这个运动，因为这是一场没有领导的示威。"在9月的一次采访中，帕特里克·布鲁纳说。

布鲁纳是整个"占领华尔街"运动的媒体公关负责人，同时，也是一个刚毕业却找不到工作的大学生，并且在运动开始后才加入，当了志愿者。在大多数媒体的报道里，这个23岁的瘦瘦的年轻人，就是示威者们的"官方代表"。

"有些人不拿我们当回事，觉得我们只是个小运动，并且马上会结束。"一位示威者比克在接受媒体采访时说，"而我们能做的只有一件事：用事实让他们睁开眼睛。"

香港凤凰卫视著名评论员阮次山先生在回答主持人提问时说："产生这场占领华尔街的风潮我们现在还不能说他是一场运动，运动要有组织者，要有领袖，要有适当的口号，可是占领华尔街这个风潮到现在除了他是乌合之众以外，看不出是谁在后面主导，看不出他领袖何在，看不出风潮所宣誓的什么样意义。"

这显然是在用传统的眼光扫描新问题！事实上，在从工业社会迈入信息社会的人类大变革当中，许多"精英"还无法真正洞察人类文明即将发生的前所未有的革命性转变。

与之前人类经历过的所有时代相比，信息社会的到来，无数个"自我"形成的澎湃力量，是任何壁垒都无法阻挡的。在信息社会，"意见领袖"就是最高的领袖，网络就是最大的组织。

甚至无须提升到"意见领袖"的高度，有时一个小小的"P（屁）民"，只要他的思想能放出光芒，就可能点燃世界范围内的熊熊大火，像"维基解密"的阿桑奇一样。

这一次的矛头是指向金融界，下一次可能又是另一个领域。他们不想推翻谁。正如美国总统奥巴马所说："为了让现实符合理想，经常需要说出令人难受的事实，并以非暴力抗争创造紧张局势。"

与传统社会相比，网络在集合力量方面变得简单而有效率。每个人都是领导者，每个人都是组织者，人类"自觉"意识的表达找到了最有价值的载体，从而形成推动变革的力量。

2011年11月16日，美国近140名百万富翁请求国会，为国家考虑，应向他们多征税。

据英国媒体报道，这些企业和商界领袖向总统奥巴马及国会领袖致函称："请做这件正确的事，提高对我们的征税。"信中提到，良好的经济曾让他们受益，现在也希望别人能得到好处。

这封信由"财政力量之爱国富豪团"（Patriotic Millionaires for Fiscal Strength）的138名成员联名签署。该组织一年前成立，当时旨在说服国会终止前总统小布什实施的富人减税政策，不过未获得成功。

"占领华尔街"运动远未结束之际,该组织又向由12名国会议员组成的"超级委员会"提出同样要求。他们正努力使两党达成协议,未来10年至少减赤1.2万亿美元,以帮助美国财政走上健康的轨道。

Computervision Corp创始人维勒斯(Phil Villers)称:"我们中能承受税收增加的人应该站出来,这是我们要向'超级委员会'传递的信息,希望他们可以听取。"

要评估"占领华尔街"运动的影响还为时太早。这样一个影响世界的激荡的民权运动,会在相当长时间内不断深化沉淀,然后才会显出其意义及在社会历史发展中的地位。

但是,无论是"维基解密",还是"占领华尔街"运动,它们对推动人类朝向更加透明、公正、民主的未来具有无可争辩的正面意义。这两件影响人类的大事同是发生在美国,绝不是偶然的事。

美国是互联网最发达的国家,是信息社会的引领者,美国同时又是工业化时代西方民主制度的楷模。上帝其实非常宠幸美利坚,"维基解密"和"占领华尔街"从某种角度看来,是美国完成从工业文明时代到信息文明时代跨越的重要标志。

如果把"维基解密"称作"线上",那么"占领华尔街"运动就是"线下",这种线上线下的互动,使得传统政客们只有招架之功而无还手之力。

正如德国媒体报道:"'维基解密''四两拨千斤',压制了全世界最强大的政府。而博弈的另一方,却始终无法找到对付'维基解密'的有效方法,只能停留在一次次的谴责声讨上。"

传统政客们的形象在"维基解密"和"占领华尔街"运动的夹击下,跌到了历史的最低点。他们从未有像现在这样带着丑陋的"伤疤"在世界公民面前来回"裸奔"。

"维基解密"和"占领华尔街"运动发起后,韩国一份最新公布的民意调查结果显示,近九成韩国人不信任国内政治和政治家——

韩国联合通讯社16日援引韩国政府特任长官办公室所作的这份调查报道,1018名韩国成年人和730名青少年接受调查,87.1%的受访成年人和85.6%的受访青少年不信任政治和政治家。

调查报告说,40多岁的成年人怀疑程度最深,91.6%的受访者不信任政治家;30多岁人群和50多岁人群中这一比例分别为91%和87.6%。

10岁至29岁人群中,85%的受访者对政治持怀疑态度;而60岁以上的老年人较为信任政治,不到80%的人表示怀疑态度。

调查问及韩国政府针对与朝鲜的统一政策和双边关系时,年长者的回答更为温和。(京华时报2011年10月17日)

如此，这是信息社会里公民对政治人物的故意刁难，还是传统政客们的命运走到了历史的尽头?! 这不能不说是信息社会全体社会成员都应该认真思考并予以回答的问题。

欧盟的成立曾经是欧洲人引以为傲，世界其他地区争相模仿的人类文明进步的样板，但欧债危机的爆发，使得人们又不得不对其到底存在哪些问题进行认真的考察和探究。

香港凤凰卫视评论员吕宁思先生在电视上评论指出："欧债危机将倒逼欧洲政治改革。"很显然，他认为问题的根源还是出在欧洲的政治家们身上。

吕宁思的这一观点似乎也得到了在北京访问的法国外长朱佩的支持。朱外长说："欧洲这么多国家使用统一的货币却没有统一的金融货币体制与税率体制，又怎么能够保证欧元稳定呢？"

所以朱佩再次提出了他的想法，也就是法国人的想法，那就是在欧洲应该实行统一的联邦制，就像一个国家那样进行统一的行政管理。问题是，关于像美利坚合众国那样建立一个欧罗巴合众国，这已经是个陈旧的理想了。

二战结束之后的1950年5月9日，时任法国外交部长的舒曼就建议创建统一的欧洲。经过几十年的努力，欧盟逐渐壮大，欧元终于诞生，已经是大大的向统一迈进了。

但是欧洲与北美不同，美国是由东部几个英语殖民地逐渐扩大起来的，没有历史的负担，而欧洲则由多个不同民族，不同语言的国家所组成，继承事实诉求多多。

所以从二战之后就提出来的欧洲一体化，由于冷战和经济政治发展不平衡等诸多原因，特别是有些国家的民众——与其说是民众，不如说是政治家们对大一统的抗拒，欧洲大陆在政治上的统一一直都是步履维艰。

为什么这个被誉为代表着人类发展方向，并被世界其他地区颇有羡慕的区域政治联盟组织，在关系到其生命线的经济领域，却显得是如此脆弱和步调不一致呢？

意大利罗马东部的山丘小镇菲力亭诺镇镇长赛拉利似乎一语中的："谁都想当王公贵族！"这是他在意大利政府为节省开支，有意合并全国近2000个小镇时作如此表示的。而菲力亭诺想借此独立。

不仅针对欧洲，赛拉利先生的话击中了世界上所有传统政客们的要害——虽然人类止大步进入信息时代，经济全球化和文化全球化的浪潮汹涌澎湃，可许多传统政客仍然沉湎于对权力迷恋和对财富贪婪的陈旧游戏而不能自拔。

中国科学院资深国际问题专家资中筠女士在其著作中质问："今后超国界、超民族，需要共同应付的天灾人祸定会层出不穷。各国政治家何时能超出狭隘、自私的'国家利益'的惯性思维和强权政治、损人利己——其实也损己的行为模式？"

世界永恒不变的是变。政治家会消失，但政治不会消失。人类历史的每一次时代的跨越，都离不开那一个时代的以新派政治家、宗教家为代表的社会精英们的助推。

历史又到了转折关头，从工业文明时代到信息文明时代的跨越，与人类历史上的任何一次跨越都有不同。在经济和文化全球化的强劲浪潮冲击下，这是人类的一次整体跨越。

在我们这样一个伟大的时代，对以新派政治家、宗教家为代表的精英们的描绘，很难不与历史有所区分。准确地说，他们是"人类意识觉醒者。"这些"人类意识觉醒者"比常人更有远见卓识，他们对人类的发展规律了然于胸，他们的所作所为的出发点和归宿都是全人类。

"我们下代的子孙恐怕很难相信，世界上真有过这样一个人。"这是20世纪最伟大的物理学家爱因斯坦所说。他说的这个人名叫"英·甘地"。今天看来，英·甘地可谓世界上最伟大的"觉醒者"之一。

美国一位政治家曾经评价他："英·甘地之所以至今在世界上还拥有这么多的尊敬，是因为他考虑问题从来不是从一个国家或民族的利益出发，而是从全人类出发。"

纵观世界伟人的队伍，甘地确实是特别中的特别，宗教与政治在他身上融合一气，他的思想又似乎是东方传统文化与西方近代思想激烈碰撞之后产生的火花。甘地说："我努力通过为人类服务看到上帝，因为我知道，上帝既不在天上，也不在地下，而在每个人心中。"

世界各国中有着"国父"之称的人物不在少数，但如甘地般竭力宣扬"非暴力"革命的人，寥寥无几。而且他做到了。他的非暴力学说和实践，不仅影响了印度民族独立运动，而且影响了美国黑人民权运动。

马丁·路德·金曾说："随着我对甘地哲学的钻研，我对爱的力量的怀疑逐渐消失。我第一次认识到，通过甘地非暴力方法所付诸实施的基督教的爱的法则，是被压迫民族争取自由的最有效的武器之一。这一原则成为我们运动的指路明灯。基督提供了精神和动机，而甘地提供了方法。"

美国总统奥巴马2011年10月16日在为马丁·路德·金铜像揭幕时说："我从甘地那里学到的一件事是，你必须坚持你的旅程，你必须继续努力，永不说放弃。甘地、马丁·路德·金和亚伯拉罕·林肯是我们不懈了解和学习的对象。但我经常为远不如他们而感到沮丧。"

奥巴马的这种"沮丧"应该受到鼓励。他让我们看到，虽然到目前为止，在人类文明的天空中，"人类意识觉醒者"的星光还有些稀疏，但我们应该有百分之一百的信心相信，总有一天会"繁星满天"。

与传统政客相比，"人类意识觉醒者"除了具有非同一般的远见卓识外，还更有强烈的正义感和羞耻感。例如，当"占领华尔街"运动风起云涌之时，英国外交大臣威廉·黑格说他"有些同情"示威者；当"占领华尔街"运动蔓延到美国西部最大城市洛杉矶时，该市议会通过决议，支持"占领洛杉矶"示威活动……

香港凤凰卫视《读书》栏目主持人梁文道先生在讽刺传统政客时说："传统版本里皇帝不知道自己没有穿衣服，但是我们现在是知道他没有穿衣服，而且他照样还走出来，他知道我们知道他没有穿衣服，但是他就出来，他就在那满街晃，我们也看着他满街晃，我们还照样装着他穿着衣服。"

而"人类意识觉醒者"的"耻感"则表现为他们把公权力全部用以创造和维护人类透明、公正和民主的社会环境，以积极开放的心态推动人类的发展、融合。他们常为自己的能力不足而懊恼，他们会为自己的半点私心杂念而愧疚。

我们在前面谈到，在现今世界上，由于各国的历史、政治、经济、文化还存在不同，人类还不能同步进入民主社会，甚至，"先进的"与"落后的"还存在巨大的差距。

但在信息社会的阳光普照下，我们会轻而易举看到，"人类意识觉醒者"的种子无论飘到肥沃的土壤上，还是落在贫瘠的田地里，都一定能生根发芽，茁壮成长！

事实上，自欧洲启蒙运动以来，一些超越一国一族的狭隘情感、具有世界情怀的政治家和知识分子，和一些由于种种原因，游走于世界各地的各色人士，就把自己叫做"世界公民"。

在英国培格曼公司出版的《邓小平文集》序言中，中国改革开放的总设计师邓小平就曾满怀深情地说："我荣幸地以中华民族一员的资格，而成为世界公民。"

但是，在民族国家时代，尤其是冷战时期，世界隔着重重壁垒的时候，对大多数地球人来说，"世界公民"显然只是个遥远的概念。现在不同了，人类已经进入了"全球化"时代，信息科技的革命让世界已经变成了"地球村"。

可以说，人人都成了"世界公民"，即使他没有跨出国门，也可能会受到外部世界的影响，也可能会对他国居民产生影响，更不用说那些经常往来于不同国家的人了。

人类发展的历史证明，政治的力量常常产生地域的壁垒，宗教的力量又往往导致心灵的隔阂，只有旅游，才能使不同种族、不同信仰、不同文化的人们走到一起，共同分享人类的文明成果。

在古代，强势的一方往往在取得战争胜利后，将自己的文化和信仰直接移植到被占领的领土上，强迫战败的一方接受。而人类文明发展到今天，这种现象几乎不再存在。

2011年，在北约空军的卖力轰炸下，经过长达8个月的战斗，利比亚反对派终于推翻了卡扎菲的独裁统治。赢得政权的"过度委员会"表示，新利比亚将以伊斯兰教立国，并暗示将实行一夫多妻制。

这令一开始便积极支持利比亚"民主斗争"的世界人士大跌眼镜。因为这实在是与民主社会格格不入的行为。这充分说明，一场战争，很难改变根深蒂固的文化。人们寄希望于新利比亚人与外部世界的更多交流。

2011年10月21日，85岁高龄，与美国等西方世界作斗争达半个世纪之久的古巴前领导人菲德尔·卡斯特罗在其官方网站上说："一场核战争的爆发，伴随的将是人类的毁灭""我们应当有勇气要求取消所有的核武器、常规武器，以及一切可以作为武器的东西"。

相信卡斯特罗的话是发自肺腑之言。人类文明发展到今天，经济全球化已经实现，文化全球化也在进行之中，传统历史中靠武力强占别国领土、消灭异族文化的政治生态几乎不能再生。任何政治决策者都不能以任何理由、也没有任何资格使用核武器。即使偶尔产生动用核子武器念头，都是一种反人类的行为。

2014年4月1日，美国《财富》双周刊网站发表一篇标题为《中国游客推动美国企业发展》的报道，记者史蒂夫·哈格里夫斯在新闻中写道：

去年，成千上万的中国游客蜂拥而至黄石国家公园，观看山景、水牛和老忠实间歇泉。

之后，至少有1600人向东跋涉200英里，来到尤克罗斯的牧场，在那里享用汉堡、烤豆和饼干。午饭后，他们欣赏了14岁的凯蒂·威廉表演的骑术。

牧场主人朱迪·布莱尔说："她的表演让他们疯狂，两国间的所有政治问题都烟消云散了。"

希伯来大预言家弥赛亚2500年前曾在耶路撒冷做出预言：终有一天，人们将把刀剑铸成犁头，把枪矛打成镰刀，国家之间不再拔剑相向，人世间不再有战争。

## 三、"世界政府"形成的基础日益巩固

"世界政府"的建立并不是一个新鲜的政治话题。早在古希腊和古罗马时期，就曾讨论过建立"世界政府"的想法。古代希腊人和罗马人预言有一天，人类为了永久和平将有且只有一个共同的政治权威。

荷兰法学家格劳秀斯在1625年写的《战争和和平法》（*De Jure Belli ac Pacis*）一书，被视为现代国际法的起源。"联邦"的概念在18世纪末赢得了不少的支持。更为突出的是，这一时期，世界上第一个民主联邦——美国，于1788年诞生了。

一直以来，欧洲的许多哲学家受到了相关思想的影响，创造了类似的理论，尤其是德国哲学家伊曼努尔·康德，他在1795年写下了《论永久和平》的短文，在这篇短文里，康德描述了人类永久废除未来战争威胁的三个基本条件：

- 每一个国家的公民宪法都应当是共和制（Republican）的。
- 国际法应当建立在自由国家的联邦制之上。
- 世界公民法应当依据普遍受到友好接待的条件加以限定。例如人们可以参观其他的国家，但未经邀请不能停留。

1811年，德国哲学家卡尔·克里斯蒂安·弗里德里希·克劳泽在其一篇名为《人类原型》的短文中，建议设立五个地区联盟：欧洲、亚洲、非洲、美洲和大洋洲，然后结合成一个世界共和国。

借鉴美国的经验，在1848年和1867年，瑞士和加拿大也分别建立起了第一批多国联盟，将不同种族、不同文化和不同语言的各民族统一在了一个共同的政府内。

随着"世界政府"理念的影响日益扩大，并因此诞生了许多国际组织。例如，红十字国际委员会成立于1863年，国际电信联盟成立于1865年，万国邮政联盟成立于1874年。

人类进入20世纪后，由于不断增加的国际贸易，各国之间的倚靠关系日益紧密，从而加速了国际组织的形成。据有关资料显示，在1914年的"一战"爆发前，共有大概450个全球性或地区性组织。

与此同时，为了配合国际组织的发展，国际法研究也取得了大的进步。1873年，比利时法学家Gustave Rolin－Jaequemyns建立了世界上第一个国际法研究院，领导并起草具体的国际法草案。

第一个世界议会的雏形"各国议会联盟"（Inter－Parliamentary Union）也在1886年由克里默和帕西开始组织，由许多国家的议员组成。1904年，这个联盟正式提议成为"一个定期讨论国际问题的国际国会"。

从古到今，政治人物向来是"世界政府"的践行者。著名的例子有亚历山大大帝及其帝国、罗马帝国、蒙古帝国和大英帝国。就大英帝国来说，它最辉煌时期拥有世界四分之一的土地和将近三分之一的人口，被誉为"日不落帝国"。这是世界曾经最接近一个共同政治体的时期。

巴哈欧拉在1852年和1892年之间，创建了巴哈伊教，并为他的新宗教确定了一个建立全球联邦的重要原则。

巴哈欧拉基于全球人民共享和共商的基础，设想了一套新的社会体系，包括一个世界立法机构，一个国际法庭和一个国际行政机构来执行立法和司法机构的决定。他的准则还包括世界通用的度量衡，统一货币，并使用一个国际辅助语言来交流。

令人遗憾的是，靠政治和宗教的力量试图建立起来的完整的世界政府，从来就没有存在过。在20世纪的前50年，企图通过建立全球性的机构，来解决国际争端的尝试，也以失败告终。

最让世人悲摧的是1899年和1907年的《海牙公约》及1919年和1938年的

"国际联盟",均未能阻止两次世界大战的发生。之后的"冷战"时期也证明,在人类的综合发展并不成熟和核心价值观存在差异的条件下谋求统一的"世界政府"无异于同床异梦。

不过,即使历经一次又一次的挫折和失败,人类追求成立"世界政府"的脚步却从未停止。相反,从"二战"行将结束到1950年,这一时期造就了"世界联邦主义运动"的黄金时期。

温德尔·威尔基的书《一个世界》,在1943年第一次出版就卖出了超过200万本。另一本作者名叫埃默里·里夫斯的《和平析》,因其在书中宣扬用"世界联邦政府"取代联合国的观点,使该书迅速成为世界联邦主义者心目中的"圣经"。

1947年在瑞士的蒙特勒召开会议,从而形成一个全球性的联合会,即World Federalist Movement,也是一个有影响的国际组织。到1950年,该组织声称在22个国家拥有56个成员组,并有156 000位成员。

1948年,该组织创始人格瑞·大卫(音译)在联合国大会上未经许可发表演讲,呼吁建立一个"世界政府",却以被警卫赶出大会而告终。随后,大卫先生放弃美国公民身份并开始注册成为世界公民,不到两年内便有超过75万人也注册成为了世界公民。

1953年9月4日,大卫在美国缅因州的埃尔斯沃思市政厅宣布,"世界政府"基于三个"世界法律",即同一上帝、同一世界和同一人类,并为此在纽约成立了"联合世界管理局",首要任务便是设计和发行世界护照。据悉,到目前为止,全世界共发行了超过80万本这样的护照。

但大卫先生的想法和做法显然没有发展的后劲。"同一上帝"便是一种不符合世界多元化潮流的"霸道"之举,仍然没有脱离宗教"整合"世界的陈旧藩篱,且同人类文明背道而驰,因为人类文明进步的标志之一便是信仰自由。

康涅狄格圣三一大学的社会学家杰姆斯·胡戈(音译)是全球政府的支持者,他认为这是顺应时势的必然选择。

胡戈说:"本世纪内应该会出现新的,为政治一体化服务的经济、文化和通信力量,而灾难性的重大威胁会让成立全球政府体系成为一种刚性需求"。他所指的"灾难性的重大威胁",指的是全球气候变化、恐怖主义和新兴科技给人类所造成的威胁。

关于可能实现的政治实体——世界政府的理念,人们普遍认为,这个政治实体解释并执行国际法,现有的国家要逐步削弱和放弃某些权力。这当然要和前面所提到的"人类意识"的增强同步进行。

令人欣喜的是,不管主权国家愿意不愿意,历史的车轮总是滚滚向前。例如,WTO的出现,就在经济领域"剥夺"了主权国家的部分经济权力。

事实上,"世界政府"将在现有的国家主权上新增一级行政级别,或为不同国家提供独立国家无法提供的协调。信息社会的来临,地球村的实现,都为"世界政府"的出现提供了必要性和可能性。

如今,越来越多的人视一些国际机构,例如国际刑事法院、联合国和国际货币基金组织,以及各种超国家和大陆联合体,例如美洲国家组织、欧盟、非盟、南美洲国家联盟和东盟等为世界政府体系的雏形。

与早期相比,这些国际组织或机构在推动人类融合和协调国际事务等方面所起的作用不可同日而语。这并非是现代人比过去的人更聪明,而是全球政治、经济、科技、文化发展的结果使然。

中国有句古话:"强扭的瓜不甜",另一句相应的话则是"水到渠成"。目前,世界上存在的各种组织,都是推动人类融合的外因,人类文明的整体进步,才是各种组织抑或"世界政府"得以实现价值的内在根本。

尤其是人类进入信息社会,随着经济和文化的全球化,人类融合和文明共享的澎湃潮流也必将推动诸政治实体合并在一起。正如胡戈所指出的那样,不管有没有敌对势力,历史的推动都将我们指向了全球政府的大方向。

对于各类国际组织而言,当人类旅游活动第三次飞跃到来的时候,"世界政府"不是出不出现的问题,而是谁将有机会主导"世界政府"成立的问题,它的"牵头人"是联合国、欧盟、七国集团?抑或其他国际组织。

第二次世界大战造成了5000万人的伤亡,而且大部分是平民。随着战争接近尾声,许多仁人志士呼吁建立能永久防止冲突的国际机构,这导致了联合国在1945年的成立,并在1948年通过了世界人权宣言。

联合国是一个由主权国家组成的综合性国际组织,到2012年为止,共有193个成员国。在"冷战"时期,联合国在维护世界安全、推动人类和平方面取到了不可替代的作用。目前,在国际政治等诸多领域仍有着举足轻重的地位。

一些著名的人士,像爱因斯坦、丘吉尔、罗斯福和甘地等,呼吁各国政府采取进一步措施,来逐步形成一个有效管理世界的"世界政府"。不过,他们所谓的"世界政府"是撇开现有的联合国另起炉灶,还是将联合国进一步改造,不得而知。

从眼下来看,联合国确实面临来自各方的挑战。"冷战"结束之后,仍按传统老路走的联合国,发现路已越来越窄。许多国家拒缴或拖延会费便是一个明证。而2013年10月18日,沙特阿拉伯拒绝担任联合国安理会非常任理事国一事更是凸显了联合国在新时期的危机。

沙特阿拉伯外交部在声明中说,鉴于在过去数十年来安理会未能有效推动中东和平,又未能结束叙利亚内乱,该国拒绝接受任命。声明还对安理会的"能力、作风和机制"提出了质疑。

BBC驻联合国记者说，外交官们对沙特作出的这一史无前例的决定感到震惊和不解。法国常驻联合国代表阿罗德对法新社记者说，法国认为沙特阿拉伯能给安理会带来非常积极的贡献，但也完全理解沙特的不满。

面对联合国越来越松散以及越来越缺乏权威性的现实，虽然联合国内部不少精英也越来越意识到联合国转型的迫切性，但面对纷繁复杂的国际形势，又似乎方向不明，无从下手。

2012年12月，笔者受联合国记者协会邀请，赴纽约参加其一年一度的颁奖会。会上该协会向包括联合国秘书长在内的500余位嘉宾，赠送了拙作和笔者关于倡议联合国颁发"联合国旅游护照"的书面演讲，引起了诸多与会人士的共鸣。

隔日，联合国有关机构再次邀请笔者，为部分联合国官员作"联合国旅游护照"的专题演讲。笔者在演讲中指出，"冷战"结束后，联合国应从传统解决矛盾、避免战争逐步转型到推动人类融合和文明共享的轨道上来；应从传统的服务国家和团体逐步转型到服务地球公民的轨道上来。

笔者认为，"联合国旅游护照"的颁发，则是这种转型的最重要标志之一。因为人类经济全球化已经实现，文化全球化也已经开始。"联合国旅游护照"的推行，无疑将大大推动人类的融合和进步，并推动人类旅游活动第三次飞跃的加速到来！

毋庸置疑，"世界政府"是由"世界公民"组成的。一个公民的"公民权"属于一个国家的政治主权范畴。像WTO向各国"剥夺"部分经济主权一样，联合国目前是"分享"主权国家部分政治权力的最佳组织。

实际上，欧盟国家正在实行的申根护照，从某种程度来说，就是"小联合国旅游护照"。虽然与欧盟相比，颁发"联合国旅游护照"难度要大得多，但只要世界各国统一认识，从金字塔端开始向下有步骤地进行，技术性操作并无难题。

联合国若能审时度势，利用现有的独一无二的政治优势，颁发"联合国旅游护照"，不仅能加大世界公民对联合国的向心力，还能为联合国未来主导"世界政府"的构建增加竞争的筹码。

更为重要的是，当最终有一天，世界上所有的公民都拥有"联合国旅游护照"时，我们千百年来赖以生存的这个地球还会有战争吗？这种想法和做法，难道不是和联合国当初成立的理念相吻合？！

与欧盟相比，联合国机构庞大、效率低下、腐败滋生历来为众人所诟病，若不进行大的改革，这一切必将会成为其今后试图主导建立"世界政府"的显著障碍。相反，欧盟很可能会以丰富的经验、高效的管理和廉洁的组织，赢得未来世界公民对它的青睐。

何况，联合国还有一个致命的短板，那就是在较长时间内，仍将是世界"头号大国"的美国，对它已越来越嗤之以鼻。这就要看联合国在全球管理民主化潮流面前，能否进行华丽的转身，从而把命运牢牢掌握在自己手里！

2012年，诺贝尔和平奖首次授予欧盟，这既是对它一路走来所取得的成果的褒赞，更预示着它有着强大的发展远景。欧盟内部虽然还存在各种不利因素，但经历了两次世界大战洗礼的欧洲人，在世界人民面前率先走出了一条消除分歧，避免战争，共享经济与文化繁荣的和平途径，实为世界其他地区的样板。

当然，随着人类历史的进步，其他国际组织的迅速崛起也并非没有可能。尤其是人类进入信息社会，网络本身就是最大的组织。当在民主浪潮的冲击下，政治人物越来越成为一种象征和摆设时，"世界政府"的形成或另辟蹊径，并不是天方夜谭！

人类的经验和教训都证明，要建立一个有机统一的"世界政府"，离不开全球化背景下新文明的形成。中国学者裴勇先生在《文明的整合》中写道：

"建立一种新的全球文明、建立一个新的世界无疑更为需要一种全球范围的新文化的培育、形成并深入人心。这个新文化无疑应该是代表世界未来发展的先进文化。这个新文化既不是'全盘西化'、也不是'全盘东化'、既不是全盘'欧化'、全盘'美化'，也不是全盘'黄化'、全盘'绿化'。因为，世界各种文明没有一种文化是完全适应未来世界发展的纯粹的先进文化。新的先进文化必然是一种南北互补、东西合璧的新型文化。在未来的全球文明建立起来的社会里，后现代化是其主要特征。这个新社会需要一种生态的、平衡的、平等的、合和的新文化，它将兼收并蓄，集各种文明精髓之大成。他的建立和培育将是全球文明得以建立的重要基础，是世界未来的先进文化……世界经济一体化与世界文化一体化必是同步的，这种交易、交流、融合是悄无声息的，潜移默化——润物细无声的。"

旅游是能达到此目的的唯一方式。

旅游整合世界，人类共享文明！

# Chapter 1
## General Introduction

# Taj Mahal

泰姬陵

# Section 1

## Tourism is a result which combines human beings' instinctive attribute and social attribute

1. Tourism view in ancient China

What is tourism? When does tourism appear? Is tourism a kind of human being's instinct or a product of social development? What contents are there in the intentions of tourism? Though the questions above seem to be simple, they are an academic difficult problem which has puzzled experts and scholars from home and abroad for a long time. In fact, there is nothing strange about it. As a kind of activity or a phenomenon, tourism has existed for thousands upon thousands of years on the earth, but tourism research just has a history of several decades.

According to textual criticism, the oldest tourism view in China may be the gua of "Guan (Contemplation)" and "Lv (Traveling Stranger)" which were mentioned in the *Book of Changes*. In the "Guan (Contemplation)" gua, there were such expressions: "One contemplates the glory of the kingdom. It will be advantageous for him, being such as he is, (to seek) to be a guest of the king", and " 'he contemplates the glory of the kingdom' — (thence) arises the wish to be a guest (at court)". It means that by contemplating the thriving and prosperous scenes of the kingdom, one will be in an advantageous state of becoming a guest of the king, and thence it can show the government treating worthy men with courtesy. Although, the idea of "contemplating the glory of the kingdom" here is still much different with the modern view of "seeing sights" in meaning, but it is the earliest original source of the word of "seeing sights".

The word "seeing sights" came into China when Shen Yue, a poet in the Liang Dynasty (502—557) of the Southern Dynasties period, wrote one of his poems with a title of "*On Sorrow*": "We are seeing sights made more charming with the annual spring, and the annual spring is enchanting travelers at the scene. While the slow lights send out brilliant colours in the morning, moisture is formed over the warm dews. Early birds fly from the tender leaves, and orchid fragrance is felt from time to time. On such a day I was cut off from my former country, and the fine moment is blocked when I was away from home ten thousand li afar." The word "seeing sights" in the poem is somewhat similar to our understanding of "sightseeing" nowadays and therefore has a connotation of "making" one's temperament delighted while enjoying beautiful scenes.

Before the Southern Dynasties, the Chinese words of "*lv you*" are two independent characters for quite a long time. There are words of "taking a rest and making a tour" in the chapter of "Rites of Study" at *the Book of Rites*. Our ancestors refered "*You*" to "an activity one makes in strolling around when he/she is full at ease and has nothing to do". It shows that the sightseeing tour described by our forefathers is an activity one makes when he/she is at full ease, and therefore has a concept that one makes tours only in his/her spare time. Noted scholar Kong Yingda of the Tang Dynasty (618—907) once made such an explanation on "*lv*" in his book entitled Rectified *Interpretation of the Book of Changes*: "*Lv* means staying away from home, and living in a place that is not one's hometown. We call it '*lv*' when one travels away from one's home and lives in another place." He stressed that "*lv*" is an activity one makes from one place to another.

The vast and numerous volumes of classical Chinese literature showed to us a vivid picture scroll of life of the ancients of all types through records of "*lv*" and "*you*". For example, *the Book of Songs* once said in its "the Schemes of the Great Yu": "I drive on my tour to find relief, and drown my homesick grief." The *Book of History* said: "Never indulge ourselves in playing." The *Poetry of the South* said in "the Far-off Journey": "Hard pressed by the world's ways and woe, oh! I'd become light and upwards go." *Zhuang Zi* said in its "Travel Free and Unfettered": "Ride on the true law of the heaven and earth, and control the changes of the six elements (the feminine, the masculine, wind, rain, darkness and brightness), as as to travel in the realm of the boundless." Among them, *Zhuang Zi* represented the first peak of tourism view of ancient Chinese, and is of epoch-making significance in the history of Chinese tourism culture.

Zhuang Zi was one of the founders and a chief representative of the Taoist School in ancient China. Just like *the Analects* which recorded the words and deeds of Confucius, *Zhuang Zi* also recorded the rich experiences of Zhuang Zi in his roaming and excursion in all his life. *Zhuang Zi* is both a philosophical book as well as travel book. When Zhuang Zi advocated the idea of "I live aside the heaven and earth, and all the outside world is in harmony with me", he was in fact hoping to reach an aloof realm in which "one can live in harmony with the outside world" and one can forget both the outside world and oneself. The mental state of "taking advantage of the outside world to make one's heart happy" has enlightened people's pure aesthetic attitude later and also the hermit culture of ancient Chinese.

Through tourism, the "*law*" was described by Zhuang Zi as extremely mysterious and abstruse, and through the utterly illusory "*law*", tourism was described by him as aloof from this mortal life, free and unfettered. The famous "Debate on Haoshui River (in today's Fengyang County, Anhui Province)" thoroughly demonstrated Zhuang Zi's tourism and amusement outlook that "one can live in harmony with the outside world" and that "I live aside the heaven and earth, and all the outside world is in harmony with me".

Houshui is located in Fengyang County of Anhui Province, east China. Huishi was a politician and philosopher in the period of the Warring States (B. C. 475—B. C. 221). When Zhuangzi and Huishi came to Houshui, Zhuang Zi found the fish swam back and forth in the river, and he said to Hui Shi: "How happy there are." Hui Shi asked Zhuang Zi: "You are not fish, how do you know they are happy?" Zhuang Zi replied: "You are not me, how do you know that I don't know they are happy?" Hui Shi explained: "I'm not you, and thus I don't know what you are thinking. And accordingly, as you are not fish, you will not know the happiness of the fish. This is quite clear!" Zhuang Zi retorted upon Hui Shi, said "Let's go back to the starting point. Just now, you said: 'how do you know they are happy', etc. This means that you knew what I mean and then asked me the question. Thus when I stood at the Haoshui Bridge, I also knew the happiness of the fish".

The this debate on "knowing the pleasure of the fish", Zhuang Zi intended to show to people an idea that when appreciating the mountains and rivers, one needs to blend one's body and mind with the nature in a bid to reach a beautiful state of being carefree and happy and forgetting both the outside world and oneself. The mental state of "taking advantage of the outside world to make one's heart happy" has enlightened people's pure aesthetic attitude later and also the hermit culture of ancient Chinese.

We can see from above, though the understanding of our forefathers on "*lv*", "*you*" or "*lv you*" (tourism) varied in specific meaning with the change of times, their understanding on tourism at least reflected common features in three aspects, namely differences with change of places, temporariness and aesthetic sentiment.

In modern, times, divergence has always existed among the views of experts and scholars on understanding tourism. The definition on tourism and tourists has not been clearly unified in the academic field. Along with the development of social economy and culture, the chaotic state on describing the essence, definition and extension of tourism has not been lessened in the slightest degree.

But from another angle, it also indicates that tourism has developed and has been enriched continuously, and people's understanding on tourism is being deepened continuously. Although the versions of definition are multifarious, and various explanations lay special emphasis on different aspects, they are beneficial to going a step further on revealing the scientific intention of tourism through the views of experts and scholars at home and abroad.

In the book entitled *Recognition Outline of Tourism and Chinese Culture*, Mr Shen Zuxiang said: "As a cultural phenomenon and a system, tourism is the most essential part in human beings' material and cultural life, and spirit. It is a composite mass in a dynamic process of a mobile touring activity made by a tourist, who as the mainstay of tourism, tries to achieve a special goal by launching active manoeuvres on tourism objects through outsides factors such as tourism media." He also noted: "Tourism belongs to the category of culture and is part of culture."

Mr. Feng Naikang said in his book named *Treatise on Chinese Traveling Literature* that "the essential starting point, the whole process and the final effect of tourism should all target spiritual enjoyment as the aim", and "tourism is not an economic activity but a spiritual activity. People get this spiritual life through aesthetic feeling and enjoyment. So travel is also an aesthetic activity, a comprehensive aesthetic activity".

The view of Mr. Xian Yanjun — author of the book *Basic Tourism Textbook*, which was published in 2001 — is quite representative. He stated: "Travel is an individual's short experience which has social, leisured and consumption attributes when one goes to a different place outside his/her abode to mainly seek appreciation and enjoyment."

In his book entitled *An Introduction of Tourism Studies*, Mr. Tian Li gave a definition to tourism: "Travel is a trip made by people when they leave their residing abodes for a trip to a foreign country or a strange land, and also the total sum of all kinds of phenomenon and connections caused by their temporary stay during the trip."

2. Tourism view of the West

In the West, the concept on tourism also varies and cannot reach a consensus.

The word of "tourism" first appeared in English in the 19th century. The *Webster's Dictionary* gives an explanation to tourism like this: a process one experiences after he/she returns to the place where he/she starts off. It is a tour which takes business, entertainment or education as the main aim, and people often plan to visit different places in the course of traveling".

A book, entitled *National Science Dictionary* and published in Germany in 1927, gave another definition to tourism: "As an understanding in the narrow sense, tourism refers to the contacts one made as a consumer of economic and cultural products, when he/she stays in the strange places after leaving one's residence temporarily to seek life and culture wants, or meet various personal desires."

The view of Austrian economist Herrmann Unsgerard is quite representative. He was one of the Western scholars who viewed tourism from the economic angle. He said: "Tourism is the total sum of economical activities which are caused by people from foreign countries or other parts of the country when they come to a non-settlement area for stays or transfers."

The view of French scholar Jean Mattson also found support among people in the West. He said: "Tourism is a kind of leisure activity, which includes travel or stays in places far away from one's settlement. The aim of it is for recreation and rest or enriching one's experience or cultural education." Mr Douglas Pearce also expressed similar standpoint, saying: "Speaking from a more technical sense, tourism is a relation and phenomenon which is caused by people when they travel with an aim of leisure and recreation, and thus stay in a place temporarily."

When we mention the development on definition of tourism, we cannot forget Swiss scholars Hunzikee and Krapf. In a co-authored tourism book which was published in the 1940s with a title of *General Outline of Tourism Studies*, the two scholars offered a definition on tourism this way: "Toursim is a total sum of phenomenon and relations which are caused by non-settlement activities and temporary stays. These travellers will not result in permanent settlemnt, and will not engage in money-making activities." This definition has a major influence on future scholars, and thus has become a set pattern to nurture "relation theory" and "intergration theory".

In 1972, British scholars Bogart and Metlik offered their definition on tourism: "Tourism is a result of migrant activity when they head for and stay in various scenic spots. It is the combination of the movement when people leave the place where they work and live in usual times and head for a traveling destination in a short period, and also the all kinds of activities as they stay in the destination."

In 1973, the U. S. National Tourism Resources Appraisal Committee gave a definition on travellers like this: "Travellers refer to people who leave one's home and travel at least 50 miles of a one-way distance out of the need of business, recreation, personal affairs, or other reasons besides one's journey to work and back home, in disregard of his/her stays for the night in the place one heads for, or heading back home during the day." A definition in Canada is also similar : "Travellers refer to those who leave one's brink of living community and head to places which are at least 50 miles away. "

The United Nations' International Union of Official Travel Organizations offered a definition on tourism like this: Travellers engage in a traveling activity when they come to a country for short stays for more than 24 hours. Their travelling aims are among the following two: (1) Leisure, which includes enjoyment, vacation, health care, research work, religious or sporting activities; (2) Business, family affairs, diplomatic activities and conferences.

In 1979, the British Tourism Services offered its view: "Tourism refers to any kind of activities which are related to people's temporary movement when they leave their daily life and workplace and head for a destination, and thus their short stays in the destinations. " In 1981, the International Association of Scientific Experts in Tourism gave its definition on tourism, which later became quite popular. Experts from the association said: "Tourism is the total sum of inter-linking relations and phenomena caused when people travel to a place, which is neither their permanent settlement nor their workplace, and stay in the place. "

3. Differences of tourism views between China and foreign countries

It is not difficult for us to see from the above definitions of tourism that scholars at home and abroad have different understandings of tourism: Most Chinese experts and scholars tend to see tourism from the aesthetical and recreational point of view, while Westerners focus more on its economic and educational functions, despite their recognition of it's recreational and relaxation functions; On tourism's denotation, some Chinese experts and scholars seem more willing to "narrow" it and confine it into the category of "eating, residing, transporting, touring, entertaining and shopping"; while the Westerners, on the contrary, tend to "extend" the denotation of tourism, which they see as a "comprehensive" activity, combining relaxation, business, education, culture and experience, etc., i. e., the so-called "sum total of all relations".

Through comparison of the views on tourism at home and abroad, we also find that some Chinese experts and scholars often take tourism as a one-way consumption behavior. We can get a glimpse of this from Mr. Xie Yanjun's definition, which defines three basic characters of tourism: consumption, relaxation and sociality. In his opinion, "tourism during its whole process neither provides any consumable materials for the society nor for the individual tourists. On the contrary, it licks up tourists' savings and labor products of others". And that "The aim of tourism is obtain aesthetical experience by means of various recreational activities. Tourism in its whole process should be dominated by a natural, free randomness and by a motivation for relaxation and amusement, which is similar to any other recreational activities".

About the sociality of tourism, Mr. Xie Yanjun said, "The sociality of tourism exists as the aesthetic awareness is the prerequisite to tourism. Besides, under different social conditions, people's desire for tourism may be influenced by and branded with the characters of the time".

Mr. Xie also cited *Observation and Cultivation—Brief Introduction to Tourism and Chinese Culture by* Shen Zuxiang as saying, "Tourist activities in ancient times seemed to be a refractor of Chinese culture, revealing more or less the cultures of different times and the soul of Chinese culture, such as the obscurity of pre-Qin Dynasties, the decadence of Wei and Jin dynasties, the enthusiasm of Sui and Tang dynasties and the tranquility of Ming and Qing dynasties…" Here we can conclude that the so-called sociality of tourism by Xie was not drawn from the "total social relations" perspective, but from the perspective that different times had different "aesthetical awareness", so it remained a "consumption" concept.

Among the views of Westerners ranging from the explanation of "tourism" when the word first appeared as "a travel for the purpose of business, recreation or education" to the present definition as "the sum total of interacting relations and phenomena brought about by people who travel to a place where they neither live permanently nor work in", none of them seemed to take tourism as a pure one-way of "relaxation" and "amusement" but regarded it as "the sum total of interacting relations and phenomena", that is to say tourism is not only a "consumption" behavior which "licks up tourists' savings and labor products of others", but a two-way investment activity to enlarge knowledge, enrich experience and increase wealth.

As a matter fact, Westerners had much in common with ancient Chinese scholars in their understanding about tourism. The ancient Chinese scholars did not consider tourism as only a recreational behavior for amusement and aesthetic satisfaction, but a learning process to enlarge their scope of knowledge and broaden their mind. Confucius, the Chinese ancient thinker and educationalist is a typical representative of this opinion.

On tourism, Confucius had his famous words about mountains and waters. He said: "The wise find pleasure in waters and the virtuous find pleasure in hills." Confucian was fond of the orderliness of nature and hoped that the country and the people could maintain a natural and harmonious relation as the nature does. To keep the nature and the society in a harmonious unification is the core value of the Confucian "heaven-human oneness" thought. The renowned scholar of the Song Dynasty — Liu Yi also had another well-known saying which is "Reading ten thousand books and traveling ten thousand miles". He took tourism as of the same importance as reading, and thought that tourism and reading were complementary to each other and indispensable in mental cultivation and human growth.

4. A new definition of tourism

Given the various different views on tourism between Chinese and Westerners from ancient to present, it is pragmatic to seek common ground while putting aside all the differences, as searching for the truth is the prerequisite to science. According to the author, human beings up to date has not yet formed consensus on the nature, connotation and denotation of tourism, but it is no doubt a scientific way for us to stand on the giant's shoulder and track the origin of tourism within the existing framework and study the roles of human beings' instinct and the society in tourism.

Mr. Xie Yanjun, a representative of the opinion that tourism was the product of social development, said in *Basic Tourism Theory*: "Tourism is essentially an aesthetical and recreational process from which mental delight is obtained and it became one of the human beings' fundamental activities when the human society had developed to a certain level."

This definition emphasizes that tourism, as "one of human beings' fundamental activities" is a product of the society with certain development level. Nevertheless, according to many Chinese and foreigners, if that is true, to what extent the human beings have developed should tourism be "produced"? It is hard to define in terms of time.

Mr. Xie Yanjun believed that tourism in its true sense came in the North and South Dynasties when the word "tourism" first appeared. It came in a time "when tourism activities began to boom and the aesthetic awareness of natural grandeurs emerged", "the tourism activity and its background at that time were almost the same as today with the only difference shown in form and manner", so he thought that "the prior travels and the travels afterwards not for the purpose of relaxation, amusement and aesthetics should not be counted as tourism".

As for such a proposition, we must not rush for a conclusion. We can seek the answer from history.

In Qin and Han dynasties, there appeared a new phrase called "wandering and gazing about". Li Si expressed in his *Report to Emperor the Second of Qin Dynasty* that there was a prevalence of wandering-and-gazing-about activities after the management of the drive roads, which showed the great merits and virtues of the emperor. According to the people of Qin and Han Dynasties, tourism had four functions: Firstly, it could help to assess social-political atmosphere. As mentioned in *Royal Regulations of the Book of Rites*, "The emperor carried out a hunting visit in every five years and sent Chen Shi, the court teacher out to observe the social atmosphere"; Secondly, It promoted physical and mental wellbeing. Among the seven "catholicons" Mei Chen mentioned in *Qi Fa*, there were three kinds of "wandering and gazing about", which could provide extreme enjoyment; Thirdly, it helped to gain knowledge by investing things. Wang Bao in Western Han Dynasty once said in *Eulogy to a Wise Emperor Who Gets a Liegeman*, "I am now isolated in the State of Shu in the west. Having been born and grown up in a shabby house of a poor alley, I do not know anything without going out wandering and gazing about ". That is to say that he felt ignorant without traveling. From that we could see that even people in remote ancient times had realized that traveling was the source of knowledge, wisdom and talent; Lastly, tourism could provide amusement for life. That was the most marvelous advance made in Qin and Han Dynasties and we had the same opinion today.

Among the tourism activities enjoyed by the people of Qin and Han Dynasties, the spring outings and autumn outings most prevailed. For example, March 3rd in lunar calendar, was the Shangsi Festival, which was originally a sacrifice activity to dispel evil and bring luck and later people went bathing in steams on that day. Afterwards, the activity of "floating wine cups along the winding water" was invented. People introduced water into a winding and circled channel, which was called "winding water", and then a goblet was put on the water. As it floated down the water and stopped before a guest, he would drink it up and compose a poem for amusement. This is so-called "drinking in succession from the goblets as it floated down the stream".

There was a recordation in history about the great calligraphist Wang Xizhi, who made a much-told story of composing poems when drinking from the floating goblet. Such is the story: on March 3rd in the lunar calendar, the Shangsi Festival, at the ninth reign of Emperor Yongle, Wang Xizhi, the famous calligraphist and the court auditor of Jin Dynasty, together with his relatives and friends like Xie An and Sun Chuo totaling forty two people convened in Orchid Pavilion for the evil dispelling activity. As Wang Xizhi wrote in the *Orchid Pavilion Preface*, "There was clear water flowing around the pavilion and we diverted it into a winding channel to flow goblet and got seated one by another. We composed poems as we drank and felt much contented even with the absence of the music played with bamboo and string instruments".

People of Han Dynasty had extensive spring outing activities. Zhang Heng expressed in his famous work *Southern Capital Rhapsody*, "That is the good thing about wandering and gazing about, which brings delight both for the eye and ear". He also made the vivid description about the grandeur of tourism in Shangsi Festival of Han Dynasty: "people go to the riverside for auspicious and amusement during Shangsi Festival." On that day, not only the officials and the grassroots but also the emperor with the empress and concubines went washing by the water to get rid of dirt and dispel evil. Besides the spring outing, Han people also had autumn outing on Double Nine Festival when they climbed high and drank chrysanthemum wine. The spring and autumn outings were the most popular biannual traveling activities for the people of Han Dynasty.

According to Xie Zhaohang's *Wu Za Zu* of Ming Dynasty, "The Shangsi Festival was carried on to Wei and Jin Dynasties. It actually started from Han Dynasty although not on the 3$^{rd}$ of March". This showed that these activities had started from Han Dynasty.

In ancient times, scholars traveled mostly for the purpose of lobbying, pursuing career and giving discourses, mostly motivated by personal gains. But people in Qin and Han dynasties began to travel for pleasure, which made the recreational function of tourism obvious, representing a milestone in the history of tourism. With the development of the society, the recreational function of tourism gained full development in later dynasties. It was promoted by so many travelers, especially by poets and literati that the other functions of tourism were almost ignored.

Given the development of tourism in Qin and Han Dynasties, it is obviously not a convincing proposition to regard the South and North Dynasties as the watershed for tourism. Especially, the concept of "incidental travel behavior" itself is quite obscure and is hard to define in both time and scale.

As said by Robert Lanquar in *The Sociology of Tourism*, "tourism started when human beings were born". This view was agreed by Fan Nengchuan, a Chinese scholar, who said in the preface of *China's Tourism History* by Zhang Bigong, "The history of tourism started and ends with human beings". These opinions were no doubt based on the cognition that tourism was an indispensable part of human life. We can also verify these propositions from physiological and psychological perspectives.

There is an old saying in China: Flowers have various colors, and human beings have seven emotions and six carnal desires. What are the seven emotions? According to *Conveyance of Rites* of the Chinese ancient classic *The Book of Rites*, "joy, anger, sorrow, fear, love, hate and desire are what we are capable of without learning". Thus, emotions are the forms or mental activities of joy, anger, sorrow, and desire is one of the seven emotions.

Then, what are the six desires? According to Gao You, a philosopher in East Han Dynasty, "the six desires are the desires for birth and death, the desires from ear, eye, mouth and nose". It is obvious that the six desires were referring to the physiological needs and desires of human beings. To survive and lead a colorful life, human beings need to eat with mouth, taste with tongue, see with eyes, hear with eyes and smell with nose. These desires were inherent, without learning.

According to Maslow's hierarchy of needs, human beings' needs from low to the top of the hierarchy are physiological needs, security, sociality, respect and self realization. We could deduce from this theory that human beings could feel two kinds of delights, one is physiological delights and the other is mental delights. The former are shared by animals and the latter are only possessed by human beings.

Just imagine, could the primitive people ever had the curiosity for the outside world beyond the mountains? Could it occur to them to revisit some hunting places with tasty food, beautiful views and nice sound? The answer is affirmed. Just as Xie Yanjun said in *Basic Tourism Theory*, "as a matter of fact, people in ancient times to a great extent had worship in the remote areas, which could serve as the massive driving power for people to make their first step of tourism".

It would be no easy to judge the ancient people's satisfaction by only considering their physiological delights. It should be more convincing if their physiological and mental delights are both taken into consideration.

However, the sporadic tourism activities in remote ancient society driven mainly by human beings' instinct should not be counted as true tourism. Only as the productivity developed, people had leisure time and aesthetical awareness, and the tourism phenomena appeared in the society, tourism in its true sense was generated.

At the end of the primitive society, with the use of metal tools, agriculture and animal husbandry industry gained fast development, and handicraft industry were promoted to become a separate industry, which lead to the second social division of labor in human beings' history, i. e. the separation of handicraft industry from agriculture and animal husbandry industry. Subsequently, people began to enjoy more leisure time and have strong aesthetical awareness and more aesthetical needs.

What is the "aesthetical awareness"? Aesthetical awareness is a unique thinking activity possessed by human beings and different from animals. In brief, it is a fixed thinking logic about esthetical things formed by human beings in the process of socialization. Aristotle in his *Nicomachean Ethics* made a detailed feature description about the super-utilitarian aesthetical experience: "That is an extremely delightful experience from seeing and listening", "The delightful experience is only possessed by human beings. Other life forms have their own delights, but mainly from smelling and tasting while human beings could obtain the aesthetical delights of the harmonious feeling from the eye and ear" ···From this, we could see that the psychological delight gained by human beings is essentially different from the physiological delight.

Due to the differences, "aesthetical awareness" developed along with human civilization and social development.

According to Karl Marx, "Labor creates everything". As Grosses wrote in *the Beginning of Art*, "Production industry is truly the life force of all cultural forms", "Comparing with the basic cultural phenomenon of production, all other cultural phenomena are derivative and lesser important". Therefore, "aesthetical awareness" is tied with labor activities. It will be enriched as the contents of labor get enriched.

From the above, we could conclude that tourism, as "one of the human beings' most basic activities" has both the nature instinct character and the objective social character. We could also see from the domestic and foreign tourism history that tourism will develop as the society develops and views on tourism may change as the society develops.

In today's "globalization", facing various academic views on tourism, how we should see tourism, from the narrow and pure "amusement" point of view or from the transcend vision and "sum total of relations" point of view, is a pressing subject for not only Chinese experts and scholars, but experts and scholars of other counties.

Hegel once said, "Whatever is reasonable is real and which is real is reasonable". Chinese and foreigners have given different explanations to tourism from different angles, which have enriched people's cognition and understanding about tourism. Based on all these explanations, the author tries to give a new definition for tourism: ***Tourism is the sum total of various relations when people move to a destination to fulfill their various aesthetical needs.***

This definition is different from traditional ones in that it gives prominence to "various aesthetical needs". It emphasized that human beings' "aesthetical needs" are diversified. Tourism is not only for find pleasure in water and mountains, but for knowledge enlargement, political fulfillment, religious worship and business and trades, etc. For example, the scholars in ancient Chinese Spring & Autumn and Warring States period, lobbies around either for political career or for fame and gains. Although they had strong political motivations for their touring of various countries, they must have obtained some aesthetical satisfaction from their long-term travel and increased their aesthetical thinking on tourism.

Just like Liu Deqian, deputy director of the Tourism Research Centre of the Chinese

Academy of Social Sciences, said while commenting on the essence of tourism: "What is the essence of tourism? My opinions are: The common essence of human traveling activities is the communication of the mankind. This communication not only contains the exchanges between man and nature, the exchanges between man and history, but also includes the exchanges among men themselves. Although the tourism usually means a kind of traveling action for leisure, entertainment and spending a holiday, along with people have more individual. demands, more variety of traveling ways must be in vogue and occupy the leading position gradually."

With the development of human's society and the enrichment of social activities, people's "aesthetical needs" will become more diversified. Sometimes even in one travel, tourists may have diversified "aesthetical needs". They will not only seek "pleasure" in natural mountains and water, but satisfy their "aesthetical needs' from various tourism activities related to culture, sports, science and technology, business, religion, adventure, study and health care, etc.

The definition has a relatively broader denotation than those of some other Chinese scholars' definitions, but the nature of tourism to meet "aesthetical needs" has not changed. The definition also has definite difference with the "total sum of relation" point of view by some western scholars, who regarded tourism as a sack which could wrap up everything. It also unveils the core value of tourism. People's fondness of tourism is because it can satisfy their needs for appreciation and enjoyment of the beauty of nature, art, science and technology and life.

Sometimes, people may tour around just for meeting their curiosity, which has no apparent aesthetic characteristics. But considering their mental and spiritual activities, they have harvested a great deal of satisfaction and happiness, which are surely aesthetic experience.

According to this, Liu Deqian, Professor of Tourism Research Center of CASS, said in an article that "the aesthetic appreciation of human is also some sort of communication, during which the appreciators appear dynamic and positive while the aesthetic objects are static (in some cases) and passive".

*Introduction to Tourism* says "tourism is a comprehensive aesthetical activity, combining the beauty of nature, society and art, a mixture of cultural relics, historic sites, architecture, carving, painting, calligraphy, music, choreography, drama, folk customs as well as gourmet food. It can not only satisfy people's various aesthetical needs to a maximum extent, but fulfill their physiological and cognitional needs and desires".

In addition to all these mentioned, the definition distinguishes tourism from some similar activities like travel, migration by stressing the aesthetical character of tourism.

In the early phase of human society with a lower productivity, our ancestors were forced to leave their residences once and again in their combat with the unfavorable living atmosphere. Even in the Neolithic Period, they had not yet escaped from this "moving around" fate. This kind of migration life where people had neither material foundation objectively nor "aesthetical" needs mentally but lived only for survival, is essentially different from the travel activities evolved later and even far more different from tourism in today's sense.

Although migration is also to leave a fixed residence, it is not a "temporary experience" and it is not aimed to come back again but to seek a better habitat. Travel and tourism are identical in form, both featuring "alien area" and "temporariness", but it is sometimes hard to demarcate them in content. Taking the inspection tour of ancient emperors for example, the tour was mainly for political purpose, but who could assure it did not contain the elements for "aesthetics" and "recreation". Of course, there were other cases which could be easily demarcated, such as the well-known story about Da Yu's Water Control, which was an arduous traveling activity for survival.

In order to find the ways to control water, Da Yu stayed away from home and did not enter in when he dropped by his home three times. His footprint had almost covered the Yellow River and Yangtze River areas. He eventually realized the unification within four seas throughout the country. Da Yu's traveling for water control represented the hike of traveling activities of primitive human during their combat with and conquest of nature.

Travel could be of any purpose, but tourism must be for the purpose of joy. Travel is not equal to tourism, but they may become obscure in concept with the development of the society when people have more "aesthetical needs" and the connotation of "aesthetics" constantly changes with more rich contents. Nevertheless, theoretically speaking, it is widely recognized nowadays that tourism must be realized through travel but not all travels are tourism.

Tourism and Tourism industry also easily cause confusion for people of today in concept. The two could be clearly distinguished: tourism is an individual behavior of tourists while tourism industry is a collective behavior for tourist enterprises. Tourism industry could be understood in its broader sense and narrow sense. In its broader sense, it is related to any consumption behavior of tourists. It is a comprehensive industry creating convenience for tourist activities and providing tourist with tourist products and services; in its narrow sense, it is an enterprise providing products and services to bring aesthetical pleasure to tourists.

## Section 2

## Tourism in ancient times is an activity belonging to the rich, the powerful and the carefree

1. Tourism in ancient China

As we can see from the above, tourism is one important activity for human beings. There had been recordation of tourist activities since human being began recordation with characters.

As a unique social activity of human beings, tourism has the combined character of consumption, aesthetics and sociality, which distinguish tourism from other social activities. As pointed out in the summary of tourism characters in *Introduction to Tourism*, "Tourism is a high-level consumption activity", "tourism is an activity for amusement featuring aesthetics", and "tourism is a social activity of human beings".

Such characters of tourism had determined that tourism was only the privilege of a few people under the undeveloped productivity in ancient times. To be more exact, it is an activity for only a few people who have power, wealth and leisure. The development of tourism either in quality or quantity is a low-to-high transition process.

China is an ancient civilization of the world and also one of the countries with the earliest emergence of tourism, which could be traced back to B. C. 2250.

Due to the low productivity of the early stage of primitive society, almost all people in the society were fighting arduously with the nature for survival. With the completion of the twice labor division, productivity gained a full growth and classes appeared. Wealth and leisure time were gradually entitled to a few people and that made tourism realized in its true sense. In ancient China, tourism was mainly carried out by emperors' tour of inspection, scholars' lobbying, literati' wandering, religious pilgrim, geographical inspection and diplomatic travel, etc.

(1) Emperors' tours in various forms

The emperor's tour of inspection was for the highest ruler of past dynasties to inspect and tour his country and territory within his authority. Through the tour, the emperors could on the one hand, enhance his authority and reign throughout the country by showing of his sovereign power, assessing political atmosphere and observing the customs of the people; and on the second hand amuse himself by enjoying the beautiful scenes to his heart' content and setting up altar to offer sacrifice to Heaven and Earth.

During the period prior to Qin Dynasty, The tourism activities were mainly carried out by a few slave owners represented by the emperors and leuds to take on an inspection tour, offer sacrifice to Heaven and Earth, Convene and make oath of alliance, hunt and travel for recreation, etc. For example, it was said in Chuci Lisao that Xia Taikang "was so indulged in recreational activities that he did not care about the future". It was also written in *Shuoyuan Zhengjian* about Qi Jing Gong, the emperor of Qi Kingdom, who "took a voyage trip and enjoyed it so much that he didn't go back until six months later". The voyage broke the record of early times for marine tour.

The earliest record about emperor's tour of inspection in China's history was the westbound journey made by Zhou Mu Wang, the king of Zhou. It was said that Mu Wang had a dream one day, in which he was invited by a person called Hua Ren to travel the country of Hua Ren. So on a propitious day, designating Zao Fu as the wagoner, who was good at horse raising and riding and escorted by warriors in seven troops, Mu Wang started his journey from Cheng Zhou (the southeast of today's Luo Yang city). He headed for the north along the west side of Taihang Mountain, passed the Jili Mountain ridge located in the southeast part of Qinghai province and reached at Kunlun Mountain, where he paid visit to the West Goddess, offering her the pearls, gems and other gifts he brought and had a happy gathering with the host. Afterwards, he went north to Wakhan in Pakistan and came back from Kashi.

It took more than two years for Mu Wang's westbound journey of over thirty thousand *li*, passed through Henan, Shanxi, Hebei, Inner Mongolia, Qinghai, Gansu and Xinjiang and other places and up to the middle part of Asia of today. The route was basically the same as taken by Zhang Qian who was later sent on a diplomatic mission to the West Region. So he was indeed a great traveler in China's history.

Qin Shi Huang, the first emperor of Qin Dynasty, was the first important representative of the imperial tours in the feudal society. During his reign of 11 years, he made five distant tours, on which he made decrees to set up stone tablets and inscribe his great merits and achievement of nation unification on the tablets, among them are the famous Tai Mount Tablet, Huiji Tablet, Jieshi Tablet, etc, with the recordation of the grandeur of those tours. Qin Shi Huang did not forget about appreciating the landscape of various regions. Offering sacrifice to Heaven and Earth was his main activity. On Tai Mount, he named the pine tree which saved his life as "Wu Da Fu Pine Tree". When he sailed on Dongting Lake, he almost fell over the ship due to the surge of the water. So under his anger, he ordered his attendants to go up to the Jun Mont and burn out the Temple of E Huang and the Temple of Nv Ying, and permanently sealed the mountain by carving the words "permanent seal". Qin shi Huang died on the way up to Xian Yang on his last tour due to fatigue at the age of 50.

Emperor Han Wu Di, Liu Che made similar tours to Emperor Qin shi Huang, but he exceeded Emperor Qin shi Huang with more than ten short or long distance tours. According to *Suo Zhi*, after climbing to the top of Tai Mountain, Han Wu Di appreciated the highness, extremeness, greatness and uniqueness of the mountain and also felt confusion. On Tai Mountain, Liu Che set up the famous wordless tablet, implicating that his merits and virtues were beyond description. On Song Mountain in Henan province, it was said that when Liu Che was climbing the mountain, he heard the words "long live" with a sudden wave of the surrounding pine trees. He thought that was the God's will and named the mountain "Long Live Mountain". During Han Wu Di's reign, the nation was strong and prosperous. Its border constantly explored. The constant attacks launched by General Wei Qing and Huo Qubing in Liu Che's order to get the traffic open to the Northern Desert, Su Wu's diplomatic mission to the Xiong Nu Minority and Zhang Qian's trip to the West Region were all wonderful stories about tourism in China's history of tourism.

Among the imperial tours, Sui Yang Di had the largest scale and most extravagant tour. According to *Da Ye Za Ji*, on the tour down to Jiangdu, Sui Yang Di was riding on a dragon boat of 45 Chi in height, 50 *Chi* in width and 200 *Chi* in length. It was of four stories. The empress and concubines were each on separate boat. In addition, there were 36 boats prepared for the court beauties and over 1000 boats for the maids of honors. Following these boats were the storied boats for court ministers, shaman and foreign guests as well as the officials under the fifth level, among which were the 52 five-story boats for court ministers and the 120 three-story boats for shaman. The whole team of tour was composed of hundreds of thousands of people inclusive of the attendants and the crew. When the tour started in the Grant Canal, the boat fleet last for more than 200 *li* with the head and the stern of the boats connected. People within the 500 *li* circumference of *Sui* Yang Di's visit were required to offer gourmet food and jewelries. The leftovers of the food would be thrown into the water and those who offered the most jewelries and moneys would get promoted to a much higher level.

Sui Yang Di made three tours to Jiangdu in his life time and made much waste of both property and manpower, leading to a great number of beggars all over the street. When he made his third tour, a nationwide revolt by the peasants broke out, but he was still dissipated until he was cut off his head by the insurgent peasants.

Hunting was always treated as a comprehensive military training and recreational activity by feudal emperors and their subordinates. At the early age of Ming Dynasty, the emperors often went hunting in Nan Yuan, a place beautiful landscape, which featured low-lying land and densely spread marshes, abounding in water and grass and birds and beasts, located in Da Xing District, the western suburb of Beijing. Every spring with winter just passed, the emperors would come here hunting. Emperor Yong Le set up a Shanglinyuan Administration and build a Xanadu. Since the middle period of Ming Dynasty, most of the emperors were not capable of hunting with their weak constitution caused by their dissipated life.

In Qing Dynasty, the hunting activities became popular again. Since the Emperor Shun Zhi, Qing Dynasty had regulated "Prohibitions on Hunting", and also promulgated the "Hunting Provisions". Emperor Kang Xi decreed the biannual hunting. He was a good hunter and went hunting every autumn and winter. It was said that he went hunting forty-eight times in Chengde District in his life time. Emperor Qian Long ascended the crown because of Emperor Kang Xi's appreciation of his bravery in hunting. After becoming the emperor, Qian Long became even more obsessed in hunting and he did not stop hunting until he was eighty.

Offering sacrifice and paying a visit to the ancestors' tombs was one of the activities the feudal emperors engaged in to advocate fealty and solicit protection of the county by their ancestors. The emperors of Qing Dynasty visited their ancestors' tombs very often, almost up to thirty times each year, more often than the emperors of other dynasties. Each tour to their ancestors' tomb almost became a spring outing or autumn outing of the emperors. They hunted around and climbed Chang Bai Mountain in the name of offering sacrifice to the mountain or went boating on the Song Hua River. According to *the Records of Lin Yu County*, Emperor Kangxi, Qianlong, Jiaqing and Daoguang went to Shan Hai Guan up to nine times on their tour to their ancestors' tombs, climbing on the Temple of Jiaoshan in the north and visiting Cheng Hai Zhou in the south, holding banquets and composing poems as they enjoyed the nice natural landscape.

Emperors of Ming and Qing Dynasties liked to launch inspection tours. Their aims were quite clear: On one hand, they wanted to assess folk life and strengthen the frontier defense; On the other, they were earger to search for celestial beings and visit virtuous scholars besides feasting their eyes on famous mountains and waters, experiencing the small-bridge-and-floating-water country life and enjoying delicious game to their heart's content. During the 22 years from 1684 to 1707, Emperor Kangxi went on six tours of inspection along the Yellow River and giving instructions on the river control. At last he was consoled with "the completion of river project". Meanwhile, by taking the advantage of the inspection tours to the south, he investigated the situation of the people and approached the scholars in the south and won their loyalty to him. What he had done made outstanding contribution to the political stability and economic prosperity of China in the 18$^{th}$ century.

In the sixty years reign of Emperor Qianlong, he made six tours of inspection to the Yangtse River Delta in the wake of Emperor Kangxi, and he regarded the tour to the Yangtse River Delta an important activity besides the military campaign. Different from Emperor Kangxi who was thrift and simple on his tours, Emperor Qianlong's tours were much a stir and wasted both money and manpower. Preparation for his tour was carried out one year in advance, building bridges, paving roads and establishing xanadu. He was accompanied by as many as 2500 people and more than 1000 boats with the head and the stern connected. Along the bank of the river were officials riding on houses ready for his order at any time. The local officials within the circumference of thirty *li* of the river all came to meet him in court costumes and the old and young stood on both sides of the river welcoming him. Extravagant food was provided everyday.

However, different from the dissipated Sui Yang Di, Emperor Qianlong was after all an emperor of achievements. His knowledge and military capabilities had made some contributions to China's unification of the multiple nationalities. When he made his sixth tour to the Yangtse River Delta, he was already seventy-five years old. At the end of the tour, he composed a poem: "The sixth tour to the Yangtse River Delta has come to an end, and I would revisit it in my dreams."

(2) Tours by scholars with clear utilitarianism

The Spring and Autumn Period (B. C. 770—B. C. 476) and the Warring States Period (B. C. 403—A. D. 21) witness the disintegration of the slave society and the gradual establishment of the feudal society. At that time, a number of scholars, on behalf of the benefits of different classes, wrote books to promote their doctrines and make debates, led the disciples to tour kingdoms for carrying forward their politic views and propositions in order to obtain appreciations and high posts. Confucius, Su Qin and Zhang Yi were the prominent representatives of the touring scholars seeking for dignities in those years filled with featured political lobbying activities.

Confucius (B. C. 55—479) also named Qiu or Zhongni, was born in Zouyi, Lu Kingdom (southeastern Qufu, Shandong Province), was a thinker, a statesman, an educationalist and the founder of the Confucianism in the later Spring and Autumn Period. The essence of Confucius' thought is "benevolence" which means "loving others". He regarded "benevolence" as the standard and target for "implementation of benevolence" and promoted the interaction of "benevolence" and "ritual", encouraging the rulers to "cultivate the people with truth and restrict them with rituals" for further realizing his dream of "Great Harmony".

"Tianshan Mountain wins universal respects because of its loftiness, where grasses and woods are prosperous, universal things are booming, flying birds are swarming and beasts are roosting. Contributing a lot to the surroundings, it stands higher than the clouds and guides the people to be unique in the world. Thus the sky and the earth are built and the states are peaceful. It is the reason that the benevolent persons enjoy the mountains", according to the *Unofficial Biography of Han Dai*. It is no difference with Confucius' view on tourism which says "the benevolent enjoys the mountains while the wise the water". Humanitarian connotation is involved in this view. It starts to shake off the direct physical utilitarianism to landscapes and replace that with transcendental spiritual utilitarianism.

Confucius spent 14 years to tour Song, Wei, Chen, Cai, Qi, Chu and other kingdoms for widely spreading Confucianism. In his kingdom traveling, he rebuked the tyrants by saying "tyranny is crueler than tigers" at the sight of the homeless and miserable civilians. In his daily tour and at the sight of endless flowing river, he sighed "time goes on and on like the flowing water in the river, never ceasing day or night" to encourage the later generations to grasp the time and move upward. Confucius' experience of long-term tour forged the Confucianism view of "man and nature combined into one" which preaches the union of harmonious nature and society.

Confucius also raised the tourism view of "when your parents are alive, one should not stray far from home". It refers to "travel" and "work in other cities". This point reflects the feature of an age with low production forces. The target of Confucius' tourism view is to realize the policy of benevolence of "the old to live in peace and comfort, and the young to be taken good care of". So, it is apparent that Confucius never regarded travel as a pure leisure activity simply. He always melted travel into Confucian thoughts on benevolence, ritual, loyalty and benefit, archaism esteem and "enjoying happiness with civilians", leaving magnificent influences on the posterities.

In order to publicize Confucian's thought of "benevolence is the root", Mencius, like what Confucius did, also traveled among kingdoms. He said to Song Goujian "Do you like to lobby the emperors of kingdoms? Let me tell you how to lobby them: Be composed and contented no matter the others understand you or not". The opposite asked: "How to be composed and contented then?" He replied: "Paying homage to morals and fondness to benevolence may realize composedness and contentedness. So scholars neither violate benevolence in the event of poverty and frustration nor breach the moral principles in the event of illustriousness and exhilaration. Scholars can be composed and contented if keeping benevolence and loyalty in case of poverty and frustration. Civilians shall not lose trusts on them if the scholars do not deviate from benevolent government. Ancient scholars oblige the civilians when achieving their ambitions and cultivate themselves to emerge in the society when failing in their ambitions. To sum up, in obscurity, scholars would maintain their own integrity; in times of success, they would make perfect the whole empire. "

Other scholars were not so spectacular. But they also played necessary roles at the moment of truth. Some of them released their masters from dangers, and some of them defended their kingdoms' dignities. For instance, Fan Sui from the Wei Kingdom had to serve for Xu Gu, a senior official of the state, since he had no travel expense and introduction fee for his ambitious state-travel and lobby plans. Once, he went to the Qi Kingdom with Xu Gu who was reproved by King Qi Xiangwang without any disproval. Fan Sui stepped forward boldly and disproved with justice, King Qi Xiangwang leaving frustrated.

King Qi Xiangwang still bore in mind constantly of Fan Sui's bold behavior in the imperial court after the meeting. At that night, he sent somebody to persuade Fan to stay in Qi Kingdom to assume an office of alien minister. Fan refused with dignity and justice: "The envoy and I left our kingdom together. If I do not return with him together, I am not loyal and honest. Then how can I live in the world fair? " Receiving the reply, King Qi Xiangwang esteemed Fan greatly and awarded him 10 *jin* of gold, oxen and spirits etc.

The idiom of "volunteer one's services as Mao Sui once did" has been spread in China over 2000 years. Mao Sui becomes the popular designation for self-recommended persons. Mao Sui, an originally unknown sponger under Lord Pingyuan of Zhao Kingdom in the Warring States Period (B. C. 403—A. D. 21), develops into an eternal name with the popularization of the idiom.

In B. C. 260, Bai Qi, a general from Qin Kingdom, led an army to attack Zhao Kingdom. Altogether 450000 soldiers of Zhao Kingdom were demolished in Changping Battle, leaving a severely wounded and frightened Zhao Kingdom. Zhao Sheng, i. e. Lord

Pingyuan, decided to select 20 spongers who were well versed in both polite letters and martial arts to go to Chu Kingdom for supports.

Although Zhao Sheng had decades of hundred spongers, even less than 20 elite among them can assume the responsibility. Then, a sponger named Mao Sui made a self-recommendation. Zhao thought Mao had no outstanding performances for three years and wanted to refuse him. Mao persuaded Zhao for the adventurous mission with just grounds.

Zhao and his suite met great difficulties in lobbying the king of Chu Kingdom, who still hesitated on resisting Qin Kingdom with Zhao Kingdom shoulder to shoulder after Zhao's half-day efforts.

Mao Sui, quite discontentedly, walked up the step with hand on his sword and said to Zhao: "The advantages and disadvantages for jointly resistance to Qin Kingdom are apparent enough to be explained in one word. Why do you talk so long?"

The king of Chu Kingdom angrily rebuked him: "I am talking with your master. It's none of your business."

Mao stepped forward and said: "You may rely on Chu Kingdom's great forces and strength to rebuke me. But now, we are face to face and your life is controlled in my hand. Your forces cannot help you right now."

After threatening, Mao changed the topic to praise Chu Kingdom's strong forces and dense population with the blame of its submission to Qin Kingdom. Then, he continued: "Bai Qi, just a small potato, led tens of thousands soldiers to assault Chu Kingdom, capturing Yan and Ying cities, burning up Yi Ling, demolishing Chu Kingdom's ancestral temple and insulting Chu Kingdom's ancestors. Even our Kingdom feel ashamed for you, but you actually ignore that. We advocate the resist to Qin is actually for the benefits of Chu Kingdom."

The king of Chu Kingdom was rendered speechless by Mao Sui's words. So, he gave an order to jointly resist Qin Kingdom. Having returned back to Zhao Kingdom, Zhao Sheng sighed: "I dare not profess to identify talents any more." From then on, Mao Sui was respected as a distinguished guest.

Of all the scholars living in the Spring and Autumn Period (B. C. 770—B. C. 476) and the Warring States Period (B. C. 403—A. D. 21), Su Qin and Zhang Yi are the most famous ones. The Warring States Period is a turbulent age with seven kingdoms battling for the throne. The rise of Qin Kingdom threatened others in the battles among the kingdoms. The statesmen at that time held two kinds of distinctly different political plans. One was vertical integration of six kingdoms to resist Qin Kingdom with Su Qin as the image spokesperson, the other was horizontal integration with Qin Kingdom with Zhang Yi as the brand ambassador. They shuttled among the six kingdoms to urge the kings to accept their propositions.

Traveling around all kingdoms, Su Qin lobbied the kings in the courts with his unparalleled eloquence, leaving their ministers without an argument.

Actually, Su Qin's success is not smooth. Born in a poor family, he suffered a lot from poverty in his early years. After submitting ten written statements to the king of Qin Kingdom without any responses, he had to leave the kingdom and returned to his hometown since no clothes and money to support his living.

When he arrived home, languishing, ragged and shameful, his wife was busy for weaving and didn't greet him. His sister-in-law didn't prepare him meals and his parents didn't respond him. At this, Su Qin deeply sighed: "My wife doesn't regard me as her husband, my sister-in-law doesn't regard me as the brother-in-law, nor do my parents regard me as their son. That's all my faults!"

So, he opened all his bookcases at that night and found a book of tactics written by Master Jiang Ziya named *Yin Fu Script*. He concentrated himself into the book the whole night. While feeling sleepy, he took an awl to stab his leg with blood flowing to the heel. "Why can't I lobby the king and enable him to award me treasures and high positions?" He blamed himself seriously.

One year later, he thought he had mastered the know-how. "Now I'm confident to lobby the kings with my knowledge." he said to himself. So he paid a formal visit to King Zhao Suhou in a splendid palace of Zhao Kingdom. King Zhao appreciated his talents greatly and appointed him the prime minister of Zhao Kingdom with the title of Lord Wu'an. He was also granted with lots of chariots, silk, jades and gold for promoting his strategy on breaking up horizontal integration and striking the powerful Qin Kingdom to other kings.

When he was in success and dignity, Su Qin had lots of valuable treasures and endless attendants, highlighting the road. All the six kingdoms worshiped him deeply, thus the position of Zhao Kingdom was greatly improved. When Su Qin passed Luo Yang on his way southward to lobby the King of Chu Kingdom, his parents got the message and cleaned roads, prepared music and banquets to meet him in the suburb. His wife, standing silently to listen to him, didn't dare to look at him. His sister-in-law knelt down and required for pardons for four times. Su said: "Why are you so humble now while that arrogant before?" "It is just because that you are lofty and rich now." said his sister-in-law. "Alas! When one is in poverty, even his parents do not regard him as their son. But when he captures wealth and rank, even his relatives are scared by him. So, how can one ignore power, wealth and rank in his life?"

Zhang Yi, a poverty-stricken scholar from Wei Kingdom, went to Chu Kingdom to lobby its king who refused to interview him. A county magistrate of Chu Kingdom received him as a sponger. But Zhang was doubted to steal a rare jade of the county magistrate just because of his poorness and beaten ruthlessly.

Zhang returned to home with frustration. His wife, caressing the injuries, said with affection: "You will never suffer grievance like that if you do not study and seek for rank."

Zhang opened his mouth and asked: "Is my tongue still there?" His wife replied: "Surely it is there." "I never worry about my future if the tongue is good." said Zhang.

Later on, Zhang Yi, relying on his eloquence, won the trust of Huiwen King of Qin Kingdom and assumed the prime minister of the kingdom. Meantime, the six kingdoms were organizing vertical integration. In B. C. 318, Chu, Zhao, Wei, Han and Yan Kingdoms built a united force to assault Hangu Gate of Qin Kingdom. Since the five kingdoms didn't make concerted effort due to their internal contradictions, they were defeated easily by the strong army of Qin Kingdom.

Qi and Chu are the bigger ones of the six kingdoms. Zhang believed it was necessary to break the union between Qi and Chu Kingdoms for realizing horizontal integration. So he lobbied in Chu Kingdom and contracted enmity with Qu Yuan, resulting in the latter's exile to the wild and a tragic death for drowning himself in the Miluo River.

Above scholars hoped to achieve their political ambitions and the content of self-realization through frequent travels to the kingdoms. Embracing ambitions and braving bad weather, they regarded the experience as happiness instead of bitterness, showing a kind of special aesthetic realm. By the West Han Dynasty, spongers supported by leud still continued the lobby tradition.

(3) Man of letter's colorful and pleasurable trips

In the Qin and Han Dynasties, some Brahmins became wealthy, educated and leisurable with the thriving of social economy. They returned back to the tranquil countryside from the prosperous metropolis and gave infinite sighs inspired by the enthusiasm to the nature. "Touring at countryside, reveling in the landscape and forgetting to return" and "Instruments are not necessary, the landscape gives crystal sound".

In the East Han Dynasty, some Brahmins hated the darkness of the officialdom and placed feelings on landscape due to the failure in official career. Tourism was regarded as an ideal lifestyle for reclusion, exclusion of difficulty and anxiety and preservation of one's moral integrity. Chuang Tzu's view in Free and Easy Wandering was reemphasized and contributing themselves into the nature became a kind of life delight of Brahmins and hermits. It is vividly presented in a poem: "Even one cannot live a long life, he always worry about a much longer period. If the daytime is short while the night is long, why not burning a candle light? Enjoying the life at the time, never waiting for the uncertain future."

In the North Wei and Jin Dynasties, the trend of Brahmins reclusion due to the frustration of their political careers was unprecedented and unrepeatable, highlighted as the first culmination of Brahmin tourism in Chinese history. At their will, they toured much and enjoyed a lot. Some built huts for seclusion and some traveled among mountains and rivers for playing chess and studying paintings, far away from the hypocritical earthliness.

It is also not difficult to find the representations to landscape and nature in the literatures before the Qin Dynasty. But the purpose in those literatures was not to know the beauty of the nature. Cao Cao (Cao Mengde), a lord of both civil and military ability living in later East Han, was the first prestigious one to highly praise landscape with aestheticism. His masterpiece *The East Sea* says:

"I come to view the boundless ocean

From Stony Hill on eastern shore.

Its water rolls in rhythmic motion,

And islands stand amid its roar.

Tree on tree grows from peak to peak;

Grass on grass looks lush far and nigh.

The autumn wind blows drear and bleak;

The monstrous billows surge up high.

The sun by day, the moon by night.

Appear to rise up from the deep.

The Milky Way with stars so bright.

Sinks down into the sea in sleep.

How happy I feel at this sight!

I croon this poem in delight."

In the poetry, the poet actually expressed a kind of hero-like narcissistic appreciation through the eulogy to Jieshi Mountain and the East Sea.

According to *The New Dao*, "Seven Sages of the Bamboo Grove", i. e. Ruan Ji, Ji Kang, Liu Ling, Ruan Xian, Wang Rong, Shan Tao and Xiang Xiu, hating the treacherous political struggles amid the East Han's Sima Family, often went outing and had parties in the wild. *History of the Jin Dynasty* records that Ruan Ji, enjoyed the landscape and immersed himself in the nature for several days. He specially selected narrow roads when riding forward randomly and cried bitterly in the cart. It is also recorded in the book that Sun Chuo "has lived in Kuaiji to indulge in the nature beauty over ten years" and Sun Tong, his brother, "lives in Kuaiji, loves sceneries … and gratifies his interests in known mountains and rivers to a great degree".

Xie Lingyun, born in an aristocratic family with high talents, was the most prestigious traveler living in the $4^{th}$ to $5^{th}$ century. To release himself from his unsuccessful political career, Xie usually banished himself into fantastic and magnificent mountains and rivers. When he was an official in the court, Xie often made journeys, leaving the position vacant without any previous applications and arrangement, resulting in being deposed from his office by the court. From then on, he decidedly started his traveling and integrated himself into the nature.

Moreover, Xie specially designed a pair off wooden shoes with blocks fixed on them, named Master Xie's Shoes, for the convenience of climbing. It is said that Xie took off the front block when ascending and removed the back block when descending. Armed with Master Xie's Shoes, it is so joyful, just like walking in plain when hiking in the rugged mountainous region.

A grand brigade, consisting of his friends and servants for paving the way, always followed Xie for his trips each time. Sometimes the mighty brigade made great noise when opening up the road and aroused numerous civilians' attention.

Xie's colorful and well-informed tourism career brought him a prominent achievement in literature creation. His work of *Travel Notes on Famous Mountains* was deemed as the birthmark of Chinese ancient itinerary literature. Particularly, his poetries on landscape greatly enriched and explored the realm of this literature form thanks to his tranquil and refined style and the clear and pure description, overturning the metaphorical tradition inherited from the East Jin Dynasty and establishing the position of landscape poetry which became a genre in Chinese poetry development history from then on. Xie Lingyun was laurelled the father of landscape school's poets.

Tao Yuanming, living in the same era with Xie, resolutely "removed the royal chop" and returned back his home in Xunyang (Jiujiang, Jiangxi Province) since he wouldn't "bow himself for the official salary of 5 *dou* of rice". At the foot of Nanshan Mountain (Lushan Mountain), he and other peers chanted and composed poems leisurely in the embrace of the nature. *Peach Blossom Source*, written by Tao in early years of the Song of the

South Dynasties (the 5<sup>th</sup> century), presents a utopian society, expressing the poet's complete denial to existing social systems and immense admiration to an ideal world. Tao Yuanming, as the inaugurator of the pastoral poetry school, pioneered a new field in Chinese poetry forum and gave a profound brand to the idyllic poem genre in the Tang Dynasty. So, Tao was also titled an "idyllic poet".

The Tang Dynasty (618—907) saw the culminating period of Chinese feudal society. The political enthusiasm of the middle and low-level scholars was greatly ignited due to the practice of an imperial examination system. The decadent psychosis of those landscape-indulged intellectuals was ultimately changed.

In Tang Dynasty, "tourism for official career" and "tourism for investigation" were prevailing. "On one side, they appreciate the mountains and rivers and verify the history records; On the other side, they made friends and exchanged poetry to pursue improved scholarship." (excerpt from *Introduction on Tourism Study*). Although some of the learned intellectuals were so proud and would not participate in the imperial examinations, there were great differences between them and the aforesaid hermits in Wei and Jin Dynasties. They always toured to remote areas with the ambition of assisting the society. "Presentation of ambitions via specific objects" in their tours is a sort of higher level tourism form. Li Bai, Du Fu, Liu Zongyuan and Ouyang Xiu were the outstanding representatives for this type of tourism.

Li Bai (701—762), also named Li Taibai and Green Lotus Hermit with original family home based in Chengji, Long Xi (Qin'an County, Gansu Province), was the greatest poet in romanticism. He was born in Suiye, Anxi Area in 701 and moved to Qinglian Township, Changlong County of Mianzhou (Jiangyou County, Sichuan) at the age of five with his father. Li Bai received good family education in his juvenile year. Li had versatile hobbies, capable to recite poems, read various books, compose poetries and practice fencing at the age of ten. He showed great capabilities in writing articles at 15 and started traveling in Sichuan Province to enjoy the grand views after 20.

In 726, the 26-year-old Li Bai, bidding farewell to families with a sword in hand, began his 16-year-long traveling centering around Anlu (Hubei Province) with footprints impressed in nearly half of the Chinese land covering Hunan, Hubei, Jiangsu, Zhejiang, Henan and Shanxi etc.

Li Bai, at the age of 42, was recommended by a friend to assume an office of the member of the Imperial Academy in Chang'an (Xi'an), the capital of Tang. At the beginning, Li, full of excitement, left the lines of "embracing the world full of confidence and optimism, I am not an ordinary person absolutely!" (*Bidding Farewell to Children in Nanling and Marching toward the Capital*). Unfortunately, he soon found out that the governing Emperor Tang Xuanzong, indulging himself in sultriness without managing the politics, was muddleheaded and decadent. Li Bai, suffering the pain of disillusion of his dreams, started the first step of his 11-year-long $2^{nd}$ traveling with Liangyuan (Kaifeng) as the centre. "Living a wandering life with poetries and liquor as the comforts" (Liu Quanbai *On Mr. Li, Former Member of the Imperial Academy in Tang Dynasty*,) is a vivid expression of Li Bai's life in those years. In Autumn, 745, Li Bai met Du Fu and Gao Shi in Luoyang and Bianzhou respectively and toured Liangyuan and Jinan happily with them together. From then on, Li Bai and Du Fu built their life-long deep friendship, the line of "sleeping under the same quilt after being drunk at night, walking together shoulder to shoulder in the day" witnessing their fellowship (Du Fu, *Looking for Fan's Hut with Li Bai*). Li achieved his creation peak at the period in the period and authored magnum poetrys like *Mount Skyland Ascended in A Dream*, *A Song of Farewell*, *Bringing in The Wine*, *An Ode to North Wind*, *Song for Liangyuan Garden* etc.

Li Bai reached great achievements in poetry creation though he failed to realize his political dream. He reveled in tourism with footprints covered nearly the whole Chinese land, leaving lines of "Since the world can in no way answer our craving, I will loosen my hair tomorrow and take to a fishing boat" and "Never worrying about distance for visiting immortals in grand mountains, ardently loving traveling around famous mountains". He spent numerous writings in praising the grandness of the landscape and expressing his great love to the country. Precipitous mountain roads, majestic peaks, roaring rivers and rushing falls were vividly and grandly presented to the readers. For instances, his lines on the Fall of Mt. Lushan say "The 3000-foot-long fall is straight to fly, is the Milky Way falling from the sky"; he sighed for the roughness of the roads in Shu: "Oh, but it is high and very dangerous! Such traveling is harder than scaling the blue sky!"

Du Fu and Li Bai, representing two great genres, had been esteemed as two giants in the poetry field of Tang Dynasty. Du, born in Gongxian, Henan Province, grew up in a downfallen aristocratic family. He spent great efforts on learning from early years and also visited many noted mountains and great rivers. The prosperity of Tang Dynasty was described in his lines of "Rice and millet are nice and sufficient, official and civil barns are abundant. No robbers across China on the way, and no tiredness for traveling far away." At the age of 20, Du went to South China and traveled the area of ancient Wu and Yue Kingdoms. He returned back Luo Yang four years later but failed in the imperial examination. Not defeated by the failure, he visited eastward to the territories of historical Qi and Zhao Kingdoms, living a juvenile "rich and noble" life. In his Mt. Tai tour, he wrote "I must ascend the mountain's crest; It dwarfs all peaks under my feet", clearly showing a young man's heroic spirit. He met Li Bai in the tour and composed a poem *Presented to Li Bai* with renowned lines of "Also planning for touring areas of Liang and Song Kingdoms, hoping to get good results and gains", expressing the poet's beautiful desires for the future.

Du Fu authored many poetries related with tourism. Some of his poems on objects and landscapes contain a profound affection to the country and the people. For example, in his well-known spring outing theme poetry of *On the Beauty* with popular lines of "In a fresh day in spring, many beauties go to the riverside", he showed his attitude through the description on their clothing and food instead of direct rebuke to the dissoluteness life of Yang Guozhong (the brother) and Yang Yuhuan (the sister). Du Fu was honored as the "Sage Poet", parallel with Li Bai, the "Immortal Poet".

Thanks to the developed economy and the prosperous culture, no poets didn't like mountains and rivers and no intellectuals didn't love tourism and travels. They toured for studying while learning and toured for offices while securing official position. Once failed in the political career, they renounced the world to revel themselves in landscape for relief. Liu Zongyuan, one of the Eight Great Literary Masters during Tang and Song Dynasties, was a typical representative for this lifestyle.

Liu Zongyuan, being a reformist for Tang Dynasty's literature circle, had been frustrated in political career. Demoted to be a local officer in Yongzhou (Liling, Hunan Province) in his early years, he cast his eyes on the elegant landscape during his 10-year-old stay in Yongzhou due to the hate to the ugliness of the officialdom. Deeply reveled in the landscapes and melted them in the articles, he wrote down numerous noted pieces on landscape. Itinerary notes represent his peak achievement in prose creation. *Eight Travel Notes about Yongzhou*, Liu's masterpieces, have been shine out brilliantly in Chinese literature treasure.

Nowadays tourists can still pay homage to Liu Zi Temple built for the commemoration of Liu Zongyuan in Liling, Hunan Province. In 810, Liu settled down in Ran Xi where he wrote Eight Poems on Yu Xi Brook after rename the place as Yu Xi Brook (*Yu* means stupidity here). *Preface to Yu Xi Brook Poems* is a prelude for the eight poems in question. Why did he rename it as Yu Xi Brook? Liu gave three points: first, its water level is to slow to irrigate fields; second, its water is turbulent and full of protrudent rocks, which hinders the approach of big boats; third, the riverbed is narrow and shallow in a remote place, having no attractions to dragons to rain. He teased himself that there was nothing else, except the Brook, are more stupid than him in the world since his behaviors were often out of swim even in the peaceful age. The wise and cynical comparison between the Brook's stupidity and his clearly showed that Liu's tourism in mountains and rivers were not just for appreciation but for the expression of the discontentment and the empathy of his persistent dream.

Song and Yuan Dynasties saw an age with many great travelers, some traveled at home and others even went traveling abroad.

Su Shi (Su Dongpo) was a "versatile" Chinese ancient talent, boasting pretty high attainments in literature and arts such as poetries, Ci poems, Fu poems, proses, paintings and music. As for tourism, Su also displayed his branded free and grand style. The regions he toured were so vast and the results he obtained in his tours were so extensive that nearly no one can achieve.

Su Dongpo, born in a bureaucratic family, went to the capital for the imperial examination with his noted father Su Xun when grew up. He had held posts for 26 times covering 11 provinces and 16 counties, which enabled him to visit scenic spots and historical sites everywhere on his way fro/to the posts and have the time to compose a great deal of majestic poems to glorify the nature.

Su had twice been the official of Hangzhou where he cherished the West Lake intensely. Intoxicated by the scenery of the Lake, he nearly viewed the Lake everyday. A description in *Record of Hangzhou* says: "Su Donpo tours the West Lake when he holds the office in Hangzhou. His attendants go there through the Qiantang Gate while Su rows through Yongjin Gate with one or two veterans. After having meals in Pu'an Court, he strolls around Lingyin and Dizhu Temples. Equipped with officials and files, he arrives at Cold Spring Pavilion and quickly sweeps away the disputes and lawsuits at ease. Then he drank happily with the peers and officials. At dusk, they ride back together." According to statistics, he wrote above 300 poems and *Ci*-poems with the West Lake as the theme.

On Su's second trip to Hangzhou, the West Lake became shallow and smaller with rampant weeds covering half of the water due to lack of maintenance. To improve the dilapidated lake, Su arranged 200 thousand civilians to dredge up the lake and built a causeway with the excavated slurry linking the south and north banks of the lake. Moreover, bridges were erected and the West Lake came back to the vastness and beautifulness. "Spring Dawn at Su Causeway" has become a noted charming and gentle view from then on. Residents of Hangzhou sent Su's favorite pork to him for expressing their gratitude. Su asked the servants to send the pork and spirits to the civilians. While cooking, the civilians mistakenly cooked the pork with spirits due to mishearing Su's instruction. Unexpectedly the pork stewed with spirits was more delicious and fresh. So, Dong Po Style Pork was spread and honored as a historical famous dish in Suzhou and Hangzhou.

Even at the time when he was demoted and dispatched to Huangzhou, Huanggang County, Hubei Province with "relatives and friends depart from him because of fright", he still went boating in the Changjiang River, stood in the pavilion to view the scenery and composed the lines of "East flows the mighty river, sweeping away the heroes of time past…" in his best-known masterpiece of *Nian Nujiao*, *Meditation on the Past in Chibi*.

In the late years, Su Dongpo was demoted to Danzhou, Hainan. Even under the situation of "no meat for meals, no medicine for diseases, no room for rest, no friends for outing, no heating for winters and no water to drink for summers" in his hard and lonely exiled life, Su also traveled around happily like before. Having concentrated himself completely into the nature, he achieved a life realm of "extreme consummation" and "adaptable to everything".

Similar with Su Dongpo, great travelers with successes in itinerary literature, history and arts living in Song and Yuan Dynasties also include Fan Zhongyan, author of *Thoughts on the Yueyang Tower*, Lu You, auther of *Touring Shanxi Village*, Sima Guang, author of *History as a Mirror*, Wang Anshi, inspired from tourism to articles, Ouyang Xiu, prestigious for tourism and itinerary notes, Zhang Kejiu, enjoying fantastic sceneries himself, Zhu Xi, Fan Chengda and Xin Qiji etc. It is really an age of tourism inspires literature and tourists highlight the literature brilliantly.

(4) Hard geographical investigations

Just as the name implies, survey of travel refers to the practice with the combination of learning and tourism based on the later generations' textual research on the correctness and errors of the posthumous works of the early generations or the exploration of the myths of the world. This is one of the Chinese outstanding traditions since the ancient times, i. e. Reading makes a full man; practice, a competent man. Some scholars or those who are longing for learning have made great academic and scientific achievements through long-term painstaking field survey and travel, and meanwhile, become famous travelers.

Sima Qian, whose style name was Zichang, was a great historian and litterateur in Western Han Dynasty. He was born in a well-known official family in Hancheng City Shaanxi province. The family learning with a long history had deep influence on his road of learning. At the age of 20, he followed six people including court academician Zhutai for "travel", and began his life of travel.

According to *Taishigong in the Records of History* and *The Story of Sima Qian in the Book of Han Dynasty*, he "made southward trip to Changjiang and Huaihe River, climbed up Huiji Mountain, explored Yu's cave, Jiuyi Mountain, crossed Yuan River and Xiang Rivers; crossed Wenshui and Sihui rivers in the north, and gave lectures in the capitals of Qi and Lu to observe the relique of Confucius, visited the Zou, and Yi. He was trapped in Po, Xue, and Peng. He passed by Liang and Chu, and then returned." Therefore, the later generations can know that Sima Qian set his feet on Huiji (Shaoxing, Zhejiang), Gusu, Huaiyin, Fengpei, and Chu…he surveyed Meng Changjun's official shire; in the states of Zou and Lu, he offered sacrifice to the hometown of Confucius and Mencius to have an understanding of the Confucianism. Besides, he passed Zhuolu and climbed the Great Wall in the north, and traveled to Yuan Xiang, and set his feet to Kongtong Mountain in the west. Grand travel broadened his horizons and enriched his knowledge.

In B.C. 99, he was imposed castration punishment due to Li Ling's Event, which greatly provoked him mentally, but he encouraged himself with people in the adversity such as Confucius, Qu Yuan, Zuo Qiuming, Sun Zi and Han Fei. Finally, he endured humiliation and lived with astonishing willpower, thinking that "Though death befalls all men alike, it may be weightier than Mount Tai or lighter than a feather." Finally, he accomplished the great work, *the Book of History*, which remained as a magnum opus that "explores the boundary between heaven and people, and understands the changes of past and present, thus formulating words of a new school".

*The Book of History* is the first biographical history book of China, and it initiated the grand beginning of biographical history works. The book was highly lauded by Lu Xun, the great Chinese modern writer, as "the apex of historical books and rhymeless 'Li Sao'". It was worth the praise. Sima Qian was the earliest and most outstanding representative for academic survey and travel in ancient China.

Li Daoyuan, whose style name was Shanchang, was born in Zhuolu, Fanyang (Zhuozhou, Hebei Province). Born into an official family, he sojourned in Shandong along with his father. He had thorough travel to the mountains and rivers in Shandong. After he grew up, he often followed Emperor Xiaowen in Northern Wei Dynasty (386—581) to make tours of inspection to Shanxi, Henan and other places, where he made survey of the rivers and water systems and the geographical styles and features.

Since childhood, Li Daoyuan had dream for geographical research, especially fond of research on the hydrological geography and natural scene. He made full of the opportunities of being officials in various places to conduct field survey. He set his feet in many places including Hebei, Henan, Shandong, Shanxi, Anhui, Jiangsu, and Inner Mongolia. In each place, he would travel around famous places of interests, mountains and rivers, and conducted careful investigation into current and topography. Besides, he paid visit to local superiors to understand such information as the change of watercourses in history and the origins of rivers as well as the areas through which the rivers flow. In this way, he obtained a great deal of first-hand materials. Meanwhile, he read lots of ancient works on geography, for example, *the Classic of Mountains and Rivers*, *Yu Gong*, *Zhou Li Zhifang*, *Han Works: Geography*, and *the Classics on Waters*, laying a solid foundation for his geography research and writing.

*The Classics on Waters*, a geography book written by Sang Qin in the era of Three Kingdoms, briefly recorded the watercourse situations of 137 major rivers in the country. The book with only more than 10000 Chinese characters, recorded quite briefly, was lack of system. It did not record the geographical situations of the watercourses and the areas through which the rivers flow in a detailed and specific manner. Therefore, Li Daoyuan used the rich first-hand materials under his control, and on the basis of the Classics on Waters, he finally completed Commentary to the Classic of Waters, a masterpiece on geography.

In order to write Commentary to *the Classic of Waters*, Li Daoyuan went on a journey twice along with Emperor Xiaowen of Beiwei. In two years of time, he covered ten thousands of miles. He followed the suit of Sima Qian before writing *the Book of History*. Wherever he went, he visited many aged gentlemen and historic sites, which enabled him to obtain a great deal of unheard-of materials.

With a quote of lots of books and stele materials, the book boasts marvelous style of writing with high value in history and literature. Li Daoyuan was thus recognized as the originator of travel literature describing mountains and waters.

Shen Kuo was an eminent scientist and politician of the Northern Song Dynasty (960—1127). He was born into a scholar-official family. When he was young, he followed his father and made journey to many places. According to history records, he "would visit people including doctors, those on streets and lanes, or children, so that scholar-bureaucrats and anchoret in mountains wherever he went".

After survey of the Yandang Mountain with beautiful scenery and stiff and strange peaks, Shen Kuo ascertained that the formation of the strange peak on Yandang Mountain was like this, "at that time, the valley was swashed by flood. Gone were the sands and dusts. Only huge stones remained to stand upright". When he passed by the foot of Taihang

Mountain on a diplomatic mission under orders, he found " there are usually snail and clam shells as well as stones like bird eggs on the cliffs", thus he guessed, "This is the seashore in the past". Sand and mud filled up and formed land. These judgments have been validated by the science today, and thus Shenkuo was the first to have given scientific explanation of the terrain formation in North China.

During his diplomatic mission to Khitan, Shenkuo conducted field survey of the local situations of mountains and rivers, human relationship and custom. After his return to court, he prepared China's first relief map, i. e. Map for Khitan on Diplomatic Mission. When he held a post on the border in the northwest, he found a substance locally called "grease water (Zhishui)" and cementitious oil (Niyou), and ascertained that "it would prevail in the future". This is one of the indispensable resources in our modern life, i. e. petroleum.

Shen Kuo spent eight years of time in his old age in sorting out his notes carefully. Since the spring in front of his residence was called Mengxi, so his notes were called *Mengxi Bitan (Dream Pool Essays)*. In hid notes, he made a detailed record of the scientific development and production technologies at that time, for example, compass, movable-type printing, and the methods for steel-making and copper-making, and "made them pass on to the future generations".

*The Travels of Xu Xiake*, written by Xu Xiake (1586—1641), the great geographer and traveler of the Ming Dynasty, gives a diary type of literature with a detailed record of what he saw and heard during his travels, including mountains, rivers, climate, vegetation, custom and human relationship etc. With rich literature style and significant scientific value, the book was an early work on Karst landform in the world.

Xu Xiake was born into an aristocratic family. Since his childhood, he received good family education, and had special interest in books on history, geography, and travel notes. When he grew up, he was discontented with the dark politics in late Ming Dynasty, and had no intention to attend imperial examination. So he aspired to travel around the country to visit famous mountains and rivers".

At the age of 22, the beginning of Xu Xiake's travel career was started. With Long Travel Hat woven by his mother, he left his family and started his 34-year-long exploration and travel in his lifetime. He travelled to Beijing and Hebei in the north, Fujian and Guangdong in the south, and he climbed up the Peak of Taihua Mountain in the northwest, and reached the border of Yunnan and Guizhou in the southwest. His footprints could be found in the 16 provinces, i. e. Jiangsu, Zhejiang, Shandong, Shanxi, Henan, Hebei,

Anhui, Jiangxi, Fujian, Guangdong, Guangxi, Hunan, Hubei, Guizhou and Yunan.

Xu Xiake's travel and survey was greatly supported by his mother, who inspired him, "Man should aim higher". His mother, who even disregarded her old age of 70, accompanied Xu Xiake to travel Gouqu (Yixing, Jiangsu Province) and other places.

During his travel, Xu Xiake was diligent to keep notes. Wherever he went, he would take a careful survey and examination of the direction, division and continuity of ranges, as well as the causes of formation of odd mountains and waters. Sometimes, in order to explore the origins and ranges, he would travel to some places again and again, even returned without expected results many times.

According to his own travel experiences for many years, he summarized a set of regional comparative methods for systematically observing and comprehensively describing geographical environment, and expressing geographical characteristics, and other methods for explaining geographical phenomena and causes of formation. This kind of modern geographical research method was 200 years earlier than those of western geographers. His record of the lime rock physiognomy in the southwest of China was also 200 years earlier than Europeans. Therefore, Xu Xiake was considered as the pioneer of modern geography.

In 1636, Xu Xiake's mother passed away. He was 51. Due to lack of kindred care, he left his hometown for Yunnan, his farthest destination for travel and survey, via Jiangsu, Zhejiang, Jiangsu, Hunan, Guangxi, and Guizhou. The five years of travel turned out the last and the longest travel in his lifetime.

In order to survey geography, Xu Xiake rushed about in wild mountains and forests over the years. He suffered from not only the tests from the nature, but also the challenges arising from various human factors. With cloth shoes and luggage, he had rough meals and stayed at temple for night. During his last survey and exploration, he suffered from theft three times and ran out of food four times. He was trapped in the state of hunger and cold. Under the circumstance of extreme hardship, some people with good intentions tried to persuade Xu Xiake to stop survey and exploration at risk. "If I concluded my survey and exploration and returned to my hometown in case of difficulty, my wife and children would not simply allow me to renew my survey in the future. So my willpower for further survey won't be changed." He said, "I have brought the tool for excavation, where cannot I bury my bones if I die?"

To explore the profound mysteries of the nature, Xu Xiake sought novelty and explored the dangers. He would climb the highest mountains, and visited the deepest caves. Once when he was in Chaling, Hunan Province, he intended to explore the "evil cave" in the local legend, MaYe Cave. At the news, the local people were aroused. They rushed here from all directions, and stood around Xu Xiake with great surprise. Some people said "there are magic dragons in the cave", some uttered "there are evils in the cave" …Xu Xiake, however, feared nothing at all, took off his clothes, and went into the cave for exploration with a torch. In the cave, he did not encounter the various magic dragons or evils, but experienced the grand phenomena of "strange shape of stones with various textures and inspirations".

Xu Xiake covered 19 provinces and cities in his lifetime, reaching Yunnan and Guangdong in the south, and Beijing and Hebei in the north. He was the first great traveler in Chinese history, who without shouldering government mission and assistance, traveled to make a survey and exploration for upholding landscape and practical learning out of his pure personal interest, which was different from worship of Buddha of religious travel, and from the romance of the wandering of scholar-bureaucrats. *The Travels of Xu Xiake* became the first field survey records and outstanding geographical work in China. With lifelike type of writing and detailed contents, the book is praised as "authentic work, great work, and marvelous work in the world" and "No. 1 travel notes in ancient and modern times".

Ming and Qing Dynasties in China witnessed the seeds of local capitalism, and the gradually shrinking feudalist society faced a new round of change. Many aspiring intellectuals stepped out of their studios and traveled and pondered in the nature, seeking the good plan for assisting their generation and benefiting the common people. Li Shizhen, the author of *Compendium of Materia Medica*, was such a great historic figure who could develop his skills to the full.

Li Shizhen (1518—1593), whose style name was Dongbi, and called Binhu, was born into a family of doctors in Qizhou (present-day Qichun County, Hubei) in the 13th year of Wuzong Zhengde of Ming Dynasty (1518). He became a Xiucai (one who passed the imperial examination at the county level in the Ming and Qing dynasties) at the age of 14. In the nine years that followed, he went to Wuchang three times to sit the examination for Juren (candidate in the imperial examinations at the provincial level in the Ming and Qing dynasties), but failed in the competitive examination. Therefore, he gave up his intention to secure an official position through imperial examination. He devoted himself to medicine instead. He persuaded his father and showed his determination, "I am like a boat against the current, and my heart is harder than stone. Hoping my father to help me to fulfill my wishes, I would fear no difficulty till death".

During more than ten years of his practice of medicine, Li Shizhen read up more than

10000 volumes of medical books in over 800 kinds. Besides, he read a lot of masterpieces on history, geography, and literature.

In the process of compiling *Compendium of Materia Medica*, it was the confusing of the name of herbs that troubled him most, causing his to be unable to decide which is right. Under his father's inspiration, Li Shizhen realized that Reading over ten thousands of books was necessary, but walking over ten thousands of miles was indispensable. Therefore, he traveled far to remote mountains and wild fields, visit famous doctors and scholars, seek folk proved recipes, and observe and collect specimen of Chinese herbal medicines. He first gathered information in his hometown Qizhou. Later, he went out to gather medical information many times. Besides Hubei and Hunan provinces, he had been to many places including Jiangxi, Jiangsu, and Anhui. His footprints could be found on Mt. Lu in Jiangsi and Mt. She, Mt. Mao, and Mt. Niushou in Nanjing which were all rich in Chinese herbal medicines.

For Li Shizhen, he would pick up and observed the herbal medicines one by one instead of only survey for a superficial understanding through cursory observation. At that time, betelnut palm produced in Wulong Palace on Taihe Mountain, in the eyes of Taoists, was the "saint fruit that could make people eternal". Every year, they picked up the fruit, and paid tribute to the emperor. The local feudal authorities forbade other people to pick. Li Shizhen did not believe the nonsense of the Taoists, so he took the risk to pick up a "saint fruit" regardless of the opposition of the Taoists. After research, he found its efficacy was the same as ordinary peaches and apricots, which can only promote the production of body fluid and relieve thirsty. It is only the anamorphic fruit of elm without any special efficacy.

After long-term filed survey, Li Shizhen finally completed *Compendium of Materia Medica* in 1578. With about 2 million Chinese characters, the book included 52 volumes with 1892 kinds of medicine, 374 kinds of newly added herbal medicines, 1100 attached pictures and more than 10000 prescriptions. It has established a monument in the history of pharmacy of China, and has made outstanding achievements in animal and plant classification and many other aspects. It also covers such fields as astronomy, geography, and science and technology. It was lauded by Darwin as the "Encyclopedia in Ancient China".

(5) Persistent religious expeditions

Religion derived from human mental activities. In early years, human beings had no clear understanding of wind, rains, thunders, rivers, lakes, and seas, mountains, valleys, sun, moon, and stars etc. So people became awesome to such natural phenomena, and then began worship and pray activities. After becoming rational animals from the animality, human beings began to ponder over the causes and effects of the nature, human society, and themselves. Religious hike is an ancient way of travel with the purpose of worshipping Buddha, praying for good luck, and preaching. It has a long history. Even in modern times, it is still a kind of far-reaching way of travel.

In the Wei, the Jin and the Southern and Northern Dynasties, Buddhism became increasingly thriving with the support of the imperial government. For instance, in the Southern and Northern Dynasties, there were more than 500 temples in Jiankang alone. Du Mu, a great poet in Tang Dynasty, wrote in the *South Riverside Spring* (The Seven-Character Chinese Metrical Poem), "Over the red-dotted green vastness, gold birds are singing, the riverside towns decorated with inn-banners fluttering. 480 temples built up during the South-Dynasty, all the pavilions cling to raining in the misty". The poem was a real portraiture of the style at that time, "temples" were those obliged by officials, and those privately built were called "Zhaoti". Later, Buddhist temples are generally called "Cha", so there are such names for fanes as Fancha, Chancha, and Gucha. Cha is the Sanskrit transliteration, meaning field and state.

Buddhist temples are mostly built on famous mountains, so there is such saying that "monks reside in many famous mountains all over China". The Taoist "fairyland" described in Golden Elixir Chapters of the Book of the Master Who Embraces Spontaneous Nature, including such mountains as Huashan, Taishan, Huoshan, Hengshan, Songshan, Shaobaoshan, Changshan, Jingshan, Zhongnanshan, Daughter Mountain, Difeishan, Wangwushan, Baodushan, Anqiushan, Qianshan, Qingchengshan, Emeishan, Jianshan, Tiantaishan, and Luofushan, most of which are famous tourist attractions in China.

In order to pray for good weather for the crops and free from disasters, ancient people early started the activities for paying sacrifice to the god of mountains. According to historical records, at that time, 451 mountains were respected as god of mountains, and poor people and rulers were no exception. According to Offering Sacrifices to Heaven in the Records of History, emperors offered sacrifices to famous mountains and rivers, deeming the Five Famous Mountains in China as the Three Government Officials, and Four Channels as seigneurs. Seigneurs offered sacrifices to the famous mountains and rivers in their realms.

Various temples are built on famous mountains, thus forming the objective phenomenon that "monks reside in many famous mountains all over China". In turn, the said mountains are famous for many old and famous temples. Since ancient times, people visit famous mountains mostly for pilgrimages to offer incenses. It is the case even at present. The old say was proved true that what matters most for a mountain is not its height, but its heavenly inspiration.

During the period of Wei and Jin, the temples and their owners had many privileges, for example, land, pay, trade, and feneration. Soon, temple economy developed fast, which provided economic and material conditions for religious travel. Going on a pilgrimage for and spreading Buddhist scriptures, and the activities of cultivation according to religious doctrines became increasingly frequent, and many monks and believers joined the travels to seek dharma and cultivation.

The Buddhist travel in the Wei and Jin, basically could be divided into two categories. One was the travel of pilgrimage for and spreading Buddhist scriptures. During the period, sea and land route transport was relatively developed; so many foreign monks came to China to spread Buddhist scriptures. The person who was came to China first from land route for this purpose was Yicun from Dayueshi (current Afghanistan). He came to China in the late West Han Dynasty. Afterwards, Dharmaraksha and Kashyapamtanga came to Chang'an and Luoyang via Dunhuang. They were buried in Baima Temple in Henan after death. During the regime of Sun Quan in Three Kingdoms, monks came to China from Viet Nam and other South Asian regions. After Bodhidharma from came to China from Tianzhu (India today), he had deep influence on Chinese culture. According to historical records, he had been to the temples in Guangzhou, Jiankang (Nanjing today), and other regions in succession. Finally, he settled down on Songshan Mountain, where he initiated the Buddhist zen school of meditation for self-cultivation, and established Shaolin Wushu with great fame all over the world.

Foreign Buddhist scriptures spreaders during the period promoted and prospered Chinese Buddhist culture, and propelled the progress of Chinese monks to travel to the west to seek dharma. According to textual research, Zhu Shixing, the first Han monk who introduced Buddhism to Central China from India in Caowei Period. He was from Yinchuan (Henan today). During his routines of eulogizing Buddhist scriptures, he felt that some reading books lacked contextual continuity. Whenever he saw foreign Buddhist spreaders, he would have the intention to go abroad to seek dharma and trace the source. After him, ten monks including Kang Falang went to Western Regions, India and other places to seek dharma, of whom, the most famous one was Fa Xian, a renowned monk from Wuyang, Pingyuan County, Shanxi. *Records of Buddhist Countries*, written by him according to his experiences, plays a very important role in the current research on the ancient history of South Asia.

During the Wei and Jin period, foreign monks came to spread Buddhist scriptures and Chinese monks traveled to the west to seek dharma, marking the beginning of China's first international travel of scale from religion, which served as an initiator for the development of Chinese Buddhism and the cultural exchange between China and foreign countries.

Besides monks' journey to the west, another form of Buddhist travel is the travel where local monks cultivate themselves and talked about Buddhist theories in the nature. The famous monk travelers at that time included Fanlan, Zhi Daolin, Shi Daoan, and Huiyuan et al. In their eyes, people could "seek recreation in the nature", mould their temperament, enjoy mountains and waters, and learn from each other by exchanging Buddhist theories in the nature, which was a kind of grace of accomplished monks.

Huiyuan was one of the favorite students of Shi Daoan. At the age of 45, Huiyuan left his master for the south alone in order to carry forward Buddhist theories. When he passed by Luoshan Mountain, he found "Lushan is wild and spacious where he can get rid of sundry ideas", so he set up Longquan Jingshe in the Xilin Temple, and then moved to Donglin Temple. During the long period of 36 years, he "stayed on the mountain and kept away from the common people", and explained Buddhist theories. Thus, he became the representative figure of one of the famous and important schools of Buddhism.

Taoism is the local religion of China. In the Qin and Han Dynasties, to become immortal, Emperor Qin Shihuang and Emperor Wu assigned excellent persons to visit marvelous mountains and waters. The activities of these excellent persons were called Xianyou (Immortal travel). During the period of Wei and Jin, with the prevailing of Taoism, Taoists were not the only participants. Literators, officials, and common people joined them.

Ge Hong was a famous Taoist leader in Eastern Jin Dynasty. He was good at immortal Taoism. He studied medicine and Taoism and Confucianism. With rich knowledge of various schools and profound thoughts, he wrote a rich variety of books. He not only made great contributions to the development of Taoist theory, but made achievements in metallurgy, medicine, music, literature and other aspects. In order to collect Taoist immortal methods, he made "a long and hard journey from afar", traveled to famous mountains.

Due to the booming of religions, Buddhist temples and Taoist temples welled up constantly, and the number of ordinary believers became bigger. Although these believers could wander around like Taoist pope Fangshi, many of them went to religious sites to visit and offer sacrifices when they were free from farming work, especially on the occasions of holidays and sacrifice-offering, which made the scale of religious travel increasingly expand. However, during the period of the Sui and Tang Dynasties, economy and culture thrived, and religious travel prevailed during the said period.

In the Tang Dynasty, Zen began to boom, and more and more zen monks joined the travel for seeking Buddhist theories from their masters. Buddhist travel became a special way of self-cultivation. The Buddhist travel mentioned herein was different from sightseeing in ordinary sense. They made journey around and communicated with various great masters and famous schools for Buddhist theories and insights.

As a unique way of self-cultivation, Buddhist travel is the embodiment of the fundamental thoughts of Zen. Zen emphasizes that "no focus on one specific aspect is the nature of human being", so it is vital to "seeking explanation by oneself instead of from others", "seeking solutions through travel instead of understanding", and overtaking masters instead of focusing on them.

The so-called "focus" means focusing on one aspect. According to Zen, if a person owns something, his "mentality" will be tied by something. The more one owns, the more his "mentality" will be tied. Only when a person minimizes what he owns will his mentality be free from too much mixed ideas, and he will be free from any troubles and interferences from the society. Therefore, monks on Buddhist travel, generally, experienced the state of leisure and carelessness through the way of roaming. Without any purpose for material gains, they could become friends with mountains and rivers, and integrate with the nature.

Buddhist monks often roamed around mountains and rivers. As time passed by, they absorbed the essence of the nature, and forged extraordinary cultivation. Their experience of the nature was different from that of ordinary people. The difference was shown in their poems. The difference from traditional landscape poems by scholars could be found, and it added new contents to the ancient poem field of China.

They usually chose Buddhist temples as the topics, and they always focused their imago points on deep valleys and remote mountains, deserted temples and white clouds, moonlit nights and pine trees and the like, from which they could experience the Zen pleasure and interest. *Take Composed upon Po Shan Temple's Hou Chan Chamber* written by Chang Jiang for instance, "Entering the temple in the morning, the rising sun shines on the high trees. Winding paths lead to the deepest places, Zen houses among woods and flowers. Mountain light takes pleasure in the bird's character, with the shadow of the lake preempting the eye's mind. While all voices are silent, you only hear the bell". The poem highlighted the silence and quietness of the mountain temple so as to make the Zen mechanism and style outstanding. It was really a famous poem describing mountains and temples. Another example, *Gift to Qinseng*, "Remote antiquity sound flows from fingers, Zen house seemed chilly at the moon-lit night, doleful wind and streams sobbed frequently, the sound remained wonderful even in silence"; *Forgotten Anxiety*, "Unconsciously it is hot summer after spring, cicadas sing in the autumn shade. Strong wind broke the thatch door, fallen leaves seemed frost on the ground"; *Shade and Moon*, "Shade and moon mixed at night, one monk sits on one cattail hassock, sitting in tailor-fashion till midnight, flying moth put out the lamp before Buddha", and more examples like these are the masterpieces describing the visional state of Zen.

With the development of economy and culture, it was an emerging climax for Buddhist monks to travel to the west to Buddhist theories in the west in Tang Dynasty. Some of Buddhist travelers made their travel further to foreign countries. This kind of travel was covered with sort of mysterious style due to long and hard journey. Xuan Zang, the prototype of Tang Monk in the Journey to the West, one of the four masterpieces of China, was an initiator of this kind of travel.

Xuan Zang (600—645), family name Chen, was called Hui. He was born into a Confucianism family in Goushi, Luozhou (Goushi Town, Yanshi, Henan). He was very bright since childhood. It was said that at the age of 8, when his father taught him *The Classic of Filial Piety*, he talked about "Zeng Zi dodged a seat". Suddenly, Xuan Zhuang tidied up himself and stood up. His father asked him what happened. He said, "Zeng Zi dodged a seat at the order of his teacher. I followed your kind teaching. How could I sit with ease?" Xuan Zhuang learned various classic theories introduced into China. When he found much differences and discrepancies, he made up his mind to settle these issues. He chose to travel to the west to seek Buddhist theories, hoping to find the classics in India to unify the domestic Buddhist theories.

In 629, Xuan Zhuang left Chang'an (Xi'an today) to the west. Under the assistance of Gao King of Gaochang, Khan of West Tujue, and other headmen in the Western Regions, he passed through the 19 states in the Western Regions, and great snow mountains, and another more than 10 states, and then he entered the State of Lanbo in India. In 633, he reached the Nalanda Temple, the center of Buddhism of India at that time. There were tens of thousands of resident monks in the temple. Xuan Zhuang learned philosophy, Buddhism, logic, medicine, craftwork, and rhythm etc. After five years, he became one of the ten Buddhist masters accomplished in 50 volumes of classics. Then, he left the temple, and traveled to East India, South India, and West India, and finally, he returned to the temple again. In the temple, he had the chance to learn *A Buddhist Pilgrim on the Silk Road* and other Buddhist classics, where he realized his original wishes.

After the learning, Xuan Zhuang digested Buddhist Pilgrim and Madhyamika. Besides, he wrote on *Buddhist Theories*. Thus, he was famous in India. Later, he wrote *Insights into Treatment of the Evils*, which was lauded by Jie Xian as "Second to none in the world." When Xuan Zhuang stayed in India, a person of Lokayata hanged 40 pieces of viewpoints at the gate of the temple, and invited people for argument, saying in case of failure, he would extend thanks beheaded. Ordinary people dared not to go but Xuan Zhuang. After several rounds, the person was defeated, asking to be beheaded as agreed upon. Xuan Zhuang did not allow him to do so, but asked to seek the power of Buddhism.

Before Xuan Zhuang returned to China, King Harshavardhana held farewell ceremony to him in Kanyakubja. At the ceremony, Xuan Zhuang proposed his viewpoints in On Buddhist Theories and Insights into Treatment of the Evils. In 18 days, no one questioned him. So the honorary tiles of Mahāyāna-deva and was recommended and granted to him.

On the $24^{th}$ day of the first lunar month in 645, Xuan Zhuang reached the west suburb of the capital of Tang Dynasty. Hundreds of thousands of people welcomed him back. The capital was rather crowded so that he had too much difficulty to enter. At that time, Emperor Tang Taizong was in Luoyang. After he met the emperor, he was asked to write down his experience in the Western Regions, and tried to persuade him to secularize and engage in politics. Xuan Zhuang only consented to the first request.

When Xuan Zhuang returned, he brought back 657 Sanskrit classics. In the nearly 20 years after his return, he translated 75 classics with 1350 volumes. Besides, he wrote *Traveling Notes of the Western Regions in Great Tang Dynasty* and other works. Some of his memorials, documents, and letters were collected in the *Life of Hiuen Tsiang Si-Yu-Ki*.

The stories of Xuan Zhuang attracted great attention of the monks in Tang Dynasty. Later, many monks took Xuan Zhuang as example and traveled to the west to seek Buddhist scripture unswervingly. *Tales of the Hierarchs Searching Buddhist Scripture in Western Regions of Tang Dynasty* recorded such 60 monks. They feared nothing all in face of hardships and dangers. They never cower or accept destiny. With surefooted and religious attitude, they walked steadily, which became a historically much-told story passed on generation after generation.

Taoism, an indigenous religion in China, gained unprecedented development in Tang Dynasty. As Li Er, the founder of Taoism, has the same surname with the Emperor of Tang Dynasty, Taoism enjoyed equal privileges as those for Buddhism in the dynasty. A large number of Taoist temples sprung up across the nation, "The Three Divine Officials (namely the official of heaven, the official of earth and the official of water)" temples in particular.

Numerous influential folktales such as "Zhangxian Bringing Sons", "Zhongkui Captures Ghosts" and "The Eight Fairies" are all originated from the Tang Dynasty. Affected by the idea of "Taoism is hidden in forests", many well-known Taoists including Yuan Danqiu, Li Ye and Huang Pusong, either lived in mountains or roamed around, intoxicated with the enchantment of the great nature. In a sense, compared with Buddhism, Taoism is closer to the essence of mountains and rivers, and the nature of travel as well.

(6) Ingenious and brave diplomatic visits

A diplomatic trip is to fulfil political or economic purposes of a state. This kind of trip originated before the Qin Dynasty, and was popular in confusing and turbulent times. Scholars frequently canvassed among kingdoms. Su Qin and Zhang Yi were typical representatives of this kind of persuasive talkers. In West Han Dynasty, Zhang Qian, a famous diplomat, travelled to the West Region twice. This is a significant event in Chinese travel history.

Before the Han Dynasty, the West Region was strange to all the people living in Middle China. In early West Han, although people began to know about the West Region from merchants who went between the west and the east, people in Middle China could not grasp specific information about the West Region due to the traffic limit.

During the period of Emperor Wu in Han Dynasty, the northern border area of Han Dynasty was often invaded and disturbed by Hun people. In B.C. 138, Emperor Wu sent Zhang Qian to the West Region to ally with the Great Yeh-chin to fight against Hun.

Zhang Qian was born in Hanzhong. Chen Shou, writer of *History of Three Kingdoms*, said: "Zhang Qian was born in Chenggu, Hanzhong (present Chenggu County in Shanxi Province)." When Zhang Qian started the trip, over 100 people followed him. When Zhang Qian's delegation passed Hun area in B.C. 139, he was captured by Hun and was detained for as long as ten years. Meantime, he concealed his talents in order to spoof the enemy. One day, Zhang Qian escaped with a few attendants. When he returned from the west to the east, he was captured again by Hun. Later, he escaped back to Chang'an during inner strife in Hun. Zhang Qian spent 13 years to finished the trip. When he returned back to Chang'an, only one attendant followed him.

This trip is the first official trip to communicate with states in West Region in Chinese history, and establishes links between Han Dynasty and those countries. The political purpose required by Emperor Wu is not fulfilled, but a great deal of geological knowledge and folk custom about the West Region is acquired through observation of the delegation. People in Middle China began to know specific details of the West Region. Moreover, the information encouraged Emperor Wu to expand the territory. Later, he initiated a series of wars against Hun.

In B. C. 119, Han Dynasty sent Zhang Qian to the West Region again in order to ally with the State of Wusun. Zhang Qian led more than 300 people to prevent from attacks of Hun, and the delegation arrived at the State of Wusun safely. Thanks to in-house conflicts in the State of Wusun, the alliance purpose was not reached. Zhang Qian and envoys from the State of Wusun together returned to Chang'an. When the envoys came back to Wusun, they talked to everybody about the prosperity in Middle China. Afterwards, Han Dynasty and the State of Wusun frequently exchanged agricultural products, and finally established marriage relations.

The two brave and hard trips executed by Zhang Qian enhanced the relations between the West Han and minorities in the West Region. Zhang Qian's mission trips enriched geological knowledge of Chinese people, and advanced commercial and cultural exchanges with the West Region. Elaborate Chinese handcraft products, in particular silk, lacquer products, jade articles, and bronze ware, were taken to the West Region, and natives in the West Region, such as clovers, grapes, walnuts, guavas, sesames, horsebeans, cucumbers, garlics, carrots, woollen products, furs, fine horses, camels, lions, and ostriches, were brought to China in succession. At the same, western music, dances, paintings, sculptures, and acrobatics were also disseminated to China, and western art had active effects on ancient Chinese culture and Zhang Qian's trips established an important road in inland Asia, started official friendly exchanges with the West Region in culture and economy fields, and pioneered the land traffic from Gansu and Xinjiang in China to present Afghanistan, Iran, and other places, which is known as the famous Silk Road. Therefore, Zhang Qian is worthy of the name of the first Chinese people going to the world.

After functioning for over 140 years, the Silk Road was almost cut off by disturbances from Hun in late West Han and early East Han, so Ban Chao was sent by Han Dynasty to the West Region on a diplomatic mission.

Ban Chao was born in Xianyang. When he was young, he studied hard and decided to contribute to the country like Zhang Qian. After the foundation of East Han, the economic situation gradually recovered after fifty years of rehabilitation. In A. D. 73, Ban Chao led a delegation to the State of Shanshan. He learned that the king of Shanshan didn't dare to be friendly with them, because Hun people were supervising Shanshan people. Then, Ban Chao set a fire on Hun camps. The King of Shanshan eliminated worries after seeing such a brave envoy from East Han, and made up his mind to submit to the authority of East Han. Other states in the West Region then became friendly with East Han after this event. Since then, states in the West Region resumed relations with Han and sent emissaries to Han. The Silk Road was reused after being blocked for more than fifty years. On the southern road of the West Region appeared a peaceful and harmonious scene of travellers without soldiers.

Meantime, Ban Chao sent Gan Ying to visit the Western Roman Empire. Although Gan Ying only got to the Persian Gulf and returned due to various causes, he obtained valuable information about the states in Middle Asia. Ban Chao stayed in the West Region for altogether more than 30 years, and established friendly relations between East Han and over 50 states in the West Region.

A well-known nautical specialist in Yuan Dynasty—Wang Dayuan, styled name is Huangzhang. He was from Nanchang of Jiangxi Province. He was called "oriental Marco Polo." When he was a child, he had already traveled Quanzhou of Fujiang — the largest commercial port of the world, meanwhile, it was the largest commercial port of China in that time, with his seniors. People who had various colors and said different languages jostled each other in a crow in Quanzhou Port, and all kinds of products from China and foreign countries were piled up mountain-high in the port. He was so exciting for all of them. Especially, he was curious to the exotic conditions and customs which was described by the merchants and sailors from China and foreign countries.

In 1330, Wang Daquan was just 20 years old. He came to Quanzhou. and went on his first long journey by Quanzhou oceangoing merchant ship. In autumn of 1334, he traveled back to Quanzhou. In those several years, he started from Quanzhou, passed through Hainan Island, ancient Vietnam, Malacca, Java, Sumatera Utara, Myanmar, India, Persia, Arabia, Egypt, then crossed the Mediterranean Sea and reached to a northwest country of Africa, Morocco. After that, he returned to Egypt, then came to Somalia through the Red Sea and traveled to south to Mozambique. He crossed the Indian Ocean with the merchant ship and reached to Sri Lanka, Sumatra, Java, Australia, Kalimantan Island and Philippines, at last he returned to Quanzhou.

The long-range voyage expanded the vision of Wang Dayuan who has been curious. In 1337, Wang Dayuan started for the first time from Quanzhou to the islands in the southern sea, the Arabian Sea in the west of the Indian Ocean, the Persian Gulf, the Red Sea, the Mediterranean, the Mozambique Channel, and places in Oceania, and he returned back to Quanzhou after two years.

When Wang Dayuan returned, he started to compile the Island Foreigners, preparing for recording the economic and social situations in each state that he passed during the two voyages. Later on, Wang Dayuan went to Nanchang, his hometown, and extracted the book into *A Brief Description of the Island Foreigners*, which was printed and issued and further spread in public.

When Wang Dayuan compiled *Island Foreigners*, he was very serious. Once he said: "All information in the book was witnessed by himself, and no legendary stories were recorded." Ma Huan, who followed Zheng He during the seven voyages to the western sea in Emperor Yongle period of Ming Dynasty, said: "Following Zheng He, I passed many states and saw the local situation. Then I know that the content in the *Island Foreigners* is true."

The extracted *A Brief Description of the Island Foreigners* talks about over 220 states and regions. The book has information about Taiwan and the Pescadores Islands. According to the book, Taiwan was administered by the Pescadores Islands, which was subject to Jinjiang County of Quanzhou. Salt tax and other taxes were collected by Jinjiang County. The book also recorded the information about overseas Chinese people for many times. For example, merchants from Wuzhai of Quanzhou lived in the current Timor Island; some officers and soldiers of the troop sent by Yuan Dynasty to Java still stayed in the current Granville Island; in Shali Badan (current Nagapatnam on the eastern shore in India), there stood a Chinese style brick tower built by Chinese people in 1267, and on the tower was Chinese characters saying: "By Chinese workers in August of the Third Year of Xianchun Emperor"; there lived Chinese people in the State of Zhenla (currently Cambodia); there lived Chinese men and women in Longyamen (currently Singapore); and even the chief of Malujian (the current Marag in northwest Iran) was born in LinZhang, China.

Information about the Oceania was also recorded in *A Brief Description of the Island Foreigners*. At that time, Chinese people call the Oceania as Luosuosi, and called Darwin Harbour area as Manali. Merchants and sailors from Quanzhou thought the Oceania was the end island on earth, so they called it an End Island. With regard to living conditions of people in the Oceania, Wang Dayuan wrote: "Men and Women look very different. They don't wave or wear, but cover their bodies with bird feathers. They don't cook with fire, but eat both furs and blood of an animal. They live in caves in group." He also wrote: "They wear colourful short jacket made of raw silk and skirts made of cloth." Wang Dayuan also said a place in northern Oceania was "surrounded by water". In fact, this place refers to the large swamp to the east of Darwin Harbour. The Anheng Peninsula on northern shore of the Oceania and 800m-high Jipeili mesa, which was described as "strange peaks are like running horses and the place is by the sea", were recorded by Wang Dayuan and later proved to be true.

The book, *A Brief Description of the Island Foreigners*, which is famous for detailed records and exact words, has important historical value in the research of historical geography. Therefore, the book attracted much attention from foreign historians. Since 1867, western scholars began to read and study the book, and translate it into many languages. The book has many records about the natural conditions and products in the Oceania, these records are supposed to be the earliest written recordation about the Oceania in the world. However, most western scholars dare not or would not accept that Wang Dayuan has ever been to the Oceania, because European people learned to know the continent almost 200 years after Wang Dayuan's tour to the Oceania.

2. Tourism in ancient world

Outside China, travel activities emerged in ancient civilized nations of Egypt, Babylon, and India, as well as ancient Greece and Rome with advanced economic, political, and cultural development.

(1) Traveling activities in countries with ancient civilizations, such as Egypt, Babylon and India, etc.

As early as before B. C. 1000, Egypt was a famous tourist site, and a large number of travellers visited Egypt by water and land every year. Some nobles appreciated the landscape down the Nile in boats with delicious foods, and some nobles travelled to the pyramids in sedan chairs and carriages.

In the time of pyramid, Egyptian business was extremely prosperous. There appeared surplus agricultural products and handcraft products, so nobles had to take up commercial activities outside Egypt. They went to some places by ship or land and exchanged products or bought something with currency in order to meet their demand for luxurious lift. Before B. C. 2700, Egypt carried out frequent overseas trades with the Island of Crete, Phoenicia, Palestine, and Syria.

Many a people did religious trips in Egypt, and there were several large-scale religious festival assemblies. During festival period, people travelled to the assembly site by boat. Men played flutes, and women accompanied. They danced and performed in every town along the river. When they arrived at the assembly site, they sacrificed their offerings, and held various ritual ceremonies. All people enjoyed in the spectacular activities. From 1501 to B. C. 1480, Egyptian Queen Hatshepsut went to Punt (Red Sea area) to have a visit, and this is deemed as the earliest travel in the world.

Mesopotamian civilization originated between Tigris and Euphrates, i. e. the present Middle East including Iraq and Iran. The land in this area was fertile, and there were a great deal of products. Moreover, the rivers, the Mediterranean, the Persian Gulf, and the Red Sea provided convenient traffic conditions for local commerce.

In the Hanmorabi age before B. C. 2100, the social economic and cultural situation was unprecedentedly flourishing in Babylon. Teams made up of numerous merchants and camels were not limited to go between large cities, they traded with foreign merchants through convenient river and sea shipping. At that time, there was a famous commercial centre, the Commercial Travel City. People nowadays can imagine the ceremonious scene at that time from inscriptions and arrow-headed characters. Mesopotamian industries, laws, politics, cultures, astronomy, and calendars were spread to other places by merchants, sailors, and conquerors.

American scholar Will Durant wrote in the *Civilization History of the World —— Our Oriental Heritage*: "The current western civilization, that is, the European-American civilization, was originated from the Near East, instead of Crete, Greece, and Rome, because the Aryans didn't create any civilization actually, and their civilization was originated from Egypt and Babylon. The Greek civilization admired by the world was largely originated from cities in the Near East, which is the root of western civilization."

Phoenician sailors and merchants controlled the Mediterranean before Greek people controlled it. About B. C. 3000, Phoenician people, called the Nation above the Sea, had advanced commerce and handicraft industry, and its shipbuilding technical level was at the top place in the world. This provided chances for business trips. Owing to voyage experience for years, Phoenician people were acquainted with the Big Dipper, called by Greek people as the Phoenician Star. Phoenician people got to Estrecho de Gibraltar in the west, to the Baltic Sea in the north, and to Persian Gulf and India in the east. The Phoenician people carried Egyptian letters to the western world through their trips. This is the greatest contribution of the people to the world.

Persian Empire is one of the earliest countries that have business travels. Persian Empire is on the key traffic path from the East Asia and South Asia to the west, and has been playing an important role in cultural exchanges between the west and the east. During convergences of various cultures, therefore, diversified travel cultures developed in the empire. Partial Mesopotamian and Egyptian civilizations was inherited by Persian Empire.

When Persian Empire was powerful, the emperor ordered to build up many roads in order to control distributive governors in different places and expedite delivery of political, military, and commercial information. In the middle period of the $6^{th}$ century B. C., the empire built up two imperial roads. The first one was from Susa, the capital of Persian Empire, to Ephesus in the Mediterranean, with a total length of 2400 km. Another road was from Babylon city to the border of India. This road later acted as the western segment of the Silk Road.

In ancient times, India was the remotest state known by western people who thought that Indian people lived in the ease where the sun rose, and there would be a wild desert to the east of India. In spite of spatial distance and different cultures, India and the western world have been communicating with each other. In B. C. 975, a western fleet might take ivories, apes, and peacocks to India for spices. It is said that some educated travellers might get to Athens and discuss philosophy with Greek philosophers. When Socrates was asked about the purpose of studying philosophy by Indian people, he answered "to explore the world". Indian people smiled: "How can we recognize the world before we communicate with the God". If this record was true, the travel communication history between India and the western world would be revised.

Greek people communicated with India people in a very early time. Voltaire once wrote: "Before the time of Pythagoras, Greek people travelled to India for study." It is recorded that when Alexander reached the north of India, he found Indian traffic system was as advanced as the one in Persian Empire. On the sides of those roads, trees were planted, wells were dug, and public security sites and inns were established.

(2) Tourism in ancient Greece

The Island of Crete on the sea is a key strategic place between Italy, Egypt, and Greece. In about B. C. 2500, nobles migrated to the city and built up many ports to trade with Egypt and Syria. From B. C. 2000 to the $15^{th}$ century B. C., a powerful fleet from the island controlled the sea. According to *Homer Epic*, there were more than 90 cities on the island, and the prosperity and strength was also amazing to people nowadays. The Island of Crete is the origin of Greek civilization.

In the $8^{th}$ century B. C., Greek people began to trade with Phoenician people, Egyptians, Syrians, and Etruria people. Greek people used their wines, oils, furs, minerals, pottery, weapons, luxurious products, and books to exchange fruits and meat from Phoenicia, fishes from the Black Sea, nuts from Asia Minor, copper from Cyprus, and tin from England. In order to attract foreigners, Greek people issued a series of preferential policies. Advantageous ports in Athens were open to everyone, and foreign merchants were allowed to take away their earned gold and silver. Meantime, the Mediterranean region became the first large-scale community market in the world.

In a time in ancient Greece, it was popular to take a short-distance travel by boat.

When it came to the period of Easun and the legendary Argonaut hero, people thought that travel was more interesting than everyday life. In Greece, in particular in Athens, keeping open doors was deemed as a kind of virtue. A strange traveler was always welcomed, and an invited guest was always allowed to bring a stranger. Many hotels in cities were funded by the rich, so travelers were treated friendly even though they were not introduced.

Ancient Greek philosophers, including Thales, Pythagoras, Plato, and Aristotle, were famous travellers who thought travelling was a process to observe the world, reflect life, and share life. Knowledge acquired from voyages and trips about the actual world expedited the formation of natural sciences and philosophy in ancient Greece.

Thales's natural philosophy is some kind of metaphysics about earth. It is said that he was born in Miletus in Asia Minor, where various cultures assembled. When he was young, he did business in various places. When he visited Egypt, he ever measured the height of a pyramid. He considered the height could be measured when the shadow of a human being was equal to the actual height of him. He brought what he learned abroad in relation to mathematics, astronomy, and geometry to Greece, and proposed that the root of the earth was water. His theory laid a foundation for Greek philosophy.

Pythagoras was born in Samos, a commercial city in Greece. He studied hard when he was young, and he spent over 30 years on travelling. He's ever been to Arab, Syria, Phoenicia, India, and Gaul. When he summarized his life as a tourist, he told the travellers: "Get rid of prejudices of your own state when you travel abroad", which means do as the Romans do.

Plato has ever been to Egypt, Asia Minor, and Italy, and has visited believers of Pythagoras. Aristotle learned from Plato at 17, and spent over 20 years in Plato's lyceum. After Plato died, Aristotle travelled to Athos and other places. Plato and Aristotle might be the earliest visiting professors in tourism in the world. Aristotle was accustomed to teaching when he took a walk, so his school was called the Peripateticism. Alexander who later conquered the world was the most famous Peripatetic student.

In fact, the most renowned traveller in ancient Greece is Herodotus who combined a cultural anthropologist, a geographer, a nature study scientist, and a historian. His journeys covered all the Mediterranean, and he was awarded Father of Historian by Cicero, a noted politician in Rome. Although Herodotus concentrated on Greco-Persian Wars in his traveling works, he recorded various cultures in the Near East and Greece. His traveling experience and oral materials collected during traveling made his narration very vivid. He liked to contrast Greek culture and non-Greek culture and analyze local custom, and drew a conclusion: "The custom dominates the world and mankind, and leads the God."

From the historical material about Herodotus, we can say he has ever been to many places, including cities in Asia Minor, Greece, Macedonia, Egypt, Phoenicia, Syria, the Black Sea, south Italy, and Sicily. At that time, it was not easy for one to travel to so many places. Therefore, he was called the Father of Traveler later.

The period when religious trips were most popular is in ancient Greece age. Delos Island, Delphi, and Mt. Olympus were famed religious sanctums. In Olympia where the Temple of Zeus was built, Olympian festival was the most celebrated activity, and there were a great number of participants. During the festival, horse races, carriage races, running contests, and wrestles were held. During the time recorded by *Homer Epic*, Greek people began to carry out various sport activities. People gathered from all sides and competed to see their icons.

The ancient Olympic Games started in B. C. 776, and was abolished by Roman people in 394. The athletic meeting was held per four years, and lasted for one over 1000 years. The game was a happy festival in a real sense for Greek people, and without doubt it drove tourism in Greek and activated every game place. This game evolved to the modern Olympic Games. The old Olympia ceremony was totally a religious activity, pushing religious travelling. Later on, religious travel gradually was popularized throughout the world and became an international travel activity.

(3) Tourism in ancient Rome

The Roman time is the most prosperous travelling age in world travelling history. Seneca, a distinguished historian and write in ancient Rome, once said: "Many people would like to suffer long journeys for remote landscape." In ancient Rome, many roads were built with the centre at Rome. The road management mode was similar to modern traffic management mode. For instance, each region is responsible for a certain segment of road.

When conditions suitable for travelling got mature, some rich people who had enough spare time started to travel for pleasure. Their trips were different from the old ones for business and religious purposes, and they travelled to appreciate art, temples, and buildings and to make a healthy life.

Varo (B. C. 116—B. C. 27), a renowned Roman writer, once said: "Perhaps you've travelled to many sites. Have you ever been a place that is more beautiful than Italy? How can we list all the interesting places of note?" During holidays, Roman people went to watch the Olympic Games, went to hot springs, and went to the cinema. During this time, the earliest sightseeing tour emerged. Lakes in north England, river valleys in north

Greece, the Nile, Rhine, and rivers in Asia Minor as cultural symbols, were popular tour sites. In addition, travellers were attracted by pyramids in Egypt, temples in Greece, distinguishing custom in Spain and Gaul, and new cities in North Africa. Plutash said: "World travellers spent the most precious time in their lives on hotels and boats." According to history record, luxurious villas were built along the road from Rome to Naples for travellers.

Thanks to frequent large-scale voyages, geography developed rapidly in Roman time. Geographers were acquainted with Europe, Southeast Asia, South Asia, and North Asia, as well as custom in these areas. Poseidonius (B. C. 135—B. C. 51) was a celebrated philosopher, geographer, and runner. He's traveled to many places in Rome Empire and wrote down many travel notes. He predicted that a navigator would get to India from Spain after sailing for 8000 miles (12874.4 km).

Strabo (about B. C. 58—A. D. 25) was the most distinguished traveller and geographer. He was well educated. When he was young, he's been to many places in Europe, Asia, and Africa. He emphasized on studying geography by combining natural knowledge and human knowledge. His works, *Geography* and *History*, consisted of configurations of mountains and rivers, climate, earth quality, animals and plants, minerals, local products, custom, traffic, and historical development in details, having positive effects on subsequent study. The *Geography is an important source of modern geography.*

*Strabo* was good at observing the nature and human beings on his journeys, and paid much attention to preceding research results. He wrote: "I ever started from Armenia to the west, and from Euxine Sea to the border of Ethiopia. My tour scope is the biggest among all geographers. Those who went to deeper places in the west never reached remote east, and those who went to deeper places in the east were behind me in the west. The situation of the north and south is the same. Most of local information comes from dictation of other people, so some of what we said is the same with others. However, some people insist on that only the things that have been seen can be knowledge, and they don't believe in what people said. They never know that what is heard is far more important than what is seen in terms of learning."

Strabo divided the world into three parts of Europe, Asia, and Libya (Africa). He asserted that the whole earth on which people live accounts for only one third of the total land. Beyond this space, there are one or more worlds in which people live. Lebon, a modern human geographer, said: "Ancient geography reached its climax at Strabo."

Gaius Plinius Secundus (23—79) is a productive natural historian. His 37-volume

*Natural History* is a masterpiece. At the same time, he is a geographer, traveler, lawyer, and military man. He ever acted as the captain of Nordic cavalry and the commander of West Roman Fleet. Depending on his post, he stepped over almost every corner in Rome.

The *Natural History* covers mathematics, cosmography, geography, anthropology, zoology, botany, medicine, mineralogy, and their applications. He referred to works of more than 400 writers and marked quoted ideas in his book. After Aristotle and Strabo, Plinius also thought the earth was round. There are some mistakes in his book of course. For example, he thought Europe was the largest continent on earth, and accounted for 5/12 of total area of the earth; India accounted for one third of total land with people living on and expanded to both the east and the west. With respect to aesthetics, he affirmed copying from the nature instead of other artists. He thought the nature was the source of beauty. Plinius exhausted almost his whole life in traveling. In 79, he died in the eruption of Vesuvius.

Lomi (90—168), a geographer in Rome, had the most elaborate discussion in respect of the earth in *Introduction to Geography*. The journeys and contribution to geography of Marlin, a traveller and geographer from Tier, were also recorded in the book. In addition, Avien, a Roman poet, translated a famous travel book called *World Travel Note*. The travel records about the Mediterranean, the Black Sea, and the Caspian Sea in the first volume in the book were reserved.

(4) Tourism in the Arabian empire

Arab Empire, crossing the three continents Asia, Europe and Africa, was unprecedented prosperous during $7^{th}$ and $8^{th}$ centuries. The post roads extended to all directions and the traffic and transport was developed unprecedentedly. The posthouses not only provided traffic means such as horse, mule and camels, but also guest houses for travelers. As Moslemism had acquired a legal position in the empire then and it stipulated a pilgrimage system which made each and every Moslem aspire after a long distance trip. During the pilgrimage time, Hajji teams across the world swarmed in Mekaa, so did the merchants and artists for business or showing their arts. The posthouse bureau had composed many travel instructions which were useful for Hajji, travelers and merchants.

Arab is a representative nation of seeking knowledge and loving travel. Traveling for seeking knowledge and study was very popular in Arab Empire. Mohammed once instructed Hajji, "Even though the knowledge exists in as far as in China, we shall seek for." For example, al Masudi, traveler and historian, nicknamed Herodotus of Arab Empire, had once visited Egypt, Palestine, India, Ceylon (today's Sri Lanka) and China. In his book *Golden Grassland* he had referred to China for many times. He praised highly the craftsmanship of Chinese and said they were good at making statues and believed Chinese was the wisest nation in the world.

Another traveler of Arab Empire was Battutah who had visited China during 1345 to 1346. He had traveled for 28 years and his works *Travels in Asia and Africa* recorded the cities, commercial ports, products and customs of China.

Italian traveler Marco Polo (1254—1324) arrived in China accompanying his father who was a merchant after crossing the Euphrates and the Tigris River drainage areas, surpassing Iran Plateau and Pamirs Plateau. He arrived in the capital of Yuan Dynasty Shangdu (northwest of Duohua County, Inner Mongolia Autonomous Region) in 1275 and was trusted by Kublai Khan, Yuan Shi Zu. Marco Polo acted as official in Yuan Dynasty for many years and had visited different cities. In 1292 Macro Polo returned his motherland crossing Sumatra and India by the sea route. *Travels of Macro Polo* recorded information of many countries in Central Asia, Western Asia and Southeast Asia, especially rich and prosperous China.

(5) Tourism in the Middle Ages in Europe

Travels in Europe in the early days of the Medieval Times were mainly activities for missionary purposes. At that time, people mainly lived in the manors with the castle as the center. Rigorous manual labor and durance of religions made people hardly have money and time to enjoy pleasure of the worldly life. However, with development of trade, especially the civilization exchange and integration after the Crusades, the cultural atmosphere of Europe had been getting loosen and people started to seek for knowledge and pleasure. In late Medieval Time, a series of Renaissance activities restarted the tourist industry in Europe.

Dante (1265—1321), a great cultural master at the same period of Marco Polo, is the founder of cultural renaissance of Europe. In order to search classic literatures and arts, Dante traveled to Naples and Rome and composed *Decameron* in 1348, which had become world famous later. The book questioned Roman Church and encouraged people to seek the roots and the truth of the doctrines of Christianism. And the book also ignited the religion reform started by Martin Luther in the 16$^{th}$ *Century*, shaking the foundation of Roman Church.

The ultimate purpose of Renaissance is to revive long-confined humanism of ancient Rome and Greece and liberate people from the pressure of religion. However, it is Francesco Petrarca (1304—1374) who truly opened the gate of Renaissance. He was born in Arezzo and had visited Pisa, Genoa, Bologna and Milan where featured thick cultural deposits. In Rome, he cried out "what's left in our history except admiring Rome", calling on people to study classic culture. He visited Paris, Flandres and Cologne in 1331. In 1336 he bought a villa near Vaucluse where he lived a reclusive life and involved himself of composing.

With his works, Petrarca inspired passion of the people to classic culture, expressed wishes of the people caring about and enjoying life with simple but convincing diction and stimulated reviviscence of humanism and connoisseurship with unique charms. He is not only "the father of Renaissance" true to the name, but also a genuine traveler of the humanism time.

The Renaissance activities, originated from Italy in the 14$^{th}$ Century, expanded to the whole Europe with influence lasting until the 16$^{th}$ Century. Cultural and art renaissance activities liberating humanity in various places of Europe boosted development of cultural tourism.

Jacob Christoph Burckhardt, famous researcher of Renaissance, saw Renaissance as one of man's joyous new discovery of the world about him and himself: the former refers to discovery of the external world, impersonal, while the later refers to the individuality of man, subjective. "Return to the nature" and "return to the classical antiquity" were very popular saying.

The famous Italian litterateur wrote, "Men go forth, and admire lofty mountains and broad seas, and roaring torrents, and the ocean, and the course of the stars, and forget their own selves while doing so".

"On this point, as in the scientific description of nature, Aeneas Sylvius is again one of the most weighty voices of his time. ··· He here claims our attention as the first who not only enjoyed the magnificence of the Italian landscape, but described it with enthusiasm down to its minutest details, whose chief delight was in nature, antiquity, and simple, but noble, architecture, appears almost a saint. In the elegant and flowing Latin of his 'Commentaries', he freely tells us of his happiness. His eye seems as keen and practiced as that of any modern observer. He enjoys with rapture the panoramic splendor of the view from the summit of the Alban Hills from the Monte Cavowhence he could see the shores of St. Peter from Terracina and the promontory of Circe as far as Monte Argentaro, and the wide expanse of country round about, with the ruined cities of the past, and with the mountain-chains of Central Italy beyond; and then his eye would turn to the green woods in the hollows beneath and the mountain-lakes among them. He feels the beauty of the position of Todi, crowning the vineyards and olive-clad slopes, looking down upon distant woods and upon the valley of the Tiber, where towns and castles rise above the winding river. The lovely hills about Siena, with villas and monasteries on every height, are his own home, and his descriptions of them are touched with a peculiar feeling." (Jacob Burckhardt, 1979)

Da Vinci, great master of Renaissance, emphasized that artists shall imitate the nature while bringing into play one's imagination and the artist shall compete with the nature and excelled the nature. He wrote in his works *Leonardo da Vinci: Treatise on Painting*, "the holy natures of painting science turns the spirit of the painter as holy as the divinity. The painter freely thinks over the production of different things, for example animal, plant, fruit, scenery, garden, hillside and fearful places; and those delightful, tender and pleasing places, the grassland with colorful flowers free from rainstorm but enjoying breezing; rivers pouring from the high mountain as flood, tearing up trees, wrapped rocks, roots, earth and foam and all the things that were unwilling to die but struggling for life. It can also create ocean under the storm, where the sea water and gale fighting fiercely. The huge waves destroyed the wind when they dropping, besieging, encaging, destroying and splitting it and mixing it with the stagnant foams. Thus the raging sea cools down. However, it was beaten by the wind and fled from the ocean into the high bank of the neighbor cape, crossing the peak, falling into the valley on the other side. Then some of the sea water turned into flying foam, becoming capture of the storm; and some fled away from the wind and turned into shower to return to the sea; some fallen to the high cape, indulging in destroying and sweeping all things resisting its death, heading on huge waves from time to time; they fought with each other, flying into the sky, filling the air with mixed foam fog which was broken by the wind at the edge of the cape, producing the black clouds tracking by the wind".

Renaissance movement not only revives the humanism with classic culture and arts as the main content, but also stimulated leapfrog development of nature sciences in the 300 years. Roger Bacon, encyclopedia natural historian, predicted with experiments that man could produce machine such as automatic ship, submarine and aircraft. The predictions had been realized step by step, enlarging the traveling scope of the human being.

(6) Columbus and Magellan

The emerging industrial revolution in the 15$^{th}$ Century in the western country and description of the eastern world in the Travels of Marco Polo attracted merchants, navigators and feudal lords to engage in the adventures. Columbus (1451—1506) was a famous Espanola navigator, herald of the grand geographic discovery.

Columbus was of Italy nationality, devoted to sailing and adventures when he was a child. After reading *Travels of Marco Polo*, he yearned for visiting India and China. At that time, the idea of a spherical earth had prevailed. The Italian had asked for funds to kings of Portugal, Spain, the UK and France for his plan sailing to the west to arrive in the oriental countries but was refused. In addition to traditional silk, porcelain and tea, the western countries also required spices and gold the most important. The spices, in large demand, were necessary materials for the living, drinking and cooking of European. The goods were mainly supplied through traditional sea and land transport. Columbus lobbied to realize his plan. Ten-old years later, queen of Spain persuaded the king in 1492 and even funded Columbus with her case dough.

On August 3, 1492, Columbus, appointed by the King of Spain, headed for sharp west from Burrows Port of Spain, with letters of credence to the king of India and empire of China and three 100-odd tons sailboats. With 70 days and nights sailing, he finally saw the land on early October 12, 1492. Columbus thought he had arrived in India. On March 15, 1493 Columbus returned Spain. And he repeated his sail toward west for three times and landed on many beaches of America. He thought where he arrived was India till his death in 1506. Later Amerigo, an Italian scholar, found with more investigation that where Columbus arrived was not India, but a new unknown continent.

The long voyage of Columbus is beginning of the grand navigation time. In 1498, Portuguese Da Gama discovered the new sea route rounding Cape of Good Hope of the south end of Africa. The opening of the new sea route changed the process of world history. It changed the overseas trade routes from Mediterranean Sea to coasts of the Atlantic. Since then the western world finally stepped out of the darkness of medieval time and emerged in the world irresistibly. These western countries wrote their rulership history over sea in the following centuries. A brand new industrial civilization became the mainstream of the world economy.

The long voyage of Magellan is a great epic of the voyage tourism industry of the human being. It was the first voyage of the human being when he circled the earth during 1519—1522.

At that time Columbus had discovered America and Da Gama had returned from India with great fortune from the oriental countries. In 1505, Magellan joined in the overseas expedition to start his adventure life of voyage. In this adventure to India, Malacca and Malaysia, the expedition fought with Arabic merchants and local people to fight for the trading domain of Arabs and Magellan was wounded for three times.

On the trip back to Portugal, the expedition ran on the rocks. While all the members lost their hearts, Magellan stood out to head them to fight against difficulties. Due to his outstanding performance, he was promoted captain and stayed in India. Since then Magellan joined in the colonial war in India and Southeast Asia and explored and traveled there.

In 1515 Magellan returned Portugal. He had repeatedly asked the king to permit him to organize a fleet to explore the world but failed. Despairing Magellan came to the commander of Seville, Spain, who appreciated his capability and ambition. The commander married his daughter to Magellan and recommended him to the king of Spain. Magellan's plan of voyage around the world was approved by the king who signed a long voyage agreement with him.

Magellan headed a fleet, consisting of over 200 members and five ships, departed from the port of Seville of Spain to start his long voyage exploration in September 1519.

With over two months' voyage, the fleet arrived in a vast bay in January of the next year. The sailors thought they had arrived in the south end of America. However, they found the sea water became fresh water when they advancing along the bay. It turned to be an estuary, estuary of today's La Plata River of Uruguay.

Two months later the fleet found another estuary at 52 degree south latitude. The strait was extremely zigzag with changing width, interlaced branching streams and billowy waves. Magellan sent a ship to explore the route, which changed the direction and fled away back Spain. Magellan had to head the rest three ships to sail in the labyrinth-like strait. After one month of sailing, they finally sailed out the strait and saw the vast sea. The strait was named Strait of Magellan in memory of the great achievement of Magellan in the exploration.

Magellan's fleet sailed for over three months in the ocean where kept calm. Therefore they named the ocean "Pacific Ocean".

In early March 1521, when they suffered from fatigue and shortage of water and food, the fleet reached the rich land of Mariana Islands where they were welcomed by the local people. In late March the fleet arrived in Philippine Islands. When the servant Magellan took from Malacca spoke with the local people with Malay, he knew he finally reached the oriental world after sailing toward west.

However in a conflict with the local tribe Magellan was killed. His assistants headed the remaining two ships with spices to return Spain in September 1522, after crossing Malacca Strait, Indian Ocean and the Cape of Good Hope. Only one ship and 18 crew members were left in the adventure. Magellan and his members finally completed the voyage circling the earth one time in three years for the first time of the human being.

(7) An era of "Greater Travel" in Europe

The 17$^{th}$ and 18$^{th}$ centuries was the time witnessing fast spread of sciences and culture in Europe and close international exchanges. The Grand Tourism affecting the whole Europe not only became a fashion mode of that time, but also laid a foundation for the spread of culture and thoughts across Europe.

"The educated class of Europe had never formed a more cosmopolitan society ever. They often traveled abroad, with French as the universal language. This is a great tourism time-especially in the first half of 18$^{th}$ century when wars were seldom seen." (Alan Bullock, 1997)

"The Treaty of Utrecht" in 1713 started the relative peaceful period of Europe and the continent was open to the tourists again. Many young men started to travel around Europe and discovered wonders: Amsterdam, Versailles, Florence, and Rome in particular. At that time it became the vogue for each young man from the blue blood to travel abroad for one year or two with one servant or a tutor directing their behaviors and study.

"Grand tourism becomes important content of education for young nobles and the blue blood of the whole Europe shared the same culture. When talking about the international conflict must be ended, Jean Jacques Rousseau said, 'We are all European, sharing similar interests, similar passion and similar life style.' Whichever French nationality, or German nationality or other countries, politicians, philosophers, scientists and artists all were aware of they were European." (Jayer, 2000)

Rousseau also called on "grand tourism" and he believed returning the nature was the best way of education. He often traveled to other countries of Europe on foot. Since the 17$^{th}$ Century to middle 19$^{th}$ century when the mass tourism rose, grand tourism was welcomed as one important mode of education for the young people. As in Europe there had always been the sayings of "educating people with tourism" and "traveling fosters the next generation", the purpose of the young people to travel was to learn a new language, discover new customs or get familiar with arts and etiquette.

During the 18$^{th}$ and 19$^{th}$ centuries, grand tourism had been popular in Europe, especially in the U.K, Germany, Russia and northern European countries. The tourism activities became important means fostering administrative talent and political leaders at that time. Tourists normally started their journey of Grand Tourism with a venerating heart to the classic civilization and modern culture. While visiting the rivers, famous mountains and ancient cities, they studied a new language, culture, arts, social etiquette and customs from one place to another, expanding their views and enriching their thought.

While British scientist and philosopher Francis Bacon's *Of Travel* is a very famous work at that time. Here, let us enjoy the whole text of the work:

*Travel, in the younger sort, is a part of education, in the elder, a part of experience.*

*He that travelleth into a country, before he hath some entrance into the language, goeth to school, and not to travel. That young men travel under some tutor, or grave servant, I allow well; so that he be such a one that hath the language, and hath been in the country before; whereby he may be able to tell them what things are worthy to be seen, in the country where they go; what acquaintances they are to seek; what exercises, or discipline, the place yieldeth. For else, young men shall go hooded, and look abroad little.*

*It is a strange thing, that in sea voyages, where there is nothing to be seen, but sky and sea, men should make diaries; but in land-travel, wherein so much is to be observed, for the most part they omit it; as if chance were fitter to be registered, than observation. Let diaries, therefore, be brought in use.*

*The things to be seen and observed are: the courts of princes, especially when they give audience to ambassadors; the courts of justice, while they sit and hear causes; and so of consistories ecclesiastic; the churches and monasteries, with the monuments which are therein extant; the walls and fortifications of cities, and towns, and so the heavens and harbors; antiquities and ruins; libraries; colleges, disputations, and lectures, where any are; shipping and navies; houses and gardens of state and pleasure, near great cities; armories; arsenals; magazines; exchanges; burses; warehouses; exercises of horsemanship, fencing, training of soldiers, and the like; comedies, such whereunto the better sort of persons do resort; treasuries of jewels and robes; cabinets and rarities; and, to conclude, whatsoever is memorable, in the places where they go. After all which, the tutors, or servants, ought to make diligent inquiry. As for triumphs, masks, feasts, weddings, funerals, capital executions, and such shows, men need not to be put in mind of them; yet are they not to be neglected.*

*If you will have a young man to put his travel into a little room, and in short time to gather much, this you must do.*

*First, as was said, he must have some entrance into the language before he goeth. Then he must have such a servant, or tutor, as knoweth the country, as was likewise said. Let him carry with him also, some card or book, describing the country where he travelleth; which will be a good key to his inquiry. Let him keep also a diary. Let him not stay long, in one city or town; more or less as the place deserveth, but not long; nay, when he stayeth in one city or town, let him change his lodging from one end and part of the town, to another; which is a great adamant of acquaintance. Let him sequester himself, from the company of his countrymen, and diet in such places, where there is good company of the nation where he travelleth. Let him, upon his removes from one place to another, procure recommendation to some person of quality, residing in the place whither he removeth; that he may use his favor, in those things he desireth to see or know.*

*Thus he may abridge his travel, with much profit.*

*As for the acquaintance, which is to be sought in travel; that which is most of all profitable, is acquaintance with the secretaries and employed men of ambassadors: for so in travelling in one country, he shall suck the experience of many. Let him also see, and visit, eminent persons in all kinds, which are of great name abroad; that he may be able to tell, how the life agreeth with the fame. For quarrels, they are with care and discretion to be avoided. They are commonly for mistresses, healths, place, and words. And let a man beware, how he keepeth company with choleric and quarrelsome persons; for they will engage him into their own quarrels.*

*When a traveller returneth home, let him not leave the countries, where he hath travelled, altogether behind him; but maintain a correspondence by letters, with those of his acquaintance, which are of most worth.*

*And let his travel appear rather in his discourse, than his apparel or gesture; and in his discourse, let him be rather advised in his answers, than forward to tell stories; and let it appear that he doth not change his country manners, for those of foreign parts; but only prick in some flowers, of that he hath learned abroad, into the customs of his own country.*

In the middle of the 18th century, with the fast development of science and technologies in the West, Europe also witnessed emergency of scientific exploration and adventure with predatory purposes. For example the UK had organized expeditions for plundering colonies, including natural scientific workers who studied the sea route, animal, plant and geology. The expedition headed by Captain Cook had made three times of voyage around the world. Darwin had reviewed South America on site on the journey and found explanation to origin of species and created the great theory of principle of evolution. The journey with scientific meaning at that time had brought important impact to the advance of the human being.

3. Tourism spheres and forms of the ancients are limited

Tourism is one of the basic requirements of human being. With development of the civilization, people have richer and deeper understanding to tourism. In various tourist activities in the ancient time in China, the word "tourism" has been recorded with poems by scholars by species.

For example, tour has the meaning of lobbying, just as that in *Guanzi*, "making him tour around and expressly recruiting able and virtuous people". Leisure tour means travel leisurely just as what Ban Gu, historian of East Han Dynasty said, "all of them travel leisurely, enjoying beautiful poems." Fugue, means visiting mentally. Shen Yue, litterateur of South Dynasties once wrote, "although I stay under the high and steep porch, I has visited the rivers and mountains mentally." Ramble means visiting freely. Yuan Jie, litterateur of Tang Dynasty said in his poem, "there is no limit in distance for ramble and there is not time limit to ramble." Happily tour means traveling agreeably. Liu Yuxi, litterateur of Tang Dynasty, wrote, "leave beautiful rhyme and enjoy the rivers and mountains happily." Ambitious tour, just as it implies, a tour with a lofty ideal. Yuan Dynasty scholar Yuan Jue wrote in his poem, "The ambitious tour enabled me to write poem with open-minded; the clarion from ancient garrisons sound sorrowful." Or enjoying vivid travels or pictures instead of visiting the places in person, as what Ni Zan, painter of Yuan Dynasty wrote, "the chrysanthemum in the field works as the sacrificial vessel; I enjoy the rivers and mountains painted on the wall instead of visiting the places in person." And emperor's tour, as wrote by Gui Youguang, litterateur of Ming Dynasty, "during the wheat harvest season, the golden carriage goes out of the palace with the emperor to make a tour." All these poems indicate that the ancient people in China had understood and acknowledged tourism to a high level.

However, due to the backward production tools and underdeveloped productivity, the tourist scope of the ancient people was limited. Especially in the early time, even the potentate or the rich could hardly go far and comfortably, constrained by the scientific and technical development. Even during the Grand Tourism Time of Europe, the travelers had to face difficulties such as hardships and dangers on the road, shabby hotel, weird food, infectious diseases and robbers and pickpockets. Some young men from the rich families often took a team of servants to help him handle the difficulties on the trip to ensure comfort and safety of the master.

Including walk on foot, the ancient people had to select carriage, horse or wooden ship for a journey. Thus they had to spend most of the time on the way, wasting not only time, but also energy.

China is one of the first countries using carriage. It is said that during Huangdi reign Chinese had learned how to make a carriage. There was a tribe specializing in making carriage during the reign of Yu named Xue Tribe of which a person named Xi Zhong who once worked as Carriage Officer of Xia Dynasty in charge of carriage production, keeping and usage of Xia Dynasty. In order to facilitate sledge and carriage moving, the people were aware of leveling off and expanding the road and changed the narrow footpath suitable for walking on foot to wide road.

The earliest traffic means on water is canoe. According to *Yi Xi Ci*, the ancient people "hollow out the trunk as canoe, and sharpen the wood as barge pole". In another word, the ancient people hollowed out the huge trunk to make a canoe and chopped the trunk to make a flat oar. Since the canoe was made, the people could cross rivers and exploit new space of tourism.

The ancient people not only were limited by backward productivity, but also constrained by the political turbulence and social changes. According records of the ancient books, as early as West Zhou Dynasty in China, King of Zhou Kingdom set up 12 sentry posts at the borders, which were believed the earliest toll gate in the history of China.

During the Spring and Autumn Period and the Warring States Period, it was common for different kingdoms to set up sentry posts as the powers fighting for the hegemony. With special functions, the sentry posts had an important position, impacting the safety of the military, economic and social cruxes of the kingdom. Therefore it was not easy for a common person to pass through the sentry posts. Sometimes even some "celebrities" of that time failed in passing through the post in disguise. For example, Shang Yang, Qin Dynasty, was killed by a cruel punishment because he failed in muddle through the post; Wu Zixu, on his escape to Chu Kingdom, was so anxious that his hair turned into white over one night because he could not go through Shaoguan Pass.

The history books also recorded that in West Zhou Dynasty there was a certificate named *Fuchuan*, similar with today's ID card, but only for temporary purpose. When a citizen was to emigrate or travel, he/she must first apply for a *Fuchuan*. The tourist was not only checked for *Fuchuan* from time to time during the journey, but also had to present the certificate when passing through a city gate or in a curfew or a state of siege if requested. What's more, *Fuchuan* only could be used for one time and must be handed back on time after the journey. Otherwise the holder would be punished.

In the ancient time, the travelers would face huge dangers sometimes fatal to life on the journey or in the hotel. Sometime it was the same for a king. For example Emperor Zhaowang of Zhou Dynasty encountered storm when he made a tour of inspection and died in a sunken ship unfortunately. Xu Xiake was robbed for three times and ran out of food for four times on his journey. He caught diseases in Yunnan when he was 55 years old and died the second year when he returned home… As there were so many dangers the ancient people had to face on the journey, they were especially superstitious and would normally practice divination and fortune telling when planning a journey. Divinatory Symbols for Tourism in the *Book of Changes* mentioned above were used for foretell good or ill luck of the traveler on the journey.

*Classics of Mountains and Seas* recorded more than 60 natural dangers that one might encounter on one's journey such as "anyone who would die if see this", "something that could eat human being" and "something that when one saw it would flood", which shall be avoided by the travelers then. And more than 130 kinds of food recorded in the books such as those that "one would not feel hungry if having this food", "one would not die young if having this food" and "one would not feel cold if having this food" were often magic weapons for the ancient people to survive on the journey.

In order to facilitate traveling of the mass, as early as the $10^{th}$ century, the central government then had appointed dedicated officials in charge of similar affairs and set forth relevant system of greeting guests and rules of tourism. According to *Yi Zhou Shu*, the feudal government then had stipulated that the local government must build roads for the merchants and travelers, dig a well every 10km and set up hotels every 20km. And those who defended the city must offer exchange service of small changes.

During the Spring and Autumn Period and the Warring States Period, more and more private hotels were opened due to there were so many merchants and travelers. Ni Lv (inn) is the earliest private hotel in China. Qin Kingdom and Wei Kingdom had stipulated rules especially to govern such hotels. *The Master of the Multitude of the Earth Office in Zhou Li* has such recordings, "Along all the roads in the country, hostel shall be set up every 10 *li*, where food and drinks shall be offered. And every 30 li, lodging stations shall be set up and in the lodging stations guest rooms shall be provided. And every 50 *li*, there shall be a town where there are larger hotels which have reservation of food and drinks." These hotels built in the cities and along the traffic trunks and the borders shall be the earliest hotels ran by the government.

In a word, in the ancient time tourism was normally activities of kings, emperors, nobles, officials and landlords and the scholar-bureaucrat and the common people only made a trip at the festivals, for example to the temple fair. The domestic travelers normally aimed at making technical investigation, stimulated by the thought of "read thousands of books and march thousands of miles". In the ancient time the tourist activities were closely connected with the social, political, economic, cultural and technical development of the time and the indicator of social civilization advancement. When the country was in peace and prosperity, the tourism was prosperous, otherwise it was sluggish. Therefore, tourist activities will bear brands of the times with the development of the human being, showing different contents and styles.

In the ancient time, the cross-border tourism was normally in the modes of political exchanges (for example envoy exchange) and for the religious and economic and business purposes. With relative backward scientific and technical level, the journey, no matter the long voyage or journey on the land, was full of hardships and would take one months, years or dozens of years. Therefore, it was not easy in the ancient time to make a journey.

# Chapter 2

## A new epoch of tourism opened for humans amid scientific and technological development

# Cristo Redentor

巴西基督像

# Section 1
## Several important inventions affecting mankind's tourism activities

During the one hundred years from the mid-1700s to the 19$^{th}$ century, Europe step into the period of the Industrial Revolution. Mankind's civilization got a huge progress because of a rapid development on science and technology. In this period, most workers already went to the small towns or factories from village agriculture to join city life. The work time of the middle bourgeoisie was cut short and the holiday was increased. The demands in many aspects increased by a large margin, such as treasure, education, leisure time, or in the aspect of leisure traveling life.

1. Steam engines

It underwent a very long process when people began to understand and use the steam. In 2$^{nd}$ century B. C, the ancient Greek already made a kind of engine which used the steam's jet to produce the reaction.

In 1698, a French physicist named Denis Papin (1647—1712) designed cylinder and piston installation creatively.

After that, a British engineer, Thomas Savery (1650—1715) revised Papin's conceive and in 1698, he designed and invented the first steam engine which can be used to draw water in mine-shaft. First, steam was become a kind of industrial motive force indeed. But due to an inefficient of this kind of machine, so its work was limited, meanwhile, it was also not safety.

In 1705, a British forging named Thomas Newcomen (1663—1729) invented the atmospheric steam engine. It was more practical. He separated the working machine which drew water from mine-shaft and steam installation which offered the motive force completely to ensure the steam engine working safely.

James Watt (1736—1819) was born in a small town, which is close to Glasgow, Scotland, on January 19$^{th}$, 1736. His grandfather and uncle were both the machinists. He father was also a shipbuilding technological worker in his early years. Watt followed his father to study all kinds of craftsmanship when he was a child, meanwhile, he cultivated the good habits of think independently and probing mystery.

Due to he was weak and always fell ill, Watt did not receive the regular education. But under a guide of his father and mother, he had studied independently. In 1753, Watt went to Glasgow to be an apprentice. Next year, he went to a instrument and meter repairing plant in London to be an apprentice continuously. Because he was diligent in his studies, he had learned to make those instruments and meters which have a high difficulty quickly.

In 1756, Watt's ability brought to attention from a professor of the Glasgow University. Due to his introduction, Watt became a repairer of teaching instrument in Glasgow university.

In 1763, Watt repaired a Newcomen steam engine for Glasgow University. Through a great deal of experiments and analysis, he made a thorough study to the old style steam engine and found the main reason of its inefficiency.

In spring of 1765, Watt suddenly had a inspiration when he was walking: the condensation of steam happened in the cylinder was the main reason that cause an inefficiency of Newcomen steam engine, why could not the condensation was made out of the cylinder?

So since 1766, Watt surmounted various difficulties during more than three years and made the first prototype of the steam engine in 1769. In the same year, Watt gained his first patent because he invented the condensation machine. Although the first steam engine which had the condensation machine had been successfully trial-produced, but compared with Newcomen steam engine, its dynamic machinery still had not made substantial progress except the hot efficiency was raised markedly.

In 1781, Watt derived inspiration from the circular motion of planet moves round the sun, and developed a gear driving installation which was called "the sun and the planet" to change the reciprocating straight motion of piston into a circular motion of gear wheel finally. In the end of 1781, Watt gained his second patent because he invented the mechanical driving installation which had gear and pull rod.

In 1782, Watt trail-produced a new type cylinder which had a two-way installation and gained his third patent. He refitted the quondam one-way cylinder installation into the two-way cylinder installation. For the first time, he changed the low-pressure steam which was poured into the cylinder into the high-pressure steam, and it was the third leap in the process that Watt improved Newcomen steam engine. Due to those three technological leaps, Newcomen steam engine was evolved Watt steam engine completely.

Due to Watt changed the reciprocating straight motion of the Steam engine into a continous and symmetrical circular motion, it could drive all kinds of machines to run through the gearing. The steam engines became an "all-purpose power machine" which could be used in the Industry and the Transportation Industry commonly.

The British, Watt invented steam engine and raised the curtain on the human being's industrial revolution. Because steam engine had a scientific structure, it could produce an unprecedented power for human being. But the steam engine was used in the field of colliery for drawing water at first. In the early days of 19$^{th}$ century, hundreds of steam engines were used for mining coal widely.

How to use this "weight-lifter" to bring benefit to mankind? Scientists had been considering this question. In 1769, a French engineer, Mr. Cugnot developed successfully the first steam car of the world. The steam car had three wheels. When the car made a performance on the street at a speed of 4.5 kilometers per hour with four persons in it, people really could not understand what paractical value it had unless feeling surprise. It showed that any important inventions would almost experience a "naive stage".

In 1801, a British colliery engineer named Trevithick developed successfully the first steam locomotive which can go on the railroad. It was a single-cylinder steam engine and could go on the railroad of colliery with five railway carriages. Although its speed was slow, it had the basic feature and function of the train and could made colliery never to depend on horse as its motivity in transporting coal.

Afterwards, a British called Headley developed steam locomotive continuously. He raised the speed of the locomotive to eight kilometers per hour, while pulling eight railroad cars. His improvement laid the function for the naissance of real train.

2. Trains were invented

George Stephenson was a British. He was deprived of education when he was a child and became a fireman. Through self-studying and hard studying, he grasped the structure and function of the steam locomotive. When he was responsibility for designing the first commercial railway of the world in the northern part of Scotland, he changed the rail which was made by iron into the steely rail, and design to lay the sleeper under the steely rail. Thus the problem that the rail used to rupture because of shocking was solved, and those two aspects that raising train's speed and increasing freight volume were possible.

On 27$^{th}$ September, 1825, the locomotive called "The Travel", which was designed and driven personally by Stephenson, drew 12 freight railway carriages and 20 passenger railway carriages to proceed along the railway with a speed of 24 kilometers each hour. When more than 400 passengers reached to the destination safely, people hailed warmly. Since the day, the world had the train, a transportation which could be used in traffic and transport. It ushered a new era in world vehicle history and traffic history. Stephenson also was called the inventor of the train.

In the 19th century, in Britian, Stephenson was not made the train alone, some consortiums also invested for researching and making the train because they saw its developing prospect. They were unwilling to be outshone and not convinced each other. How to attain a goal of survival of the fittest? Through the way of launching a "contest", the British government carried out their aim to choose the type of the engine.

On October 6, 1829, on the railway from Liverpool to Manchester, a "contest" in which three trains participated was hold. Every train must draw a railway carriage which was filled with stones, and the weigh of the goods must be three times to the weigh of the train. They were asked to go 20 times back and forth on a line of 2.4 kilometers continuously. The winner would get 500 pounds as a premium.

The boiler of the train Strangeness boomed soon after it was hitched the railway carriage and began to travel. The one of the other two trains although could start when it was hitched the carriage filling with stones, but it just could to forward slowly and at last "palsied" on the railway.

Lastly, Stephenson's train "Rocket" started off, it drew the heavy carriage and went back and forth reposefully with an average speed of 28 kilometers per hour, and reached the terminal point in a high-speed of 46 kilometers per hour. Stephenson's achievement and contribution were acknowledged by the society. He was also praised as the inventor of the train.

In 1825, the railway from Stockton to Darlington, which was constructed by George Stephenson, who was called the "Father of Railway", was began to ply regularly. Hereafter, the railway in various places of Britain were begun to sep up. Thomas Cook, an British who was acknowledged as the first real travel agent, chose the train to be the means of transportation when he firstly formed a group for a trip.

In July of 1841, relying on the language art and enthusiasm, Thomas Cook persuaded 540 persons who advocated to give up drinking to take the train in Waltham Forest, and through a 12 hour's journey to went to Loughborough for attending a giving-up-drinking meeting. It is the first time to rent a train for a travel by a group. Afterward, people who entrusted him for arranging the journey became more, so he actually was a organizer of the short-distance travel. In 1846, he successfully set up a travel guide which was the earliest guide in the history. In 1851, he formed more than 160000 tourists to visit the first "Expos" which was launched in the "Crystal Palace of London". In 1872, Cook launched a

220-day global travel with nine travelers attended in,. so he was praised the founder of modern tourism industry.

In 1879, Siemens Electric Company of Germany developed the first electric locomotive. It had a weight of 954 kg, and only was shown once in Berlin Business Exhibition. On October 27, 1903, the first practice-electric locomotive, which was developed by Siemens Electric Company and General Electric Company, was put into using and its had a top speed of 200 km per hour.

In 1894, the first petrol locomotive was developed successfully in Germany. It was used in railway transportation and ushered in a new era of locomotive in the world. But it had a high consumption of energy because it needed to burn petrol to be a motive power, so it is difficult to popularize and engineers had developed a newer product.

In 1924, the diesel locomotive was developed successfully in some countries, including Germany, the U. S. and France, etc. and used widely in the world. In 1941, a new-type gas turbine, which regarded diesel as its fuel, was developed successfully in Switzerland. It was adopted generally by industrial countries for its excellent property.

3. Automobiles and aircraft came into being

Since the 19$^{th}$ century, the steam-motive-power steamship was popularized and developed rapidly. In 1807, the steamboat Claremont already started to ply by a regular voyage number on the Hardson River for transporting people and goods. In 1838, the British steamship "Sirius" crossed the Atlantic Ocean successfully and shortened the time and distance enormously when passengers traveled between Europe and America.

It should attribute the success to invention of internal-combustion engine that the automobile and aircraft could come out. Due to the steam engine which was invented by Watt was clumsy and inefficient, scientists and engineers had found a kind of high-energy exchange machine. Thus the appearance of automobile and aircraft gave the credit to the invention of internal-combustion engine.

In 1862, a French engineer named Beau de Rochas mentioned a theory of four-stroke internal-combustion engine. After 10 years, the German engineer, Otto made the first coal-gas internal-combustion engine of the world. In the middle of 19$^{th}$ century, owing to the development of petroleum industry and appearance of diesel oil, petrol and kerosene, the inter-combustion could be transformed ulteriorly.

In 1883, the Germany inventor Daimler created the first petroleum internal-combustion engine, which was better than the traditional internal-combustion on performance. In 1892, another engineer of Germany invented a automatic ignition internal-combustion which regarded diesel oil as its fuel.

In 1885, Daimler, the inventor of petroleum internal-combustion and his compatriot, Karl Friedrich Benz invented the three-wheel automobile separately which took petroleum internal-combustion as an engine. Several years later, Karl Friedrich Benz created the four-wheel automobile. In 1892, an American named Ford also invented the first automobile of the U. S.. Karl Friedrich Benz and Ford also ran their own automobile companies to produce automobile in batches. Afterwards, they formed a pillar-industry of economy — the automobile industry. In 1908, Ford Company also built the first productive line of automobile in the world and made a rapid advance to the automobile industry.

The invention of internal-combustion engine also changed human's dream of flying in sky into a truth. In October of 1900, Wright brothers made their first glider. In the next year, through many transforms they created another glider. It could aviate at a height of 180 meters. One day, when they saw an automobile stopping at the gate of their house, they had a brainwave and found that maybe they could use automobile's engine to drive the aircraft.

Through numerous experimentations, Wright brothers came to seaside for test flight again with their new aircraft. Although the test flight was failed, they absorbed many experiences from it. In the mean time, an inventor named Langley also made an aircraft with a petroleum-engine by trust of the government of the U. S.. But it was a misfortune that the aircraft fell into the sea in the process of test flight.

When Wright Brothers got the news, they came to investigate and wanted to draw a lesson, and got more experiences. Afterwards, they checked every part of their airplane strictly, and made a strict operating stipulation. On December 14, 1903, they came to the Kitty Hawk for a new experience of test flight.

In the afternoon of the day, they stopped their airplane at the railway first. The aircraft just taxied for a distance of three meters, it rose in the sky with a whistle. But the planer reduced its speed soon and dropped onto the ground. The whole flight time was just less than four minutes.

The brothers thought over from different angles and checked the plane carefully. Finally, the younger brother Orville Wright found the reason. He said: "On the slope, our plane just slid for a distance of three meters and took off. But the airscrew could not run at a high speed, so it fell off soon."

At ten o'clock on December 17, 1903, the sky was covered with dark clouds and the cold wind chilled people to the bone. Orville Wright got on the plane and sit in the control cabin. Soon, the engine began to thunder and the airscrew also ran. The plane started to slide and rose into a height of three meters. Then it aviated forward smoothly and steadily.

Several presents who were invited to view the experience cheered and began to chase the plane. After the plane aviated for a distance of 30 meters, it touched down steadily. Wilbur Wright was so excited that he threw himself at his younger brother and shouted with tears were full of his eyes: " we are success, we are success!" when the news spread quickly and people lost no time telling everybody. The government of the U. S. paid much attention to it and decided to let the Wright brothers make a performance of test flight. On September 10, 1908, the weather was fine. The space where the plane was going to aviate was full of people to wait for the performance excitedly.

At about ten o'clock, Orville Wright drove their plane flied into the sky amidst loud cheers. It was just like a hawk flying in the sky in people's vision. The plane had flied for one hour and fourteen minutes at a height of 76 meters with a brave passenger sit in it. When the plane was about to land, people gathered round it from all directions. Through the support from the government, Wright brothers set up a flight company. Meanwhile, they established a flight school. From then on, the plane became another advanced means of transportation to serve for human.

Before 1914, people still did not know what changes would happened in people's life when automobile and airplane were invented. But mankind stepped into the 20$^{th}$ century, many things, including people's travel way which had changed continuously and the inventions were closely linked.

## Section 2
## A qualitative leap in tourism spheres and number of tourists

Due to the industry revolution of capitalism, the productivity of enterprise was improved greatly. The wealth of capitalist and employees were also increased at an unprecedented pace. Thus, the number of tourists and tourism spheres increased more. A few middle classes who were growing preferred to make a short-term travel in the scenic spots and resorts nearby. But some members of the upper strata had more time and money to travel in foreign countries.

Although in the 20th century, the new-type means of transportation were still in a embryonic stage when automobile and airplane appeared, it meant that people's work and lifeway were happening an unprecedented change. The sphere of people's travel activity was extended with an unprecedented scale when the automobile and aircraft came out. Such aspects, like convenience, comfort and effectiveness in the process of trip, happened an earth-shaking changes. In the middle of the 19th century, no matter domestic or international tourism in various countries of the world also had a huge development.

Relying on the features of speediness and safety, railway was to be the main means of transportation in tourism. The development of railway could not only transport more passengers, but also make people travel to the place which was more far away with a less money. In the period of carriage-transportation, a person need to spend three weeks to go to Chicago from New York. But after 1857, it just need three days. Due to traveling by train could not save time, but also save expense, more and more people at middle and lower levels joined the tourism industry. The travel agency industry which was founded by Thomas Cook established its station gradually, and became an important sector in tourism cause. The ancient social activity-travel, was to be a kind of economical activity.

The Industry Revolution accelerated the course of urbanization and transferred the core of people's work and life into industry city from countryside. The various agricultural labour, which was regular along with changes of farming season, began to be replaced by uninteresting, single and repetitive machinery industrial labour. The change created a favourable conditions for workers to have a holiday and made people have a strong requirement of being on furlough for getting a breathing spell to adjust themselves. People need to avoid the rhythm-strained city life, and crowed and noised environmental pressure properly. They looked forward to enjoy a natural environment which was full of freedom and peace no matter for subjective or objective reason.

In the end of 19th century, many similar travel organizations were set up in European continent. In Britain, a climbing-mountain club was established in 1857 and a tent club was founded in 1885. In 1890, France and Germany also established the sightseeing clubs. In 1938, the Thomas Cook Travel Agency set up more than 350 branches in the variety of places of the world. It also created the travel cheque which could be used in banks of various cities in the world. Besides, the travel agency compiled and edited Travel Gazette — the earliest travel magazine of the world, which was once translated into seven languages. In early the 20th century, America Express, Thomas Cook Travel Agency and The Railway Sleeping Car Company of Belgium were three largest travel agencies enjoyed equal popularity.

Due to science and technology developed the mode of tourism, the travel scenic spots and installations were improved and constructed swiftly. For example, restaurants and stores along the railway became more, synthetic corporations which had advanced entertainment establishment and comfortable environment were built gradually, and many scenic spots and bathing beaches which were enjoyed by the upper strata of society specially were opened to the average person all the year round.

Although the travel activity in modern times has developed greatly, it could not form a kind of independent economical industry. Making a general survey of the whole modern times, it was just a kind of travel agency industry operated by individual person in some areas.

## Section 3

## Tourism in modern China

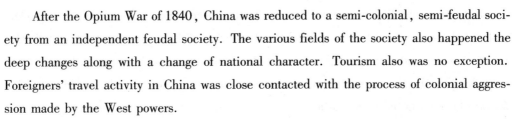

After the Opium War of 1840, China was reduced to a semi-colonial, semi-feudal society from an independent feudal society. The various fields of the society also happened the deep changes along with a change of national character. Tourism also was no exception. Foreigners' travel activity in China was close contacted with the process of colonial aggression made by the West powers.

Wang Xiaoyun once wrote in his book named *Stories of Chinese Tourism* : During this period, the change of tourism had such features: First, due to the aggression of the West, Chinese's conception on tourism was changed greatly. The populace class joined the group of tourism. The second, along with a development of modern transportation, the travel-style also got more promotion. More and more people began to enjoy travel and they preferred to visit those places more far away. The communication between international tourism became frequent. The third, for adapting to the development of the traveling trend, the folk tourism organizations which provided services to the tourist formed an independent industry gently.

Since 1840, the imperialists opened the Gate of China, which had been cut off from the outside world by the ruling class, with indestructible warship and cannon. Many foreign businessmen, missionaries, scholars and adventurers came to China one after another. Some even built the houses in Chinese well-known scenic spots, like Beidaihe seashore and Lushang mountain, for living. China was almost a paradise preferred by foreign adventurers.

Meanwhile, the number of Chinese travelling to foreign countries also increased more. Some of them were the tourists who traveled abroad for invest and visit. Others were students wanting to seek knowledge, such as Hong Xiuquan, Kang Youwei, Yanfu and Sun Zhongshan, etc. they were who found the truth to the West earliest.

After the Opium Wars, some officials of Qing Dynasty (1644—1911), like Lin Zexu and Wei yuan, put forward a suggestion of "studying foreigner's strong points for subduing them". *Records and Maps of the World* written by Wei Yuan, was an enlightened work which made China, a country still closed itself to international intercourse and looked at the sky from the bottom of a well, understand how great the world was and some "advanced Chinese" had a requirement of moving towards the world. Since 1840s, many Chinese went to Europe, America and Japan to visit and study, like Zhang Deyi who once toured in Europe. He wrote his personal experiences into his travels in what introduced economy, politics, science and technique of the West, which were help to widen Chinese's field of vision and liberate their thought.

In 1870s of the Westernization Movement, the government of Qing Dynasty sent many students who were from 12 to 14 years old to the U.S. and European countries to study Occidental science and technology for fostering the qualified persons who could handle "foreign affairs". The first railway engineer — Zhan Tianyou was one of little students studying abroad who went to the U.S. earliest.

The great revolutionary forerunner, Dr Sun Zhongshan, went abroad to study when he was just twelve years old. He traveled to and fro between, such as the U.S., Britain and the various countries of southeast Asia. During the period of the Reform Movement of 1898 in Qing Dynasty, whose leading spirits, Kang Youwei, Liang qichao and Tan Sitong and represented the interests of the liberal bourgeoisie and the enlightened landlords, a great deal students studying abroad were sent to foreign countries. Until 1906, the number of students who studied abroad on state scholarship and at their own expense increased to more than 8000. Most of them worked hard and had gone through the test of the democratic thought of the capitalist class. So many students studying abroad, such as Huang Xing and Chen Tian-hua, etc were all the active to propagate and carry out the democratic revolution of the capitalist class.

Although travel activity was appeared in ancient China, the tourism industry was began to change into a kind of economic career in 1920s. In 1923, the Travel Department of the Shanghai Commercial & Saving Bank changed its name into China Travel Agency, which was the first professional travel agency in China. Before the travel department was established, many foreign tourists were accepted by China-based foreign travel setups when they came to China, like the Thomas Cook Travel Agency of Britain. Because they were not versed in Chinese conditions, foreign tourists traveling in China were often left with simple contacts and even misunderstanding on China's scenic spots, history, customs, local delicacies, culture and arts, thus hindering the development of China's travel business. Therefore, the establishment of the Travel Department of the bank received quick and warm welcome, and developed rapidly.

# Chapter 3

# Tourism is a process transmitting human civilizations

Africa Land 非洲大陆

# Section 1
## Tourism is a bridge linking different civilizations

From above expositions, we know that although people has the different understandings to tourism at all times and in all lands, they have a common understanding to the characteristic of tourism-a movement from a place to another place. The essence of tourism decides that the travel activity can propagate as well as accept civilizations.

For understanding the indispensable function of tourism in the process of exchanging human's civilization, we must have a clear understanding to human's civilization from an philosophic angle firstly.

Like other various subjects, scholars at home and abroad have the multifarious understandings to civilization. The word of civilization was appeared in the book named *the Book of Changes* in China earliest, in which said: " The dragon appears on the field, thus the world is full of rich and bright colours, and becomes bright. "

Liang Qichao, the well-known figure in the modern China said in his book *the Spirit of Civilization*: " The civilization is visible and has its spirit. It is easy to get a visible civilization, but difficult to get a spiritual civilization. "

In the book titled *Sun Wen Theory*, the great democratic revolutionary forerunner of China — Sun Zhongsan mentioned that civilization was a result which combined material and spiritual civilization.

Liang Qichao and Sun Zhongsan all paid much attention to the aspect of spirit of the civilization. During the period of the "May 4th Movement of 1918", the famous ideologist—Hu Shi thought that the material civilization is as important as the spiritual civilization. He also thought that a kind of civilization must be formed by the material part and the spiritual part. The material part included the natural power and substance, and the spiritual part is consisted with the intelligence and ideality of a nation. Besides, he expressed that there was no a single material civilization as well as no single spiritual civilization in the world.

*The Chinese Encyclopaedia: Philosophy* explains the civilization as this: it is a summation of the material and spiritual achievements when mankind changes the world, and also a symbol of reflecting the progress of the society and how the mankind becomes civilized.

The well-known historian and master of almanac-school of France, Fernand Braudel, thought that the civilization was a space, a cultural field and a collection of aggregation of cultural feature and phenomenon.

The American scholar Samuel Huntington figured that the civilization and culture touched upon an all-around life-style of a nation. It included the value, regulation, system and mode of thinking which has been thought as the most important function by the people in a certain society.

Immanuel Wallerstein, founder of the Modern World-System, said that civilization is a special connection of world outlook, customs and structural culture—material culture and high-level culture. It forms the historical summation, and co-exists with the other changes of this phenomenon, though not always necessarily currently.

Arnold J. Toynbee, the historian of Britain, said that civilization is the inevitable fate of culture—the external and human-made state that the advanced human kind can attain— and is a finale from budding stage to ripe.

Melchor thought that civilization was a kind of unified activity in a certain degree. The relation among the various parts of civilization and the relation between parts and the whole decided each of their components.

Friedrich Engels said that civilization is a historical concept. It is antagonistic to the barbarism and imbrutement, and a kind of estate of progress when the human kind's history develops into a certain stage.

From above standpoints, we can know that the civilization includes both the material and the spiritual achievement of the mankind. It is a way to reflect the progress of human remakes and adapts themselves to nature, which is usually shown with such states, like the values, labour regulations, cultural customs and social system, etc. It is a general reflection of the material and spiritual fields of a country and a nation.

When we review the developing history of human's civilization, we can understand that the new-trail-blazing is the momentum for human's development and mostly is the synonym of the development of human's civilization. Whether a kind of civilization has a new-trail-blazed spirit will decides the civilization has the vigour, life-force and future.

Mr Duan Yabing wrote in the book named *Talk Civilization Freely*: The culture-blazing is a whole conception. It included several aspects, such as the thought-blazing, blazing new trails in scientific and producing field, and system-blazing, etc. The connection between them is that the theory-blazing is the core and precondition, the blazing new trails in scientific and producing field is the momentum and source, and system-reform is the center sector of the civilization-blazing

Jaspers, the philosopher of Germany, called the period as an 'Axis Period', which included the 10 centuries since the 1st century Before Christ. Because the main several civilizations of the mankind were fallen into the pattern. He wrote in his book titled *History of Mankind*:

"The spiritual process, which is happened during the time from 800 B. C. to 200 B. C., seems to build an axis. Let's call the time 'Axis Period'. The period is full of unusual time. In China, Confucius, Lao-tzu, Mo-tse and various schools of Chinese philosophy spring up. In India, the Buddhism is developed, meanwhile, all kinds of philosophical schools, include skepticism, materialism, sophism and nihilism, are developed. In Iran, Zoroastrianism advances an inference which is full of challenge. They think that the process of the universe is a battle between virtuous and evil things. In Pakistan, the prophets, like Elijah, Isaiah, Jeremiah and Deutero-Isaiah rise with force and spirit. In Greece, the vast number of poets and philosophers, include Homeros, Parmenides, Heracleitus, Plato, Thucydides and Archimedes, etc. are constantly emerging. All of above appears alone within the several centuries in China, India and the Western countries almost in the same time."

The cultures in the different areas appeared and grew alone for the limitations of the mankind's producing-force in the past time. So they could not influence each other. Through a development during more than 2000 years, they have taken an important parts in human being's civilization.

## Section 2
## No dissemination, no civilization

No new-trail-blazing, no civilization. In the same way, no dissemination, no civilization. The new-trail-blazing is the source of the civilization, and the dissemination is the life of the civilization. The dissemination and communication between different civilizations form a glorious picture of the development of the mankind's civilization.

The American historian L. S. Stavrianos pointed out in his book titled *World History* that the mankind's civilization was born in an opening environment for such environment was of advantage to propagate and communicate the civilization. He divided the world history into two stages with a time demarcation line of B. C. 1500. Before B. C. 1500, the variety of human being's societies were all in a segregated state each other on a different degree. But after B. C. 1500, the whole world was connected together. To a great extent, the history of later stage of mankind was main about how the activity sphere of human extended to the various regions, and then to the whole world from the local place.

In the initial stage of the human society, the land-transportation was the major traffic way. Due to the transportation was convenient between European and Asian continents, they were the heart-like region in the world history. The European and Asian continents cover nearly two-fifth of the earth's surface, and the population of them amounts to nine-tenth of the world's. The two-rive-the Euphrates River and Tigris River, civilization and the ancient Egyptian civilization can be the earliest civilization of mankind for the Middle East region is located in where the Europe, Africa and Asian meet. The terrain here is smooth, the transportation is convenient, and the business activity is developed. So the economy here also was developed earlier.

Except the European and Asian continents, the world is main formed by Africa, America and Australia which had none of connections each other. The North Africa, where appeared the Egyptian civilization, was linked to the European and Asian continents. But the South Africa almost had no any well-known civilizations because it was separated by the desert. The original inhabitants of Australia had lived in the continent and were cut off completely for 30000 years with the European and Asian continents. So their development was impeded seriously.

Franz Boas, the well-known anthropologist who was called the "Father of American Anthropology", said: " human's history proves that whether the culture of a social group can make a progress usually is decided by if it has the opportunities to draw on the experiences from other social groups. The various discoveries which are gotten by a social group can convey to other groups. The more they communicate, the more they will get the opportunities to study each other. Mostly, the tribes, which have been cut off with the world for a long time, always have the most original culture for they can not draw on the experiences from the cultural achievement which are gotten by other tribes in the vicinity. So if the geographic conditions are same, then the key of mankind forge ahead is the communication and influence between the various nations each other. Only the nations which are easiest to be closed and have the most opportunities to affect with other nations each other can advance by leaps and bounds. "

When a place is cut off from the outside world, the development of civilization main rely on the creation. When the whole world is connected together, then the development of civilization depend on propagation. Comparing with the creation, the propagation is easier and more simple. It needs a great deal of manpower and material resources for developing a new technique or a new invention. For example, when the Four inventions of China were propagated to the outside world, they would be the common treasure of the whole mankind.

Many inventions and creations are originality, so it is impossible to invent or cream them again and other people just can study to the inventors. The Industrial Revolution of Britain is a typical example with an originality. The industrial revolutions in the other European countries were a result of learning from Britain. Some countries in Europe even had the more excellent conditions of industrialization, but they could not carry out the industrialization successfully. Because it was not a result which could be chosen by those countries on their own initiative. So to happen the industrial revolution is far more difficult than to study the achievement of the Industrial Revolution. By reaching for human's history, we find that the more important and larger civilization areas on the earth all develop by communicating with outside world frequently.

The competitions have been kept between the variety of civilizations, because the competitions are an important force to propagate the civilizations, due to feeling the pressure and threat from the competitions, people have to learn from the other nations for drawing the advanced experiences and keeping a same step to fore ahead. Along with the development of civilization, the world is connected together gradually and the various civilizations are more closely linked with each other. The competitions will be more tense and sharp.

Before 1500 years ago, the various areas of the world were almost cut off between each other. Te competition was not so intense and the backward civilizations still could exist. After 1500 years later, the world was linked together gradually. Especially up till now, along with the knowledge-oriented economy comes, the development of communication technique and the world economic integration, the information transmission is becoming easier and easier. The earth is becoming smaller and smaller, just like a "earth-village". Under these circumstances, all of civilizations must step into the "arena", and the civilization is developing quicker and quicker. The competition between the civilizations is also being sharper and more intense. So the propagating speed of civilization is being quicker and the sphere it touches upon is becoming wider.

An opened environment is of advantage to the development of civilization, but in closed environment, the civilization only retrogresses, instead of makes progress. It is was a typical negative example that Chinese civilization retrogress seriously in the Qing Dynasty in China because of the policy of cutting off their country from the outside world adopted by the ruling class.

In the 17th and 18th century, many huge changes were happened in the world sphere. The great scientists emerged one after another, such as Nicolaus Copernicus, Galileo Galilei and Isaac Newton, etc. The science became a strong motive force of the development of the productive force. But in the same time in China, it was a different status completely.

In the period of Emperor Kangxi (1654—1722), people could be allowed to have trade relations with the foreign countries in the four ports, but in the period of Emperor Qianlong, it was just in Guangzhou. In the period of Emperor Kangxi, the missionary were allowed to travel or stay in China, and they brought the variety of natural knowledge, including astronomy, mathematics, calendar, geography, physics, chemistry and medicine, etc. but in the period of Emperor Yongzheng, the missionary was all driven out.

Due to self-closing and self-satisfaction, the Chinese of the time, even the most advanced scholars, could not understand the circumstances of the world, and even know how large Britain and France were, as well as where they were?

In 1792, George Macartney, the special envoy of Britain, led a delegation to come to China. The delegation had a large scale with several large ships, more than 700 members and 600 boxes of goods. Among them, there were the most advanced scientific instruments, like globe and astroscope. The large-scale instruments filled a large house of Yuanming Garden when they were installed. Besides, there were the mode of foreign ship and some advanced arms.

It was originally a very good opportunity to study the foreign advanced culture and understand the situation of the world when the British delegation visited in China, but the Chinese just missed the golden opportunity for arrogance and ignorance of the Emperor Qianlong.

Macartney once said when he made a report to the British emperor: "the Qing empire is just like a tagged first-rank warship. It has not sunk in the past 150 years because it has supported by a group of lucky, capable and vigilant officers."

In the late period of Emperor Qianlong of the Qing Dynasty, the total economic output of China ranked the first in the world and its population made up one-third of the whole globe. Besides, it had long operated with trade surpluses. But just within 100 years, China fell into a position of being a backward country to be invaded by foreign countries. Karl Marx once commented: "That a giant empire, containing almost one-third of the human race, vegetating in the teeth of time, insulated by the forced exclusion of general intercourse, and thus contriving to dupe itself with delusions of Celestial perfection-that such an empire should at last be overtaken by fate on the occasion of a deadly duel, in which the representative of the antiquated world appears prompted by ethical motives, while the representative of overwhelming modern society fights for the privilege of buying in the cheapest and selling in the dearest markets. This, indeed, is a sort of tragical couplet stranger than any poet would ever have dared to fancy."

The time of stating modernization in China and Japan is almost same. The activities of Meiji Restoration of Japan and the Westernization Movement of China also happened in the same time. But Japan had not any misgivings and went forward in a large step, so its national power was raised rapidly and invaded China on the contrary.

A renowned professor of the Harvard University of the U. S. once made a speech in Taiwan. When talking about why the U. S. has ranked first position in the world on its global competitive power, he said: "The more a society opened, the more it would has a strong competitive power. The capital, science, information, inexpensive but elegant commodities and excellent talents will all come to the country." The other negative example is in Japan. Form the later stage of 1970s to the initial stage of 1980s, the global competitive power of Japan was arranged in the first position in the world. But during the ten years from 1990 to today, it was not the No. 1. What is the reason? People always say that there are two Japans, the one is known well by people which has the advanced electrical equipment and automobile industry. The other is a unopened and conservative Japan.

(1) Dissemination of Chinese civilization

Huang Di is the first ancestor of the Chinese nation. It was said that Huang Di was used to travel outside. He not only toured the five well-known mountain of China, but also traveled in various places with his wife. When he returned back, he would told what he saw and heard, such as making weaponry, engaging in sericulture and weaving cotton cloth, etc. to his tribe for increasing the their ability of understanding and conquering the nature.

After the Silk Road was started, more silks of China could be transported into the foreign countries. In the $1^{st}$ century B. C. , the Roman noble, Caesar (about B. C. 100—B. C. 44) once wore the robe making by the Chinese silk to view the play and caused a sensation in the audience. The sericulture was spread into Arabian countries and Egypt in the $7^{th}$ century, into Spain in the $10^{th}$ century, into Italy in the $11^{th}$ century and into France in the 15$^{th}$ century. Nowadays, the main breed of silkworm in the variety of countries are all from China.

The traveling activity in the far ancient times also brought the iron-smelting and irrigation technology into the Middle Asia and Europe. The country named Dawan also learned to dig the well from China.

Before the Papermaking Technique was spread out from China, people of Korea and Japan were used to write on bamboo slips and silks, the Indian used white bark and the leaf of palm to write, the European regarded the sheepskin as the paper to write. Above things had different disadvantages, such as some of them were heavy, some were too fragile and expensive.

It was said that it needed to use 300 piece of sheepskins for writing a book entitled *The Bible*. So most of above materials were not suitable to use largely. The propagation of the Papermaking Technique greatly promoted the popularization of culture and education, developed the dissemination of the world science and culture, and exerted a deep influence to the course of the world civilization.

Francis Bacon, an British scientist once said when he appraised the Four Inventions of China: "They change the whole face and state of the things in the world, and make them happen the numerous changes. None of an empire, a religion or an illustrious figure can give play to such more power and influence in developing the human's cause than those mechanical inventions."

The Silk Road was once a tie to link the civilizations of the East and the West. In 395, the Rome Empire was broken up into two parts — the East Rome Empire and the West Rome Empire regularly. The East Rome Empire had a vast territory which included where was from the Balkan Peninsula to the two-river valley and Egypt. In a certain times, it took an important part in the transportation and communication between the East and the West. For breaking the monopoly of Persia in intermediary trade, the East Rome Empire even sent the envoys to go to Axumite Kingdom — a powerful country which extended across the two side of the Red Sea.

In the Sui (581—617) Dynasty, for one thing, the Emperor Suiyang let the minister named Pei Jun to mobilized the businessmen of the Western Regions to come to the inland for engaging in trade. For another, he ordered to build the new business engineering. After it was finished, for welcoming the envoys, businessmen and tourists from the various countries, he gave another order to rectify the appearance of the city, and the whole Luoyang City was decorated with lanterns and coloured streamers in the first month of the Chinese lunar calendar every year. The Tianjin Street which had a distance of about four kilometers outside Duanmen and inside Jianguomen, was changed into a opera-area. The Fengdu City of Luoyang was started to be an international market. The businessmen here wore the gorgeous clothes and prepared enough rare treasures for receiving the consumers and guests. The government also established the Sifangguan to dispose the diplomatic and foreign-trade affairs roundly. All above ensured that the international trade activities could carry out smoothly.

The Tang Empire (618—907) paid much attention to operate the land-silk-route for a consideration of keeping the political prestige and economic communication with the foreign countries. The development of the land-silk-route in the Tang Dynasty was more prosperity. Unless the south, north and middle routes which were opened in Han Dynasty (B. C. 202—A. D. 220), there were two new routes opened too.

In the early stage of Emperor Taizong (reigned 627—649), the government defeated the East Turk, but the West Turk, which lived in the western part of the Altai Mountains was still powerful. In 639, the Emperor Taizong made up his mind to reoccupy the Western Regions and dispatched troops to the Gaochang (Qara-hoja). In the next year, the Tang government established Duhufu in the City and moved it into Qiuci to commanded where were called the Four Towns of Anxi in the history, which included Qiuci, Suiye, Yutian and Shule. The measures ensured the safety and prosperity of the Silk Road. Along the Silk Road, the business groups of China and the West countries were in an endless stream.

The association of the person was an important precondition in the communication between two kinds of civilizations or cultures. In the capital of Tang Empire—Chang'an City, a great number of foreigners from the various places of Europe and Asia lived here. In the time, the local people of Chang'an were influenced by the Western people. The women had the Indian shawls draped over their shoulders and wore the Persian earrings, and the men put on the foreign caps. Since the Emperor Taizong, on the 1$^{st}$ day of the first month of the Chinese lunar calendar, the envoys of the various countries and representatives of the variety of minorities would come to Chang'an City to attend the annual meeting of the Tang Dynasty. The people who has all kinds of colours of skin and facial features, dresses, languages and dances got together. The whole city had an exceptionally grand occasion and became an international metropolis gradually.

Due to the international communication and traveling activity was more frequent increasingly, the Chang'an City was becoming a center of communicating economy and culture between the various Asian countries gently. Many countries sent scholars and students studying abroad to China for taking a more advanced course of study or training. The highest-rank institution of higher learning — the Guozijian in Chang'an, had a number of 8000 foreign students, among them, the Japanese and Korean students are most.

The Korea once sent 105 students to come to China. They were well received by the government of the Tang Dynasty and allowed to attend imperial examinations. When the Korean students returned back to their country, they could not only take the knowledge that they learned, but also brought a great deal of Chinese ancient codes and records. The Buddhism, Buddhist scripture and carving-printed technique were also propagated into Korea. According to recording, the capital of Korea—Pyongyang was built by imitating the style of Chang'an and Luoyang Cities. Even the setup of government post for the civil and military officials, calendar, reign title and the dress of people in Korea were almost similar with the Tang Dynasty. So the Emperor Xuanzong (reigned 712—756) of the Tang Dynasty praised that the Korea was the Land of Gentlemen because the Korean understood the poetry and was reasonable, just like the Chinese nation. In the meantime, the music and specialty were spread into China and enriched the life of Chinese.

The cultural communication between China and Japan also reached a high-tide in the period of Sui and Tang Dynasties. According to the historical record, China sent the envoys and business-ships to Japan for 32 times totally in a time of 62 years from 841 to 903. But the Japanese envoys and students who were sent to China were more, sometimes there were even 500 persons in a group.

The Japanese students studying abroad who learned a lot of knowledge promoted the development of Japan actively. Under their encouraging and helping, the Emperor Xiaode of Japan made the Taika Era reforms. The reforms required the centrality and localities to study to the Tang Dynasty in many aspects, including politics, economy, culture, education, medicine and many other techniques. In 719, the Emperor Xiaode issued an imperial edict to change the Japanese clothes by imitating the clothes-style of the Tang Dynasty. From then on, the kimono has been a national clothes in Japan.

The exchanges between the Tang Dynasty and the countries of the South Asia, West Asia and Europe are also more frequent. In the process of communicating with each other, the astronomy and medicine of India were propagated into China. The Chinese national medicine, such as the ginseng and Chinese ephedra were propagated into India. Besides, the techniques of engaging in sericulture and planting the mulberry entered into Persia. The Persian not only master the sericulture, but also drew the technological features of Chinese silk fabrics to develop the Persia-style tapestry satin.

At that time, the international business travel were more brisk. The Persian businessmen, who had a tall nose and whiskers, led the camels, or rode the elephants or donkeys with a great deal of commodities, came and went between China and different countries busily. The businessmen of the Arabia Empire, which was situated in where the Europe, Asia and Africa meet, exchanged their perfumes for Chinese teas, porcelains and textiles. The great Arabian businessman and traveler—Suliman once engaged in trade while traveled in China in about 851. A unnoted Arabian author wrote a book named *Travels of Suliman in Orient* to describe what he saw and heard in China and other oriental countries after he returned to his country.

In the process of communication on civilization between China and foreign countries in the ancient times, it really can be called an unparalleled feat that Zhen He went to the West for seven times. The original name of Zhen He was Ma Sanbao, he was a famous navigator in the Ming Dynasty (1368—1644) of our country. After Zhu Di, the emperor of the Ming Dynasty ascended the throne, he ordered Zhen He to organize a large-scale economic and cultural diplomatic missions and make the ocean-going voyage for publicizing the Ming Dynasty and developing the international trade. At that time, people used to call the waters in west of Sumatra and Malaysia peninsulas to be the West. On July 111407, Zhen He led a huge mission with a number of 27800 people, including translators, sailors, artisans, doctors, secretaries, and mathematicians, etc. by 62 ships separately on which were filled with all kinds of goods, such as silks, porcelains, teas and gold, etc. started from the Liujiagang Port of Suzhou. They passed through the East Sea and South Sea to get to Java, Malacca, Indonesia and the west coast of India. Then they returned to Nanjing of China by taking 27 months.

Zhen He visited to the West during at the seventh time during 1431—1433. Except visiting the most countries and regions which he visited in the past times, he also paid a visit to some new countries. In the Mekka City, Zhen He realized his intension of proceeding to the "Holy Land" for worshiping. He saluted devoutly in front of the tomb of Islamic prophet—Mahomet. Zhen He died of illness in Nanjing after he finished his last long-distance voyage. After that, although the marine trade and exchange with the foreign countries were still rich and colourful, but the similar large-scale navigational activity was never appeared.

Zhen He took 28 years to sail more than 100000 nautical miles, he and his missions swept through the length and breadth of the Pacific Ocean and the Indian Ocean. They left their footprints in more than 30 countries and even reached the east coast of Africa. It was not only a precedent in Chinese navigated history, but also a rare magnificent feat in the world navigated history. They brought the great achievements of China to Where his ship-groups got, and were welcomed by the local people warmly. The Sanbao Long, Sanbao Temple and Sanbao Pagoda, which has been in a well protection in Java, Thailand were the witness of the friendly diplomatic relation. The books, includes Zhen He's navigated record —— *Zhen He Navigated Picture*, and his book entitled *Zhenwei Pian*, and other books which were written by his retinues have been the valuable date in the navigated history of China and world. Zhen He is not only an outstanding navigator in the navigated history of China and the world, but also an ambassador of civilization for propagating the Chinese civilization abroad.

If we talk bout who is the first man in the communication between the West the the Orient, it is absolutely the Italian traveler——Marco Polo. He is the first man who traveled to China from Venice of Italy through the sea route and land route, and then returned to Europe again. His footprint extended all over the Asia and Europe continent.

In 1271, Marco Polo began to travel to the orient with his father and uncle. They walk along the ways in the southern part of the Taklimakan Desert, by passing through He Tian and Luobupo, they got to the Dunhuang area and reached the Shangdu City of the Yuan Dynasty (1271—1368). They were successful on their hard journey of crossing the Europe and Asia continents in 1275 finally. Due to Marco Pole was wise and farsighted, in addition he also mastered many kinds of foreign languages, he was kept by Kublai Khan in the Yuan court to hold the office. Until 1291 when he returned to his homeland, he had traveled and lived in China for 17 years.

Kublai Khan once sent him to Ganzhou and other places for several times to check the revenue and also let him travel to the Southeast Asia and India. The Lugou Bridge, which stretch over the Yongding River in the suburb of Beijing, once was called the Marco Polo Bridge because it was described in the book entitled Travels of Marco Polo. It said: "This beautiful bridge shows a superb bridge-built technology of China. It has an ingenious carving with an excellent modeling craft. The whole bridge looks like a rainbow and affords a magnificent view." He also praised the capital and palaces of the Yuan Dynasty heartily: "There are a splendid palace and many beautiful residences in the city. You should know how large the palace is, just like I see. The whole palace is built on the smooth land. The roofs of the palace are so high, and the walls of the palace and rooms are decorated by gold and silver all over with all kinds of the figures, like dragon, animal, bird, rider and many other things are drawn on them. There is the huge hall in the palace for storing the weapons which are used to guard the city. The streets in the city are so straight that you can see the both ends when you stand on the streets, and you also can see the other gate form the gate where you are at."

The travel routes which Marco Polo walked along in China were where the post roads of the Yuan Dynasty passed through. There main were two ways. The one was the post road from Dadu to Yunnan and the other was from Dadu to Quanzhou. Above post-road system was the important infrastructure of the Yuan's ruling. Marco Polo praised that there were many roads started from Dadu and lead to many places.

Marco Polo also recorded the social life of the Hangzhou City in greater detail and especially mentioned the conditions of the tourism industry in Hangzhou. He said: " when I come here, I know that it is really a glorious , famous and precious city which can not be described by any beautiful words. The city is so large with 12000 stone-bridges in it. The bridge is so high that a big boat can pass though under it. It is not at all surprising that there are so many bridges in the city. Besides, there are numerous big or small boats on the lake for making merry to the visitors. Every boat can hold 10, 15 or more than 20 people. The length of the boat is from 15 to 20 steps and the bottom is smooth and wide. A boat is enough for who want to visit with the family, and there are tables, chairs and other necessary things. The boat-man can paddle the boat to where you want to go."

Marco Polo and his father and uncle began to miss their homeland after they stayed in China for many years. Now there was finally an opportunity to realize their desirability. When Marco Polo just returned from India, the Tartar, who had lived in the eastern part of the Mediterranean, sent three emissaries to seek a marriage alliance to Kublai Khan and asked him to send a princess. Marco Polo suggested that he and his father and uncle would escort the princess and the three emissaries to return through the seaway, Kublai Khan complied with his requirement. Marco Polo and his father and uncle got to the coast the Black Sea in Turkey by the land-way firstly, then went to Constantinople and returned to Venice in 1295.

In the sea-battle between Genoa and Venice in 1298, Marco Polo was taken prisoner and bought to Genoa. There he knew the royal author named Rusticiano. He told his experiences to him and Rusticiano wrote the well-known book entitled *Travels of Marco Polo*. In the introduction of the book, Rusticiano wrote:

The book of Marco Polo was undoubtedly born of the mind of a travelling businessman. His observations betray his roots as a practical merchant with an eye open for possible markets. He makes notes on transport, economy, obstacles, sources of food and water, and is always quick to list the primary sources of trade in the regions through which he travelled. Such inside information would have been useful to enterprising tradesmen and Western merchants searching for new marketplaces and regions for export.

Polo takes a practical and uniform approach to his descriptions. He describes "fine" towns, "large" provinces, "principle" cities. He notes religious persuasion in each area, encountering Christians, Mohammedans, Idolaters, Nestorian Christians, amongst others. Polo often details local laws and customs. He also discusses local people and notes who governs them. In some of the longer passages of the book, Marco Polo tells of legends, history and tales native to the area.

Travelling through a province called Tunocain, Polo describes a great plain, where "according to the inhabitants, took place the battle between Alexander and Darius". Further on he describes a place where horses were said to have directly descended from Alexander's horse, Bucephalus: "they were all born with a horn on their head, like their descendant, Bucephalus." Bequeathed to a vengeful widow, the breed was destroyed "so that it is now extinct". Fact and fiction frequently intertwine in this way throughout the narrative.

Marco Polo's book is almost unique in its accurate reportage on the geography, topography and make-up of nations. He was an observant traveller. However, many of his descriptions contain inaccuracies. Some may be attributable to Rustichello's own, undoubted embellishments. Others, such as his stories of Prestor John may be more attributable to common belief of the day than to recorded history. When considering such inaccuracies within the narrative, it should always be remembered that some thirty years had passed between the journey starting out and the writing of the book. The accounts were drawn from memory.

After the *Travels of Marco Polo* was published, it was well received by various readers and translated into Latin and all kinds of Italian dialects.

(2) Dissemination of Western civilization

In 13$^{th}$ century, the most Europeans knew the Asia by depending on their imagination and hearsay. For example, some people said: " The explorers traveled to the far places and they will face a strange and new world where the half-man and half-animal devils, mystical animals and races who have the unusual customs live in." Other people said that the local woman looked like the human, but the man was like dog or according to the trusty data, there had lived the human-shaped devils, their heads were as same as the human, but their face looked like the dog and with the cow-roof-shaped foot. They could speak two kinds of human's languages and cry out the third language like a dog. Some people even said with certainly that they once found some human-shaped monsters when they crossed the desert. They just had one hand which was in the center of the chest and one leg. The two monsters used a bow together and could run so fast that even the horse could not catch up them. They used their legs to jump, and when they were tired, they would touch the ground with their hands to jump continuously. Their bodies turn from here to there just like the wheels.

The legends of that sort, on one side made the Western people feel convulsed with fear when they mentioned the orient. On the other side, they also stimulated their curiosity to have a stronger desire on understanding the mysterious orient. For satisfying their curiosities and getting more business opportunities, a great deal of European travelers opened up a new prospect on traveling in Asia from Europe.

It was said that when Marco Pole returned to Venice, he was regarded as a vile character who told about some strange stories just for entertainment in the ballrooms and recreational arenas in Venice. When he was approaching his end, his relatives and friends urged him to confess his sins to God and admit his fault of lying for saving his soul. But Marco Polo said that he did not lie, and what he told to the people were less half of what he viewed.

In the end of the 15$^{th}$ century, the two hordes of forces intruded into India. One was the Portuguese who came by the seaway, the other was the Moguls who came by the landway and were going on the expeditions in the Middle Asia. The arrival of the two hordes of the forces made India take place a huge and lasting change. Until 1526, Babur established the Mogul Dynasty of India in Delhi and began a ruling of Moslem force.

In the West, the Portuguese was who entered into India earliestly. The book entitled *The Tourism History of the West* told:

"In 487, Pero da Kovilia, a philologian, soldier, spender and diplomatist, was sent as an envoy to India by the king of Portugal by the land-way for collecting the intelligences about this country. Kovilia could speak Arabic. He got to Cairo and Aden along the traditional routes of the businessman. Then he went to Calicut of India by a Arabian single-mast sailboat. He reconnoitred the west coast of India — the Malabo port, and returned to the east Africa by taking a Arabia ship. In the east Africa, he visited many Arabian cities and towns. Then he went back to Cairo again and finished his whole trip in Abyssinia. Before he left Cairo, he summarized his findings and wrote a worthy report and post it to Lisbon."

"In the period after him, what the occidental was proud of was the openning of the new navigation line. Vasco da Gama (1469—1524) arrived in India in 1498. In a time of 50 years afterwards, the Portuguese occupied an area which had a length of 96.5 kilometers and a depth of 48 kilometers on the Goa coast as their trade strongpoint. Afterwards, they occupied a great number of ports and forts in the southern part of the country and sent the envoys each other with the Mogul Dynasty in the northern part and the various states in the southern part of India."

"The Portugueses uses the trade-exchange between Lisbon and Goa to launch an important commercial revolution. Actually, it makes India, even the whole Asia accede to a single global exchang-system finally. After the groups of Portuguese ships returned to Lisbon from Goa, they sailed to the royal 'commercial firm' of Antwerpen. They developed the North Europe trade which was developing more thoroughly more than any times before."

The book also said: "it must recognize that the profits of trade, especially the profits of the transport trade between India and Afric, Arabia, Melaka, the Perfume Islands, China and Japan prop up the whole economic mansion of India — the vassal state of Portugul. The trade and the taxations which were imposed to the trade with a legal way or a corruptive means, bear the expenses of armies and officials. The trade also made the missionary activities extend to Beijing from Abyssinia."

The dissemination of the Western civilization basically began from the religion. Along with a development of commerce and navigation industries, the determination of European to propagating the Gospels to the the pagans was stimulated greatly. The John II of Portugal even sweard that "unify the whole world that human can live into the Christianity".

The Pope paid much attention to that how to carry out the direct domination of church all over the world. Spain and Portugal all belonged to the sphere of influence of the Roman Catholic Church. Along with the development of colonial expansion abroad, the Catholicism was disseminated into America and Asia. when some people asked Vasco da Gama what was the motive force to impel him to go to India, he answered predicatively: " it's Christian and perfume."

In 1500, the Portuguese commander—Cabral, led a troop to go to the Orient for developing the trade. Besides, eight ordinary believers and eight Franciscans traveled together with them. They would go to the Indian coast for propagating the Christianity under orders. But three of them were killed within two months unfortunately. The other missionaries did not shrink back and had lived there to do missionary works.

When De Almeida took office of the first Governor-general of India in 1505, more missionaries went to India for doing missionary works. During the 40 years before the members of the Societas Jesu stepped into India, the main activity sphere of the missionaries was the nearby coasts where regarded Goa as the center. They also set up the area under Madras Franciscan Archishop's jurisdiction. Their missionary activity has gone on until the 19th century.

In 1707, the last ruler of the Mogul Empire—Aurangzeb (1618—1707) was died. Afterwards, India was began a colonial rule by the UK. India was changed into a society which was influenced by the West deeply from a typical Non-Western traditional society.

In the early and middle stage of the $17^{th}$ century, the British, Hollander and French opened the commercial firms in the Surat District, the Gulf of Cambay in India continuously. After 1665, the economy of Surat developed rapidly. At the port where the ships gathered, there were full of a great number of simply sheds for sailors from Europe or other places to live temporarily. According to the recordation, the number of the permanent residents in Surat was about a million, the city could even be compared with Lyon. Except the prosperous commercial scene, the variety of nations and religions in the world also gathered here and formed an other kind of scenery.

Due to the products in various areas were rich, the trade-travel in subcontinent of India was more prosperous. In those where closed to the ports and rivers, the trade caravans transported the goods into the vast inland areas continuously through the land-way.

In $16^{th}$ and $17^{th}$ centuries, the missionary works of the various Catholic groups developed continuously. Many preachers of Societas Jesu from Portugal also regarded India as a base to do missionary activities to other places. Such as the Franciscans did missionary works, went to church, and received the visit of who had the identity in some areas of Ceylon. In every larger village and town, there were the missionary schools built. In some large Christian communities, people usually could hear the sacred song which was sung with Latin and Tamil. Some missionaries also left the travels described about India in the $17^{th}$ century. Such as the renowned book entitled *Travel Notes*. It told the experiences of Manrique, a Spanish missionary in Bengal in 1612. The book also described the fertile Ganga River area, the gorgeous cotton goods, the respect of the local people to cow and the Ganga River, and the rare activities in some areas, such as offering sacrifices to gods by sacrificing one's life.

From the $16^{th}$ to $17^{th}$ century, along with the trade and commerce developed more prosperous, more and more Western travelers came to India. Nicolas Conti and Dela Wale separately visited India by carrying their families in the $15^{th}$ and $17^{th}$ centuries. It made clear that the travel culture of India was so developed in those days.

The clergymen of the disseminated the modern Christianity in the world sphere most successfully. In 1514, Loyola became the leader of the Societas Jesu. He announced that all the followers of the religions were Christian brothers. Through the hard work of clergymen of the Societas Jesu, a religionary group which had a strong attraction was come into being in the partial Catholic areas in Europe. The ambition of the clergymen of the Societas Jesu was not only limited in Europe, they wanted to propagate the Gospels of God to every places in the world.

For insuring the missionary activities abroad could effective, the church would sent the more reliable people who were selected carefully to go. It meaned that those missionaries must have both ability and integrity. Through a series of preparations, from the middle of the $16^{th}$ century, the missionaries of the Societas Jesu began to missionize to India, China, Japan and the New Continent. The content of their activity included education, preaching the Gospel, providing the relief and other kinds of missionary activities.

As early as the period of Sui and Tang Dynasties, the foreign religions were propagated into China in accompany with a development of communication between China and foreign countries. After the Buddhism, the Islam and Christianity were spread into China one after another in the initial stage of the Tang Dynasty. In 742, the first mosque of our country was built in the Chang'an City. besides, the foreign musical instruments and recreational acitivities also were bought into China, such as the Huxuan Dance of the northern minorities, the Persian Konghou, an ancient plucked stringed instrument, and the acrobatics of Rome Empire, etc. Due to a popularity of Huxuan Dance, the dresses of such minorities also became the fashionable clothes received by people. Today, people can see the patterns of Huxuanwu on the carvings and murals in Dunhuang, Xi'an and Yanchi (Salt Pool).

Because the Ming and Qing Dynasties adopted the closed-door policy, the foreign travelers could seldom travel to China. According to the historical records, there were only 1200 foreigners traveled in China in the $21^{st}$ year of Yongle Emperor in the Ming Dynasty, and the international tourism was in a stagnating. But the transportation were becoming more convenient along with the science and technology developed day by day, the number of the missionaries coming to China from the West increased rapidly on objective. While the missionaries spread the religions, they also played the part of emissary of civilization in the cultural, scientific and technological communication between China and the West. Michele Ruggieri and Matteo Ricci were the most well known.

On March 29, 1578, Michele Ruggieri, Matteo Ricci, Francois Pasio and the other 13 clegymen of the Societas Jesu left Lisbon to start their voyage to the Orient. On September 13, 1578, they got to Goa. In April, 1579, Michele Ruggieri took a ship to China and reached Macao on July of the same year. Through a two-year study, Michele Ruggieri, who was already 36 years old, recognized 15000 Chinese words and could read Chinese books gradually. He was even trial to translate the Chinese volumes. Finally, he finished a book called *The New Catholic Veritable Records* or *Catholicism Veritable Records*, which introduced the creed of the Christianity in a systematic way. It was the first programme of creed which was written by a European in Chinese, and was cut blicks for printing in Guangzhou in November, 1584.

Since December, 1580, Michele Ruggieri got into the prosperous city for many times in company with the Portuguese businessmen who were allowed to carry on trade in Guangzhou City, and began his missionary activities in Guandong Province.

For gaining the trust of the Chinese officials as early as possible, he rehearsed a play for raising the prestige of the missionary and guiding the Western businessmen study Chinese ceremony and propriety, such as kowtow, kneeling down, modest attitude, etc. by helping of Canero Bishop of Macao. For a long time, some Portuguese businessmen were disgusted by the Chinese officials because they objected to Chinese overelaborate formalities. Due to the clergymem had an important position in the Western religions and social life, their opinion on public affairs had certain deterrent function. Through the enlightening and education by Michele Ruggieri, the Portuguese businessmen gave up their vulgar actions. Meanwhile, due to he was wise and kindly and never carried arms with him, he was asked to bear witness on the spot when the official paid a formal visit every time.

东京（Tokyo）

He also built the personal friendship with the officials of Guangzhou and gained a right to live here temporarily for launching the small-scale missionary activities. In September, 1583, Michele Ruggieri and Matteo Ricci went to Zhaoqing City, in where the government office of the Governor-General of Guangdong was. After gained a nod approval of Wang Pan, the prefect of Zhaoqing, they began to built churches and did missionary works in the city, and expanded into other places of Chian gradually. In 1588, Michele Ruggieri left Macao and returned to Europe. He never came back to China as a special envoy of the pope and passed away on May 11, 1607.

Matteo Ricci was one who had a huge influence in China as a missionary in the period of the Ming and Qing Dynasties. He was born in Italy and graduated from the Roman Theological Seminary. Due to the Chinese people had seldom gotten in touch with the Western Churches, just like Michele Ruggieri, Matteo Ricci also was not successful in the early days of missionary process. For attracting the Chinese people, he showed some scientific products which were made by the Western people, like the clock, etc. in the churches, and hung a self-made world map on the wall. He intentionally drew the position of China in the center of the map and signed in Chinese for trying to gain the favourable impression of the Chinese people. When he won the confidence of some local officials, he did his missionary works in Nanjing, Nanchang, and Suzhou, etc. successively, meanwhile, visited the historical sites throughout the journey. Then he was recommended to go to Beijng and called in by the Wanli Emperor of the Ming Dynasty. The emperor bestowed him a residence and allowed him to build the Catholic church in the area of Xuanwu Gate of Beijing, and the court would offer the whole funds he needed.

Matteo Ricci had lived in China for 29 years. Except doing missionary works and explaining scriptures, he spent the most time to introduce the Western culture and translate the books. The survey and drawing technique of the West was introduced in China by him. He surveyed the longitudes and latitudes of the Chinese south coast, north boundary and some cities, like Beijng and Guangzhou, etc. successively. He drew many kinds of world maps which made Chinese understand a conception of the Eastern Hemisphere and the Western Hemisphere. He translated many natural scientific books into Chinese, such as *Geometry Principle*, *Surveying Principles*, which enriched the natural knowledges and were conducive in enlightening the scientific and technological wisdom of the Chinese.

# Chapter 4

## The integrating force of tourism is an accelerator on developing human civilizations

# Eiffel Tower
埃菲尔铁塔

# Section 1

## Tourism has a "hard" integrating force with widespread intensions

1. Tourism industry is the largest mixed industry in the world

American scholar Daniel Bell mentioned in his book "*The Coming of Post-industrial Society*" published in 1973 that the tourism is the largest mixed industry in the world and it was impossible to compare contents which were contained or related in tourism with any other industries. He pointed out that the correlated industries of tourism not only influenced but also constrained each other.

The research and statistics made by some experts show that there were 180 nicknames for tourism, such as "tourism is the peace emissary", "tourism is the global passport", "tourism is just as lubricant to promote economic growth". And it is rare to find such phenomenon in any other industries.

The reasons for there are so many nicknames for tourism according to the writer come from two aspects. One reason is that all people have not a full and further understanding about tourism so far, just as the blindman feels an elephant. And the other reason is that the tourism has a big inclusiveness and wide correlation.

The concept of "integration" originates from the Europe theoretical circle. It is pointed out in Oxford Advanced Learner's Dictionary of Current English with Chinese Translation that "interstate" means "to make into a whole by bringing all parts together".

From a static perspective, tourism integration is to optimize the allocation of resources through the adjustment of industrial structure and the organizational reform under the condition of market economy and its goal, also the ultimate goal of the tourism industry development, is to achieve the best results and conditions of industry combination and industry competition. From a dynamic perspective, tourism integration is to achieve a process of abovementioned result and condition.

Tourism integration also accord with the above characteristics. From the perspective of the economic and cultural attribute of tourism, it also can be divided into hard integration and soft integration. And the hard integration means substance power expressed by the industry chain or the industry group of tourism.

What is the industry chain of tourism? From the economic perspective, the development of tourism is not only to stimulate the service industry which provides services for tourism such as traffic, accommodation, catering, entertainment, commerce, scenic spot and etc. but also to drive the development of the correlated industries.

Taking restaurant industry for example, the increase of hotel must drive the development of architecture, building materials, furniture, decoration and other related industries. And catering industry needs agriculture, animal husbandry, fishing, forestry and other industries to expand the production capacity and increase product supply. As a comprehensive industry, tourism associates with other key factors, industries and systems. The first one is the factor association. The six key factors of tourism—food, shelter, transport, travel, purchase and entertainment—are inter-contacted and mutual-dependent. The second one is industry association. Besides the tertiary industry, tourism has relations with many other industries and sections such as the primary industry including agriculture, animal husbandry and fishing, which provide tourism with material support, and the secondary industry including light industry, heavy industry and construction industry and the telecommunication industry, finance industry, insurance industry, public service industry, health and sports industry, culture and art industry, education industry, information consultation service industry as well as the tertiary industry including tourism administrative bureau, customs, border control and etc.

According the statistics of relevant department of Australia, the supply of tourist product associates with 29 economic departments and totally 109 industries. The development of tourism drives the development of these departments and industries, while these departments and industries provide powerful material foundation to drive the development of tourism. The third one is the systemic relation. The tourism is composed of five systems—tourist attracting system, service system, transportation system, marketing system and information supporting system. And the sustainable development of tourism needs them to associate with each other organizationally and coordinate interactively.

The industry group of hard integration simply means the high dense association between the same enterprises or the same supporting enterprises.

Industry cluster has become a world-wide economic phenomenon. And it attracts the attention of many governments of different countries and regions. The industry group model of localization, specification and socialized division attracts more and more travel enterprises to come towards industrialized regions or objective. For example, the three city communities—Suzhou, Hangzhou, and Shanghai; Zhujiang delta region as well as Beijing, Tianjin and Hebei—was called troika of China economy. And tourism, which energizes among hot industries of the three metropolitan economic circles, has shown its integrated development trend at different levels.

The Yangtze River Tourism Coordination Region has realized the integration of the tourist resources and the supporting factor of tourism firstly and becomes the biggest economic output region in China's tourism. Shanghai, Jiangsu and Zhejiang provinces have made the associations with 150 scenic spots along 14 coastal cities of Shanghai, Jiangsu and Zhejiang provinces actively with the goal of establishing the "big Shanghai" tourism distribution center. And the three provinces package and bring out 36 cross-region tour routes and gain tourism income of 230 billion yuan in three years. Guangdong Province takes advantages of the city group brand of Zhujiang delta and the radiation of Hong Kong and Macao markets to bring out the "big tour circle" concept, from which Guangdong Province gains the return of 126.083 billion yuan, and show the special advantages of big tour region.

2. The integrating force of tourism cannot be replaced

We can say that the human economy will not have development and the human civilization will not have progress if there's no tourism. Tourism develops together with the development of human productivity and boosts the progress of human productivity with the constant growth and vibrancy of itself.

Mr. Zhu Changqin contributed an article to *Global Travel Weekly* on October 14, 2006: "tourism has turned into a super big industry touching every corner of our life. Tourism has become a universal industry in the world and all countries attach importance to tourism. Tourism has got breakthrough in time and space and is no longer exclusively enjoyed by the rich, the power holder and the leisure class. It is no longer an elegant subject of "The wise find pleasure in water; the virtuous find pleasure in hills". Every region is tapping tourist resources and developing tourist industry. It's difficult to estimate the development speed and broadness of engagement. For the boosting of the tourism, a multiple of relative industries also get leap-forward development. The grow up of tourism is startling."

Mr. Zhang Guangrui, director of the Tourism Research Center of China Academy of Social Sciences, makes it more specific: "the people's understanding on tourism has seen significant changes in the less than 30 years development period." It has changed from "non-governmental diplomacy" into "foreign currency creating industry", "non-smoke industry" and "intangible trade", later it is called as "pillar industry", "advantaged industry" and "pillar industry", now people begin to call it as "environmental friendly industry", "learning industry", "culture industry" and "power industry". Mr. Zhang's account has clearly explained the relations between tourism and other industries and the key contributions to the development of world economy and the progress of human civilization.

Tourism is a recognized emerging industry in the world. Some countries regard tourism as fundament to the building of a nation, some countries and regions only have tourism, e. g. Maldives, Hawaii and Athens. Athens is a city of 4 million populations. It only has two industries, of which the bigger one is tourism and then comes textile industry. The textile industry only engages 180 000 populations and the others are also fed by tourism. The water city Venice only has two industries, one is tourism, the other is shipping. Shipping also serves for tourism. The city with only 1.6 million populations has about 60 million person/times of visitors every year.

Related study shows that every one dollar of direct tourism income can bring forth U. S. $2.5 worth indirect tourism income. In 2005, the total tourism income in the world surpassed U. S. $6000 billion, occupying 10% of the gross world production and the practitioner number has come to 221 million. According to this figure, it can be deducted that tourism has boosted GDP to increase by U. S. $15000 billion and total benefit will come to U. S. $21000 billion.

The boosting effect of tourism is ever bigger in China. According to the estimation of relevant study, every one dollar of direct income in tourism can bring U. S. $3.12 indirect tourism income; if the tourism income increases one yuan, the output of the tertiary industry will increase 10.7 yuan. If the tourism earns one U. S. dollar of foreign currency, the foreign capital utilization volume will increase U. S. $5.9. China's domestic tourism income in 2005 was 528.8 billion yuan and the international tourism income is U. S. $29.3 billion yuan, the GNP growth tourism boosted is 1600 billion yuan and U. S. $170 billion.

The report on China's tourism development— "Sowing the Seed of Growth" of World Travel and Tourism Council (WTTC) said that the direct added value of China's tourism is U. S. $44.5 billion, equivalent to 2.8% of GDP; the total added value of tourist economy is U. S. $217.8 billion, equivalent to 11.7% of the GDP; the number of persons directly employed by tourism is 14.2956 million, occupying a share of 1.9% of the total employed of the country; tourism has created a total of 64.6251 job opportunities, occupying 8.6% of the total employed of the country; investment in tourism is U. S. $100.3, occupying 9.9% of the total investment capital and government expenditure in tourism is U. S. $8.3

billion, occupying 3.8% of the total government expenditure.

Yu Yingshi, director of the Tourism Research Institute of The China Senior Professors Association mentioned in his book: "one industry requires an industrial group to support its production, e. g. in the steel-making industry, the mining and smelting can all be included in the industry, but the situation to tourism is rather complex. Tourism hasn't an independent industrial group and the industrial group of tourism belongs to other sectors. Tourism relies on the industrial group of the society to realize its industrial purpose, which is the characteristics of the tourism industry."

The development of tourism has boosted the integration and interaction of a region in resources allocation, economic growth, infrastructure building, ecological environment, labor and employment, social culture and opening up. At the same time, regional economic development can boost the growth of tourism consumption and the raise of consumption level, while the bettering of the infrastructure and supply level and the improvement of ecological environment have ensured the development of tourism.

Resource integration degree of the tourism is higher than any other industries. Traditional industries and sectors can only select resources suiting product production, but the situation in tourism is different. Tourism can combine matters of several thousands and even more than ten thousands years ago with modern society; it can even combine resources in such aspects as economy, culture folk custom and society and even psychology together; it may integrate materials, spirit, culture and religion, as well as history, geography, architecture, hydrology, geology, biology, botany, zoology and micro-organism for the tourists.

Mr. Chi Guowei said in his article entitled *My Word on "Tourism Unifies the World"*: "While common people are gradually changing their views on tourism activities, scholars are also changing their views on tourism activities and joining in the ranks of serious research. Unlike what they did in the past, the scholars no longer view tourism as an apparent and approximate activity and action, which is characterized by the 'temporary' contacts and exchanges between visitors and the host and thus cannot precisely help people know the objective world. They now put tourism onto a level which can help various nationalities and race groups to mutually understand, equally treat each other amid rich cultural exchanges. This new recognition is also based on the traditional cognition and rational understanding on the society and culture with a deepened historical depth and extent. So naturally, tourism helps reorganize many subjects while many subjects also bring tourism into their spheres of research."

"For example, agriculture now covers rural tourism, anthropology explores the relation between visitors and their hosts, commerce now pays attention to hotel investment while ecology seeks to see elements relating to tourism and nature. Economics studies cast their eyes on tourism economy, education is keen on extending tourism education, geography has a new subject named 'Tourism Geography' while history begins to focus on issues relating to tourism history. Hotel management is eager to explore issues relating to hotel management and services, legal studies now touch legal problems relating to tourism, recreation and reproduction are keen to see the relations between the recreation and reproduction of visitors, market transaction discusses matters relating to transactions in tourism market and political science widens its macro research on the boundless world. Psychology now aims to deepen research on tourism motivation, religious studies have interest in issues relating to pilgrimage tourism and relevant religious rites, sociology has a new subject called 'Tourism Sociology', transportation now has great interest in issues relating to tourism transportation such as aviation while urban and district planning now casts its eyes on tourism development problems, tourism safety, diseases, social gender, ethnic self-identity and media, etc."

Mr. Chi said further in his article: "Nowadays, tourism has become the largest and fastest-developing industry in the world, which brings forward a series of completely new subjects to the world economy, politics, environment, resources, employment, cultural exchanges, management and globalization while posing great challenges to them."

We can feel in our life that as a leading industry of modern services, tourism has rather strong integration and wide radiation. Modern tourism nearly includes all contents of the tertiary industry. Among these industries, some are old industries which didn't grow up in the past decades but rise up with the development of tourism. The postal and telecom industry is just a typical example. According to the statistics of the telecom department, the income brought by migrant populations and tourists occupies 46% of the total income of the industry every year.

Tourism plays a leading role among numerous industries. The development of tourism decides the development of many other industries. The sudden prevalence of "SARS" in 2003 troubled many governments. In order to cut off the spread via tourism, many countries promulgated orders to stop all tourist activities. Although other industries are not stopped during this period, these industries fell into depression for the termination of tourist activities. After "SARS" was under control before long, these industries restored together with the restoration of tourism. This testifies that tourism determines the development of other industries.

# Section 2

## Tourism has an immeasurable "soft" integrating force

1. What is "soft force"

American scholar Joseph S. Nye created the word "soft force" in the second half of 1980s. Soon after, the word was frequently used by political leaders, editors and scholars all over the world.

What is "soft force"? To make it simple, it is the capacity that one country attracts, not "orders" or "compels" other countries to do something or make certain option. According to Joseph S. Nye, just for relying on "soft force" —the wide spread of American-styled democratic and value concept, the U. S. defeated the former Soviet Union and won the final victory. As a scholar ever acted as the assistant defense minister of the U. S., Joseph S. Nye's idea has great influence in the political circle and provides a theoretic basis for the U. S. to lead the world.

According to the analysis of Joseph S. Nye, soft force is the power of attraction and persuasion, while hard force (the capacity to compel) comes from the military and economic strength of a nation. Compared with the "hard force" based on military, sci-tech, education and economy, the resources of soft force mainly include three aspects: culture, ideology (or outlook of value) and international criterions and institution.

According to an article contributed by Zhou Qing'an to *Global Times* a country which is affluent in soft force resources is not necessary a strong player of soft force. When Bruce Lee introduced Chinese *Kongfu* to western film in 1960s, kickboxing has become a common event in Western countries. Zhou wrote in his article that "the modern history shows that there's no necessary relations between the soft force resources and soft force. In international politics and history, several important traditional culture centers in the world, such as East Asia, Aegean Sea, Tigris and Euphrates drainage area and South-Asia Continent, have not had soft force center influencing international political discourse system. There are two reasons, one is there are more developing countries in the region and the long-term backwardness has influenced their image; the other is that culture is not soft force. Whether a thing can play an effect of force depends on the communication and application result. "

According to Zhou Qing'an, the soft force product must experience three stages if a country which is affluent in soft force resources wants to turn into a strong player of soft force.

"Firstly, good package is required if a cultural product wants to develop from existence to an important mean of the soft force of a nation. The reason for calling this kind of force 'soft force' is not only that the contents are easily to be recognized, but its form is more easily to be accepted."

"Secondly, whether the cultural products of a nation can turn into an effective means of soft force depends on the internationalization degree of the products. Kickboxing is just such kind of typical soft force. The display of cultural products and the output of cultural means are all soft forces."

"Finally, soft force requires the sufficient integration of resources. The functioning of soft force is a long-term process. Any kind of soft force resources can't be independent. In the promotion process of kickboxing, South Korean government, commercial institutions and non-governmental organizations have utilized such mass media means including TV & film, audio products and website and kickboxing club for promotion. Objectively, the integration of these channels has made kickboxing a comprehensive cultural carrier. It is also a vertical sign of the national cultural resource brand of South Korea. This is also a reason for soft force to be 'force' and the source of 'force' is integral and all-round after all."

According to the soft force model of Joseph S. Nye, soft force has appealing in culture, ideology and outlook of value, as well as in shaping international rules and deciding political issues.

Tourism-related conceptual product is a kind of soft force worthy of the name. It is a conceptual product with obvious theme, conspicuous feature and strong culture sense. It is not only the theoretical distillation of tourist products, but adds wings to tourist products. Dalian's registration its city trademark as "capital of romance" is a typical example.

Dalian is situated in the south tip of Eastern Liaoning Peninsula. It is adjacent to Yellow Sea in the east and Bohai Sea in the west. There's no severe coldness in the winter and sweltering heat in the summer. The yearly average temperature is 10 ℃. Dalian is an outstanding tourist city, hygienic city and garden city in China. On June 5, 2001, the United Nations elected Dalian to the rank of "Global 500 Roll of Honor" in environmental protection.

Dalian tourism is based on the sea and relied on the green. With the agreeable city environment as the brand and large-sized tourist activities as the carriers, Dalian is a city full of charm for such elements as fashion city, football city, hometown of track and field event and city of night views. By centering the objective of building Dalian into "an important international city in Northeastern Asia", Dalian makes all-out efforts to implement the "capital of romance" tourist brand strategy. After years of efforts, State Administration of Industry and Commerce agreed to accept the registration application of Dalian as "capital of romance". This is the first time for a city to apply for trademark with an overall tourism image.

At the same time, Dalian made an all-round registration of 43 products related with "capital of romance", which makes Dalian a city which changes scenery into capital. Experts of Tourism Organization said: the intangible asset value of the tourist brand of "city of romance" is 100 billion yuan.

Presently, the U. S. is not only popularizing its tangible products in the world realm, but is spreading its cultural and spiritual products in the world and enlarging the influence of its outlook of value, living mode and commercial management mode. The output value of its cultural communication industry has come to U. S. $2640 billion, occupying 20% of the GDP in 2006. 349 listed companies have possessed a capital market value of U. S. $380 billion. Time Warner, one of the top 10 media companies, had more than 100 000 employees in 2001 and the business income was U. S. $37 billion.

Till the present, the right of voice owned by western society enables it to include the mainstream vale, ideology and even cultural trend of the west. The development of soft force even surpasses the estimation of Western scholars themselves.

2. Tourism is the best way to use "soft force"

The inherent characteristics of tourism determine that the impact and guide to the people's thought and concept is rather huge. No other thing in the world can narrow the distances between different countries as successful as tourism and make the exchange between different countries as extensive as tourism. Tourism is a multi-form, multi-tier, multi-channel, large-scope and all-round contact and interaction.

Tourism has cultural and economic dual attributes. Combination of culture and economy is a conspicuous characteristic of tourism. The essence of tourism is culture and there's no tourism without culture. Although a large amount of funds and construction is required at the early period of tourism development and economic nature occupies a dominating role in tourism. When tourism enters the developed stage, the culture nature will gradually occupy the dominating position for the intensifying of culture consumption of the tourists.

Undoubtedly, culture is soul to tourism and the most important appealing factor to the public. Culture is normally carried by specific substances and architectural relics. When it comes to Egypt, people may think of Pyramid, when it comes to China, people may think of the Great Wall and the forbidden city. These tangible and intangible Oriental civilization and buildings reflect century-long historical civilization of the Chinese nation at the time of bringing forth visual impact. This is also the spirit carried by these cultural heritages. It has the charm of breaking through special and geographical limits.

The present times is an era of constant progress and integration. Political reform, economic rules or cultural activities are all promoting international communication and exchange. However, it becomes more and more clear that any other activities have such extensive roles in integrating the world, promoting exchange and sharing civilizations.

Zhu Changqin pointed out in the "Thoughtful Newspaper Proverb" that: "integration includes tangible integration and intangible integration; material integration and spiritual integration. Tourism not only has promoting, regulation and integration roles to world economic development, but what mentioning is that it has unconquerable integration on the diversified civilization stage. No other industry in the world has so big compatibility, sports and diversification as tourism. Tourism enables a multiple of culture and information get tangible and intangible or realistic or rational exchange, integration and distillation in the evolution process. Tourism has no national boundary and language choice. It enables people to make extensive and free communication at the time of appreciating the world. Only in the realm of tourism, can people be free from wars and disasters. Therefore, tourism is the most civilized, most harmonious and best communication mode in human life, as well as the best method for obtaining great harmony. This is the charm for tourism to turn into 'global village'. This kind of lasting and potential force has profound significance to the future."

Deng Zhitao, director of Gansu Bureau of Tourism, said: "tourism is an industry boosting the civilization and progress of the entire society. Tourist activities can not only boost economic development, but are important contents of people's spiritual and cultural life. Productivity development and the growth of economic indicators are not the representatives of the core value of the society, only exchange makes an isolated small mountainous village to see the dawn of civilization and progress and enjoy the achievements of spiritual and material civilizations. Therefore, we can say that tourism is an industry combined with material civilization, spiritual civilization and political civilization. A pure political movement can't attain this effect."

Here, we shall further learn the soft unifying force of tourism and we can probe into "cultural invasion" by taking this opportunity. For a long period of time, culture and civilization spread are accompanied with "anti-cultural invasion".

We know that invasion is an intentional conquering of one country or race to another country in order to acquire material or spiritual fortune. Then, when one country or government propagate its outlook of value, political concept, living mode and cultural concept, it is also "invasion"?

In China's history, Buddhism was disseminated into China and became a state religion. No one regards its cultural conquer a kind of invasion. At the same time, Chinese characters are also deeply embedded in Japanese characters and become an intrinsic part of Japanese culture. Japanese is also very upset for this kind of invasion. Today, white collars in non-English-speaking countries often chat in their native language with English words blended in, which is not regarded as an "invasion" of national dignitary, but a fashion.

In the "Analysis of 'Culture Invasion'" by Mr. Wu Zuolai: " 'culture' doesn't involve sovereignty, what matters is whether this kind of culture is more advanced, whether it is rich and diversified and humanistic. Culture is a kind of 'manner', it can be exchanged, spread, studied, used and copied. Culture is different from war. Culture is a symbol not aggressive. It is a manner in which one person, group or nation's soul and ideology are voluntarily being conquered and the outlook of life, outlook of world and production and living mode are changed accordingly."

Culture spread is a process of contradictory movement, including cultural contradiction and adaptation. If there's no new culture input and one nation exists and develops within a limited scope, there's no culture conflicts. Of course, there's no tensile force brought forth by such conflicts and no development and progress of local civilization. Therefore, culture not only has no sovereignty, but involves no invasion. There are only backward and advanced cultures. The backward culture voluntarily accepts advanced culture in non-violent manner, which is the development rule of human civilization.

In 1980s, Japanese and American cartoons flood China's domestic TV screen. Some one then cried "cultural invasion" on the excuse that China's cartoon industry was on the down-slope trend. But in fact, the reason for Chinese cartoon films to fail in international appraisal is conformism. Later after China has realized this shortcoming, it began to absorb new idea of alien culture and rose up then.

A news report entitled "Well, China Finally Carries Out 'Cultural Invasion' on the U. S." on September $20^{th}$, 2005 issue of *Hunan Daily* mentioned that Hunan Sanchen Company, China' biggest cartoon art manufacturing basement, has signed a contract with the

U. S. -based Sino-American Trade Development Association. The cartoon film "Blue Cat" created by the company has entered the U. S. market. The following is the detailed report:

The gentle and lovely "Blue Cat" will enter the U. S. market to amuse U. S. children. This is a deal reached by Hunan Sanchen Company and Sino-American Trade Development Association at Guangzhou Expo. Consul of the U. S. consulate in Guangzhou, relevant leaders from State Administration of Radio, Film and Television and mayor of Changsha attended the signing ceremony.

Hunan Sanchen Company is the biggest cartoon art making basement in China. The "3000 Whys of Blue Cat" created by the company is deeply loved by Chinese kids and the yearly sales output is more than 100 million yuan. The international version blue cat cartoon newly packaged by Taiwan branch of the company is widely favored by all once it is launched in the market. Chairman of Sino-American Trade Development Association Mr. Robert who ever acted as the far east economic counselor of president Nixon acted as the match maker and helped "Blue Cat" to export to the U. S. .

It's said that the "Blue Cat" exported to the U. S. has a total of 900 parts and will be broadcasted all over the U. S. four months later, helping American children to learn China. This is the first time for Chinese cartoon works to export to the U. S. . On the signing ceremony, Mr. Robert said: "American children begin to watch 'Mickey Mouse' when they are kids. This kind of cartoons is funny, while 'Blue Cat' is gentle, lovely and clever and American children can have more understanding on China through these cartoons." Tan Zhongchi, mayor of Changsha, said: "Chinese children know more on the U. S. , which is benefited from American cartoons to certain degree. There are not only the comic classic as 'Mickey Mouse', but the tragic class as 'Snow White'. China's cartoon making shall learn from that of the U. S. ."

This example shows that if we take alien culture for granted, "Isn't it delightful to meet friends from afar" and carefully discriminate, absorb and digest alien culture, and combine it with outstanding part of Chinese culture, there's possibility for us to launch a counter-attack.

It can be easily seen in the realistic world that normally it's countries and regions with a relative backward culture often cry for "anti 'culture invasion'". Upholding the banner of protecting "national culture", they often distort alien culture, but they failed finally and all that shall enter have entered. Tourist activities are just an activity containing this kind of "attack".

The development of human civilization history shows that cultural interaction can not only generate new culture, but huge economic benefit. At a certain time, the "soft" force can turn into concrete "hard" force. If Dalian further develop the commercial value of the "capital of romance", the economic benefit from the use of trademarks of 43 series products is immeasurable.

Although some industries are not directly connected with tourists, the development of tourism can not only upgrade the reputation of a city or region, but the reputation of products in the tourist destination, creating new business opportunities. Tourism also has the special functions of turn the foul and rotten into the rare and ethereal. Places and substances seemingly have no value can be forged into an expected tourist sites.

Disneyland is a tourist destination constructed on an isolated desert. The holding of one session of Olympics accelerated the development of Sydney for 10 years. The 2002 FIFA World Cup not only freshened the image of South Korea in our mind, Korean pickled vegetable also become one of the most important export products of the country. Therefore, we shall comprehend tourism from a broad sense. We can't only see the tourism has boosted the development of relevant industries, but shall understand its material and spiritual contents. The spiritual force generated by tourism can have unimaginable explosive force which can boost the all-round development of a city or region in politics, economy and culture.

Linfen in Shanxi Province was the capital city for Emperor Yao more than 4700 years ago according to the recordation of historical book "China starts from Yao". Therefore, Linfen is crowned as "the 1$^{st}$ ancient capital in China". After the founding of Yuan Dynasty, Kublai Khan ever issued an imperial edict to rebuild Linfen. For the destroy of chaos and earthquake, Yao capital is gradually neglected in history. Till 2000, Linfen people decided to all-roundly rehabilitate Yao capital. In 2003, China Hua Gate, a large building displaying the 5000 year long Chinese civilization was constructed in Yao capita. Different from tradition, the tourist site has rather big innovation. Leon Bertrand, French Minister of Tourism said when holding a talk with the chief designer of Hua Gate Su Qingping: "I admire your creation very much. Although Hua Gate is new at present, it will turn into historical heritage several thousands later and it will show its charm and value then." Hua Gate is then crowned as "the first monument of Chinese civilization" and "China's first cultural and tourist site".

Several years ago, when Hua Gate's chief designer and head of Yaodu District Su Qingping put forward the concept, many people criticized that this is an "image project" and it's better to build housings to shelter people than to construct a temple for an ancient people. But Su Qingping presented this cultural and innovative work in front of all despite pressures from all sides.

Hua Gate is now not only the highest gate in the world, but its unique cultural connotation has reflected huge cultural influence. It is dubbed as "the first monument of Chinese civilization" and "China's first cultural and tourist site" by media. In just one year, the ticket income of Yaomiao Scenic Spot that Hua Gate is increased by 100 times and such tertiary industries as transport, catering, hotel, trading and information are developing at an unprecedented speed.

What the digits reflected are only material effect, the spiritual effect is dozens and even hundreds times of the material effect. Presently, Hua Gate has become a symbol of Linfen and the symbol of the source of Chinese civilization. And Linfen people have regained the lost pride. A Hong Kong businessman who didn't expect to invest in Linfen changed his attitude after viewing Hua Gate. It's said that the foreign investment in Linfen rose up significantly after the building of Hua Gate. A local cadre said that: "Linfen people are more proud after the construction of Hua Gate."

We can see from many incidents that the development of tourism has big impact on people's thought and concept. For the development of tourism and the holding of tourist activities, the distance between countries will be shortened. The way of thinking and living custom upheld for more than 1000 years may change through the multi-form, multi-tier, multi-channel, large-scope and even all-round contact and exchange of tourism.

圣彼得堡（St. Petersburg）

# Chapter 5

# Development of Human-Civilization Increases the Value of Tourism

# Sydney Opera House
悉尼歌剧院

# Section 1
## War is the Main Channel for the Transmission of Human Civilization in Ancient Times

According to the previous chapters, tourism is a flowing bridge for disseminating mankind's civilization. The low productivity resulted in small-scale traveling activities involving relatively few tourists, which failed to exert great effects on the society. Thus, the main channel to disseminate mankind's civilization is war instead of travel in the history.

War produces a great impact to the communication and development of civilization. When the war destroys a civilization, it often gives birth to another civilization. Marx once said: "violence is a midwife in every old society who will help to give birth to the new society."

When Alexander defeated the Pharaoh of Egypt decisively, he not only destroyed the civilization of Pharaoh, meanwhile brought the advanced Grecian and Roman civilization into Egypt. Due to the war launched by Alexander, many Grecian scholars came to the Orient to explore its science, technology, culture and art. Alexander City of Egypt was the greatest cultural center of Greece at that time.

The war often changed the territory of a country, the attribute of political power, the living way of a nation and their religious belief forcefully and violently. Some political powers, countries and nations were destroyed and replaced by other stronger counterparts. The war even could break off the function of a civilization and force it to develop into another way. Besides, the war could also promote the development of science and technology with its special function, and strengthen the communication between different countries and nations, all of which help people change their ways of living.

From ancient times, conflicts between tribes and countries broke out frequently because of the reasons of territory, population and belief. Peace can be maintained only if two countries are well matched in strength; otherwise, a war would break out at any time if the balance is broken. Generally speaking, it is the side enjoying a more advanced civilization that stirs a dispute up.

The war itself is a way to realize cultural fusion. Because it is of vital importance to the country's safety and people's life, so the most advanced science and technology, the bravest warriors of the tribe will be firstly used in the war.

For example, in the Period of Spring and Autumn (770 B. C – 476 B. C.) and Warring States (475 B. C – 221 B. C.) of China, more than 200 principalities fought and annexed with each other, eventually formed a situation in which seven powers fighting for hegemony, including Zhao, Yan, Chu, Qin, Wei, Han and Qi being called "the seven powerful states of the Warring Sates Period" in Chinese history.

Successive years of tangled warfare among these states required no only advanced weapons like chariots and spears, but also a think tank At that time, scholars-the talented persons who had the professional expertise were recruited by princes, marquises, and dukes. Accommodating and recruiting scholars became so prevalent. According to historical records, the four princes of the Warring States period-Mr. Mengehang, Mr. Pingyuan, Mr. Xinling and Mr. Chunshen, recruited thousands of scholars, and most of them were proficient in a particular field. The prime minister of Qin State, Lv Buwei, once recruited more than three thousand scholars.

The scholars of the pre-Qin period (before the First Emperor of Qin united China in 221 B. C.) included such great thinkers like Lao Dan, Kong Qiu, Mo Zhai, Meng Ke, Zhuang Zhou, Zou Yan, Xun Kuang and Han Fei, the statesmen, like Guan Zhong, Zi Chan, Yan Ying, and Shang Yang, the militarists, such as Wu Qi, Sun Wu and Sun Bin, the diplomats, such as Lin Xiangru, Su Qin and Zhang Yi, the historians, like Zuo Qiuming, the poets, like Qu Yuan and Song Yu, the orators, like Hut Shi and Gongsun Long, the medical scientists, such as Bian Que, the hydraulic experts, like Li Bing and Zheng Guo, and the astronomers, such as Gan De and Shi Shen, etc.

Worldwide speaking, it is also the case in the ancient Greece. From the 5th century B. C. to the 4th century B. C., a large-scale military conflict-the Greece-Persia War broke out between the West and the East. At last, the war came to the end in Persian's failure. During the war, the democracy of Athens stepped into its flourishing period and the economic and political rights of citizens were protected by the government who at the same time encouraged poor people to attend cultural and political activities. In this time, poetry, literature, play, historiography, construction and modeling-art of Greece achieved a glorious success.

In the early of the 4th century B. C., the monarchical state came into being in the Macedonian area in the north of Greece.

Along with its political, economical and military force strengthened day by day, it controlled many a city-state of Greece rapidly and became a powerful country in the area of the Mediterranean Sea. In 336 B. C. , Alexander ascended the throne and began to launch the massive aggression to the East.

In 34 B. C. , Alexander set off on his expedition. He led his army to go across the Asia Minor, Syria and Egypt and reach the Persian Plateau and the Caspian Sea. Afterwards, they went southward towards the Sistan area, through which they passed through Afghanistan to reach Bactria, then crossed Hindu Kush Mountains and arrived at Indus's mouth of the sea.

He conquered the Mediterranean world region, Persian Empire and the north part of India by military force. The armed expedition of the Macedonian played role in disseminating the Greek culture-where the army arrived, where the Greece culture came in. It was a kind of communication and collision of the civilizations on the European and Asian continent in the 4th century B. C.

When Alexander the Great defeated the Persian Empire, he combined the whole civilization areas of the Mediterranean and unified a great empire including the Indus basin, Egypt, the Middle Asia and even Greece, which promoted the cultural development of the area, and made the Greek culture exert a great influence on the development of the Western culture. The Hellenistic era saw an unprecedented communication and mixture of culture between the West and East.

The direct influence of the expedition to India brought by Alexander seemed little, but to the history of India, its influence was indelible. The estrangement between the East and West was broken, and the traffic line was linked up. All of these provided an ascendant condition for the development of traveling activity and the dissemination of civilization. The Indian art was influenced greatly by Greece, Gandhara sculptures in particular. Due to coming into contact with the Greek culture, the Buddhism of India also had undergone drastic changes, for instance, the icons worshiped in the Buddhist ceremonies were in response for the influences of the Greek culture.

Under a storm of aggression of Rome, Greece was occupied. In 395, Greece was incorporated into the Byzantine Empire (the East Rome). Although Rome conquered the Greek by armed might, meanwhile, the old Greek culture conquered the Romans who were comparatively backward in culture. Romans studied the advanced philosophy, rhetoric, poetry, sculpture, science and technology, upgraded Christianity as their state religion, and decided Greek as the official language. The Byzantine Empire was changed into a Hellenistic country gradually.

Caesar was a high-ranking military officer of Rome who was diligent and cherished high ambitions. His whole life was full of legends and adventures. It was said that he was once seized by pirates on his journey who asked for a ransom of 20 Talents of gold.

Caesar chided that the pirates underestimated his social status and raised it to 50 Talents, then asked his servants to returned and borrowed money. When the ransom was gathered enough, the pirates released him, who went back to Milidu immediately to gather his troops and ships to catch up the pirates. They seized and killed the pirates, taking back all the ransom.

Caesar gained the political power by his convincing speech and smart political tactics. In 58 B. C., he carried out a six-year subjugation to Gaul and wrote an oft-quoted and widely-loved book titled "Tile Warring Notes of Gaul." This book not only recorded all previous battles they engaged in, but also described many a tribe of Gaul as well as the geographical features of the many regions including the distribution of rivers, mountains and forests which in a sense can be called a worthy travel book.

In the process of subjugation and ruling, Caesar brought Roman political system and cultural achievement into Gaul. He gave Roman-citizen-like treatment to the people of Gaul. So there was a folk rhyme putting: "hand in hand, Caesar and Gaul people walk in the triumphal ceremony, leading this country to build up congress system. Gaul people put off military uniforms and take on Roman robes."

Caesar used to stroll about in the places he conquered. The Warring Notes of Gaul recorded one of his travels: "Caesar receives a very warm welcome from all the autonomous cities and colonies because it is the first time for him to visit those places after conquering the whole Gaul territory. All the means are employed for decorating city gate, streets and every place where Caesar will pass through."

The late period of the Roman Empire experienced a series of barbarian aggressions and withered. The unity of the Mediterranean area came to an end; the barbarian culture and Christianity influenced each other and the Roman church split with the Greek Church. All of these factors influenced the establishment of European civilization in the Middle Ages.

Since the 11th century, the Christianity world of the Western Europe launched two wars to Islamic world of Palestine and the south part of Spain: "the Crusades and Recovering Movement". Eventually, the disputes existing for several centuries between Christianity and Islam were settled by war.

The Crusades is one of the most important events in the Middle Ages in the European history. The war lasted for two hundred years, which was a mixture of men's soul liberation and commercial benefit competition. Along with the religious fanaticism, commercial expansion, knight spirit and crusade zeal, the conflict and interchange between all civilizations reached the apex in these dramatic evens.

From the 7th century, the pilgrimage to Jerusalem was a way for believers to express their religiosity and atoning for their crime. In many places of Europe, the travelers wore intersecting Palestinian signs, meaning they had already finished the pilgrimage who were called palm marchers. But from the year 1070, the marchers began to bring back the news that the believers of Christianity were oppressed and the Turk blasphemed against gods, which became one of reasons to lead to The Crusades.

The other reason of Crusades Expeditions was many cities of Italy had strong desires to expand their territories. After Christian recaptured Sicily from the hand of Muslim, they began to get involved in the trading activity in the west Mediterranean area. Some commercial cities of Italy, such as Pisa, Genoa and Venice, were getting increasingly stronger. They dreamed to capture Muslim's commercial hegemony in the east coast of the Mediterranean area to open the East market. So they actively supported and joined the Crusades Expeditions.

In fact, Crusades soldiers were vagrants, adventurers, knights advocating armed might, feverish priests who felt bored toward life, the tenant-peasant who run away from feudal lord's lands, merchants who wanted to seek the new market for their goods, young people expecting to expand the new world in the East and army prostitutes. Their motives of joining the Crusades were as complicated as the identities of the members.

The first time expedition, Crusades started off in 1096. After a long and hard trek, they reached Jerusalem in 1099. When Jerusalem was occupied, they butchered and plundered frenziedly Jews and Muslims living in the city. After worshiping in the Church of the Resurrection and leaving the protectors to preserve the Holy Sepulcher, they returned proudly to Europe in a triumphant. On the journey of withdrawal, they built many independent Christian Latin kingdoms in Palestine, Syria and Turkey. Since then, the West Europe launched seven expeditions during the two centuries.

Christianity's expansion evoked strong repercussions in the Muslim world. They launched the "Holy War" following the Koran to resist the aggressors. From 1148 to 1149, the 2nd Crusades Expedition was defeated by Muslims led by Nureddin, and the mythology that Frankish could not be defeated was broken. In 1192, Saladin, a hero of the Muslim world beat the Crusades again in their 3rd expedition. Both sides signed the peace treaty, and Jerusalem was returned to the hand of Muslim, but Christian enjoyed the freedom of worshiping. The 4th expedition was waged between Rome and Byzantium, and Constantinople was captured and plundered in 1204. In 1291, the strongpoint of Crusades in Palestine was attacked and occupied by Muslim. Soon afterwards, the Latin kingdoms set up by the Christian were retaken by Muslim one after another. The Crusades disappeared from the history of Europe eventually.

The wars between different civilizations promote the interchange of civilization, although it is a reluctant communication. A 200-year seesaw war between Christianity and Muslim made the civilization of the East and West collide innumerably. Many Western travelers began to show interest to the far away East. From then on, the Westerners never stopped their steps to explore the mysterious East.

A direct result of the Crusades Expedition was the prosperity of translating activities-an academic activity to translate the ancient scriptures of Rome and Greece kept by Muslim and Byzantium into Latin.

Because of the large-scale translating activities, the European civilization traditions established contacts with other civilizations of the world. The intellectuals of Europe began to touch the Greek and Roman scriptures which were brought back by the Crusades from the East Muslim and Byzantium since the 12th century. Meanwhile, through their bridge-like function, the Arabian cultural traditions, scientific achievements, and culture, science and technology of other areas of the world were transfered into Europe. To a great extent, it stimulated Europe to reconsider seriously on its own civilization tradition and other civilizations' achievements.

Thus, the modern science-a new civilization was possible to take root and develop in Europe. Just as what Whitehead said: "the modern science comes into being in Europe, but its root is in the whole world." The most valuable treasure left by the Middle Ages of Europe to the world was the establishment of university, which was the inevitable outcome brought by the widespread translating activities.

In the modem time, the world-scale conflicts between civilizations started from Columbus. When Columbus came into America, he had the conflicts with the inhabitants of Cuba and Haiti. In 1519, when Magellan left Seville to make a world travel, Hernan Cortes also left Cuba and started his expedition to the Aztec Empire of Mexico, thereby a bloody conquering era came.

In March of 1519, Cortes commanded a troop of hundreds of people to attack the Aztec Empire. Europeans' heartless indifference, courage and excellent equipments showed a huge predominance. They took advantage of the internal conflicts of Indian to destroy them one by one. They captured the capital of Aztec in August of 1521 and butchered frenziedly.

The other notorious conqueror in the history is Pizarro. He commanded 180 soldier troop to cross the Andes Mountains and enter Peru.

Chapter 5 Development of Human Civilization Increases the Value of Tourism curious, the emperor of Inca Empire visited Pizarro officially. Pizarro followed the example of Cortes to imprison the emperor and killed his corteges. He asked the Indians to stack a room fully with gold and silver for atoning for the emperor. When Pizarro got the gold and silver, he broke faith with the Indians and killed the emperor. Then he plundered Cusco, the capital of Inca. Their behaviors encouraged the followers; as a result, Indians of America were butchered and enslaved in a larger scale.

The historians usually believe that before Columbus came into America, the total number of Indian was 25 million. But to the middle of 17th century, only 9.5 million of them were still living there. The colonists of Spain butchered in America frenziedly, and then they began to sell and hold slaves who established their colonial rules with armed might and colonial culture.

To get a lawful excuse for their massacre, the juristic advisor of Spanish King, Carlos V, even proved the necessity on launching the war to Indians with their argumentation:

"First, in India, at least before they were controlled by Christianity, their customs were all uncivilized. Most of them were vicious barbarous people who could not be able to read and did not have the prudent reasons. They were nothing but savages lack of reason, according to Saint Thomas, and many of them incompletely developed due to the reason of climate. They had many vices who were as wild as animals. The second one was that the crimes of the barbarous people violated the natural rules. These barbarous people fell into the crimes deeply because they went against the natural rules." (Travel History of the West)

The colossal empire and the global business net brought uncountable treasures to Spain, and the national power of Spain was unprecedentedly strengthened. The Spain historian, Gomera wrote in his book titled History of India: No nation in the history could capture and conquer so vast land in such a short time just like what we did. We were also unparalleled in the aspects of disseminating holy Gospel and making adorers convert to Christianity. So Spain deserved commendation in every place of the world.

War is a double-blade sword on civilization dissemination, not only transferring civilization, but also bringing the civilization too.

According to the above-mentioned contents, Roman defeated the Greek; however, they were fascinated by the old Greek culture. The Roman studied the Greek culture with great concentration and upgraded the Christianity to be the national religion, meanwhile, regarded Greek as the official language. The Byzantium Empire changed into a Hellenistic country step by step.

In Chinese history, there is also the same example. When Mongolians and the Manchu captured the regime of the Han, they were still in the monadic period, so they all abandoned their own "cultural sovereignties," mixing into the rivers of Han culture.

The Yuan Dynasty (1271 – 1368) was a great dynasty established by Mongolians. In 1271, Kublai Khan, the grandson of Genghis Khan, founded the Yuan Dynasty in Dadu- today's Beijing. Form then on, Beijing gradually became the political, economic and cultural center of China in about 700 years. The Yuan Dynasty is the first nationwide political power ruling the country as minority. The Mongolian not only conquered the regions of Central Plains and the southern part of the Yangtze River, but also seized the whole Western Asia and became a dynasty with the largest territory in Chinese history.

Mongolians led a nomadic way of life, so their productive forces were lower. After they stepped into the Center Plains, the rulers adopted their economic mode and management approaches. The livestock husbandry was replaced by Agriculture; meanwhile, they developed commerce and handicraft industry energetically. The international economy of the Yuan Dynasty was resumed rapidly. Because the territory of the Yuan Dynasty was expanded into the West Asia, the connection between China and the West Europe became more frequent, so was the communication in technology.

Due to adopting many advanced material and cultural achievements, the rulers' life of the Yuan Dynasty became more and more luxurious with a variety of material treasures. Especially in the later stage of the Yuan Dynasty, the emperors almost led luxurious lives. To satisfy their avaricious material requirements, those rulers collected various taxes on people continuously. The Hans could not stand any more and began to resist their tyrannical governing by all kinds of forms. In 1368, under assistance from many generals, like Xu Da and Chang Yuehun, Zhu Yuanzhang captured Dadu. The ruling of the Yuan Dynasty came to an end and the Ming Dynasty was founded.

The Qing Dynasty was the last dynasty of Chinese feudal society. It was founded by the Manchu aristocrats. In 1644, the farmers' leader Li Zicheng led his troops made up by farmers and overthrew the Ming Dynasty. The Qing army seized the opportunity to enter the Shanhaiguan, where the Great Wall meets the sea, and defeated the Li Zicheng's farmer army. In the same year, the Emperor Shunzhi (1638 – 1661) was welcomed into the Shanhaiguan by Duo Ergun; the Qing Dynasty was established and made Beijing the capital.

After the Manchus stepped into the Centre Plains, they almost absorbed all the productive mode and economic management of Hans, even following their way of life. In the middle of the 18th century, the feudal economy of China developed into a new peak which was called "Kangqian Flourishing Age" in the Chinese history. In the later period of the 18th century, the population of the Qing Dynasty already reached about 300 million. The largest territory of the Qing Dynasty even reached more than 12 million square kilometers.

Since the Ming and Qing Dynasty, the handcraft industry of China has developed, but it was not developed enough to take the road of capitalism. Especially, in the end of the Qing Dynasty, the stupid policy of "closing the pass and locking the country" demolished the comparatively developed shipbuilding industry, seafaring and international business in the coastal areas, meanwhile, kept the advanced science and technology of the West out of our country.

In 1720, 29 ships of Europe came to China bringing some mechanical products, like striking clock, woolen cloth and glass. The British people imported such goods as tea, porcelain and silk, etc. from China. It was a pity that the historical opportunity of communicating with the civilization of the West just flared briefly. From the reign of Emperor Qianlong to the end of the Qing Dynasty, there were four customs of dealing in business activities with foreign countries, only one existed-Guangzhou City.

The well-known scholar of China, Gu Zhun expressed in his book titled Collected Works of Gu Zhun: Taking for granted that the capitalism will come into being in every country is absolutely ridiculous. China-a proud nation could not be woken up by the Sino-British Opium War and Sino-French War held by the united army of Britain and France in 1884, slightly woken up by the Sino-Japanese War in 1894 and finally woken up completely in the year of 1900 and 1901, so it is impossible for China to take the road of capitalism.

Judging form this, the start point of Chinese modern civilization is from the war. After the Sino-British Opium War broke out in 1840 along with the imperialism invasion into China, the court of the Qing Dynasty signed a series of unequal treaties with aggressors. China was changed into a semi-colonial and semi-feudal society. But on the other hand, because of the aggression from the West Imperialist Powers, China eventually opened the window to have an insight into the world and began to breathe the fresh air blew from overseas. In 1911, the Xinhai Revolution broke out and the Qing Dynasty was overthrown. The more than two-thousand-year feudal monarchy in China came to an end from then on.

Mr. Pei Yong said in his article named Integration of Civilization: Opening a New Era for Civilization of the Earth that since the 16th century, the Christian civilization of the West developed and became stronger gradually. It occupied a leading position in the world. The civilization created the social political system and economic developing mode which are still applied in today's world. Especially, the development of science and technology originating from the Christian civilization made the West world believe it was the most excellent and advanced civilization, so they would like to disseminate their civilization into all corners of the world. Along with a rapid development of science and technology as well as the stronger economic and military forces, the West began to impose its civilization on the mankind's developing course. So its civilization, especially the religion was propagated in the world with its global colonial expansionism together. In the more than 300-year of colonial expansions made by the West Imperialist Powers, benefit between the West countries spread and extended into many a country and almost reached all corners of the world.

## Section 2
## War Can Disseminate Civilization and Also Can Damage civilization

Although the war has a function to transfer the civilization, it also breaks the social natural order, destroys the environment and damages the social treasure. What is more, it kills the most valuable thing that can create the treasure and civilization-people. So actually, wars can lead to the greatest destructiveness.

Liu Bang, an emperor of the ancient China, founded the Han Dynasty, because the ruling class understood that the war would damage the society and bring a huge pain to the vast number of people, since then, they adopted a new policy of rehabilitation, so the national force of the Han Dynasty resumed gradually. However, during the reign of Emperor Wu, he adopted a policy of fighting with the barbarian neighbors and constructing numerous royal palaces and gardens. These glorious projects consumed much of the treasure left by Emperor Wen and Jing. This is the foot-dragging burden brought by wars to civilizations.

Maya was the original inhabitants in the Middle America who lived in today's Mexico, Guatemala and Honduras with a highly developed ancient civilization. They firstly planted corns and their astronomy and calendars were also very perfect.

Around the year 800 B. C. , the Maya civilization reached its top, but a great suffering also came along: the Maya who lived in the southern lowland abandoned their flourishing cities and temples turned into wastelands and the habitat of wild animals . when European colonist got to the American continent in the 16th century, butchering and plundering, the Maya civilization declined completely.

According to Archaeologists, although the identity of its opponent had not been confirmed yet up to now; the Maya was believed to be defeated. The Maya were wiped out by the conquerors and the civilization of the whole city was almost destroyed completely. The war came to an end, but the city became an empty ruin.

In the history of mankind, the two World Wars badly destroyed the civilization. The First World War breaking out on August 4, 1914 and ending on November 11, 1918, lasted four years and three months. More than 30 countries and about 1,500 million people joined the war, making up 67% of the total population of the world at that time with 73. 51 million people going to the front. In countries, like French, more than half of the male citizens went to the frontline.

According to the statistics, during the Second World War, about 9 million soldiers immolated on the battlefield, and the number of the wounded exceeded 20 million. Besides, about 10 million populations died because of hunger and disease. The direct economic loss of the belligerent states mounted to $180. 5 billion in total and the indirect economic loss also reached $151. 6 billion. It is estimated by the experts that the industrial productive capacity went backwards at least for 8 years on the main battlefield of Europe.

The Second World War was the largest scale war in mankind's history which caused an enormous loss and unprecedented catastrophe. In the life-and-death war, more than 60 countries and regions were engaged into the war, which affected 2,000 million populations (making up 80% of total populations of the world). The flames of the war spread to Europe, Asia, Africa, Oceania, the Pacific Ocean, the Indian Ocean, the Atlantic Ocean and the Arctic Ocean. The battlefield extended as vast as 22 million square kilometers and the number of soldiers of both sides reached 110 million. More than 55 million soldiers and civilians died. The direct military expenditure amounted to $1,300 billion, making up 60% to 70% of the total Gross National Income of the belligerent states.

According to incomplete statistics, about 35 million Chinese were butchered or bunged up by Japanese aggressors, making up 42% of the total number of dead people of the belligerent states in the Second World War. About 21 million Chinese died, and there are 300, 000 Chinese were butchered in the " Nanking Massacre". Counting by the parity index of 1937, the Japanese aggressors made a direct economic loss of ＄100 billion and an indirect economic loss of ＄500 billion in China.

The loss of USSR (the Union of Soviet Socialist Republics) made up 41% of the total loss that the belligerent states suffered in the Second World War. Because USSR was the main battlefield to resist the German fascist, according to the data publicized by Russia, during the period of the War of home dependence from 1941 to 1945, about 27 million Russians died, including 8.6684 million Red Army soldiers of USSR. Counting by the parity index of 1941, the material loss reached 679 million Rouble.

The U.S. and Britain were the main members in the anti-fascist alliance. According to the historical data, more than 400,000 Americans and 270,000 British soldiers died in the war.

Germany and Italy were the prime criminals to launch the Second World War who met tough resistance and be punished sternly by the people of the anti-fascist countries. According to statistics, about 13.6 million Germans were dead or held captive in the war. 6 million German and Allies' soldiers died on the USSR-Germany battlefield. On Chinese battlefield, Japan lost about 1.5 million people, and among them, including 1.28 million Japanese surrendered to China. On the battlefield of the Pacific Ocean, more than 1.2 million Japanese and 160,000 Italians died.

The populaces of Germany, Japan and Italy also suffered deeply from the war of aggression launched by them. In the metropolitan territories of Germany, there were four million populaces dead and more than 14 million people homeless. In August of 1945, Hiroshima and Nagasaki of Japan were bombed by A-bomb of the U.S.; 200,000 Japanese died and left tremendous mental scar in the mind of local people.

After the Second World War, the most tragic one was the war between Iraq and Iran who were branded as two military powers in the Middle East. All advanced weapons, such as F14, F4, Mirage fighter and Scud missiles except the A-bomb were applied in the war which lasted eight years and millions of people died. Finally the two sides exhausted, so the war pulled down the curtain. The economies of the two countries were nearly collapsed. It was commented on a typical example to make a low-lever war with the advanced weapon by the world military circles.

The total number of dead people who died in the war of Iraq and Iran was 12 times as many as that of four times of the Middle East War. The direct economic loss was five times as much as that of the whole economic loss in the First World War. In Teheran, the capital of Iran, about 200,000 women lost their husbands, leaving so many broken families. Innumerous Iran soldiers were blind or deafened because of poison. Before the war, Iran had a foreign exchange reserve of more than $ 30 billion, but when the war ended, it had an external debt of $ 100 billion. A great deal of oil from the bombed oil tankers flowed into the Persian Gulf and resulted in serious pollutions.

The two sides lost more than 400 aircrafts, 3,500 tanks, 2,700 cannons and 31 naval vessels together. Nearly 500 ships were attacked. The direct economic loss caused by the war reached $ 900 billion. Teheran, the Iranian capital, was attacked by 133 missiles with 1,700 Iranian dead and 8,500 people injured.

These numbers may not make people feel clearly the tragedies the Iran-Iraq war brought to their people and even to the world. A military officer told the journalists that the missiles and the chemical weapons brought a mortal suffering to Iran. In the early summer of 1988, Iraq used a large number of chemical weapons to force Iran to accept the ceasing-fire agreement. Numerous soldiers were poisoned and became blind, deaf and dumb, even some died tragically.

In the backward and exclusive environment of the ancient times, the traffic was not convenient, so some wars had the special function to promote communication. In spite of all these, most of wars were still brutal massacre and destroying. When mankind's history stepped into modern times, and it became easy for the people of different countries to connect, communicate, and trade with each other peacefully. In this case, provoking wars was an absurd and stupid activity. This is why we feel painful and sick of the endless conflicts happening in the Middle East.

According to statistics, during the one hundred years of the 20th century, more than 300 wars repeatedly happened in the world in which mankind butchered themselves with weapons created by them. The innocent people were pushed into the flames of war. Life withered and civilizations were destroyed flintily. Human beings are so fragile amidst the disasters of war, which rings the bell of warning once again and meanwhile men begin to understand more deeply about war than ever before.

# Section 3
## Developing Trend of Human Civilization in the Future

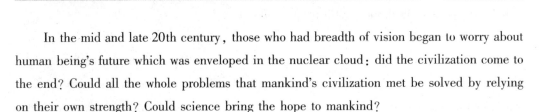

In the mid and late 20th century, those who had breadth of vision began to worry about human being's future which was enveloped in the nuclear cloud: did the civilization come to the end? Could all the whole problems that mankind's civilization met be solved by relying on their own strength? Could science bring the hope to mankind?

When we stepped into the 21st century, the conception of the "earth village" is becoming clearer and truer along with the development of traffic and communication technology.

Many scholars pictured the development of mankind's civilization for us: People's increasingly enriched life with the closer and frequent exchanging between civilizations.

Which direction will mankind's civilization head to? What prospect will mankind's society have? Here are three representative viewpoints:

1. Pluralism

Pluralism believers think that the development of civilization will be more and more multi-faceted. Meanwhile, only by adhering to a variety of civilizations can it develop better. The development of the multi-civilization follows the same developing course as other civilizations, also at the same time will experience contacting, communicating, clashing and mixing within all these civilizations.

In the age of agricultural civilization, due to the backward production and the inconvenient traffic conditions, the communication between civilizations was at a rather slow speed. When the society stepped into the age of industrial revolution, along with the productive forces developing increasingly, transport facilities got great improvement. Telephone, telegraph and mass media, such as newspaper and book could be seen everywhere.

Nowadays, internet and popular media can spread the news to every corner of the whole world in the twinkling of an eye. So the communication of civilization turns easier and faster.

For a long time, the relationship among the Islamic civilization, the Hindu civilization, the Chinese civilization, the Japanese civilization and the West European industrial civilization is to and fro in the process of merging and conflicting. It is clear that the way of communicating and results between different civilizations are various, for instance, the new changes of American and European industrial civilizations, the new civilization of Russia, the transition of Latin America to industrial civilization, the development of industrial civilization in South and Southeast Asia, the development of East Asian civilization, the modernization in the Islamic world of the Middle East, the great rejuvenation of African. All of these changes are mutually exclusive and clashing, at the same time absorbing and merging with each other.

It is true up till now that culture is pluralistic. But is the pluralism of culture eternal and universal? Someone wants to prove it with the story in the Bible- "Building the Babylon Pagoda": At the beginning, people's language is identical, so the pagoda is built rapidly on the basis of mutual understanding. Later, God makes people speak different languages. So it becomes difficult to communicate and the project of building the pagoda fell fruitless. The story proves a truth: the culture of mankind can not be merged together because that will pose a threat to god.

Although the story is full of religious color, the development of modern electronic technology seems to be coincident with this kind of viewpoint. William (Bill) H. Gates once described the conditions of life in the future network society: Network is a pass to help you enter a new media way of living. The distinct feature of the new communication technology is that it can shorten the distance between people. The network just like a road-net made up by many small paths of village, and people can see and do things they like.

The development of electric propagation and network technology make people's association in a more personal way. Everyone can express his or her own opinion on the network. The most important thing to a network organization is everyone is a focus and Internet is becoming a "center at the intersections" in the future earth village.

John Nesbit thought that it was a turning point upon the celebration of the bicentenary of the U. S. A. in 1976. From then on, the force of the non-concentrated tide became stronger continuously and overwhelmed the concentrated tendency which was disappearing gradually. He said: "In daily life, along with the development of global economy which is depending on each other more and more, I think the rejuvenation of language and culture is coming." In a word, the Swedes will more Swedish-like, Chinese are Chinese-like, and Frenchmen will be more French-like

Alvin Toffler had the same opinion. He said: "In fact, if we want to press onward to the future, we must break away from the standardized product, characterless art, unspecialized education and vulgarized culture. With the development of social technology, we are facing a juncture of dialectical changing. Technology will not limit our individuality, but will provide more choices and freedom for us.

Along with mankind moving ahead, more and more differences are appearing in today's society: the awareness of one's own homeland is becoming stronger. " The more a thing has a national feature, the more it will be accepted by the world. " In pace with an improvement of democratic system, people are paying more attention to the regions and communities where they are living. There are a variety of goods, and even education is changing to satisfy the demands from different people. The traditional pyramid-style social structure is disappearing and a new network-style society is shaping up.

In the future society, politics will be more democratic, social formation is more diversified and people's ways of living are various. More and more sub-cultural groups will appear in the national culture. (Excerpts from Reflections on Civilization)

2. Unanimity

William (Bill) H. Gates said that Information Highway will break down barriers between countries, and promote a world culture. Or at least, it will let people enjoy the same cultural activity and value together.

The old "Great Harmony" is the predecessor of the "Unanimity". Confucius put forward the idea "There will be great harmony in the world", and its core is to carry out a cultural harmony in the world. But does great harmony mean identical completely or much the same, or with minor differences? It is a problem should be considered seriously.

According to the ancient cultural codes and records of China, the thesis "There will be great harmony in the world" advocated by Chinese ancient philosophy dose not discriminate against those who hold different views. It looks forward to a unified culture of harmony, while keeps their own features.

In 1974, 85 years old Arnold Toynbee, a well-known British historian and Ikeda Daisaku, famous politician of Japan, founder of Komei Party, carried out a ten-day discussion on the problem of the destiny and foreground of mankind's history in London. Then they reached a mutual conclusion that the world civilization would be unified finally.

According to Arnold Toynbee, when human beings develop to take shape a single society, it may be a good time to carry out the unity of the world. In the atomic energy-dominating period, it is impossible to accomplish the unity by armed force but by the traditional means which has unified the majority parts of the world. Meanwhile, such kind of peace and unity forecasted by me will be certainly realized revolving around geography and culture and grows extensive step by step. Unifying the world is an approach to avoid human from committing suicide. China makes a full preparation-a nation who has been transformed and formed a unique mode of thinking in 2,000 years.

Although Ikeda Daisaku agreed with Toynbee's view point that the human being's developing trend will move towards unification, he also thought that the way to carry out unification will not take any civilization as the dominant one; instead, it will be a mixture of a variety of civilizations. He said that the direction of the world would develop into unification rather than centalization. It may adopt a united way, which means different countries would make a consultation with equal grounds and qualification. Personally speaking, the endeavors of the European Communities may be such a model.

The well-known scholar of the U.S.A., founder of "the Modern World System" Immanuel Wallerstein had a similar opinion with Toynbee. He analyzed the historical experiences of some countries, like Netherlands, Britain and the U.S.A. and elicited a conclusion of "the hegemony was short-lived." He held that the world system of capitalism was full of unfair crackdown and exploitation causing complex classes and political struggles which would destroy the world system of capitalism. It would be replaced by a new world system with higher efficiency and more logical distribution system which will contribute to establishing a socialism-world government.

3. Theory of global civilization

The global civilization means to set up a civilization and set of values which can be received generally by people all over the world.

Global civilization is also called Universal civilization. In terms of this conception, some people thought it was mentioned earlier by scholars of the West. Mr. Samuel P. Huntington also expounded the concept of Universal Civilization. He said: "generally speaking, human being is moving towards a shared civilization in which different nations of the whole world are receiving a common value, religion, direct, practice and system."

In fact, the Universal Civilization or the universal culture value is an old ideological view. In China, Confucianism represented by Confucius once mentioned a political conception " there will be Great Harmony in the world" and Catholic universal belief claims that all men are brothers.

Many scholars thought that the developing trend of mankind's civilization was a long process in which different civilizations of the world were propagated, communicated, mixed and synthesized, and ultimately shaped up a shared civilization system finally. But as for specific operation approaches, there were two sharply contrasted opinions. Some West scholars thought that the so-called universal civilization was the Western civilization or globalization of the Western civilization. But others thought that the Western civilization was declining day by day. They emphasized that Chinese culture of harmony might be a philosophic base for future global civilization despite some differences.

Many serious scholars of the West also opposed the viewpoint that modernization means being westernized. For example, John Nesbit once said: "does the globalization mean Americanization? With regard to culture, what the U.S. benefits from the world exceeds what it contributes to the world. Actually, it is the world that is changing the U.S.A. The people of the world are working hard to strengthen their own cultural characteristic. I put forward an anti-thesis to such phenomenon: the more we become globalized, the more our activity becomes nationalized, which is the very cultural feature."

In the book named "Unity of Civilization," Mr. Pei Yong said: "absolutely, the two World Wars are the disgrace of the Western civilization, and also human being's grief.

The exhausted resources, ecological crisis and homicidal weapons abusing resulted from industrialization all reflect an anti-cultural feature and the veiled murderous intentions of the Western civilization, such as excessive consumption, violence and destructions to the nature."

He also wrote: "in the minds of the westerners of the colonial times, Africans were branded as slaves in the mind of the Westerners, Indians and aborigines savages, and Asians idolatry. They should be enslaved, completely extinct or controlled who have no rights to enjoy equality, democracy and freedom. In the period of new-empire, the Westerners thought they should transfer the ideas of equality, democracy and freedom, because they hoped other countries were westernized completely and unified them with the Western civilization to keep a firm hand on them. The aim of the West was to monopolize the world and enjoy the benefit, instead of bringing benefit to the people of other countries with different civilizations. Once any country became more powerful due to carrying out democracy, they would like to let them retrogress to the stage of despotism, as long as the leader was obedient enough." What an American president said is a typical example: "I know he is a brute, but he is ours."

The director and researcher of the Chinese Culture Research Institute of the Art Research Institute of China thought that globalization of economy and the universalizing of modern civilization are the inexorable trend, but it is impossible, and unnecessary to unify the economical modes and civilizations of different countries. A course of modernization of a country can not be succeeded alone in a condition of being cut off from the outside world.

The relations between various nations with the different cultural backgrounds are interdependent. The West and the Orient can not develop without each other. Similarities and differences are the channel for achieving the goal, but the final result is the same. Book of Changes once said: "They all come to the same (successful) issue, though taking different paths; there is one result, though there might be as many as a hundred schemes."

The relation between modernization and globalization is relatively close. Only under the circumstance of modernization, can the economic forms be expended to the whole world. The modernization is the conditions of globalization and the globalization is the necessary outcome of modernization. The author of Reflections on Civilization, Mr. Duan Yabing said: "modernization, as a great change of human beings, is a worldwide development process. It integrates every nation and society into a 'worldwide society' and makes the world become an intrinsic integration."

The starting point of globalization can be dated back to 1971 with a history of over 30 years. In 1990s, the new economy promoted the trend of globalization. However, at the end of 20th Century, many countries found that the globalization is unfavorable for weak countries, and posed a threat to small countries that are getting progress. Many theories about anti-globalization appeared worldwide and the most famous one was put forward in Malaysia. Asian financial crises occurred in 1997; the premier Mahathir of Malaysia declared that Ringgit would be withdrawn from the international monetary market and depreciate significantly to benefit exportation. He also freezes capital and transfer abroad. The Mid and South America countries, have experienced liberalization for more than 20 years, however, the economic growth for most countries was worse than that in 1970s. A new economic plan was proposed by the new president of Brazil, Lula, but he still kept many government-owned enterprises and the market is not completely opened.

Facing with more and more contradictions brought forth by economic globalization, the most persuasive saying is that we can not use economic theory (globalization) to determine the direction of civilization.

"At present, the world is also in the transitional period. Building a new global civilization and a new world will undoubtedly need a cultivation and formation of a new culture in people's minds in the global scope. The new culture undoubtedly represents the advanced culture of the future development of the world. The new culture is neither "total westernization", nor "total easternization", neither "total Europeanization", nor "total Americanization". Among all world civilizations, none is the advanced culture that completely suitable for the future development. New advanced cultures will definitely complement the south and north and combining the eastern and western elements. In the future society based on global civilization, the post-modernization is its main characteristic. The new society needs an ecological, balanceable, equal, and harmonious new culture, which swallows anything and everything and integrates the essence of every civilization. The building and cultivation of this culture will be an important foundation to build global civilization, which will be an advanced culture of the future world. (Integration of the Civilization)

# Chapter 6

## Tourism, the Last Choice of Integrating Human Civilization

# Section 1
## Peaceful Development is Gradually Becoming a Common Understanding among Human Beings

1. Enjoy civilization together

Currently, the disadvantages of western civilization that was once booming and excellent are exposed gradually. In the two World Wars, resource exhaustion, ecological crisis and weapons abuse resulting from the industrialization disclose the western civilization's negative impacts on nature and society.

According to the estimation of International Energy Agency, from 1997 to 2020, the global demands for major energy sources will increase by 57% but the reserve is not limitless. It is predicted that the reserve of crude oil will run out in 41 years, gas 63 years and coal 218 years. If the human being did not find the new substitute energy, we would not survive. Such a fragile world can not withstand any conflicts, especially violent actions.

Helmut Heinrich Waldemar Schmidt, former Chancellor of Germany, opposed Huntington's "Civilization Collision Theory" and believed: "In the era of globalization, it is imperative to set up a popular will in which other civilizations and religions are respected. Such tolerance is not equivalent to indifference but should be built on the basis of respect and recognition to all extant or past beliefs in the world."

When Hu Jintao, President of China, gave a lecture on the campus of Yale University, he also emphasized the "diversity of civilization" and said: "A single note can't compose a beautiful rhythm and a single color can't make up a colorful painting. In the history, all kinds of civilizations have made great contributions to the progress of human beings. The diversity of civilization is not only the objective reality of a society but also the primary characteristic in the world and also an important driving force of human progress."

However, the diversity of civilization doesn't mean the cold-war like conficts. In Hu Jintao's speech, he also mentioned: "According to the past experience, to exchange human civilizations, we should surmount not only the natural obstacles but also break the fetter of thought should be broken. In addition, various prejudices and misunderstandings have to be overcome. The different ideologies, regimes and development modes shouldn't become the obstacle of exchanges of human civilizations and cause conflicts."

In February 2006, over 500 scientists in the US signed a statement publicly expressing their skepticism about the contemporary theory of Darwinian evolution with the words of the drafter that read: "We are skeptical of claims for the ability of random mutation and natural selection to account for the complexity of life. Careful examination of the evidence for Darwinian theory should be encouraged."

For more than a century, the contemporary theory of Darwinian evolution has shaped the development of natural science while affecting virtually every corner of our society. At the same time, people with visions can not but make the same thinking : is *the law of the jungle* a phenomenon or a rule in the progress of civilization?

What future will the Darwinian evolution theory bring if such progress is to continue, especially when science and technology have increasingly become *a double edged sword*? Will there be any future at all? Stephen Hawking recently said: "I don't think we will survive another 1000 years without escaping beyond our fragile planet." Is that pure scaremongering oraneducated prediction?

According to SIPRI (Stockholm International Peace Research Institute), world military expenditure totalled $1.8 trillion in 2014. Meanwhile, the World Bank put the number of people in extreme poverty worldwide in the same year to 1.2 billion, based on a per capita daily expenditure of USD 1.25.

It means that it costs us only 5475 billion USD to eradicate poverty, raising the question: Mankind is still developing weapons for self-destruction using already limited resources when we have achieved economic globalization and are at the dawn of cultural globalization. Is this really the civilization we have hoped for?

In 1980s, Capra, a U. S. scholar, published Turning Point, and believed the western society was faced with crises. However, he didn't believe the crises would result in the end of the world. The human progress will continue but the western civilization must be fundamentally changed.

However, Capra's criticism on the western civilization and centralism is not advocating setting another center of the world, not the Eastern-civilization centralism, such as the Chinese-civilization centralism, Indian and Arabian civilization centralisms. Capra considered that any centralism will result in hubris and the final declination. For example Chinese once regarded China as the center of the world and finally witnessed the declination.

Every civilization has its own weakness and strength, so all civilizations should assimilate other civilizations' essence through exchanging. A nongovernmental organization promoted a " concept of pursuing the best lifestyle" in the world, including the U. S. economical and timesaving dietary mode of eating snacks as lunch, regardless of wealth and status; the Chinese healthy and economical drinking mode of tea drinking, the British dressing mode "two suits are enough to make a gentleman" the former Soviet housing mode of concentrated apartments, not only offering spacious room, but save land and resources, the Japanese working mode in which every employee being hard working and the French romantic love mode.

Franz Boas, a well-known historical anthropologist, said: "The human history proved that a social group's cultural progress was influenced by the chances of assimilating neighboring social groups' experience. One social group's new discoveries can be learnt by other groups and the more exchanges can bring about more learning opportunities. Generally, the tribes with the most primitive culture are the ones who separate from the outside world for a long time. Only those most accessible nationalities have the most opportunities to interact with other nationalities and the most probabilities to make great progress. However, isolated nationalities will grow stagnant."

One must understand that people is an integral part of the nature, interdependent on each other, so do all nations and nationalities. The human progress should be based on an interdependent, harmonious and sustainable development. Either eastern or western civilization has its own weaknesses and strengths so we should learn from each other. Only based on the establishment of new world and civilization concepts and the achievement of diversification and globalization, the various conflicts be eliminated and the real equality, democracy and peace can be attained.

However, we must emphasize that we shouldn't deny the existence of universal value while we respect and maintain "diversity". When the development of sciences, technologies and productivities reaches to a certain level, not only does the West need the industrialization but also the East does. Hence, the industrialization and its achievements also derive from the civilization. On the other hand, all people pursue equality, democracy and freedom, which also are the universal achievements of the development of human civilization and the rights every people in the world should enjoy. Science and democracy are not the West's patents. The West only promoted science and democracy earlier and achieved more results than other regions. Therefore, it is not rational to keep equivalent the achievements of science and civilization to the outcome of West's civilization.

Due to different histories, economies and cultures in different countries and regions, human being can't develop and co-enter the democratic society at the same time. Therefore, the countries and regions that have stepped into the democratic society should respect the democratic progresses of the "underdeveloped" countries and regions, helping to accelerate their democratic progress instead of compelling them to speed up. In addition, the countries and regions that have not achieved the democracy must rationally consider the rule of development of human civilization and should fully understand that the so-called "diversity" is not the excuse of underdeveloped regimes and cultures. The "diversity" should be a kind of active existence state and an "optimal diversity". However, someone wants to commit crimes against humanity in the name of diversity, which is inconsistent with the essence of "diversity".

The human progress has advanced the great industrialization into the automatization or the informatization and the productivity has been pushed to a higher level. The number of factors that will cause the wars remarkably decreases. "Developed" or "underdeveloped" countries or regions should understand the democracy in one or few countries is not the real democracy. Only the democracy promoted to the whole world is the real democracy.

Currently, although the wars die hardly in the world, all people in senses are repelled by the form of war. With the development of material and spiritual civilizations, all people in the world have recognized the importance of negotiations and more and more disputes are handled by the way of nonviolence.

In the new era, all peoples share their civilizations through the tourism based exchanges, mutual understandings and respects so as to attain the goal of sharing the civilization of all human beings.

2. Mitigate contradictions

Though there were numerous "peace tours" or "journeys of mitigating contradictions" to handle disputes between nations, nationalities, clans and parties in history. That Richard Milhous Nixon's visit in China in 1970s was the prominent one. Here are following records on Diplomatic History of China:

*On February 21, 1972, Nixon set foot on the Chinese mainland for his "journey for peace".*

*At 11:30, the aircraft smoothly landed in front of the terminal building. After the cabin door was opened, President Nixon who was dressed in an overcoat and his wife, Thelma Catherine "Pat" Ryan, walked out from the door. Nixon saw Premier Zhou Enlai standing in the cold wind without a cap on his head. In addition, Vice President Ye Jianying, Vice Premier Li Xiannian, Guo Moruo, Vice Chairman of the Standing Committee of the National People's Congress, and Ji Pengfei, Minis-*

ter of Foreign Affairs, were standing aside.

When Nixon walked down to the middle of the accommodation ladder, Zhou Enlai began to clap hands to welcome him. After an instant pause, Nixon also clapped hands in return according to the Chinese tradition. When Nixon reached the last three or four steps, he extended his hand to Zhou with a smile. Zhou Enlai also extended his hand and then they held each other's hands tightly for nearly one minute. At that time, Nixon was aware that one era had gone and another new era was coming.

Nixon excitedly said: "Premier Zhou, it is my privilege to visit your great country."

Zhou said: "President, welcome to China."

This historic event was recorded by the video cameras and broadcasted to the whole world via satellites.

Then Zhou Enlai and Nixon together boarded an upscale Hongqi saloon car with curtains. When the car left from the airport, Zhou Enlai said: "Mr. President, you have extended your hand and held mine across the widest ocean. 25 years had passed before we rebuilt diplomatic relation!"

On that evening, Zhou Enlai held a welcome banquet in honor of Nixon at the Great Hall of People. Zhou Enlai accompanied Nixon couple and Kissinger to sit around a table.

The PLA Military Band performed America the Beautiful for all guests. Such warm scene was transmitted to the live program of U. S. TV stations, which evoked great echoes among the Americans.

When Zhou Enlai gave a toast, he said: "Invited by the Chinese Government, President Nixon comes here, which provides an excellent opportunity for leaders of two countries to hold face-to-face communications normalize the diplomatic relations between two countries and exchange opinions on issues of common concern. That is in conformity with Chinese and Americans' wills and a great event in the diplomatic history between China and the U. S. A. .

"The American people are a great people, so are Chinese people. People from the two countries built close relation long ago. Due to reasons known to everyone, exchanges between Chinese and American peoples have been broken off for over 20 years. Currently, thanks to concerted efforts, we get a good opportunity to normalize our relations. Based on the straight-out exchanges of opinions, we hope to find our common interests and initiate a brand new relation between two countries in spite of so many different viewpoints."

In Nixon's toast, he said: "In the past, we once were enemies. Currently, there still lie many great differences between us. However, the common interests beyond those differences make us sit together. Neither side will make concession in principle. Although we can't flatten our gaps, we can bridge to make exchanges."

On February 28, China and the U. S. A. issued the well-known Joint Communique of the

*People's Republic of China and the United States of America in Shanghai. In the Communiqué, different viewpoints on important international issues of both side are listed, both sides agree their social systems and diplomatic policies are totally different, but they also emphasize they would like to address relations between two countries based on the Five Principles of Peaceful Coexistence. Both sides agree to keep contact through various channels, including the U. S. senior officials' visits to Beijing irregularly, and make further negotiations on the normalization of relations between two countries and exchange viewpoints on issues of common concern. Both sides hoped this visit would create a new situation for both countries. Both sides also believed that the normalization relations between both countries not only conforms with common interests of Chinese and American peoples but also is beneficial to ease the tense situations in Asia and the world.*

*With the improvement of Sino-U. S. relations, the triangle diplomatic situations between the U. S. A, the Soviet Union and China began to emerge and became an important factor to influence the development of international situations in a long term. The reconciliation between the U. S. A and China compelled the Soviet Union to mitigate his tense relations with the U. S. A and the Western Europe and Japan to urgently request to establish diplomatic relations with China and boosted China and Japan to normalize their relations in September 1972. As Nixon's descriptions of his visit to China in his toast at the farewell banquet, the 7-day visit he stayed in China was a "key week to change the world".*

Before Nixon's visit, owning to its support for Kuomintang's waging the civil war, the U. S. A. was Chinese irreconcilable enemy. The above mentioned records make us further understand the strength of tourism. Such strength will bring about unforeseeable achievements if it can be continuously maintained.

In the spring of 2005, leaders of the dominate parties out of power in Taiwan visited the main-land on separate occasions and initiated the "journeys for peace". In the past, the Communist Party of China (CPC) and the Kuomintang were enemies. The Kuomintang was expelled from the mainland to Taiwan. Over fifty years, the cross-strait people can't enjoy the "three direct links of trade, mail and air transportation", the travel made by the leaders of the Kuomintang and the People First Party came to the mainland was a great breakthrough in the past 50 years. Their journeys not only attracted the cross-strait people's attention but also drew the whole world's attention.

From October to November 2005, Shao Qiwei, Director of China National Tourism Administration, paid a visit to Taiwan with his delegation. The size of delegation, the levels of members and the travel range were unprecedented. Shao Qiwei was the CPC official at the highest level to set foot on Taiwan. This travel was called by the media a "tentative travel" of Taiwan which helped to open doors to the Chinese mainland's tourists.

On November 9, Shao Qiwei left Taiwan and in Macao, he said that the Chinese mainland would actively boost the implement of measures of the mainland's people traveling to Taiwan and the establishment of a tourism circle including Hong Kong, Macao, Taiwan and the mainland. Great efforts will be made to step up the exchanges and cooperation across the Taiwan strait and realize the mainland's people's dream to travel to Taiwan as soon as possible, which will be beneficial to the communications and the common prosperity and development of economy.

According to the statistics, since the Chinese mainland opened the door to Taiwan in 1988, more and more Taiwanese come to the mainland. In 2004, the number of tourists from Taiwan to the mainland reached 3.68 million and the figure increased to 4 million in 2005. Currently, Taiwanese tourists have made up a key part of China's tourism. Undoubtedly, the tourism plays a very important role in making Taiwanese people understand the economic development of the mainland and easing the political contradictions between both sides.

The establishment of the European Union is the most important example achieving the political reconciliation and the cultural and economic integration. The European history underwent frequent conflicts and wars and the political territories of all states experienced numerous changes. Especially, the Europe suffered from the ravages of two World Wars.

After the World War II, all European countries were aware that the peace could bring about development and prosperity, while wars incur poverty and damages. Therefore, the European people of insight spared no efforts to pursue the strategies to avoid the relapse of battles in Europe after the World War II. The European Union is a great achievement deriving from such efforts and makes all European countries with different cultures and traditions remove the historical hostilities and embark on the way of harmonious communications and common development.

On May 1, 2004, the biggest signature ceremony to welcome the new members of the European Union was held at Acropolis, the site of old Greece in which many famous philosophers of old Greece delivered lectures and Acropolis was also the cradle of commercial development of old Athens. Observers and analysts said the signature site choice could embody the dream of establishment of "Pan Europe".

After the expansion, the number of the European Union would increase from 15 to 25 and the population and acreage of the European Union would reach 75 million Yuan and

740000 square kilometers respectively, which means the population of the European Union will increase by 20% and the GDP will rise by 5%. Therefore the European Union's economic strength will be equivalent to the U.S.A.. The European Union expanded 4 times in 1973, 1981, 1986 and 1995.

On the signature ceremony, Constantine Simitis, the European Commission President, said to absorb 10 new members into the EU is a very important issue in the development history of the EU, which formally terminated the separation of the Eastern Europe and the Western Europe. Otherwise, it makes the European integration surmount the historical gap existing after the Cold War.

The expansion of the European benefits from the achievements of members of the EU. The EU will boost the peace and cooperation in Europe, advance the European economy and strengthen its political and diplomatic influences. For example the relevant experts predicted the expansion of the EU will inject the new driving force into the economy. Although the economic growth speed was estimated to only increase by around 0.2%, the total production value of the EU would reach Euro 1 trillion so that the EU will surpass the North America Free Trade Area to become the biggest economic and trade body. The EU forecasted the expansion of the EU would accelerate the development of the tourism of the EU owing to the abundant historical and cultural relics.

Actually, as same as the development history of the EU, the EU after the expansion will also encounter some difficulties and problems. The new members of the EU will pose influences on its cohesion. Owing to the large social and economic differences between the new and old members, the negative factors can be eliminated in a short term.

However, the expansion of the EU and the realization of the dream of "Pan Europe" is an effective way to eliminate divergences, avoid wars and enjoy peace and prosperities. Therefore, the European politicians spare no efforts to propel the development of the European integration drive. The prosperous, stable and united European Union will not only benefit the whole Europe but also bring about peace and development to the world.

3. Dialogues are necessary among religions

All religions have a remarkable characteristic of exclusivity. The monotheism advocates that there is only one god in the world, such as Yahveh (Judaism), God (Christianity) and Allah (Islam). All religions only recognize their own gods and regard others as paganism. In history, people always waged wars to maintain their beliefs. 80% of the 6 billion people on the earth believe in different religions. The "Civilization Collision Theory" actually refers to the collision of religions. The collisions are based on the exclusivity of religions.

Currently, in many countries with various religions backgrounds, many extremists or terrorists carry out all kinds of terrorist activities in the name of religions. Hence, it seems that religions have become the unsafe factor that incurs the social turbulences.

In fact, religions should not cause conflicts by nature. Indeed, violence, slaughter, robbery and enmity are not in conformity with the nature of religions. The Islamism advocates peace, the Christianity encourages fraternity, the Buddhism claims the leniency and the Confucianism advocates the traditional virtue and morality. Many religions disputes correlated with political or economic conflicts.

Actually, many Moslems don't think Bin Laden's opinions, speeches and activities can reflect the real Islam. The real Islam advocates beneficence, tolerance and friendship rather than violence, hostility and enmity. On the Internet, the writer read a representative blog. That article read: "The Moslems uphold the holy war and want to Islamize the non-Islam regions. However, after the conquest, they didn't force the pagans to convert to Islam but only imposed the poll tax on pagans. In addition, they protected the development of Christianity and Judaism and even appointed some pagans to important positions. If they only wanted to stabilize the society by such measures, which seemed understandable but were not the short-term policies. The only rational explanation must be the Ala's tolerances. Compared with the Islam's conquest, the Crusade was simply a kind of occupancy and robbery."

Religion is not only a kind of ideology and belief but also the history, civilization and ethics. As same as philosophy and science, the different religions can exchange and learn each other. Hence, if people can be clearly aware of differences between the religion and the terrorism, the reconciliation among different civilizations can be achieved.

Indeed, all religions of different nations begin to cooperation. In 1993, 6 500 religions leaders, theologists and other related people from all over the world gathered in Chicago to attend the Annual Meeting of the Parliament of the World's Religions. At the meeting, the Declaration towards a Global Ethics was promulgated and the slogan of "without new global ethics, without new global orders" was also proposed. The "global ethics" was not a new religion beyond the current religions or a force to dominate all religions. It is a kind of basic common sense of recognizing the restrictive value concepts, irrevocable standards and personalities.

In 2000, the UN held the Millennium Peaceful Conference of World's Religious and Spiritual Leaders, which was another important dialogue among religions and aimed at unifying all religious and spiritual leaders and achieving the international peace through the cooperation between the UN and the religious leaders. At that meeting, the World Peace Declaration was issued and the international consulting conference of religious and spiritual leaders was established as a new indispensable resource to prevent collisions and resolve problems.

Till today, such dialogues among different religions are still inconsistent and temporary phenomena and failing to make up a routine mechanism and practical operational method. Especially, only within one year after that meeting, the thrilling "September 11 Event" took place.

However, the religious reconciliation isn't faced with the despair. Actually, there are many examples of reconciliation among different religions and between religions and secular citizens. The Da Vinci Code was a very good example.

On May 9, 2006, The Da Vinci Code was launched in the world. In that movie, the early ecclesiastic history was made up based on a false religious script, which directly impacted the foundation of the Christianity.

Actually, The Da Vinci Code was not the first sample to attack on the religion by secular cultural works. In the past, the church often boycotted or fought against such kind of films. For example in 1988, The Last Temptation of Christ made up a history of Jesus crucified on the basis of a common person, which seriously violated the Bible. After the movie was launched, many people protested. At the Universal Studio of Los Angeles, over 25,000 people gathered to protest and even the producer received a death threat.

To the same reality, one religions leader, who had participated in the past protest campaign, accumulated the experience. He thought to protest against the movies that are against the Christianity would only deepen the people's prejudices against the Christians. People will think the Christians dare not accept the outside challenges.

Hence, as for The Da Vinci Code, the U. S. church gave up the past confrontation methods and didn't boycott or neglect that movie. The U. S. church adopted the "civilization dialogue" and actively organized various activities.

For example the priests decorated the meeting venue and provided cakes and coffee to invite people to discuss The Da Vinci Code. Some churches even provided the free iPod to attract other secular people. Certainly, the only tenet was to make people believe in the Bible and Jesus. Many churches organized the youth to watch that movie and discuss it after watching.

The producer of The Da Vinci Code, Sony Pictures, had been afraid that the church would adopt the confrontation campaigns so that it was very delightful that the church gave up the confrontation. The producer even set up a "Da Vinci dialogue" website to invite Christians and scholars to exchange viewpoints.

The church's peaceful dialogue won the compliments from the society. All common people think that Christians are open to all different opinions. Hence, some leaders of Christians believed that The Da Vinci Code provided an excellent opportunity for the Christians to set up a new image of the Christians.

It was said the Church found that people began to pay attention to the topics on the Bible. In the past, people used not be interested in the history of the Christianity but now begin to focus on it. A teacher from one of the divinity schools in the U. S. A., who offered the history of the New Testament said, in the past, the number of students attending his class never exceeded 15, but when delivering the lecture entitled The Da Vinci Code, the number of students will reach over 600.

Tom Hanks, actor of The Da Vinci Code, also said if the churches posted a notice for a class of the Bible on Wednesday, only 12 people would attended but if posting a notice on discussing The Da Vinci Code over 800 people would swarm into the church. Hence, The Da Vinci Code provided opportunities for the churches.

The positive attitude of the church also boosted the prosperity of the book market. The publishers found all books related to the Bible became best-sellers. Hence, the church changed its attitude makes the publishers find more profitable opportunities. According to the reactions from the society, the church found an effective method to dialogue with society and eliminated the impacts from the secular civilizations.

Take the Middle East for another example, which has drawn the world's attention for a long term. In Lebanon, places of the coastal regions of the Mediterranean Sea, there are serious contradictions between the Christianity and the Islam which always result in the civil wars.

In July, 2006, Israel invaded Lebanon in the name of wiping out the forces of the Party of God. During the one-month bombing, believers of the Islam in Beirut had to move to the communities of Christianity believers to shun from the war. Both believers of the Islam and the Christianity once never contacted with each other but lived together peacefully.

The Christianity believers not only didn't make things difficult for the believers of the Islam but also provided accommodation for them. All of believers of the Christianity and the Islam prayed for the termination of wars and the peace in an unprecedented harmony.

On September 12, 2006, Vatican Pope Benedict XVI quoted the saying of Byzantine Emperor of middle ages that holy war is devil, which angered the Islamic world. The following is the report:

(*Islamabad*) *Roman Catholic Pope Benedict XVI made a home visit. In the speech delivered at Regensburg University, he associated Islam with violence, evoking a storm in Islamic world and all sides ask him to make an open apology.*

*The native of German Pope Benedict quoted the saying of Byzantine Emperor of Middle Ages that holy war is devil during his visit of Regensburg University; this move has angered the Islamic world. The Islamic world asked the Pope to take back his words. Muslims in some regions also went into the street to express their discontents to the Pope's comments.*

Just when the anger of Islamic world is building up, the Pope apologized one week later. He dispatched an envoy to Islamic countries to explain and make further apology. Here is another report.

*Catholic Pope Benedict XVI said in the open address on September 17 that he is "deeply regret for the reaction evoked in some countries" for some contents in his speech given to a group of scholars in Regensburg University. He also pointed out that the saying is "regarded as offended the feeling of Muslim."*

The above incident shows that no arms are required for solving religious contradictions and the appearance of religious contradictions come from inadequate understanding. If all religions can enhance the understanding and respect each other, it's possible to find an effective way to go on a dialogue and realize harmonious co-existence and complementarities.

Although there are such religious extremist as Laden, compared to many peace-loving followers, their number is so small. The forming of anti-terrorism force in a short time shows that dialogue is the only way for different religions and beliefs to achieve a win-win situation.

## Section 2
## Modern tourism develops swiftly and actively

1. A development of science and technology and a rapid mixture of "global village"

Modern tourism grew up after WWII. The development is accelerated since 1960s and tourism is one of the sectors emerged with the fastest developing pace in the "post-industrialization society". The breakthrough in aviation and radar navigation technology during WWII has laid a solid foundation for the development of civil aviation industry and exerted great influences on tourism. The launch of Boeing 707 jet aircraft in 1958, symbolizes the arrival of the popular travel age and travel by air becomes more swift, safe and comfortable. In 1950, Letts organized a chartered travel to la Corsein the name of Horizon Holiday Tourist Company. In this experimental tourism, he adopted the method of seat reservation to effectively cut down cost and provide chartered tourist routes to the public with lower prices. In the following period, more and more tourists accept this kind of new travel manner. When it comes to the 20th Century, the first wide-body passenger aircraft Boeing 747 was put into operation. The number of tourists on board every time can come to 400, greatly cutting down the air ticket price.

With the further development of auto industry in such countries as Europe, U. S. and Japan and the construction of expressway after WWII, self-driving travel began to replace travel by taking trains and bus with an astonishing speed. When it comes to 1970s, about two persons own a car in average.

In 1980s, there were about 600 000 sets of caravans having boarding equipment in the UK. In July and August, the holiday-making group will drive along the expressway leading to France. Paris then turned into a city for foreign tourists and tourists making holiday in Paris can be seen here and there.

Spain has been listed as one of the top 3 in the tourism countries in the world since 1960s and it has created a "Spanish miracle" in tourism. When it comes to 2002, about 51.7 million foreign tourists visit Spain every year and the income of tourism is as high as $ 33.6 billion, indicating Spain to hold take the 2nd position in the world.

China has turned into Asia's biggest passenger output country. In 2005, China's outbound tourists came to 31.03 million person/times, a growth of 7.5% annual. In 2005, China received 120 million person/times of inbound tourists and 46.81 million per-son/times stayed overnight, a growth of 10% and 12% respectively. Foreign tourists have brought forth a total amount of $ 29.3 billion, an annual growth of nearly 14%.

Information technology is the most important revolution in the second half of the 20th Century. Sheraton Group began to adopt the electronic reservation system as early as in 1958. The computer reservation system appeared in 1960s. When it comes to 1990s, tourism began to adopt computer reservation system and travel dealer visual system. Three new electronic travel media make up the electronic platforms based on Internet technology, interactive digital TV and mobile device.

According to the statistics conducted by World Tourism Organization, international tourists increased from 25 million to 635 million from 1950 to 1998, an average annual yearly growth of 6.97%. According to the statistics of International Monetary' Fund, tourist reception and transportation related income reached as high as $ 50.4 in 1998, taking the first position in international trades, including auto production, chemical production, foods, gasoline and other fuels, computer and office equipment, textile products and garment and mineral products etc.

The World Tourism Organization pointed out in Manila Declaration 1980 that: "tourism is one of the basic needs of the human society. Many countries have also recognized the importance of including tourism in the development of national economy. Boosted by this kind of human civilization development concept, such behavior mode as "popular tourism", "incentive tourism" and "social tourism" have come out.

Established in November 1974, the World Tourism Organization representing 89 state governments. Its basic tenet is: "just like those existed inter-govern-mental international organizations whose call can be concerned, seek a due position for tourism." The organization plays an important role in promoting the development of tourism in the world and its members include governments and non-governmental organizations. The organization became an institution under the charge of UN in 2003.

U. S. sociologist Roland Robertson thought that globalization is not purely an economic, political, social or international issue; it is a cultural issue because the first one in the whole system of globalization is the social-cultural "system".

Marx said: "the demand of constantly expanding product sales channel boosts bourgeois to travel all over the world. They must settle down, develop and establish contacts in any place. To explore the markets, bourgeois globalizes the production and consumption in all countries. The regional and national self-sufficiency and self-seclusion in the past is replaced by the intercontacts and mutual-dependence. This principle directs both material and spiritual productions."

When it ushered into the 21st Century, with technological progress and the development of traffic tools and communication technologies, the contacts in the world realm become increasingly extensive and the exchange between civilized entities has expanded from such channels as war, trade and religion to fields like tourism, media, culture and sports.

Due to the influence of mass media, people's cultural favor and living manner become assimilated and it's easier to have a rational cognition on the status quo of the entire world and issues arousing international concerns. In addition, with the gradually disappearing of languages in the world, English, Chinese and French become popular languages in the world.

Presently, people go shopping in chain stores of the same brand, watch the same TV programs and films, and discuss gossips of celebrities even beyond the national boundary. People begin to love tourism and get familiarized with the scenery of different countries and regions. It's now possible to do sightseeing in the east hemisphere today and make holiday in the west hemisphere tomorrow; and it is common to ski in north China in the morning and swim in southern beach in the afternoon.

The appearance of informatized society with the global flow of capital and Internet as the representative makes the transnational spread of culture product and culture production mode got unprecedented development.

Human beings have many things in common, such as culture psychology, culture requirement and basic outlook of value, as well as some common interests, the cultural behaviors and creative ability. Therefore, cultural globalization is a necessary result of the melting of culture of different nations.

Cultural globalization forces different countries to view the world and culture with a new vision and perspective and people of all over the world to ponder over questions beyond their own country or region. It has promoted the contact, dialogue and exchange of different culture and enabled human beings to share world culture resources and the achievements of human civilization.

Sun Dongmin contributed an article to January 11, 2001 issue of Peoples Daily Overseas Edition: "the further development of 'global village', the violent development of economic globalization, the in-and-out of MNCs and the enlarging of external investment make economies of different countries interlocked and interdependent. The financial crisis of Asia endangers the world and the profit drop of Federal Reserve vibrates the stock market. Incidents occurring in every corner of 'global village' can be spread to other places in a short time".

The trend of globalized resource flow has no doubt boosted the development of tourism: the more the external information people has grasped, the more the people thirst for experiencing alien civilization. Presently, convenient traffic tools make it possible to take the tourists to any destination. People's increasingly open psychology has overcome the inherent exclusive, xenophobic and chauvinism so that promote the equal exchange of the humanity.

At the conference to celebrate World Tourism Day held in Iran on September 27, 2001, the World Tourism Organization put forward the slogan "Tourism, an approach for the dialogue between civilizations and peace".

2. Tourism force touches various fields of mankind

In 1992, the total income of the world tourism industry exceeded that of petroleum and automobile industry, and for the first time to become the largest industry of the world. According to related in-formation, the number of international tourist in the whole world increased to 687 million in 2000 from 25 million in 1950. Besides, the number of international tourist and the level of consumption have increased year after year. Tourism industry had developed rapidly in the world, which has almost formed an independent industry in about 170 countries and regions. In 1993, the number of international tourist in the whole world was 513 million. It was 20 times as much as that in 1950 and increased at an average rate of 7.2% per year. In the same year, the total income of international tourism industry amounted to $ 305.8 billion which was with an increasing of 116 times as much in 1950, and increased at an average rate of 11.7 % a year. The growth rate of the world tourism industry not only exceeded the average rate of the increase of the world economy, but also surpassed the average growth rate of industry which had the strongest increasing impetus (Form 1).

Form 1  The growth rate of the world tourism industry

| Item / Time | The average growth rate of the world tourism industry | The average growth rate of the world economy | The average growth rate of the world industry |
|---|---|---|---|
| 50 | 12.6 | 5.4 | 6.8 |
| 60 | 10.1 | 4.9 | 6.5 |
| 70 | 6.0 | 3.5 | 5.3 |
| 80 | 8.4 | 2.8 | 2.6 |
| 80~85 | 1.1 | 2.4 | 1.7 |
| 86~90 | 16.3 | 2.6 | 3.2 |

Although in the early days of the eighties, the developing speed of tourism industry became slow and even declined because of the influence of the world economical crisis and the radical changes of the international situation, but in the whole 1980s, the world tourism industry still kept a higher growth rate of 8.4%. Especially in the late of the eighties, the annual average growth rate even reached 16.3 %. Tourism industry displayed its good developing impetus, meanwhile indicating a bright developing prospect in the process of stepping into the 21st century.

The rapid development of tourism industry also promoted effectively a sustained and healthy development of the world economy. First, the contribution of tourism industry increased continuously. In 1992, the international and internal total income of tourism in the whole world amounted to $ 3500 billion, and it is one-ninth of the world total commodity and service consumption volume in the year. According to the research report of the World Travel and Tourism Council (WTTC), in 1990, the new rise in value reached to $ 1449 billion, making up 5.9 percent of the world total new rise in value in that year. The tax income of the world tourism industry was $ 251 billion, making up 5.6 per cent of the total direct and indirect tax paid by enterprises in the whole world in 1990. WTTC compared the new increment between tourism industry and other industries in the U.S., Britain, France, Japan and Germany (Form 2). The form shows the new increment of the tourism industry was 3.1 times of the agriculture industry, 3.6 times of the auto industry, 4.3 times of the metal industry, and 5.7 times of the textile industry in those five countries. It fully indicated that the contribution of the tourism industry had increased continuously in national economy.

Form 2  The comparing form in increment and employee number

| Countries / Industries | the U.S. | Britain | Japan | Germany | France | Total |
|---|---|---|---|---|---|---|
| employee number of tourism industry (10000) | 3300 | 500 | 2300 | 1400 | 700 | 8200 |
| employee number of agriculture industry (10000) | 900 | 300 | 650 | 200 | 190 | 2240 |
| employee number of textile industry (10000) | 900 | 200 | 700 | 400 | 500 | 2700 |
| employee number of metal industry (10000) | 300 | 80 | 650 | 120 | 180 | 1330 |
| employee number of auto industry (10000) | 500 | 200 | 250 | 250 | 250 | 1450 |
| tourism industry increment ($ 10000000) | 200 | 70 | 120 | 100 | 100 | 590 |
| agriculture industry increment ($ 10000000) | 400 | 100 | 700 | 450 | 250 | 1900 |
| textile industry increment ($ 10000000) | 100 | 20 | 100 | 110 | 30 | 360 |
| metal industry increment ($ 10000000) | 550 | 250 | 600 | 600 | 300 | 2300 |
| auto industry increment ($ 10000000) | 100 | 30 | 110 | 120 | 110 | 470 |

Source of data: sorting out from the data of "WTTC Annual Report of 1992" published on the China Tourism Newspaper on June 1, 1992

Along with the improvement of traffic technology and the rise of the living standards in developed countries (including in the developing countries), tourism was already accepted by people and became an indispensable part in their lives. The post-modern tourism will step into a "mass tourism" epoch of global and worldwide travel.

The so-called "mass tourism," means a brand-new tourism developing conception. It reflects a trend that tourism industry is developing in depth and in an all-round way-morally in the domain of economical society. The concept of the "mass tourism" is higher in level and wider in category than the traditional tourism definition. According to the industry character of tourism industry, and the close connection between tourism industry and other industries correlated, the tourism industry extends and expands scientifically and reasonably, strengthening its industrial function: it has strong comprehensiveness, a long industrial chain and covers widespread fields.

The conception of the "mass tourism" is understood by people as an interactive connection of many aspects, such as society, economy and culture. For example, tourism should be combined with commercial facilities, high science and technology, poverty aid, environmental construction, and real estate. Tourism is not only a popular merchandise in scale, but also becoming a highly specialize merchandise in quality. Mean-while, on the basis of the traditional tourism style, such as sightseeing tourism and agricultural tourism and some new traveling projects are put out, like industrial tourism, fashionable tourism and social tourism. As many specialized tourism products are put out, tourism has becomes more enriched, touching all the various aspects of human development.

**Commerce tourism** Commercial tourism has existed since the ancient times. The Silk Road, which had an important effect in our history, is one of the most well-known commercial tourism routes in the history of human development. The earliest tourism activity in the human history may not aim to delight disposition, but for commercial activity. Modern commercial activity is different from those of the ancient time in scale and intension. As for the modern commercial tourism, the process of commercial activity involves many consumption activities. Same as the traditional commerce operation, it also includes attending industry exhibition, transnational corporation's regional annual meeting, investigation and research, trans-regional product introducing meeting, and company rewarding travel.

Regarding commercial tourism as the example, although facing to a drastic challenge of the global economy in 2003, Singapore still received 1.25 million commercial tourists, making up 20 percent of the total inbound tourists. But Singapore's total population is only more than 4 million. In fact, the "Singapore-type" tourism career is not only sightseeing and local cuisine; its tourism industry pillar includes commercial tourism, meeting, rewarding tourism and large-scale meeting and exhibition. It is said the demand to global commercial tourism market will increase in a high speed. The total world tourism expenditure in 2007 will reach $870 billion, $350 billion coming from commercial tourism. Besides, in 2005, China's expenditure was $250 billion in the aspect of commercial tourism. Chinese enterprisers are becoming more active increasingly, in the meantime, more and more foreign companies began to invest in China, so the commercial tourism market will keep increasing continuously with double-digit growth and will reach $115 billion in 2020.

**Exploration tourism**   Along with the public's diversified demands and personalization, more and more people prefer to choose exploratory tourism, one of trends of traveling in the future. Exploratory tourism, with a rich scientific intension can satisfy tourist's desires of seeking novelty and exploration in the maximum limit. Many city-dwellers, who live in the blatant cities for a long time, will get a special satisfaction and sensation of pleasure when they make the mysterious, dangerous and irritant traveling investigation activities in those untrodden places, such as elephant riding exploration in Thailand and travel by sledge pulled by dogs in Denmark.

Other explorations aim to break the world records. Such as taking global travel by balloon, driving pedal plane or sailplane to pass through channel, traveling round the world by driving boat or yacht and crossing the Atlantic Ocean by canoe, etc.

There are also a great variety of explorations which regard scientific research as their main aim. Such as high mountain exploration, desert exploration, sea exploration, forest exploration, cave exploration, polar region exploration, tracking wild animals exploration, and finding human primitive clan exploration, and so on. In 2004, an American ex-service navy captain named Alfred Mclaren ran an underwater driving training school in Bahamas. Every student must pay a high tuition of $9980. Mclaren would train every student person-ally. The news reported: "it is absolutely a revolution of underwater exploration."

**Shopping tourism**   It is a special way of traveling. Shopping is an important part in tourism, many countries and regions use tourist's psychology of yearning for shopping to develop local product, handicrafts and various elegant souvenirs with national characteristics, and famous brand tobacco and wine, cosmetic and commodity to meet foreign tourist's taste. Meanwhile, it is an important method to attract tourists and make foreign exchange. For example, Singapore built a handicraft center specially and engaged craftsmen of Thailand, Malaysia, Indonesia, Hong Kong, Japan and India. The center not only made and showed the variety of local characteristic handicrafts, but also allowed tourist to visit the making process and purchase product for the souvenir. So the income of selling tourism made up 60 percent of the total tourism income. Hong Kong is called "shopping paradise" by tourist, and 61% of their consumption is for shopping.

The small commodity city, traveling shopping center is located in Yiwu Zejiang Province, the second and third floors of the west hall of the second phase occupying a total area of 100 000 square meters with an operation area of 50 000 square meters. Following the operating conception of "the sea of small commodity, the paradise of consumer," the center amasses 320 thousand of inexpensive and elegant commodities. According to statistics, about 1.64 million tourists travelled to Yi wu in 2002 and the income of traveling shopping reached more than 200 million Yuan.

**Ecological tourism** Ecological tourism is specialized in using natural and ecological resources to develop tourism projects, and attract the people at home and abroad who pay attention to ecology and other residents to visit, enjoy, experience, and investigate. The ecological tourism centers on travel activities in the fine ecological condition area, such as in forest or grassland, in desert, Gobi, and wilderness where tourists are organized to plant trees, grass to improve ecological environment.

At present, the ecological tourism is major project in those simple and underdeveloped regions where human, nature and resident can get along with each other harmoniously. The national ecological tourism is its typical delegate, such as the Suoga Bouyeis countryside of Liupan-shui city, the Tang'an the Dongs countryside of Liping county, and Longli of Jingping county in Guizhou province, depending on the national ecological museum build by the union of China and Norway to develop national ecological tourism, and attract many visitors at home and abroad to visit, investigate and research. Paying close attention to ecological environment is the basic interest of human being. Nowadays, strengthening ecological construction and environmental protection by developing ecological tourism are important choices for many countries and regions.

**Cultural and sports tourism** Cultural and sports tourism is a kind of traveling activity by making use of cultural and sports project, facilities and competition activities to develop tourism project and attract visitor to visit, participate in and experience. According to the pertinent statistics conducted by the WTIC in terms of tourist's traveling motivation in 2004. There are five kinds of traveling motivations-commerce, spending holidays, shopping, exploration and cultural experience, among which the cultural experience already ranked the first place. The main form of culture includes art festival, music festival and film festival, etc. Cultural tourism means exploration and discovery in different cultural fields, emerging distinctive features day by day. Language-studying travel is a kind of typical modern culture traveling way. At present time, along with the development of global travel, returning to culture is becoming the key content of tourism. The mixture of ecological tourism and cultural tourism is a new trend of tourism industry development.

Sports and travel are preferred by most of people. The sports tourism composing two aspects can unify people's sports talent and travel fashion, thus it will have boundless vigorous force and draw huge attraction. The sports tourism main means viewing and admiring the important international and domestic sports games, such as the Olympic Games and the World Cup. It also includes traveling by driving automobile, motorcycle and bicycle, traveling on foot, climbing mountain, exploration, field living training, gorge drift, skating, skiing, grass ski, tennis, golf and table tennis. The self-driving tour along the Silk Road, organized by Germany Travel Service and receipted by China International Travel Service, the World Cup and the Olympic Games tour are all the large-scale sports tourism activities.

**Science tourism**   Science tourism involves using scientific research, education and teaching related traveling project. It mainly attracts students, youngsters, and teachers home and abroad to study, visit and communicate. Science tourism is also called " sun-filling travel" by people because they can study scientific knowledge, and broaden their vision in the traveling activity. Especially they not only can see or listen some traveling content, but also can experience and put into practice personally. So this kind of traveling form including knowledge, interest, education and leisure is more and more finding favour in the vast number of youngsters' eyes.

The main form of science tourism is tourism studying, such as the Japanese students come to China for studying tourism which was launched in Beijing and Jiangsu. Handwriting and art travel and well-known school visiting, such as the activity of " one day in school" which was launched by Beijing University and Tsinghua University as well as visiting the space center, laboratory and research center. Science tourism belongs to industry tourism. But it has an obvious predominance in popularizing scientific knowledge and minor education. Great attentions are not only paid by schools, family, scientific research institution, educational and travel department, but also well received by adults and it will have a wonderful prospect.

**Health care tourism**  Health care tourism involves two aspects of content. First, it initiates sports for keeping in good health in traveling process, including climbing mountain, fishing, picking, swimming, drift, skiing, grass ski, camping, sunbath, air-bath, forest-bath and meal adjustment. Strengthening body through sports is its aim. Second, the aged who can take care of themselves despite some minor illness, travel and use the convenient condition to cure the disease and regain health.

In health care tourism, forest-bathing means going into the woods to experience the special fragrance. According to the latest research result of the Forestry and Forest products Research Institute of Japan, the aromatic herbage of ferries and cypresses can reduce the blood pressure and set people's mind at rest. When you take a walk in forests, besides the aroma of trees, touching the barks can also make you relaxed and happy. You can enjoy the forest-bath in forest and park or avenue in city. Comparing with the theme park or gymnasium, the forest-bath has more functions of relaxing and health care. Health care tourism combines travel and health care together, not only relaxing the traveler, but also strengthening the immune system of body. It is well received by middle-aged and senior tourists.

**Industry tourism**  Industrial producing processes, technologies, and products may be common to professional workers, but they usually are strange, mysterious and full of attraction to most of the people. For example, coal is known to everyone, but few of them real know how the coal is dug out. The coalmine roadway, mine carts, excavators and the feeling of staying in places with a distance of thousands meters to the surface of the ground can arouse the curiosity of most of people. Many countries in the world already developed a large number of industrial traveling projects. Take the Ruhr Area of Germany for example, it transformed the industrial site into an industrial site theme park and got a big hit. Haier Group of China regards industrial travel as an important daily activity and specifies certain staff to take charge of tourist reception, guiding the tourists to visit producing process, and allowing them to choose their perfect product from the sample product.

Some enterprises with vision and strength regard the industrial tourism as a long-term investment of the company and even built the industrial museum to show the industrial relics and the developing process of technology. This kind of practice is as much as to doing free market investigations, which can greatly contribute to making marketing operation, sale strategy and product improvement.

**Exhibition tourism**  Exhibition tourism is becoming a new traveling form due to its specific characteristic of the powerful compatibility, the widespread coverage, and the high commercial grade and cultural contents. At present, the developing potential of the exhibition tourism and its economical and social benefits it produces arouse great attention to many countries and regions of the world. It is estimated by the authoritative sources of international exhibition industry, the output value of the international exhibition industry makes up 1 percent of the total GDP of many countries of the world. International conference also has a huge market. According to the statistics of the International Congress & Convention Association (ICCA), the output value of the international conference is about $ 280 billion every year. In countries and regions where exhibition industry is developed, like Hong Kong and Germany, the exhibition industry's promotional capacity to the economy reaches a ratio as high as nine to one.

Beijing will launch the Olympic Games in 2008. It is predicted that tourism industry of our country will have an income increment of 5 billion RMB every year from 2002 to 2008, and the annual growth rate of traveling income will reach 18%. In 2008, the traveling income will increase $ 10 billion, and the growth rate of traveler will be 100%. The directly increasing traveling income will mount to more than 150 billion RMB because of the Olympic Games. Besides, it is also estimated that 2010 world expo in Shanghai will bring about 70 million travelers to Shanghai.

**Gambling tourism**　In the developing process of the world tourism industry, some areas surely developed tourism through the form of gambling, even developing gambling tours or casino tours. Gambling during traveling is regarded as a specific characteristic, such as Atlantic City and Las Vegas of the U. S., Monaco and Monte Carlo of Europe, and Macao of Asia. To the vast number of masses, they mainly want to spend holidays and relax in these resort cities not to take up gambling professionally or to earn money, Most of them just want to broaden their horizons because of curiosity.

Traveling abroad and traveling in the border countries of Chinese make the tourism industry an economical pillar in some border cities, and gambling is an indispensable choice when traveling abroad. So along the border lines of China, casinos are built in many countries. A country border with Heilongjiang Province in northeast of China built more than 60 casinos in four cities. There are also overseas casinos near the borders of Yunan Province, the Guangxi Zhuang Autonomous Region and Inner Mongolia Autonomous Region. According to incomplete statistics, there were more than 200 gambling houses on the border lines of China.

**Special tourism**　Special tourism has just started to develop in the whole world, but it shows a vigorous vitality. Special tourism means traveling with distinctive features to satisfy traveler's special interests and demands in the certain aspects. Thus the traveling route and project are full of new experience, stimulus and adventures. The travelers who participate in special tourism usually have the adventurous spirit and good health, and travel with those who cherish the same ideals and follow the same path. The travelers experience the world through sports, and get complacency on mind when they adventure or face a new environment.

Comparing with sightseeing travel and holiday-spending tour, besides providing accommodations, traffic service and guidance for travelers, the most important feature of special tourism is you must involve yourself in the tour with other travelers together, and use your professional knowledge to guide the travelers to carry out their traveling aim. This kind of tourism usually deals with a wide range of regions, like the untrodden and remote areas enjoying special natural and cultural environment with an extremely primitive and natural characteristic.

In most of countries, automobiles, bicycles and motorcycles are the major means of transportation. The non-competitive sports tours include skiing, rock climbing, drift, fire balloon and glide, high mountain climbing exploration, going to gorge, desert and cave. The scientific research to natural and humanistic landscape for a short-term sightseeing, explorations and visits as its main traveling belong to the sphere of the special tourism.

According to the world traveling situation in 2002 from the "Gem of Tourism Report of 2003 Edition," published by the World Tourism Organization (WTO), we can see the features of the world tourism development in the representative countries more concretely:

Top 10    Tourism Income and Numbers of tourists in different countries

| Tourists number in the world (million) | | | | International traveling income (million) | | | |
| --- | --- | --- | --- | --- | --- | --- | --- |
| Position | 2002 | Change rate% | Occupancy rate% | Position | 2002 | Change rate% | Occupancy rate% |
| 1. France | 77.0 | 2.4 | 11.0 | 1. the U.S. | 665 | −7.4 | 14.0 |
| 2. Spain | 51.7 | 3.3 | 7.4 | 2. Spain | 336 | 2.2 | 7.1 |
| 3. the U.S. | 41.9 | −6.7 | 6.0 | 3. France | 323 | 7.8 | 6.8 |
| 4. Italy | 39.8 | 0.6 | 5.7 | 4. Italy | 269 | 4.3 | 5.7 |

续表

| Tourists number in the world (million) | | | | International traveling income (million) | | | |
|---|---|---|---|---|---|---|---|
| 5. China | 36.8 | 11.0 | 5.2 | 5. China | 204 | 14.6 | 4.3 |
| 6. Britain | 24.2 | 5.9 | 3.4 | 6. Germany | 192 | 4.0 | 4.0 |
| 7. Canada | 20.1 | 1.9 | 2.9 | 7. Britain | 178 | 9.5 | 3.8 |
| 8. Mexico | 19.7 | -0.7 | 2.8 | 8. Austria | 112 | 11.1 | 2.4 |
| 9. Austria | 18.6 | 2.4 | 2.6 | 9. Hong Kong | 101 | 22.2 | 2.1 |
| 10. Germany | 18.0 | 0.6 | 2.6 | 10. Greece | 97 | 3.1 | 2.1 |
| World | 703 | 2.7 | 100 | World | 4740 | 3.2 | 100 |

Top 10 International Traveling Expenditure of the World

| | International traveling expenditure (a hundred million) | | |
|---|---|---|---|
| Position | 2002 | Change rate% | Occupancy rate% |
| 1. the U.S. | 580 | -3.6 | 12.6 |
| 2. Germany | 532 | 2.4 | 11.2 |
| 3. Britain | 404 | 10.8 | 8.5 |
| 4. Japan | 267 | 0.6 | 5.6 |
| 5. France | 195 | 9.8 | 4.1 |
| 6. Italy | 169 | 14.4 | 3.6 |
| 7. China | 154 | 10.7 | 3.2 |
| 8. Netherlands | 129 | 7.5 | 2.7 |
| 9. Hong Kong | 124 | 0.8 | 2.6 |
| 10. Russia | 120 | 20.5 | 2.5 |
| World | 4740 | 3.2 | 100 |

According to the above forms, the Western countries still hold a dominant position in the international tourism industry. Nevertheless, this dominant situation is broken because of the outstanding performances of the Eastern Asian, especially China in the international tourism industry.

Although facing to the influences of menace of terrorism, natural calamity, price-rising of petroleum, disease and other unstable political and economical factors, the development of global travel can not be stopped. In 2005, the global tourist reached a number of 808 million, and increased by 5.5% compared with the number of 766 million in 2004. The increasing rate was higher than 4.1% on average per year, a long-term aim made by WTO.

In 2005, the number of traveler increased by 42 million, about 19 million of them traveling to Europe, 11 million to Asia-Pacific region, 7 million to America, 3 million to Africa and 2 million to the Middle East region. Considering the increasing rate in 2005, Africa was the one whose tourists increased at the highest rate of 10%, followed by Asia-Pacific region, 7%, the Middle East, 7%, America, 6% and Europe, 4%.

Traditionally, Europe and America are the most popular traveling destinations. But it is reported by the WTO that Asia-Pacific region, together with the Middle East will be regions enjoying the greatest increasing potential in the world in 2006. It forecasted that Asia-Pacific region will get a growth rate of 9%, and the Middle East with a rate of 8% this year.

As to Africa, Europe and America, WTO forecasts that they will get a growth rate of 6%, 3% and 3% respectively. WTO also thinks that the global tourism industry will get a increasing of 4% to 5% in 2006.

From 2002 to 2005, the number of global traveler increased 100 million in all. Nowadays, many countries of the Middle East, like Qatar and the United Arab Emirates are all making dedicated efforts to develop their economy with huge fund investment in tourism industry. Ambassador of Syria told the writer that in the first seven months of 2006, Syria already invested more than $10 billion to the tourism industry.

The well-known American scholar, Daniel Bell said in his book The Coming of Post-industrial Society published in 1973 that the feature of pre-industrial society and industrial society is respectively agriculture and industry. Then he pointed out: the base of the post-industrial society is service industry. Along with people's extending living sphere and a growing demand and interest, the third industry begin to develop intensively, such as restaurant, hotel, automobile service, travel, entertainment and sports.

The GDP proportion of service industry and other correlated industries in the United States is 67.1% in 1980, 71% in 1987, 74.3% in 1993 and more than 80% in 2000.

In the mid-1990s, more than 120 countries in the world regarded tourism industry as the propping industry. Tourism industry is called the vigorous growth point of the economic in the world.

According to some organizations concerned, up to 2010, the total number of international travelers will be more than 1.2 billion, taking up be one-fifth of the total population of the whole world, and the international tourism income will be U.S. \$ 900 billion. Up until 2020, the traveler of the whole world will be 1.618 billion and the international tourism income will surpass \$ 2000 billion. At that time, tourism will be the important link of the social economy. The top five world traveling destinations in 2020 are China, the U.S., France, Spain and Hong Kong of China. They will receive 29% of the world tourists. The top five countries with the largest travelers group are Germany, Japan, the U.S., China and Britain. (An Introduction of Tourism, published in 2000)

**Top 10 Tourist destination of the world in 2020**

| Country and region | traveler's number (ten thousand) | Share in the world market | growth rate from 1995 to 2020 (%) |
|---|---|---|---|
| China | 13710 | 8.6 | 8.0 |
| the U.S. | 10240 | 6.4 | 3.5 |
| France | 9330 | 5.8 | 1.8 |
| Spain | 7100 | 4.4 | 2.4 |
| Hong Kong in China | 5930 | 3.7 | 7.3 |
| Italy | 5290 | 3.3 | 2.2 |
| Britain | 5280 | 3.3 | 3.0 |
| Mexico | 4890 | 3.1 | 3.6 |
| Russia | 4710 | 2.9 | 6.7 |
| Czechoslovakia | 4400 | 2.7 | 4.0 |
| Total | 70880 | 44.2 | |

Wu Jisong, dean of the College of Economic Management, Beijing Aeronautics University, forecasted in his book "New Circulatory Economy": Up to 2050, tourism industry will rank the first of the new economical top 10 industries and tourism industry, remanufacturing industry, etc. will be the top 10 industries of the world economy in 2050, except the ecology-renovating industry, hot nuclear fusion electric power industry, ecological agriculture industry, brine-desalinating industry, information industry, new material industry, sea industry and medicine industry.

Wu Jisong said that up to 2050, along with the development of the world circular economy and the construction of the circular economy system, it will be sure to develop a large numbers of cycle-style industries, and they will be the pillar of the cycle economical system. Traditional industries still exist, but they will be the industries transformed by high technology in accordance with the cycle economical conception.

He pointed that tourism industry is a low-resource-consuming industry mainly using the cycle-using traveling resources. Tourism industry also has the problem of economizing resources and cycle using. At present, the Western Europe has already begun to use internet to build up connections. The practice of exchanging lodging resources among travelers from different countries is an attempt. Along with the rise of the income of tourism industry year after year, up to 2050, it will be the largest industry of the world. Tourism industry will play a pillar-like part in the post-industrial society because of its important position in economy.

Dalian, a city of China registered the trademark of "The Romantic Metropolis". It is said that the Coca-Cola Company who at that time did not register the homophonic commodities and imitation products and its rival the Pepsi Company took the advantage and registered its commodities. Implied by this, Dalian made a comprehensive register to 43 kinds of products concerning with the city.

All "products" in this city are available to use the trademark of "City of Romance". It's the travel trademark.

In the post-industrial epoch, the development of tourism industry already infiltrates into various spheres of human beings. Just like Mr. Zhu Changqin said in his article "The Motto Full of Ideological Content": " It involves everything that human beings can touch regardless of gender or location."

Tourism has even become a part of human rights. Antonio Tajani, an expert of the industrial and business department of EU council, declared on April 19th, 2010 that EU planned to sponsor the retired, the youth and the poor to travel with public fund.

According to The Sunday Times reported—

Tajani announced the plan when he attended The eu council of ministers last week: "How to spend one's holidays is an important criterion to judge our life quality." According to a report by Sunday Tales from UK, this program aims to increase Europeans' cultural esteem and make up the gap between the northern and southern Europe, as well as to boost the tourism market in low seasons.

The tentative program will be carried out from now to 2013 before the official project's enforcement be launched. People who will be sponsored include the retired, the senior over

65 years old, the youth aged between 18 to 25, as well as some problem family and the disabled.

Firstly people in southern Europe will be encouraged to travel to the north and vice versa. Details of the program will come out later. It is estimated that 30% of the travel expense will be covered by EU who will provide a hundred million Euros every year.

The developing history of mankind proves that if the cultures between different regions and nations can be communicated frequently and deeply, the power of culture will become greater, because such kind of communication tallies with the mutual ideals and interests of mankind.

## Section 3
## The Existing Development Indicates an Optimistic Outlook

(1) Human communication has advanced two substantial leaps.

So far, the tourism activity of mankind has undergone two tremendous leaps:

The first leap occurred during the Industrial Revolution. The advent of steam engine stirred up the productivity by a large margin and brought more leisure time to people. Then the steamships and trains further displaced those traditional transportation tools dragged by animals, which caused great changed in terms of the range, experience and security of tourism were all radically changed. More importantly, tourism was no longer the privilege of a minority. The ordinary white collar and blue collar were able to enjoy it as well. Mankind began to step into the era of "mass tourism".

The second leap has started up since 1980s and 1990s. The swift and strong development of hi-tech not only breaks through national boundaries and accelerates the exchange and sharing of information, but also shortened the distance between different places, gradually inosculating the world economy as a whole, i. e. "economic globalization".

Economic globalization presents itself mainly through the liberalization of trade, the internationalization of production and the globalization of finance as well as science and technology. So far, the dynamic economic globalization has fiercely lashed against the economy, politics, military, society, culture and even thinking mode of different countries. It is a profound revolution sweeping across the whole world, with no exception to it.

At this stage, economic globalization not only hastens the large-scaled flow of resources, capitals, technologies, products and markets, but also contributes to the unprecedentedly massive exchange. Hereby, mankind transits from "mass tourism" to "global tourism".

Despite the exact time of human tourism's third leap is still unknown, "the unity of core values" will certainly be its symbol. And it is a precondition to bring about the "global village" as well.

Only "the unity of core values" is able to help root out political and religious conflicts, minimize the cost of human communication, and enable mankind to make the best of earth resources to create wealth, develop science and technology, protect national cultures, promote free communication of people from different nations, or in a word, enhance the holistic power of humanity.

When the time comes, the political, economic and cultural development of all countries will be relevantly balanced and the tourism activities of mankind will shake off all of the restrictions, such as traveling permits, expense and transportation tools. The only thing they need to do is to conquer themselves.

However, it depends to a large degree on human's "conscious" acts to determine when this marvelous vision w511 be accomplished at last. The evolvement of economic globalization urgently demands to push forward the process of unifying the world through tourism, and al-so provides realistic conditions and material foundations to fulfill such demand.

To some extent, economic globalization has been the stage and prop of tourism to unify the world and display the rugged process of cultural development.

Since it will take some time for tourism to unify the world, the integration of cultures will run through the whole process of economic globalization. The dramatic development of information technology and the advent of information age characterized with cyberspace fiercely accelerating the update of social cultures. Tourism has exerted its subtle influence on the world in this updating process.

The age of globalization brings many new traits to the evolvement of culture. The cultural diversity becomes the main feature of cultural development, the cultural imperialism be-comes a new problem and the advancement becomes the common objective different cultures pursue.

For instance, with the rapid development of Chinese economy, the soft power of Chinese culture is more and more frequently exposed in the spotlight. "Seizing the right to make a voice is the premise for China to participate in the world", Liu Changle, Chairman and CEO of Hong Kong Phoenix Satellite Television, once said in a cultural forum.

The conflicts and exchanges between civilizations are the main features of tourism unifying the world. The rapid process of economic globalization creates more chances for the collision and interaction between regional cultures and makes the conflict and exchange of civilizations more severe. Through such collisions and changes of different regional cultures, tourism gradually fulfils its mission to unify the world.

Different nations should respect each other's culture and make efforts to promote mutual understanding, thereby becoming culturally complementary. Cultural differences are easy to lead to misunderstandings or even conflicts.

The cultural differences may hurdle the communication of different nations, but they have enriched the world, boosted human intercourse by various types of tourism activities, and offered opportunities for mankind to share civilizations.

Several years ago, Bruce Lee a well-known Chinese Kung Fu star with worldwide fame, whose statues was inaugurated on the central square of Mostar City, Bosnia and Herzegovina, a middle-European nation. Gaetano, a writer of Bosnia and Herzegovina, reckoned that the statue of Bruce Lee could help to eliminate cultural differences and break through racial barriers. "Someone's meat may be other's poison, but Bruce Lee is a genuine international hero and is also the hero for all races in Bosnia and Herzegovina", said Gaetano.

Philosophically speaking, culture conflict and integration submits to the law of unity of opposites, with the former as the premise of the realization of the latter. Only through mutual competition and contradiction, different cultures can find out their own advantages and shortages, improve themselves by learning each other and then lay foundation for the cultural integration.

The effort for tourism to unify the world is actually the evolving process to bridge the mutual conflict and integration.

Different stages and levels during tourism's effort to unify the world are featured with different sorts of cultural conflicts and integration, which also contain different meanings. But in terms of the whole course of cultural development, the unity of opposites has been the main law of social progress.

In the age of economic globalization, the cultural conflicts still concentrate on the differences and values of various cultures, but each culture has paid much attention to absorb and learn nutrients from others and thereby improve its adaptability and vitality.

For different cultures, the desire to seek common ground and reserve differences has been stronger than ever before in the age of economic globalization. In the context of different regional cultures, people have been paying more and more attention to those "universal" issues, such as global awareness, global ethics, cyber culture, mass culture, consumption culture, ecological culture, sustainable development as well as modernity.

People are trying their best to find some kind of culture with universal value, so as to cope with those common obstacles faced by human society or hereby rake in enormous political and commercial benefits. To some extent, the pursuit of such common value represents the ideal situation of cultural integration.

(2) "National consciousness" transits to "human consciousness"

In the course of changes and integration, the cultural forms have been constantly evolving with new appearance. As the main body of culture, mankind has also been characterized with special cultural charms.

Reacting to Steve Jobs' death, the Associated Press appraised his as a "CEO, technologist, futurist, innovator and refiner". Meanwhile, the Wall Street Journal reviewed his achievements in the tone of individualistic heroism.

Some people attribute Job's success to the "social system" of America. But why does he not turn up in Japan or Europe which enjoy the similar "social system"? Even in America, Jobs is a peerless and incomparable innovator as well.

Traditionally, people usually ascribed this to so-called "talent". But now, they are more inclined to believe that the personal experience, belief and personality of an inventor decide the successful result. Many qualities are particularly significant to an entrepreneur.

Ms. Ye Tan, a famous economic commentator of China, insisted that Job's success resuited from "the perfect integration of Sino-Western cultural essences." She argued that the powerful technical teams, rapid logistics chains and global marketing network laid material foundation for Apple, but Jobs' strong spiritual power came from the East.

In her article published in National Business Daily, Ye Tan said, "Jobs believes in Zen Buddhism, which not only invests him with psychological support but also bestows concise life goal and aesthetic taste on him. Actually, all gadgets of Apple have been concisely and smoothly designed, helping grasp their consumers' hearts. Following neither common views nor his own thoughts, Jobs has endeavored to explore the new road." She argued that few entrepreneurs or philosophers in China could do what Jobs has done.

Ye Tan said, even the maxim of Jobs- "Stay Hungry, Stay Foolish" -was eastern style, which tallied with both Confucian and Taoist tenets. It was really admirable for an American entrepreneur to precisely seize the core of eastern culture and then integrate it into his activities.

Hollywood movie "2012" dominated box offices across the U. S. in the first weekend of its release and then ended up with the box office revenue of $225 million across the world. In China, it even broke the box office record of 210 million RMB within the first 9 days. "I'm determined to make it the most disastrous movie", Roland Emmerich, the director of "2012", once confidently said.

The theme of "2012" is rather simple- "mankind is on the path to ruin and the whole world together deals with disasters". The movie binds the fate of all mankind together and comprises the elements of diversified cultures, thereby arousing the interest of the audience on a world basis and naturally enabling the producer to profit a lot.

Nowadays, more and more "people awakened to the awareness of humanity" and begin to instill their concerns about mankind in a variety of cultural products. They are not only aiming to maximize the market profit under the background of globalization, but also attempting to project their senses of responsibility and mission to give attention to the fate of mankind in future.

Mr. LeHousheng, a well-known strategist of China, wrote in his book named "Cultural and Military Strategies" that "in the development history of civilization, the advent of each new civilization resulted from the dramatic shift of former civilization...therefore, each new civilization symbolizes a revolution in the course of civilization development". Behind all of these revolutions, traditional politicians and religious persons have played an indispensable role.

"The World is Flat" says that the development of globalization can be divided into three stages: the first stage is dominated by nations; the second stage by multinational company and the third stage by individual.

That means, with the development of human civilization, the age of "the mass making history" will finally come. It is not to deny the function of individuals. Instead, the world in future will be an age of self-expression, with countless "selves" as the leading actors.

Traditional politicians may be fed up with the frequent change of PM in Japan, or full of complaint about the "two-person" politics of Putin and Medvedev in Russia. But in a world controlled by voters, those politicians, whether transient or everlasting, are all negligible-because the direction of a nation relies on "the mass", rather than any "political individual-al.

Throughout history, mankind has developed from ignorant, mysterious and autarchic to civilized, open and democratic, which is an unchangeable law. To some extent, the whole history of humanity has been stuffed from conflicts between rulers and the ruled.

In history, whenever the ruled invented a newer and stronger way to harness the rulers, the civilization of mankind would make a great progress. For instance, the Industrial Revolution was accompanied by modern democratic system, lending magic power through a piece of ticket to curb the insolent rulers.

The governing method most vastly used by rulers is to monopolize information. In ancient ages, books and education were the privilege of the royal and noble, while ordinary people difficult to enjoy them. At present, those autarchic governments still rely on blanking off external information to prolong their domination.

Hitler's initial success during World War Two mainly relied on the effort of Joseph Goebbels, Nazi Propaganda Minister, who steered the public by manipulating information. Following World War Two, people began to prohibit rulers to control them by monopolizing information. Under the supervision of independent media, the information gap between rulers and the ruled has been shortened step and step.

In the first decade of 21st century, the U.S., the cradle land of internet, reinforced its leading position in the field of information technology through "WikiLeaks". On July 26, 2010, WikiLeaks collaborated with New York Times, the Guardian and the Mirror to re-lease more than 92 000 secret files about U.S. troops in Afghanistan, which astonished the whole world.

"WikiLeaks: Assange and His Kingdom" published in 2011 said, "as the website of WikiLeaks built up its reputation in the past year, the world politics and diplomacy plunged in-to mess. 90 000 secret files revealed the truth how Afghan War slaughtered civilians; more than 1 000 emails from leading scientists uncovered the gigantic deceit of global warming; 250 thousand of diplomatic cables humiliated the leaders of various nations. The initiator of all these was only a person and his website."

"Truth is the first victim of war, so the public of US or the whole international community are entitled to know it," said Assange. Assange, 35 years old, founded the website of "Wikileaks" in December 2006. He believed that the transparent and uncurbed exchange of information could hold back illegal governing activities and thereby countermine the government hiding the truth to maintain itself.

The act of Assange infuriated American politicians. President Obama condemned Wikileaks as "awful and deplorable"; Secretary of State Hilary commented that it was unlawful for WikiLeaks to publish the confidential documents, which was some sort of assault to the US and the whole international community and seriously frustrated the international mutual confidence; US Attorney General Holder vowed that "the US government will carry out criminal investigation into Wikileaks according to related laws like the Espionage Act and thereby mount a prosecution."

However, those supporting the Wikileaks founder argued that "we should award him the Pulitzer Prize, rather than arresting him". Please read the following news release named "600,000 Wikileaks Followers Sign Online Petition in Support of Assange" published on December 14, 2010.

*Reports of ww. news. com. au and AFP on December 14 showed that, nearly 600,000 Wikileaks supporters throughout the world had signed an online petition ahead of a second appearance in court in London by the whistle-blowing website's founder, Julian Assange.*

*The petition, hosted on the Avaaz website, called on the court in London and other related parties to "stop the crackdown on Wikileaks and its partners immediately" and to respect "the laws of freedom of expression and freedom of the press".*

*By 4 o'clock, December 13, GMT, more than 594,000 had signed this petition and the total number of signers was expected to surpass 600,000 at last. (CRI Online)*

Meanwhile, Assange topped the list of TIME's Person of the Year 2010, raking in 280,000 votes. He was 60,000 votes over the silver medalist and even doubled the contender in the third place.

Assange was fighting "one man's war" —the war for online information freedom, which aimed to: fight against the behaviors of abusing and killing civilians; oppose those governmental tricks to blindfold the public; and combat the banks' intrigues to exploit the people.

Assange insisted that the governments and large institutions had too much under the counter, which prohibited traditional media to balance their reports. Therefore, he endeavored to change such situation. He also criticized that traditional media had been dominated by the government and incapable to deepen their investigations, so all of his effort was for freedom.

This is the historical significance of Wikileaks, which challenges traditional politicians and undermines their last advantages in the field of information. The result of this war is unforeseen presently, but the political tie between different nations is becoming more and more civilized.

It is a turning point of civilization. Wikileaks indicates that political civilization of mankind has rushed into the information age. Rulers have to restrict their political behaviors and receive the public's supervision as much as possible. As Assange argued, "this activity will change world history."

Through Wikileaks, the public can glimpse at how licentious state apparatus and intelligence sections are and how inclement international politics is, thereby dispelling the mystery and authority of rulers.

WikiLeaks resembles a fragile egg that has knocked down the stone—authority. During this process, technology played a decisive part. In the cyber age, everyone is the distributer of information. Wikileaks has drawn support from cyber citizens across the world to upload information to its own platform, creating astounding effect.

Wikileaks can survive only in the cyber age, because traditional media such as newspapers, magazines, and broadcast and TV stations are easy to be controlled by ruling power, but the internet is comparatively resistant to that. Particularly with the emergence of twitter and other micro-media, everyone becomes an independent medium, which further thwart the government's controlling attempt.

Numerous "individuals" have impelled Wikileaks to become a burst of "terrible" political power, rather than a website. Anyhow, Pandora's Box has been opened and the "post-Wikileaks" era has arrived. The future will be more attractive.

On the top of unrest of "WikiLeaks", another globally influential protest, "Occupy Wall Street", broke out in the U.S. ——

On September 17, 2011, above one thousand of protesters gathered in Manhattan, New York and attempted to occupy Wall Street. They contacted with each other through the internet, pledging to convert Wall Street into the Revolution Square in Egypt. The protesters claimed that their protests were directed to struggle against the power-for-money deal in the political circle, the bipartisan tussle as well as the social unfairness.

The most well-known slogan of protesters was "we are the 99%". They argued that 99% of Americans were deprived of their properties by financial crisis, while the remaining 1% still had it all. So 99% of American citizens could not tolerate the greed of 1%.

Within less than 3 weeks, the "Occupy Wall Street" protest has spawned similar demonstrations around the U.S.. So far, more than 200 cities have echoed by holding lasting protests.

At the same time, Europe, Asia, Oceania and South America were also spotted with related protests. "Occupy Washington", "Occupy Melbourne" and even "Occupy Taibei" were fitted to the string. On October 6, hundreds of citizens of Zhengzhou, Henan, suspended a banner saying "Great Wall Street Revolution".

During the White House news conference on October 6, U. S. President Obama made his first public comment on the "Occupy Wall Street" protest, "the protesters give how our financial system works, a voice a broader frustration". He said, "The American people understand that, no one has been following the rules, that Wall Street is an example of that".

The most seriously denounced decision that this America's first black president has made was to pump 787 billion U. S. dollars into the market to bail out banks. Many people believed at that time that they would benefit from this money, but finally failed to obtain their hope. At the same time, the Wall Street companies were still paying large amount of dividends.

In his book "The Rise and Decline of Nations" published more than 20 years ago, Mancur Olson pointed out that in a prosperous nation, some industries, namely those special interest groups, had incentives to influence the government by means of money to make it enact policies partial to them. As a result of that, these industries could earn more money and hereby exert more influence on the government.

The U. S. financial groups were actually those special interest groups which relishing their strength to enjoy favorable policies and realized over development in recent years. Following the subprime mortgage crisis, U. S. congress passed through the Dodd-Frank Act to enhance the financial supervision. But Wall Street has pressed the congress and government through its strong lobbyists, thereby weakening the Act's power.

European people were faced with similar unfairness. Jenny McIntyre, a UK protester, told Reuters journalist, "we don't want the so-called democracy on the basis of pleasing those large businesses and biasing for the financial system. It is not democracy at all".

"That's not capitalism, that's not a market economy. That's a distorted economy", Joseph Stiglitz, the professor of economics at Columbia University and a Nobel laureate, showed his support to the protesters, "and if we continue with that, we won't succeed in growing, and we won't succeed in creating a just society".

A Japanese newspaper commented that a handful of wealthy people dominated the world, leaving many others suffering the poverty. "Such situation is common for the majority of capitalist nations, thereby stimulating the mood of discontentment on a world basis."

YuanPeng, a scholar of China Institutes of Contemporary International Relations, thought that "in the 21st century, the civil societies through the world, no matter what state systems they are, will undergo another round of awakening, with the people of various countries uttering the same appeal."

Beyond all expectations, this tremendous and worldwide "Occupy Wall Street" protest seemed rather undisciplined, without exact leaders, systematic organizations, exaggerated slogans or even any definite objectives.

In the first two weeks, American media took little notice of this movement, with only 60 out of 500 newspapers (i.e. 12%) on October 5 reporting the demonstration. Many then guessed that "those consortiums have long been on good terms with Wall Street tycoons, so they shielded away the coverage".

The "organizers" were rather liberal to this- "It's difficult for the media to build a narrative because this is a leaderless protest", said Patrick Bruner.

Bruner was responsible to orchestrate the public relations effort of "Occupy Wall Street". As a recent graduate, Bruner failed to find any job and then become a volunteer after he heard about the protest. For many media, this bony 23-year-old young man had been the "official representative" of those protesters.

"Someone doesn't take our protest seriously and think that it is just a small movement and will end soon", another protester told the media, "but the only thing we can do is using the truth to make them open eyes".

Mr. Anthony Yuen, a famous commentator of Hong Kong Phoenix Satellite Television, once answered the question of an anchorman by saying that we cannot call the unrest of "Occupy Wall Street" a movement. Since a movement usually has its organizer, leader and related slogan, but all of these elements are quite ambiguous in "Occupy Wall Street".

Obviously, he was examining a new problem from the traditional view angle. As a matter of fact, during the radical revolution from industrial society to information society, many "elites" feel inadequate to fully perceive those unprecedented and ultimate changes that are about to take place.

Different from all the past ages, the advent of information era and the power from numerous "individuals" will be irresistible and carry all before them. In the information society, the "opinion leader" is the highest leader and the internet is the largest organization.

Sometimes, even a "plain civilian", not the "opinion leader", can ignite the whole world just like the WikiLeaks founder Assange, as long as his idea is eye-catching enough.

This time, the protest directed its spearhead against the financial circle. Next time, it will direct to another field. But they did not mean to overthrow anyone. "Aligning our reality with our ideals often requires the speaking of uncomfortable truths and the creative tension of non-violent protest", U. S. President Obama said.

In comparison with traditional society, the internet is more swift and effective to gather power. Everyone could be the leader and organizer. The "consciousness" of human finds the most valuable carrier, thereby forming the revolutionary strength.

On November 16, 2011, nearly 140 millionaires asked the U. S. Congress to increase their taxes for the sake of the nation.

According to British media, the entrepreneurs and business leaders wrote President Obama and congressional leaders that "Please do the fight thing for our country. Raise our taxes". The letter also noted that they benefited from a sound economy and now wanted others to do so.

The letter was signed by 138 members of "Patriotic Millionaires for Fiscal Strength". The group was created a year ago during a failed bid to persuade Congress to end tax cuts for millionaires enacted under Republican former President George W. Bush.

As the "Occupy Wall Street" movement continues, the group is now making the same request of a 12-member congressional "super committee", which is struggling to reach a bipartisan deal to cut the deficit by at least $1.2 trillion over the next decade in order to help put the nation on sound financial footing.

PhilVillers, founder of Computervision Corp, said: "Those of us who can afford it should step up. That is our message to the super committee. We hope they listen."

It is still too early to assess the impact of "Occupy Wall Street". Such a world influential civil right movement will further go forward and then manifest its significance and historical position.

However, both "WikiLeaks" and "Occupy Wall Street" play a positive part in pushing the society to be more transparent, candid and democratic. It is not accidental for them to take place simultaneously.

The U. S. is the world leader in the fields of internet development and information society, an example of western democratic system to other countries. In fact, God dotes on the U. S. very much. To some extent, "WikiLeaks" and "Occupy Wall Street" symbolize that the U. S. has stepped into the era of information civilization from former ear of industrial civilization.

If "WikiLeaks" is defined as "online", then "Occupy Wall Street" has happened "offline". The interaction between "online" and "offline" confiscates the ability of traditional politicians to cope with these movements.

As German media has said, WikiLeaks "skillfully" suppressed the most powerful government throughout the world, making the latter incapable to find any solutions except futile denouncements time and time again.

"WikiIaks" and "Occupy Wall Street" seriously lashed the image of traditional politicians to its historically lowest level. They have never been so awkwardly and humbly exposed to the public on a world basis.

Following the turbulence of "WikiLeaks" and "Occupy Wall Street", an opinion survey in South Korea suggested that approximate 90 percent of South Koreans distrust domestic politics and politicians:

*YONHAP News Agency reported on October 16 that, according to a poll of 1018 adults and 730 youths by the Office of the Minister of Special Affairs, 87.1 percent of adults and 85.6 percent of adolescents said they "do not have confidence in politics and politicians."*

*The poll of South Koreans' value systems also showed people in their 40s are most skeptical about politics; with 91.6 percent of those in that age group expressing distrust toward politicians. About 91 percent of respondents in their 30s expressed a lack of confidence while 87.6 percent of those aged 50—59 were skeptical about the political system.*

*Younger members of society in the 10—29 had relatively mild distrust, with about 85 percent of them expressing skepticism toward politics. Most senior citizens over 60 were the least skeptical, with just under 80 percent expressing a lack of confidence.*

*In terms of the country's unification policy and its relations with North Korea, younger people were less accommodative than their elder peers, the poll also showed. (Beijing Times, October 17, 2010)*

Does it mean that the public in the information society is deliberately making things difficult for traditional politicians, or those politicians are approaching the end of their fate? This is really a question that all members of the information society should seriously consider and answer.

Europeans once has taken pride in the foundation of EU, which was regarded as the model of civilization progress and also attracted the remaining world to positively simulate. However, the European debt crisis awakened the people and forced them to carefully probe into the problem hidden behind EU.

Mr. Lv Ningsi, the commenter of Hong Kong Phoenix Satellite TV, pointed out in a TV program that "the European debt crisis will instead compel the political reforms in Europe". Evidently, he attributed the crisis to those European politicians.

French Foreign Minister Main Juppe seemingly embraced this standpoint as well ~ "So many European nations use the uniform currency, but there are no uniform finance and monetary system as well as regulations about tax rate. How could we keep the Euro stable under such circumstance, said Juppe when he visited Beijing.

So Juppe repeated his French suggestion, i. e. Europe should adopt the federal system and be uniformly administrated as a country. However, the idea to found the United States of Europe has been outmoded.

Subsequent to World War Two, on May 9, 1950, Robert Schuman, the incumbent French FM, proposed to unify the whole Europe. Through decades of effort, EU has been growing steadily and the uniformed Euro is introduced as well. All of these stand for great progress towards unification.

Despite that, Europe differs from North America a lot. The U. S. originated from several English-speaking colonies, without any historical burden. In contrast, Europe comprises many nations in different languages, so there are too many appeals to be coped with.

Due to the Cold War, the political and economic unbalance and other related factors, particularly the resistance from some countries' people, or politicians frankly, the political integration of Europe has been walking with many difficulties.

Why does this political federation, regarded as the orientation of civilization evolvement and admired by the remaining world, seem so fragile and inconsistent when trying to stabilize the vitally important economic development?

"It's everyone's dream to be a prince", said Luca Sellari, Town mayor of Filettino in the hills east of Roma said. The authority of Filettino planned to declare independence to fight back Italian government's austerity measures, which included merging approximate 2 000 towns across the country.

For traditional politicians of Europe and even the whole world, what Mr. Sellari said has really hit home. Although mankind is striding into the information age and the economic and cultural globalizations are making great progress, many traditional politicians are still infatuated with power and wealth.

Ms. Zi Zhongjun, a senior expert of international issues from Chinese Academy of Social Sciences, hurled a question in his book that "many natural and manmade disasters that are cross boundaries and nations will emerge in an endless stream in future. So when can those politicians of different countries ward off the narrow and selfish thinking mode of national interests' as well as the behavior mode of power politics and gaining profit at others expense but actually at their own expense as well?"

The only permanent thing in the world is change. Politicians will finally vanish but the politics will always be there. Each historical transition has been boosted by the social elites of that era, such as new politicians and religionists.

Mankind is undergoing another historical transition, namely from industrial civilization to information, which is distinguished from any other transitions in the past. Under the background of the economic and cultural globalizations, this transition has involved all humanity.

We have to differentiate the description about social elites of our era, including new politicians and religionists, from their predecessors. Properly speaking, they are "awakened people of human consciousness", more farsighted than ordinary people and acquainted with the development law of mankind, devoting all their efforts to the whole humanity.

"Generations to come will scarcely believe that such a one as this walked the earth in flesh and blood." This is the tribute to "Mahatma Gandhi" from Einstein, the greatest physical scientist of last century. It now appears that Mahatma Gandhi has been the greatest "awakened figure" across the world.

"The reason why Gandhi still receives so much respect until now is that he once did everything for the whole humanity, rather than for only a country or nation", an American politician said so.

Among all of those world giants, Gandhi was particularly special as he not only absorbed both religious and political elements but also developed his thought through the furious collision between Eastern traditional culture and Western modern thought. "I work hard to see God through my service to humanity, because I know that God is in the heart of every human being, rather than in heaven or under the ground", Gandhi said.

Even if many countries have their own "Founding Father", few of them have endeavored to advocate the "nonviolent" revolution like Gandhi. More importantly, Gandhi put it into practice. His "nonviolence" theory and practice not only boosted the National Independent Movement, but also influenced African-American Civil Rights Movement of the U.S..

Martin Luther King once said, "as I delved deeper into the philosophy of Gandhi, my skepticism concerning the power of love gradually diminished, and I came to see for the first time that the Christian doctrine of love, operating through the Gandhian method of nonviolence, is one of the most potent weapons available to an oppressed people in their struggle for freedom"

When visiting India on october 16, 2011, U.S. President Obama said, "One of the things I draw from Gandhi is that you have to be persistent on your journey, you just have to keep going on and never say die. Gandhi, Sir Martin Luther King, and Abraham Lincoln are people we are constantly reading and studying about. I'm often frustrated by how far I fall short of their example".

Obama's "frustration" deserves our encouragement. He reminds us that despite the star-light of "awakened people of human consciousness" is still rather faint, one day it will certainly lighten all the sky.

In addition to the preeminent foresight of traditional politicians, those "awakened people of human consciousness" also have strong senses of justice and shame. For instance, when the "Occupy Wall Street" movement was rolling in immense surges, William Hague, British Foreign Minister, said he was "sympathized" with protesters. When the protest extended to Los Angeles, the largest western city of America, its municipal government passed through a resolution about supporting the "Occupy Los Angeles" movement...

Leung Man-Tao, the commentator of Hong Kong Phoenix Satellite TV, mocked traditional politicians by saying that, "The king in the traditional story didn't know he was naked. However, both he and we know that he is naked now, but he still walks out, wandering about on the street. We have a panoramic view about that but pretend that he is dressed".

The sense of shame forces those "awakened people of human consciousness" to devote all the public power to creating and maintaining the transparent, candid and democratic social environment, positively enhancing the development and integration of humanity. They often felt upset for their insufficient ability and ashamed for their occasional selfish thought.

As we have mentioned above, because of different historical, political, economic and cultural development among various countries, mankind still cannot step into the democratic society simultaneously. To be worse, there are even unthinkable gap between "the advanced" and "the backward".

However, under the sunshine of the information society, we can very easily find that the seeds those "awakened people of human consciousness" have scattered, no matter in fertile soil or in barren field, will surely be able to shoot up and vigorously grow up.

Since the age of Enlightenment in Europe, some politicians and scholars who surpass the narrow boundaries of country and nation and those who wander around the world have called themselves as "world citizens".

In the preface of "Speeches and Writings by Deng Xiaoping", published by Pergamon Press Ltd, Deng Xiaoping, Chief Designer of China' Reform and Opening up, soulfully said, "As one of the Chinese people, I'm honored to become one of the world citizen".

Despite that, during the age of national countries, especially in the Cold war, when the world was fully bestrewed with barriers, the concept of "world citizen" was unreachable for the majority of the people in the earth. But now, great changes have taken place, as mankind has stepped into the age of globalization and the revolution of information technology has turned the world into a "global village".

To some extent, everybody has turned into the "world citizen". They may not go abroad, but still can feel the external influence and also can exert impact on citizens in other countries, let alone on those who frequently come and go between different countries.

The history of human development indicates that the political power leading to regional barriers and religious power results in spiritual estrangement, only tourism is capable to congregate together the people from different races, religions and cultures, hereby impelling them to share the fruits of human civilization.

In ancient times, the conquerors usually imposed their cultures and beliefs on those occupied territories and forced the vanquished to accept them. But nowadays, such kind of phenomenon is no longer in existence.

In 2011, with the help of NATO's fierce bombing campaign, Libyan opposition forces successfully overthrew the dictatorial regime of Qaddafi after the battles lasting for 8 months. After taking over the country, the "National Transitional Council" pledged that Libya will uphold the Islamic law, which means that the polygamy may prevail in new Libya.

Such decision, absolutely running counter to the democratic society, astonished those who had firmly and positively supported the "democratic fight" in Libya. It proves that a battle cannot change the bred-in-the-bone culture. People could only hope that new Libya will carry on more communication with the external world.

On April 1, 2014, the U. S. "Fortune" bi-weekly website published a report titled "Chinese tourists promote American enterprise development". The journalist Steve Hargreaves wrote in the news as follows:

On October 21, 2011, Former Cuban President Fidel Castro, who was at his 85 and had grappled with America and the rest of Western world for half century, said in his official website that, "In a nuclear war the 'collateral damage' would be the life of all humanity. Let us have the courage to proclaim that whether nuclear or conventional weapons, everything that is used to make war must disappear!"

Castro's speech is from the deep bottom of his heart. With the development of human civilization, the globalization of economics has already come into being, and cultural integrity is on the way. Those political approaches using weapons to invade other country and eliminate foreign culture will not exist anymore. Any politicians have no rights to use nuclear weapons with any purpose. Only a thought of it can be regarded as against humanism.

*Last year, thousands of Chinese tourists flock to the Yellowstone National Park to watch mountain views, buffalo and the Old Faithful.*

*After that, at least 1,600 people travel 200 miles to the east, reach to the Euchre Ross ranch where to enjoy burgers, baked beans and biscuits. After lunch, they enjoyed a 14-year-old Katie William's performance of riding.*

*The rancher's owner Judy Blair said: "Her performances make the Chinese crazy, all the political problems between the two countries have vanished."*

We prey for the Eternal universal Prophecy of the Isaiah, who said 2,500 years ago in Jerusalem that a day will come when people shall leave their swords into plowshares, and their spears into pruning hooks. Nation will not lift up sword against nation; neither shall they learn war any more.

(3) The foundation of forming "World Government" is increasingly consolidated

The establishment of "world government" is not a new political subject. Early in the ancient Greek and Rome period, the idea of "world government" was brought to the round table of discussion. And the ancient Greece and Roman foretold that for the realization of permanent peace, one day human would be governed by only one common political authority.

The book *De Jure Belli ac Pacis* written by the Dutch jurist Hugo Grotius was deemed as the origin of modern international law.

The concept "Federation" won the respectable support in the end of 18th century. The more highlighted event in this period was that the first democratic federation in the world – U.S.A. was born in 1788.

All along the history, many European philosophers were influenced by the relevant thought and created the similar theory, especially the philosopher Immanuel Kant, who wrote the essay "Perpetual Peace" in 1795, where he expounded the three basic conditions for human to permanently eradicate the threat of war in the future:

- The civil constitution of every state should be republican.
- The law of nations shall be founded on a federation of free nations.
- The law of world citizenship shall be limited to conditions of universal hospitality.

For instance, people were allowed to visit other countries, but not permitted to stay without invitation.

In 1811, German philosopher Carl Christian Friedrich Krause wrote an essay "The Archetype of Humanity", where he proposed to establish the union of five continents: Europe, Asia, Africa, America and Oceania, and incorporate to a world republic.

By employing the American experience, in 1948 and 1967, Switzerland and Canada also respectively established their first multinational coalition, united all nationalities of different races, cultures and languages under a common government.

As the influence of the idea "world government" prevailed increasingly, many international organizations were born subject to such a contribution. For instance, International Committee of the Red Cross was founded in 1863, International Telecommunication Union founded in 1865, and Universal Postal Union founded in 1874.

After human entered into 20th century, due to the growing business of international trade, the interdependence relationship between countries went further, by which accelerated the formation of international organizations. According to relevant data, before the outburst of "World War I" in 1914, there were around 450 global or regional organizations.

Meanwhile, as driven by the development of international organizations, the research on international law also had a great progress. In 1873, Belgium Jurist Gustave Rolin – Jaequemyns established the first research institute of international law in the world, he led and drafted for the specific international law.

The first embryonic world parliament, called the Inter – Parliamentary Union, was organized in 1886 by Cremer and Passy, composed of legislators from many countries. In 1904 the Union formally proposed "an international congress which should meet periodically to discuss international questions".

From time immemorial, politicians were always the carriers and pursuers of "world government". The famous cases such as Alexander the Great and his empire, Rome Empire and Mongolia Empire as well as Britain Empire. Referring to the Britain Empire, at the zenith of his millennium the country occupied one fourth of world area and close to one third of world population, famed as "Never Sunset Empire". This was a period the world at the closest to a common political authority.

Bahá'u'lláh created Bahaism between 1852 and 1892, and upheld the important principle of establishing a global federation.

Bahá'u'lláh on the basis of common share and common business for global people, conceived a suite of new social system, including a world legislature, an international court and an international administrative institution to enforce the decision of legislative and judicial institutions. His criteria also included the world's universal weights and measures, common currency, and employed one kind of international paralanguage for communication.

Unfortunately, an integral world government built by attempting to rely on the powder of politics and religions did not exist at all time. In the early fifty years of last century, the attempt that tried to establish a global institution for settlement of international dispute also ended up with failure.

What upset the people in the world was the "Hague Convention" in 1899 and 1907 and the "League of Nations" in 1919 and 1938 failed to prevent the two World Wars from happening. Later the "Cold War" also proved that under the circumstance of the human's comprehensive development was immature and core value was different, to pursue a united "world government" was nothing else but like strange bedfellows to all nations.

However, even experienced so much frustration and failure over times, the human pace to establish "world government" never stopped. On the contrary, from near the end of "World War II" to 1950, this period was the golden time for "World Federalism Movement"

In 1943 the first publication of the book "One World" written by Wendell Willkie was sold more than two million copies. Another book "The Anatomy of Peace", its author was Emery Reeves, due to the book advocated the opinion of replacing the UN by "World Federal Government", the book rapidly became the "Bible" in the eyes of world federalist.

In 1947, a meeting was held in Montreux, Switzerland, which formed a global federation called the World Federalist Movement, also was an influential international organization. By 1950, the organization declared there were 56 member groups in 22 countries, around 156,000 members.

In 1948, the founder of the organization Garry Davis addressed a speech in the UN General Assembly, called for building a "world government", but he was ended up with driving away from the assembly by guards. Later, Mr. Davis gave up his American citizenship and started to register for the world citizenship, within less than two years there were more than 750,000 people also registered for the world citizenship.

On September 4, 1953, in the city hall of Ellsworth, Maine, United State, Davis declared the "world government" was based on three "world laws", namely same god, same world and same human, for which he established "United World Administration Bureau", its primary task was to design and release the world passport. It has been reported since now there are more than 800,000 copies of such kind of passport released.

But the thought and method of Mr. Davis was clearly lacked of successive momentum. "Same god" was an "arbitrary" policy, which did not accord with the multiple diversification trend of the world, and did not release from the stereotyped pigeonhole of religion for the "consolidation" of the world, further it was contradicted to the human civilization, because freedom of belief was the progressive identifier of human civilization.

The sociologist of Trinity University in Connecticut, James Hughes was a supporter of global government, he agreed on that keeping in conformance with the time and trend was an inevitable choice. "

Hughes said: "in this century there should be new economic, cultural and communicative power to serve the political integration, and the disastrous vital threat might lead to the establishment of global government system became the rigid demand", what he called "disastrous threat" was specific to the threat to human caused by global climate change, terrorism, and new technology.

On the possible and realizable concept of the political entity – world government, people generally believed that such a political entity was to interpret and conduct the international law, and the existing nations should gradually alleviate and release a certain extent of authority. This practice certainly should be in synchronic pace with the enhancement of the previously referred "human consciousness".

What exhilarating the people was, no matter sovereign nations such as America, Russia, China and other global political forces whether agreed or not, the wheel of history was always rolling forward unceasingly. For instance, the arising of WTO deprived a part of the economic power from the sovereign nations in economic field.

As a matter of fact, "world government" would add a new administrative level upon the existing national sovereignty, or would provide the coordination to different nations, which independent nations were unable to provide. The upcoming of information society and realization of global town offered the necessity and possibility of arising of "world government".

Today people increasingly regard some international institutions such as International Criminal Court, United Nations, International Monetary Fund and other super – national and super – continental unions, such as Organization of American States, European Union, African Union, Union of South American Nations, Association of Southeast Asian Nations etc. as the embryonic world government systems.

Comparing with the early phase, the contribution from these international organizations or institutions in aspects such as promotion of human integration and coordination of international affairs is much more significant than ever before. This does not mean the modern people are more intellectual than the past people, but a sheer result from the development of global politics, economy, technology and culture.

In China there is an old saying: "An unripe melon is not sweet if picked to eat", another corresponding saying is "A channel would be formed naturally when water arrives." At present, the existence of various kinds of organizations in the world is only the external factor for promotion of human integration, whereas the comprehensive progress of human civilization is really the fundamental internal factor based on which various organizations or "world government" realizes their value.

Especially human has entered into information society, with the globalization of economy and culture, the roaring and rushing trend of human integration and cultural sharing will inevitably facilitate the consolidation of various political entities. Exactly as Hughes pointed out, no matter whether the hostile forces existed or not, the history gearing would always direct us to the general orientation of "global government".

As to various international organizations, when human experiences the third leap in the development of tourist activity, "world government" is no longer a question about to arise or not, but a question about who would grab the chance to direct the establishment of "world government", who would be the "initiator": United Nations, European Union, Group of seven or other international organizations?

The Second World War suffered 50,000,000 casualties, and most of the victims were innocents. As the war closed to the end, many people of lofty ideals called for the establishment of the international institution that could permanently prevent conflicts, which led to the founding of United Nations in 1945, and granting of Universal Declaration of Human Rights in 1948.

United Nations is a comprehensive international organization composed of sovereign nations, by 2012, there has been 193 member nations. In the "Cold War" period, United Nations played the role irreplaceable for safeguarding the world security, promoting the human peace and other aspects. At present, UN still carries a grave weight in international politics and many other fields.

Some prominent people, such as Einstein, Churchill, Roosevelt and Gandhi etc., called for all national governments to go further, and gradually form the "world government" that could effectively manage the world. However, their idea of "world government" was whether to leave aside the existing UN and build a new one, or to retool the UN, it was just remaining unknown.

By viewing the current situation, UN indeed faces various challenges from all sides. After the end of "Cold War", UN has still persisted in the way of traditional fashion, then finds out the road has been reduced narrower. It is evidenced by many nations refuse or delay to pay membership fees. In October 18, 2013, Saudi Arabic refused to be the nonpermanent member of UN Security Council, which unveiled the crisis of UN in the new era.

The Ministry of Foreign Affairs of Saudi Arabic declared, in light of last decades UN

Security Council neither did effectively develop the peace for Middle East, nor did end the civil strife of Syria, thus the country declined the nomination. The declaration came up with a question on the Security Council's "ability, work style and mechanism".

The BBC's UN correspondent said, the diplomatists were astonished and confused by the unprecedented decision Saudi Arabic made. The French UN permanent representative A Laude said to AFP correspondents, France believed Saudi Arabic could make a positive contribution to Security Council, and understood his dissatisfaction.

In view of the fact that UN was becoming loosely organized and lacked of authority, though many UN elites were aware of the urgency of transformation of UN, however, under a complicated international situation, they seemed to have no idea about the direction of development and where to set forth.

In December, 2012, the writer hereof was invited by the UN Correspondents Association to attend the annual award ceremony in New York. At the meeting the association presented my work and written speech to five hundred guests including the UN Secretary General, the content of which was advocating the UN to issue "UN Tourism Passport", it Struck a responsive chord in hearts of many participants.

On the next day, the relevant sector of UN invited the writer hereof to make a special presentation on the subject of "UN Tourism Passport" for part of UN officials. In the speech I pointed out, after the end of "Cold War", UN should transit from the traditional track of settling conflicts and avoiding the war gradually to the new track of promoting the human integration and civilization sharing; and also should transit from the traditional track of serving nations and groups gradually to the new track of serving the global citizens.

The writer hereof thinks that the issuance of "UN Tourism Passport" is one of the most important symbols for such transition. Because the globalization of human economy has already been achieved and the globalization of culture also has been started. The promotion of "UN Tourism Passport" would greatly facilitate the development of human integration and progress, and stimulate and accelerate the upcoming of the third leap of human tourist activities!

Beyond questions, "world government" is composed of "world citizens". The "citizenship" of a citizen is subject to the domain of political sovereignty of a country. Similar to WTO takes over part of the economic sovereignty of all nations, presently UN is the best organization to take over part of the political authority of sovereign nations.

As a matter of fact, the Schengen passport being implemented by European nations to some extent is resembled to the "Mini-type UN Tourist Passport". Though comparing with

European Union, to issue "UN Tourism Passport" is more difficult, as long as all nations in the world coordinate to unify their understanding, and step by step to implement such a strategy by starting from pyramid top to lower, there should be no difficulty in technical operation.

Therefore, if UN considers the current situation and utilizes the unique political advantages, to issue the "UN Tourism Passport", it could not only increase the centripetal force from world citizens to UN, but also offer UN the chips of directing the establishment of "world government" in the future.

The more significant thing is that on the day when all of citizens in the world implement the "UN Tourism Passport", then on this earth where we inhabit for hundreds of thousands of years, would any war happen again? Is such kind of thought and practice not inosculated to the principle at the very beginning of the founding of UN?!

Comparing with EU, the organization of UN is with huger size, lower efficiency and rampant corruption, which is always denounced by people. Without a huge reformation, all these shortages would certainly play critical obstacles to the future ambition of directing the establishment of "world government". Instead, with rich experience, high efficiency management and disinterested organization, EU might win the consensus of world citizens in the future.

Moreover, UN has a vital shortage, it is about in a certain long period of time America still remains the world's "first big country" but who increasingly tends to ignore the authority of UN. This depends on UN whether is able to make a graceful turnaround in front of the trend of global management democratization, and hold the fate in his own hand firmly!

In 2012, Nobel Peace Prize was first time awarded to EU, it was a prize for the achievement of the road he walked through, and more likely indicated his vigorous development prospect. Though there are still various kinds of disadvantages inside EU, through the baptism of two World Wars, in front of people in the world, European people have taken the lead and developed a peace pathway for settlement of differences, avoidance of war, sharing of economic and cultural prosperity, which play a typical sample for other regions in the world.

Of course, along with the progress of human history, the rapid arising of other international organization is not really impossible. Especially when human has entered into information society, the network itself is the hugest organization. When under the impact of democratic tidal wave, politicians gradually become one kind of symbol and decorative object, the forming of "world government" might be developed in an alternative new path. It is not necessary a story of Arabian Nights!

Human experience and lessons have proven that the establishment of an organic unified "world government" should not be separated from the forming of new civilization under globalization background. Chinese scholar Peiyong wrote in "Consolidation of Civilization":

Open a New Era of Culture of Earth Mr. Pei Yong said that it was necessary to establish a new type of global culture and a new world and to rear a new culture more and make it strike root in the hearts of the people on a global scale. The new culture surely is an advanced culture which can represent the development of the world in the future. This new culture is neither the wholesale Westernization nor the wholesale Easternization. Because none civilizations of the world is the purely advanced culture which can adapt to the development of the future world completely. The new culture must be a new type culture combining Eastern and Western civilization. In the future society with the new culture, the postmodernization is its main feature. This society needs an ecological, equal and harmonious culture which will incorporate things of diverse nature and the strong points of various civilizations. It is the important basis to establish the global civilization, and it is the advanced culture in the world to come. The world economic integration must keep pace with the cultural integration. The communication and mixture are quiet and imperceptible.

Tourism is an absolute way to achieve the goal.

Tourism integrates the world and humans share civilizations!

附录一：
# Appendix Ⅰ:

## 驻华大使解读"旅游整合世界"
## Comment on "Tourism Integrates the World" by China-based Ambassadors

首先我认为旅游业是一个巨大的产业，旅游可以为人们带来财富，同时，旅游是人们增进了解的另一种方式，它拉近了人与人之间的距离，它使人们可以了解并熟悉不同的文化和生活习惯。

——阿富汗驻中国大使　艾克利·阿赫曼·哈基米

First, I think tourism is a huge industry. It can create treasures for people. Meanwhile it is also a mode to promote understanding between people of all countries. It makes people more close and people can know and be familiar with other different cultures, habits and customs.

— Ambassador of Afghanistan: Mr. Eklil Ahmad Hakimi

"我完全同意您的观点，我认为旅游是一座桥梁，它让不同国籍、不同民族的人相互了解对方的文化和风俗习惯，同时也增进了友谊。随着科技的进步、全球运输业的高速发展，世界变得越来越小，这也使得旅游迅速成为一种产业，人们对自己国家以外的地方有了更多的了解和体验。"

——阿尔及利亚驻中国大使　贾迈勒·爱丁·格林

I completely agree with you. I think tourism is a bridge which to let people with various nationalities and races to have a deep understand on both sides' cultures and customs, as well as to promote friendship between each other. On the other hand, due to the progressing of science and technology, and especially in terms of transportation, the world tend to be smaller and smaller, this, no doubt, also to make tourism becoming a fast growing industry, people now have more understand and experience to the outside world beyond their hometowns.

— Ambassador of Algeria: Mr. Djamel Eddine Grine

旅游发展到今天，可以很好地将各种文化整合到一起。人们可以通过旅游了解各国文化。两千年前，我们的古兰经就教导我们到世界各国去看一看，先知默罕默德曾经传授给我们人生的七个要素：友谊、知识、快乐、兴趣、感知、爱和学习，旅游可以把这七条综合到一起。

——阿曼驻中国大使　阿卜杜拉·扎希尔·侯斯尼

Tourism can unify the variety of cultures together better through a long-time development. People can understand different cultures of various countries through traveling activities. Before 2000 years ago, the Koran already gave guidance to us to go to different countries for understanding them, and the prophet — Muhammad once taught us the seven essential factors of life: friendship, knowledge, happiness, interest, perception, love and study. Tourism can combine the factors together.

— Ambassador of Oman: Mr. Abdullah Zaher Al Hussni

我非常认同"旅游整合世界"的观点。旅游真的是不同国家之间相互了解、相互合作的途径。只有在相互知晓的基础上，世界才能共享文明。跟我一样，许多爱尔兰人开始了解中国都是从书本上，那时只是知道了中国传统的一面。经过这几年在中国的工作经历，我慢慢接触到中国的各个层面，多视角地了解到中国，看到了书本外的中国。所以说旅游是接触与了解的最佳方式。

——爱尔兰驻中国大使　戴克澜

I am all for the standpoint of "Tourism integrates the world". Tourism is really a fine channel for different countries to understand and co-operate with each other. The whole world can enjoy civilization only the people of various countries understand each other well. Just like me, many Irish people know China from books. At that time, I just know the traditional aspect of China. Through the working experiences in China in the recent years, I slowly get in touch with the variety of fields of China. Thus I can understand China in various angles and see a China outside books. So I think tourism is the best way to communicate and understand.

— Ambassador of Ireland: Mr. Declan Kelleher

　　我完全赞同您的观点。我认为旅游在20世纪已经形成了一种风潮，人与人之间需要相互理解。在古代，人们都生活在不同的大陆上，互相根本就不知道，后来旅行者来了，马可波罗到了中国，郑和到了阿拉伯世界，哥伦布发现了美洲大陆，旅游就是这么重要，推动人与人之间的交往，消除误解，促进民族间文化的交往。旅游不仅仅是赚钱的工具，也是传递人类文明的法宝。

——埃及驻中国大使　马哈茂德·阿拉姆

　　I'm full agree with you. I think tourism already became a kind of agitation in the last century, and we need understand each other. In the ancient times, people lived in the different continents, and they did not know each other completely. Then tourists arrived. Marco Polo traveled in China, Zheng He went to the Arabian countries and Columbus found American continent. Tourism is so important, it can promote the contacts between different people, clear up the misunderstanding and promote the communication between civilizations of every nations. Tourism is not a implement for earning money, but also a magic weapon for transmitting human being's civilization.

— Ambassador of Egypt: Mr. Mahmoud Allam

　　奥地利是欧洲的一个古老国家，而中国是一个拥有数千年文明的古国，所以我认为一个欧洲国家和一个亚洲国家的人民，通过旅游这个路子向对方展示着文化的魅力，加强了沟通交流，扩展了人们的视野，所以我认为旅游是人类整合文明差异性和多样性的最好渠道。

——奥地利驻中国大使　史伟

　　Austria is an old country in Europe, while China is a country with thousands of years civilization. So I think for a European country and an Asian country, both sides can show its cultural charm by tourism in terms of enhance communication, enlarge people's horizon. So in this sense, tourism is the best channel that conform the diversity and variety of human civilizations.

— Ambassador of Austria: Mr. Hans Dietmar Schweisgut

我完全赞同您的观点。整个世界就是一个美丽的地方。旅行是最好的教育。它是人与人之间增进友谊、相互了解的最好的方式。

——巴基斯坦驻中国大使　萨尔曼·巴希尔

I approve of your proposition. The whole world is a beautiful scenery. Tourism is the best educational way. It is also the best way to promote the friendship between the different people and let them understand each other more.

— Ambassador of Pakistan：Mr. Salman Bashir

我非常赞同您的观点，巴勒斯坦人到中国来，品尝中国的美食，了解中国的文化，分享中国五千年文明。世界各国游客到巴勒斯坦，体验神圣的宗教氛围，这都是通过旅游才能实现的。

——巴勒斯坦驻中国大使　迪亚布·鲁赫

I fully agree with your standpoint. Palestinian comes to China to taste Chinese delicacies, understand Chinese culture and share Chinese civilization which has a history of 5000 years. Tourists from various places of the world go to Palestine to experience the sacred religious atmosphere. All of said above can be carried out only through tourism.

— Ambassador of Palestine：Mr. Diab N M Allouh

旅游和文明是相互支配的，人们去旅游是为了感受对方的文化，出去旅游不单是为了个人的享乐，而是了解不一样的文明和文化，了解人类社会的多元性，这会促进不同民族间的交流和融合。我完全认同您的观点。

——巴西驻中国大使　路易斯·奥古斯托·德卡斯特罗·内维斯

Tourism and civilization are two things which can govern each other. People go to travel for feeling different cultures. Tourism is not only for enjoyment, but also for understanding different civilizations, cultures and diversification of the human being's society. It promotes a communication and mixture of different nations. I fully approve of your standpoint.

— Ambassador of Brazil：Mr. Luiz Augusto de Castro Neves

附录一：驻华大使解读"旅游整合世界"

　　　　　　　　　我完全赞同您的观点。旅游可以让你知道原来很陌生的东西。如果一个人从来没来过中国，他们就不会了解真正的中国是什么样，比如在我们国家和其他一些西方国家有关中国的不正确的传闻，可能让人对中国有一些误解，这些误解只要亲自来中国看一下就会不攻自破。旅游让了解更深入更全面。

——比利时驻中国大使　裴伯宁

　　I fully endorse your standpoint. People can know more things that are strange to them originally. For example, if a person has never been China, he will never know what is the real China. In our country and other Western countries, people may have some misunderstanding to China due to some wrong hearsay. But such misunderstanding will be collapsed of itself if they come to and understand China personally. People will know things more deeply and completely through tourism.

— Ambassador of Belgium: Mr. Bernard Pierre

　　　　　　　　这个口号非常好。我认为旅游能开阔人们的心胸，能够了解不同的民族和文化，它还可以使人不用自己的标准衡量别人，比如人们生活在不同的地方吃着不同的食物，冰岛人吃鲸鱼肉，因为这是冰岛人的传统，绝对不会造成鲸鱼数量的减少和灭绝，就像有些人不吃猪肉一样。也许你可以这么说，旅游是全球化最好的一面。

——冰岛驻中国大使　埃德尔·古纳松

　　The motto of your newspaper is very good. I think that tourism can broaden people's outlook and let them know more different nations as well as their cultures. It also can help people to judge others fairly. Such as the people, who live in the different places, eat different food. The Icelander like to eat the flesh of whale because it is the tradition of the Icelander. It will absolutely not reduce the member of or destroy the whale, just like some people have never eaten the flesh of the pork. Maybe you can say that the tourism is the best aspect in globalization.

— Ambassador of Iceland: Mr. Eidur Gudnason

　　　　　　　　我完全赞同您的观点。旅游可以促进文明之间的交流，这是很自然的。我认为旅游的作用是双重的，一方面它可以促进文化间的交往，另一方面它还可以启发其他领域的合作，比如经济和科技的合作，我们到别的国家去的时候，我们往往看到他们在经济上和科学上所取得的成就,对我们也有一定的启发作用,好的经验我们可以借鉴。

——波兰驻中国大使 克日什托夫·舒姆斯基

Tourism serves as a double purpose. On one hand, it can promote cultural exchanges between countries, and on the other, it can also invite co-operations in many other fields, such as economy, science and technology. When we visit other countries, we usually pay much attention to their achievements made in their economy, science and technology. We would be inspired on this and can draw some successful experiences for reference.

— Ambassador of Poland: Mr. Krzysztof Szumski

我非常同意你们提出的口号。如果你去博茨瓦纳旅游,你看到的不仅是风光,还会了解当地人民的生活,了解他们的文化。旅游是传递文化的过程。旅游产业不仅是赚钱的产业,更重要的是它可以促进国与国之间文化的交往,促进不同人群的共同发展。

——博茨瓦纳驻中国大使 娜奥米·埃伦·马金达

I fully endorse the motto you mentioned. If you travel to Botswana, you will not only see the sights of our country, but also understand the life of local people and their culture. Travel is a process to disseminate the culture. Tourism industry is not only a industry for making money, its particularly function is promoting the cultural communication between different countries and the common development of different people.

— Ambassador of Botswana: Mrs. Naomi E. Majinda

我完全赞同您的观点。安徒生曾经说过:生活就是为了旅行。我想大多数中国人也同意这个说法。如果你的人生很完美,你应该去过很多地方,旅行使你思路开阔,它使你对你的国家在世界上处于一个什么状况,有一个很好的了解。旅游使人们了解不同文化的价值。200年前安徒生就有这样的思想,很了不起。

——丹麦驻中国大使 米磊

I'm full agree with you. Hans Christian Andersen (1805—1875) once said that living is just for tourism. I think most Chinese would agree to this. If your life is perfect, you should have been to many places. Tourism can give you a broad mind and let you know what position your country is having in the world. People will then understand the value of different kinds of culture.

— Ambassador of Denmark: Mr. Laurids Mikaelsen

# 附录一：驻华大使解读"旅游整合世界"

交通和通讯的发展，为越来越多的人在世界范围内旅游提供了可能，如今，在德国，接待来自中国和印度的游客便是一件新鲜的事情，这无疑又为德国人民扩展了新的视野，增加了新的体验，并且越来越成为促进经济等方面发展的重要因素。

——德国驻中国大使　史丹泽

Along with the development of transportation and communication, more people can make a journey world-wide. Nowadays, it is a new experience to receive Chinese and Indian travelers in Germany. Meanwhile, it broadens German's vision Tourism is becoming an important factor to promote development of economy and other aspects of a country.

— Ambassador of Germany: Mr. Volker Stanzel

毫无疑问，在到其他国家旅行的过程中，旅游者会碰到一些过去不熟悉的文化和传统。同样，当地的居民也常常是根据旅游者的言行来评价这些旅游者所代表的国家。

——俄罗斯驻中国大使　拉佐夫

Undoubtfully, in the course of oversea travelling, travelers will encounter some different customs and traditions that they used to be unfamiliar with. In the same way, the local residents will also judge them from their languages and behaviors where the travelers are from.

— Ambassador of Russian: Mr. Razov

旅游可以从中学到很多东西，旅游带来巨大精神享受，人们都到一个城市去，那个城市就会变成一座国际化的城市。来自世界各地、各种肤色的人，聚集在一起就成为了朋友。

——厄瓜多尔驻中国大使　马里奥·耶佩斯

We can learn many things through tourism, and tourism gives us a huge spiritual enjoyment. If different people come to a city, the city will become an international metropolis. People from different lands and different colours get together and become friends.

— Ambassador of Ecuador: Mr. Rodrigo Yepez Enriquez

有的人说大众的旅游会让全世界变成一个样子，一些国家传统的东西得不到保留，对当地的文化和民俗造成破坏；有的人说旅游会推动人与人之间的交往，消除误解，促进民族间文化的交往。我个人还是赞同后一种观点，也是您的观点。

——芬兰驻中国大使  郭安祺

Some people said that the popular traveling activity would make the whole world become same completely, the traditional things of some countries could not be kept and the local culture and folkways also would be destroyed. Other people said that the tourism would promote the communication between people, clear up the misunderstanding and promote the exchange of the national cultures. I agree with the second viewpoint, it is just your viewpoint.

— Ambassador of Finland: Mr. Antti Kuosmanen

我完全赞同您的观点，用这一理论可以建立一个全新的世界。现在全世界的经济已经全球化了，而文化的全球化是更高层次的东西，旅游会更加增进人与人之间的相互了解，使地球更加和平，也会促进不同民族的文化交流，将它们整合得更好。

——佛得角驻中国大使  儒利奥·德莫赖斯

I fully agree with your standpoint. People can build a new world with your principle. The economy of the whole world already stepped into a stage of globalization, and the globalization of the culture is what on a higher spiritual levels. Tourism can promote understanding between people, and make the earth become more peaceful. It also will promote a cultural communication between different nations and unify different cultures of the world better.

— Ambassador of Cape Verde: Mr. Julio Cesar Freire De Morais

我非常赞同您的观点。旅游是很健康、干净的。经济全球化会造成很多矛盾。旅游是人类全球化最好的一面。旅游可以代表人类的性格，为了保持世界和平，旅游应该得到大力推动。

——古巴驻中国大使  阿尔韦托·罗得里格斯·阿鲁菲

I fully agree with your viewpoint. The tourism is a kind of healthy and clean activity. The globalization of economy will cause many contradictions, but the tourism is the best aspect in human being's globalization. The tourism can representative the features of human. For keeping the peace of the world, the tourism should be promoted energetically.

— Ambassador of Cuba: Mr. Alberto R. Arufe

是的，旅游对于了解和理解其他民族的文化、语言、传统和生活方式的意义重大。我赞同您的观点。

——吉布提驻中国大使　穆萨·布·奥多瓦

Yes, tourism has an important significance on understanding the cultures, languages, traditions and life-ways of other nations. I am approval of your standpoint.

— Ambassador of Djibouti: Mr. Moussa Bouh Odowa

旅游可以给不同国家和民族的人民提供一个相互交流的机会，只有这样他们才能更好地了解对方，这也为实现全世界的永久和平创造了条件。

——加蓬驻中国大使　艾玛努艾尔·姆巴·阿洛

Tourism offers an opportunity for people of different countries and nations to communicate each other, and makes them understand each other more. It also creates a condition for realizing a perpetual peace of the whole world.

— Ambassador of Gabon: Mr. Emmanuel MBA ALLO

您说得太棒了。许多津巴布韦人来中国之前，他们从电视里看到西方媒体对中国的报道，中国人还在用水牛耕地，用黄牛拉车。当他们到达中国后，发现他们在伦敦买的衬衫是中国制造，而且更便宜。电脑产品也是如此，他们在中国也能买到高质量的电脑。这都要归功于旅游。

——津巴布韦驻中国大使　K. H. 穆茨万格瓦

You are very good. Before coming to China, many Zimbabwean have seen news reports about China on TV from the Western media, and they thought that the Chinese are still plowing the lands by buffalo and pulling the carts by cattle. When they arrived in China, however, they found that the shirts which they bought in London were made in China and the prices here are much cheaper. The same thing is true on computer products. They even knew that they can buy a high-quality computer in China, too. It is a contribution of tourism.

— Ambassador of Zimbabwe: Mr. Christopher H. Mutsvangwa

旅游作为行业发展的优先和目标,就是为人类创造价值;作为联系和融合不同民族的活动,旅游对于开阔人的胸怀和增进相互的理解做出了积极的贡献。因此,旅游也就成为展示人类文明和视界链接的一个因素。在此,我愿引用中国这样一句话:读万卷书,行万里路。

——科特迪瓦驻中国大使 科南·克拉莫

The aim of developing tourism industry is to create value for human being. As a kind of action to link and mix different nations of the world, tourism makes a positive contribution on broadening people's vision and promoting understanding. So tourism already becomes a factor to link human being's civilization with historic and beautiful outlooks. Here, I just want to quote an old Chinese saying: Read extensively and travel widely.

— Ambassador of Cote divoire: Mr. Konan Kramo

一个中国旅游者到克罗地亚去,他不仅可以度过愉悦时光,而且可以了解克罗地亚的历史、文化。通过这种方式,加强了我们两国之间的友好合作关系,使得越来越多的中国人对克罗地亚感兴趣。旅游对加强两国的经济关系也很重要。

——克罗地亚驻中国大使 博里斯·韦利奇

A Chinese traveler comes to Croatia, he not only can spend a happy holiday, but also will understand the history and culture of Croatia. Tourism strengthens the friendly relations and co-operations between our two countries. It makes more Chinese people become interested in Croatia. Besides, tourism is also important in strengthening the economic relations between the two countries.

— Ambassador of Croatia: Mr. Boris Velic

我非常赞同您的观点。莱索托和中国的旅游交往越密切就越能推动双方的文化交流,只有越来越多的中国人到莱索托,才能真正了解莱索托,反之亦然。当然旅游业也会给双方带来更多的其他领域如投资领域的机会。

——莱索托驻中国大使 蒂贝利

I am approval of your standpoint completely. An intimate relation on traveling interflow between Lesotho and China would promote a cultural exchange of the both sides. Only more Chinese people travel in Lesotho can they understand our country deeply, and vice versa. Of cause, tourism also will offer more opportunities in many other fields, like investigating sphere, for our two countries.

— Ambassador of Lesotho: Mr. Anthony Rachobokoane Thibeli

与其说旅游是文明的传递，不如说旅游是文明体验的交换过程。人们通过旅游开阔了视野，因为在旅游过程中人们可以相互交流和学习对方的文化、生活方式和思维方式。从这一点来说，人们才有机会通过旅游加深彼此之间的理解、友谊和合作。我相信旅游能为人类社会的和谐和和平做出贡献。

——老挝驻中国大使　维吉·欣达翁

Rather than saying that tourism is a transmittal of civilization, it'd be better to say that tourism is an exchanging process for experiencing civilization. Tourism broadens people's vision because people can exchange each other and study culture, life-way and mode of thinking of the other side in the traveling process. Thus, people can have opportunities to understand each other more, deepen friendship and develop co-operation. I believe that tourism will make a greater contribution for the harmony and peace of mankind's world.

— Ambassador of Laos: Mr. Vichit Xindavong

旅游是增进了解和友谊的重要手段，它可以让游客了解更多的文化和美食，即物质和精神领域的很多内容。旅游让世界人民更加融合在一起。

——立陶宛驻中国大使　阿尔图拉斯·茹劳斯卡斯

Tourism is an important means to promote understanding and friendship. It makes tourists know more cultures, delicacies and many contents in material and spiritual realms. Tourism mixes people of the world together more.

— Ambassador of Lithuania: Mr. Arturas Zurauskas

人们是可以通过旅游了解文明的，中国和阿拉伯世界有很多相似之处。如果中国人到利比亚旅游，看到利比亚的名胜古迹，也会联想到中国的一些东西。旅游的频繁，人民的接触，会让这种文明世世代代传递下去。

——利比亚驻中国大使　穆斯塔法·格鲁西

People can understand civilization through tourism. There are many parallels between China and the Arab world. If Chinese people travel in Liberia, they will associate some things of China when they view the places of historic interest and scenic beauty of Liberia.

The development of tourism industry and the communication between people will transmit the civilization generation after generation.

— Ambassador of Liberia: Mr. Mustaf a M. Elguelushi

我认为您提得很好，特别是我们正面临全球化的挑战，文化和旅游使得各民族之间建立了一些友好的关系。两国之间发生冲突，就是因为彼此了解不够，在许多方面有歧视，就是因为人家不了解自己。我们在分享同一个世界和文化成果。

——罗马尼亚驻中国大使　V. 伊斯蒂奇瓦亚

I think you are right, especially we are facing a gauntlet of globalization nowadays, and the various nations can establish some friendly relations by tourism and cultural exchange. It just because they can not understand each other enough, and have divergences in many aspects, the conflicts will be happened between the two countries. We can share a common world and the cultural achievement through tourism.

— Ambassador of Romania: Mr. Viorel Isticioaia

中国有句俗话"百闻不如一见"，没有旅游就没有了解，更谈不上人类社会的发展。你们的这个口号提得很好。

——马达加斯加驻中国大使　维克托·希科尼纳

An old Chinese saying goes like this: It is better to see once than to hear a hundred times. There is no understanding without tourism, and you can not talk about the development of human being's society yet. The motto of your newspaper is fine.

— Ambassador of Madagascar: Mr. Victor SIKONINA

亚历山大大帝生活的时期相当于中国的秦朝，他为了方便自己国家的人民出游，建造了很多道路，他坚信这也必将对于整个世界有益。我个人认为，旅游是很好的交流方式，它能让不同国家的人民相互尊重和吸收彼此的文化。

——马其顿驻中国大使　法特米尔·杰拉迪尼

Alexander the Great lived in his country when China is in the Qin Dynasty, he built many roads for his people to travel conveniently. He firmly believed that it would be valuable to the whole world. Personally I think tourism is a good communicating way, and it can make people of different countries respect and assimilate cultures each other.

— Ambassador of Macedonia: Mr. Fatmir Dzeladini

旅游是人与人交流的最好方式之一,一个人到一个地方旅行一定要花时间和当地人接触……只有了解和体验旅游目的地的风土民情,才是更充实的旅游。所以我赞同您的见解。

——毛里求斯驻中国大使　钟律芳

Tourism is one of the best methods on communications between individuals, one must spend time to touch locals when he or she in traveling one site. Only to know and to experience the local customers is the real tourism with more contents. So in this sense, I agree with your viewpoints.

——Ambassador of Mauritius: Mr. Paul Chong Leung

在蒙古人中有两句谚语,一句是"百闻不如一见",第二句是交一个朋友胜过建一个帐篷。通过旅游可以交到更多朋友,旅游会推动人与人之间的交往,消除误解,促进民族间文化的交往。

——蒙古驻中国大使　巴特苏赫

There are two proverbs in Mongol, the one is "it is better to see once than to hear a hundred times", the other is "making a friend is better than building a tent". You can make more friends through travel. Tourism will promote the communication between people. It can clear up a misunderstanding and promote the cultural communication between nations.

— Ambassador of Mongolia: Mr. Galsan Batsukh

我认为您讲的很好。我来旅游,我的思路开阔了,我看到了新的生活方式新的文化新的事物,我对当地人的理解力加深了,我不再是我们国家的公民了,我成了一名世界公民,这是旅游最重要的一项功能。旅游整合了我们而不是把我们分开。世界贸易组织和世界旅游组织都是WTO,两个WTO让我们成为世界公民。

——孟加拉国驻中国大使　阿什法库尔·拉赫曼

I think you said fine. When I travel in a place, my train of thought will be widened because I see a new life-way, culture and things. I will understand the local people deeper. I will not only a citizen of my own country, I will be a world citizen. It is the most functions of tourism. The tourism unifies the people, instead of separating people. The abbreviations of the World Trade Organization and the World Tourism Organization are also WTO, the two WTO make us become the world citizens.

— Ambassador of Bangladesh: Mr. Ashfaqur Rahman

有很多中国的舞蹈团到摩洛哥演出，每次剧场都坐得满满的，如果露天演出更是水泄不通，这说明摩洛哥不排斥外来文化，当然摩洛哥也希望把自己的文化传到世界各地，这是一个相互传递的过程。旅游是完成这种相互传递的非常好的方式。

——摩洛哥驻中国大使　穆罕默德·谢尔提

When many Chinese dance groups put on the performances in Morocco, the theatre was always packed with people, if it was an open-air performance, people would be so closely besieged that not a drop of water could trickle through. Moroccan people never exclude the other cultures. Of cause, they hope that their own culture can be propagated to various places of the world. It is a process to transmit cultures each other and tourism is the better way to carry out the transmittal.

— Ambassador of Morocco: Mr. Mohamed Cherti

我认为旅游可以更好地学习另一种文化，可以促进不同文化间的交往。旅游带给世界和平。每个国家的人们，都以自己的文化而自豪。当一种文明融合另一种文明的时候，旅游就开始了。

——墨西哥驻中国大使　李子文

I think that the tourism can help us to learn other cultures and promote the communication between different cultures better. The tourism brings the peace to the world. People of every country are proud of their culture. When a kind of culture is being mixed with another kind of culture, the tourism begins.

— Ambassador of Mexico: Mr. Sergio Ley Lopez

是的，我们热爱旅游，不仅是因为它可以创造经济价值，更重要的，旅游是增进友谊的重要手段。因为如果一个国家要和另一个国家建立良好的关系，最重要的一点，就是两国的人民必须相互了解、相互信任。政府和政府之间随时可以建立和中止关系，但只要两国人民的关系亲密，两国的友谊是可以天长地久、世代相传的。

——南非驻中国大使　倪清阁

Yes, we love to travel because it not only can create more economic value, but also is an important means to promote friendship. If a country wants to establish a good relation with an other country, the most important thing is that the people of the two countries must understand and trust each other. Governments can establish or suspend relations between them at all times, but the friendship between two countries will be everlasting ad unchanging if only the relation between the people of those countries are close.

— Ambassador of South Africa: Mr. Ndumiso Ndima Ntshinga

旅游是把全世界人民有效地联系在一起的一个非常有用的媒介。旅游的含义就是更好地相互了解。这也有助于了解彼此的感受、性情和存在的问题。旅游为全世界人民提供了一个自由交流的平台，旅游是服务于全人类的。

——尼泊尔驻中国大使　纳南德拉·拉吉·潘迪

Tourism is the best medium which can connect the people of the whole world together. The signification of the tourism is that understanding each other better. It also can help people to know the feelings and characteristics of each other. Tourism offers a platform in which people of the whole world can exchange freely. It serves the whole human being.

— Ambassador of Nepal: Mr. Narendra Raj Panday

旅游促进双方文明交流的重要一点，是通过访问对方的国家，增进对对方文化的了解。文化不单是文学、艺术，还包括生活、互动。还有一点，旅游通过直接的体验，可以消除很多偏见，例如有许多人认为挪威人有保持1.2米距离的习俗，但到了挪威就知道这是不确切的，其实很多的挪威人都有拥抱等亲密行为。

——挪威驻华大使　赫图安

People can experience the history, music and many other things of a country through tourism. When people visit a new place, they can understand each other more in an increased process of exchanges. One more thing, you will have a direct experience that can help to eliminate many prejudices through traveling. For example, many people think that the Norwegians have a convention of keeping a distance of 1.2 meters between each other. But once you are in Norway, you'll see that this is not exact, as many Norwegians in fact have intimate moves, such as embracement.

— Ambassador of Norway: Mr. Tor Christian Hildan

旅游是不同民族不同国家之间的一种交流方式。如果你参观一个国家就产生了文化间的交流。一次组织很好的旅游可以让旅游者对另一个国家的文化产生很好的了解。我同意你们的观点。

——葡萄牙驻华大使　桑塔纳·卡洛斯

  Tourism is a kind of way for communicating between different countries and nations. It will has an exchange on the culture when you visit a country. A traveling activity which is organized better can make the tourists have a deeper understanding on culture of another country. So I support your viewpoint.

— Ambassador of Portugal：Mr. Antonio Santana Carlos

我完全赞同。比如拿瑞典来说，每个人都有几次出国的经历，相比之下，美国是个大国，但有出国经历的人很少，以前瑞典人喜欢去欧洲比较暖和的地方，现在他们更喜欢去亚洲，重中之重是中国。

——瑞典驻华大使　雍博瑞

  You are quite right. For example, in Sweden, everybody has several experiences to travel in foreign countries. Compared with us, the U. S. is a large country in area, but the number of the people who travel abroad is less. In the past, the Swedish like to travel to those warm places, such as Europe. But now, they prefer to make a journey in Asia, especially in China.

— Ambassador of Sweden：Mr. Carl Borje Ljunggren

我很高兴中国正在推广孔子，在贝尔格莱德有个孔夫子学院，就像西班牙的塞万提斯，英国的戏剧一样。旅游可以整合各种文化，旅游就是一个国家的窗口，人民通过旅游者的言行举止了解这个国家。旅游者传递本国的思想。

——塞尔维亚驻中国大使　米奥米尔·乌多维契基

  I am so glad that you are popularizing Confucius. There is a Confucius institute in Belgrade. Just like Cervantes of Spain and the play of Britain, tourism can unify the various cultures. Tourism is a window of a country, the local people will know this country through the statements and actions of the tourists who come from this country. Meanwhile, the tourists will transmit the ideas of their country.

— Ambassador of Serbia：Mr. Miomir Udovicki

  我非常赞同您的观点。去不同的国家旅游也是学习和受教育的过程，因为游客可以直接接触当地的人民、文化和风土民情。对其他国家人民的了解可以使全世界人民最终走到一起，共同创造一个属于全世界人民的地球村。随着科学技术的不断发展，交通工具的更加便捷，整个世界会变得如此相互依赖，未来的世界是属于全人类的。

——塞浦路斯驻中国大使　彼德罗斯·凯斯托拉斯

  I fully agree with you. It is also a process to study and receive the education when you travel to the different countries because the tourists can get in touch with the local people, culture, conditions and customs directly. Along with the science and technology are developing continuously, the transportation is more convenient. The various nations of the world will depend on each other more. The glorious future of the world belongs to the whole mankind.

— Ambassador of Cyprus: Mr. Petros Kestoras

  我认为有三个方面，第一，旅游是一个产业可以创造巨大的经济效益。比如少林寺的纪念品，还有与之相关的交通、酒店业都可以受益。第二，我认为旅游可以开阔人的视野，到不同的国家不同的地方会有不同的感受，如中国人到斯里兰卡就会对我们的文化有更深入的了解。第三，旅游可以让人与人之间的关系更加紧密，了解更全面，这样世界就会更加和平。

——斯里兰卡驻中国大使　尼哈尔·罗德里格

  I think there are three sides. First, tourism is a kind of industry which can produce a huge economic benefits. Such as the souvenirs about the Shaolin Temple and other industries which can also be benefited from it, like transportation and hotel. The second, the tourism can broaden people's vision. You will have the different feelings when you visit the different countries, such as if a Chinese come to Sri Lanka, he will understand our culture more deeply. The last, the tourism can make the people of different countries know each other more roundly and keep a very intimate relation. Thus there will be more peace in the world.

— Ambassador of Sri Lanka: Mr. Nihal Rodrigo

　　　　　　　　我想说旅游是消除偏见的最好方式。如果你没有偏见，人与人之间的了解就会增进，就会更加相互尊重，恐惧感就会消失，而相聚一起。

　　　　　　　　　　　　　　——斯洛文尼亚驻中国大使　马里安·森森

　　I want to say that tourism is the best way to clear up prejudice. If you have no prejudice, the understanding between people will be promoted, and they will respect each other more than before. The terror will disappear and they will get together.

　　　　　　　　　　　　　　— Ambassador of Slovenia: Mr. Marjan Cencen

　　　　　　　　旅游是人与人之间增进了解的另一种方式，它拉近了人与人之间的距离，你去过的地方越多，你对世界的了解就越多。传统的旅游人们只是看看风景，现代的旅游跟传统的旅游有很大不同。不管是什么样的旅游方式，都把各个国家的人拉到一起，增进了友谊，也了解了对方的文明。

　　　　　　　　　　　　　　——坦桑尼亚驻华大使　桑嘎

　　Tourism is another kind of way to promote people understand each other more, it narrows the gap between people. The more places you have been, the more you will know the world. In the traditional traveling process, people just view the sightseeing, but the modern tourism is more different with the traditional tourism. No matter what kind of traveling way, it also can make the people of various countries become close more and understand the civilization of each other. Meanwhile, it will promote the friendship.

　　　　　　　　　　　　　　— Ambassador of Tanzania: Mr. Charles Asilia Sanga

　　　　　　　　旅游影响文明，文明也促进了旅游，它们二者相辅相成。我非常赞同您的观点，这也是非常重要的一点。全世界所有国家的人，都来你们国家旅游，他们分享了你们国家的文化。所以旅游是不同文化背景的人们走到一起，相互交流，分享成果的最好的方式。

　　　　　　　　　　　　　　——突尼斯驻华大使　穆罕默德·萨赫比·巴斯里

　　Tourism affects civilization, and civilization also promotes tourism; they supplement and complement with each other. When people from all other countries in the world travel to your nation, they will then share the culture of your country. So tourism is the best way for people, who have a different cultural background, to exchange with each other and share each other's achievements.

　　　　　　　　　　　　　　— Ambassador of Tunisia : Mr. Mohamed Sahbi Basly

　　我很赞同您的观点，旅游的含义就是更好地相互理解，消除人与人之间的误解，现在的科学技术发展地很快，通讯产业也很发达，很多人通过互联网进行远距离交流，但我始终认为面对面交流是最好的方式。你光从电视或者其他媒体上了解一个地方，而不是亲身去体验，是体会不到那个地方真正的特色的。

——土耳其驻中国大使　奥克塔伊·厄聚耶

　　I fully agree with you. The meaning of the tourism is that understanding each other more and eliminating the misunderstanding. The modern science and technology are developing rapidly, the communication industry is also developed. Many people often communicate through the internet when they are far away from each other. But I think from beginning to end that the communication of face-to-face is the best way. If you only understand a place in TV or other media, instead of experiencing it personally, you will not know the real features there.

— Ambassador of Tukey: Mr. Oktay Ozuye

　　旅游是一个非常好的活动，可以促进人与人之间的相互了解，消除彼此的误解，所有的战争和冲突都是因为缺乏了解和沟通。旅游也可以促进经济的发展，互相推动。人类在建造和谐社会的过程中，旅游起着至关重要的作用。

——瓦努阿图驻中国大使　罗志伟

　　Tourism is a kind of good action, because it can make people understand each other more and clear up the misunderstanding between them. All the wars and conflicts happened are for lacking understanding and communication. Tourism also can develop economy. Tourism plays the most important part in the process of mankind build a harmonious society.

— Ambassador of Vanuatu: Mr. Lo Chi Wai

　　是的，我非常赞同这个观点。这是很自然的事情，相互加深了解会加深彼此的友谊，比如许多中国领导都喜欢喝茅台，我也喜欢喝茅台。因为了解，我们在半个小时就可以签协议。在我来中国之前，我对中国人民了解不是很多，现在我了解了普通中国人的喜、怒、哀、乐。如果你想了解希腊人民，一定要去希腊。

——希腊驻中国大使　米哈依勒·坎巴尼斯

　　Yes, I am all for the viewpoint. It is naturally to strengthen the friendship through deepening understanding each other further. Such as many Chinese leaders like to drink

Maotai, and I also like too. Because we know each other, we can sing the agreement within half of an hour. Before I came to China. We know Chinese people less. But now I understand the happiness, anger, grief and joy of the average person of China. If you want to understand the Greek, you must go to Greece.

— Ambassador of Greece: Mr. Michael Cambanis

旅游的基本作用就是传递人类的文明，旅游不仅是休闲和度假，旅游是搭建各国人民相互了解的桥梁，旅游也促进各国经济、贸易的发展。旅游是重要的资源。今年（2006年，作者注）头七个月在叙利亚旅游业的投资已经超过100亿美元。

——叙利亚驻中国大使　穆罕默德·海依尔·瓦迪

The basis function of tourism is to transmit human being's civilization. Tourism is not only for spending a holiday, but also a bridge for understanding each other between the people in different countries. Tourism is a kind of important resource, it can promote various countries' development in the fields of economy and commerce. In the first seven months of 2006, the investment was already more than U.S. $10 billion in tourism industry in Syria.

— Ambassador of Syria: Mr. Mhd Kheir Al-Wadi

旅游意味着带着了解、接受、满足好奇心、进入一个不同文化和风俗关系中的意图，从熟悉的地方向不了解的或了解不多的目的地移动……当然，旅游还意味着更加靠近其他民族，消除不了解，有助于相互认识。

——意大利驻中国大使　谢飒

Tourism means a kind of intension to step into a relation of different cultures, habits and customs with an attitude of understanding and accepting. Tourists travel to a destination which is familiar or strange to them for satisfying their curiosity. Of cause, tourism also means you will know other nations more, understanding each other better and clearing up a strange sense.

— Ambassador of Italy: Mr. Riccardo Sessa

旅游是非常重要的，通过旅游，您可以了解各国的文化，了解文明的产生过程，比如，在我来中国之前，我对中国毫无印象，现在，我去了中国很多地方，我不但了解了中国，还打算写几本关于中国的书，把中国的名胜都介绍给伊拉克人民，让他们了解更多的中国文化，了解中国的旅游，所以我完全同意你们的观点。

——伊拉克驻中国大使　穆罕默德·萨比尔·伊斯梅尔

Tourism is very important. You can know the cultures of various countries and that how the civilization comes into being through tourism. For example, before I came to China, I knew nothing about China. But now, I have been to many places of your country. I not only understand China, but also want to write several books for introducing Chinese scenic spots to the people of Iraq. Thus they will know more Chinese culture and tourism information. So I fully endorse your viewpoint.

— Ambassador of Iraq: Mr. Mohammad S. Ismail

如果不受到限制，让旅游多样化发展，对人要实现的目标是会有很大影响的。如果全世界都大力发展旅游业，不给它制造任何障碍，对全世界的经济贸易也会有很大的促进。但可惜旅游会受政治因素的影响，这样一来全世界的人们就无法掌握旅游带来的好东西。

——伊朗驻中国大使　贾瓦德·曼苏里

Tourism will exert a tremendous influence to aims that people want to carry out, if we can make it develop variedly without any limits. If the whole world can develop the tourism industry vigorously and never erects any barriers to it, it will be promote the world's economy and trade greatly. But tourism is always affected by political factors, so the people of the whole world can not enjoy those beauties brought by tourism fully.

— Ambassador of Iran: Mr. Javad Mansouri

我同意您的观点。人类出生的方式都是一样的，都有同样的大脑，这在所有国家都是一样的。相互的访问，丰富了人类的文明，旅游最先接触的就是人类的文化。不同国家的人来你们国家旅游，他们分享了你们国家的文化，同时也带来了他们国家的文化，这是不同文化背景增进友谊的最好的促进方式。

——印度尼西亚驻中国大使　苏德加

I approve of your point of view. The way of birth of people is similar and they have the same cerebrums. It is similar in the whole countries. The visiting between each other enriches human civilization, because people will touch the human civilization firstly in tourism. People from the different countries travel to your country, they share the culture of your country, meanwhile, bring their own culture to your country. It is the best way to promote the friendship between people who have the different background.

— Ambassador of Indonesia: Mr. Sudrajat

我非常赞同您的观点。作为中东地区的交通枢纽，约旦和巴勒斯坦在连接欧洲和亚洲起着很重要的战略意义。约旦的地里位置扮演着促进东西方贸易和文化往来的重要作用。直到今天她仍然在发挥作用。访问约旦你可以对东西方文明的碰撞和融合有一个大概了解，约旦完美融合了东西方文明。要了解所有这些必须通过旅游来完成。

——约旦驻中国大使　安马尔·阿·哈姆

I am approval of your standpoint completely. As the hub of communications in the Middle East, Jordan and Palestine link the Europe and Asia and has an important strategic significance. The geographic position of Jordan has decided that it has taken an important effect in promoting the trade and cultural communication between the West and orient. You will have a probable understanding on mixture and confrontation of the civilization between the West and orient when you visit Jordan, for our country combines the civilization of the West and orient together perfectly. If want to know all of those, the tourism is the best way.

— Ambassador of Jordan: Mr. Anmar A. Al Nimer Al-Hmoud

我很同意您的观点。我们现在所处的世界信息发展得很快，技术革命给我们的生活带来了许多巨大的变化，在全球化的背景下，不同的国家拥有共同的市场，国与国、人与人之间的交往非常的方便。现在的旅游包括学习旅游，商务旅游，旅游的内涵非常丰富，它的力量也非常大。旅游不仅推动了文化的交流，也推动了贸易、经济的合作。

——越南驻中国大使　陈文律

I fully agree with your viewpoint. Nowadays, the development of information is rapid in our world. The technological revolution brought many huge changes to our life. Under a background of globalization, different countries have a common market. The communications between countries and people are very convenient. Today, tourism includes studying tourism and commercial tourism, etc. The intention of tourism is very rich and its force is also tremendous. Tourism not only promotes the cultural communication, but also promotes the commercial and economical co-operations.

— Ambassador of Viet Nam: Mr. Tran Van Luat

我非常同意您的观点, 中国和赞比亚的文化交往很多, 我们都是联合国成员国, 我们两国都有丰富的历史和文化遗产, 因此只要两国加强文化交往, 就会有更好的相互了解。

——赞比亚驻中国大使　戴维·克利福德·萨维耶

I fully approve to your viewpoint. The cultural exchanges are frequent between China and Zambia. We are all the members of the UN, and the two countries have the various historical and cultural relics. So long as we two countries strengthen the cultural communication, we will understand each other more.

— Ambassador of Zambia: Mr. David Clifford Saviye

其实, 现在人们去旅游不仅是看风景, 而是了解当地的历史……旅游可以促进和平, 旅游可以增进人与人之间的了解, 很多地方都存在共同点, 但也是千差万别的, 最重要的是一方要学习和尊重另一方不相同的地方。旅游使全球化的步伐加快。

——智利驻中国大使　费尔南多·雷耶斯·马塔

Actually, people are not only for seeing sight when they make a journey, but also for understanding local history. Tourism can promote the peace, and makes people to understand each other more. various places differ in thousands of ways, meanwhile they have their common grounds. It is important to learn and respect the differences of the other places. Tourism quickens the step of globalization.

— Ambassador of Chile: Mr. Fernando Reyes Matta

(以上内容摘自《环球游报》"总编与大使对话"专栏)
(Above content comes from "Chief editor-Ambassador dialogue" Column in Groble Travel News)

**附录二：**

## 在 2012 联合国记者颁奖大会上的书面演讲——
### 旅游整合世界　人类共享文明

尊敬的潘基文秘书长和来自世界各国的嘉宾们，

女士们先生们，

大家晚上好！

　　非常感谢会议组织者邀请我参加今年的联合国记者大会，并给我一个书面演讲的机会！此时此刻，能和在座的嘉宾们一道，分享我对人类和平研究的学术成果，我感到万分荣幸！

　　各位嘉宾们，人类的历史，是一部追求和平的历史。两千年前，东方哲人孔子，就用"天下大同"来阐述人类政治的终极目标；希伯来大预言家弥赛亚 2500 年前也在耶路撒冷做出预言：终有一天，人们将把刀剑铸成犁头，把枪矛打成镰刀，国家之间不再拔剑相向，人世间不再有战争。

　　不幸的是，虽然先哲们为人类的未来描绘了美好的愿景，虽然诸多政治家、宗教家们以及无数仁人志士，为了实现人类和平的夙愿，一直生命不息，奋斗不止，但数千年过去了，我们这个地球，仍然矛盾重重，甚至因为核武器的存在，人类稍有不慎，就有灭顶之灾！

　　日复一日，政治家们仍然在说：我们所做的一切都是为了和平；

　　年复一年，宗教家们仍然在说：我们每天都在为和平而祈祷；

　　美国学者亨廷顿在其著作《文明的冲突》中却告诉大家，因文明的差异，世界必将发生战争……

　　悲观者在哀叹，人类文明是否走到历史的尽头？！

　　而在乐观者眼里，当历史和真理的面纱渐渐抽去，人类终于发现：政治的力量常常产生地域的壁垒，宗教的力量又往往导致心灵的隔阂，只有旅游，才能使不同种族、不同信仰、不同文化的人们走到一起，共同分享人类文明的成果！

顿时，我们才醒悟：旅游，从来就以一种隐形的方式和历史随行！

在这里，我要和大家讲一段中国古代的历史——

在中国的春秋战国时期，最多时，曾经有两百多个国家，后来经过长期的兼并战争，只剩下七个，号称"战国七雄"。那时，有一个知识分子阶层，叫"士"，由于他们各有所长，所以成为诸侯国竞相招揽的对象。

在诸侯国争夺天下的"世界大战"中，"士"们或著书立说、争鸣论战，或率领门徒周游列国，弘扬政治主张。孔子就曾经带领他的弟子周游列国十四年。

在长期的游历中，孔子对大自然的井然有序倍感崇尚，从而产生了社会也应该像大自然一样有序的感慨。渐渐地，形成了他影响中国乃至整个东方的"天人合一"的儒家思想。

士人中还有一位代表性人物值得提起，他的名字叫张仪。他是一个穷书生，在外东奔西跑游说君王多年都遭到拒绝。有一次在旅行途中，他所寄居的富豪人家丢了一块宝玉，便怀疑是他所为，把他抓起来打得死去活来。

回到家里，张仪的妻子心痛地说："你如果不读书，不出去游说君王，哪会受这样的委屈。"张仪却张开嘴，问妻子："我的舌头还在吗？"妻子回答："舌头当然在。"张仪说："只要舌头在，就不愁没出路。"

果真，在后来的周游列国中，张仪凭他的"三寸不烂之舌"，终于说服秦王接受了他的政治主张，当上了秦国的"外交部长"。并帮助秦王，打败了其它六国。

秦国兼并六国后，把原来各国所建的防御城墙都连接起来，这就是后来的万里长城。

在春秋战国那个百家争鸣、群雄争霸的年代里，像孔子、张仪这样的士人成千上万，他们常年车旅在外，与山水为伴，与日月为友，历经风吹雨打，但他们不以为苦，反以为乐，表现出一种特有的精神境界。

现在看来，与其说那些"士"是辅助君王争霸天下的政治家，还不如说他们是满怀政治理想的旅行家。在那个战争唱主角的古代社会里，虽然士们的作用还有限，但他们却在人类历史上，第一次彰显了旅游和旅行者在整合世界中的伟大力量！

当玄奘带着印度佛经回到中国；当郑和的船队满载着东方瓷器，七下西洋；当马可波罗的足音，响彻欧亚大地……无数的事例，都不断地证明旅游是一种整合世界的有效方式。

世界发展到今天，虽然战争的硝烟还未在地球绝迹，但人类的理性已将战争的形式唾弃。世界各国人民普遍增强了对话意识，以非暴力方式解决分歧已经成为世界的主流。

人们越来越清楚地看到，地球上没有任何一种活动，能像旅游活动那样，将世界各国的距离拉得如此之近，使不同民族之间的交流变得如此之广。纵观历史，人类的旅游活动迄今已经进行了两次大的飞跃——

第一次出现在工业革命时期，由于蒸汽机的发明，人类第一次脱离了以动物体力为交通工具的时代。旅游不再是少数人的专利，普通白领、蓝领也踏上了旅游的征途，人类由此拉开了"大众旅游"时代的序幕。

第二次飞跃始于上世纪八九十年代。由于冷战的结束，加上以信息革命为中心的高新技术的全面发展，"地球村"日益显现。"经济全球化"给人类带来前所未有的大规模的交流，人类由此进入到"全球旅游"时代。

虽然人们还无法预测人类旅游第三次飞跃的准确时间，但人类"核心价值观的统一"将是旅游活动第三次飞跃的重要标志，也是人类"地球村"真正实现的前提。

只有全人类"核心价值观的统一"，传统的政治、宗教矛盾才能真正消除，人类才能将地球上的有限资源最大限度地用于提升人类的整体力量，而非浪费在制造屠杀人类自身的武器上来。

而这美好愿景的实现是早是晚，很大程度上取决于全人类的"自觉"行为！

我非常认同 2012 年的诺贝尔和平奖颁给了欧盟。我对评委们高超的判断力和对人类文明发展潮流的非凡洞察力表示由衷的赞赏。

尊敬的嘉宾们，我们可以试想一下，在突如其来的欧债危机面前，发生债务危机的希腊，如果是在过去，会是一个什么状况？或许，它从其他国家得到的，除了嘲笑、幸灾乐祸，可能还有战争，因为这种事例在历史上不只发生过一次。

但这一次，欧盟的成员国却像家人一样，搀扶着这位第一个摔倒的兄弟前行！

虽然欧盟内部还存在各种不利因素，但经历了两次世界大战洗礼的欧洲人在世界人民面前率先走出了一条消除分歧，避免战争，共享经济与文化繁荣的和平途径，无疑为世界其他地区的和平与发展提供了有益借鉴。

所以，我认为，2012 年诺贝尔和平奖不仅是颁给了欧盟，而且是颁给了人类的未来！

1922 年，当年仅 28 岁的《泛欧论》（*Pan－Europa*）作者库德诺夫·卡雷尔基先生在回忆自己童年的生活时写道："和我们一起用餐的还有我母亲的匈牙利籍贴身女佣，我父亲的巴伐利亚籍私人秘书，我们的捷克人总管家和一位俄语教师。我父亲的土耳其语教师、一位阿尔巴尼亚籍穆斯林也经常和我们一起用餐。"

这种四海一家，其乐融融的生活场景，相信在人类的未来，随处可见！

尊敬的嘉宾们，以知识为基础的"后现代社会"正在向人类扑面而来。未来的世界，是一个"文化混血"的时代。毫无疑问，旅行者是"文化混血"的先行者。

中国自古以来就有"读万卷书，行万里路"的哲理名言；丹麦伟大作家安徒生也说过："旅游就是生活。"

在此，我衷心地希望和来自五大洲的朋友一道，发起和成立一个"全球旅游和平组织"，以倡导和推动"联合国旅游护照"的施行，为地球上那些对人类和平有重大贡献或有能力作出重大贡献者，颁发全球免签的"联合国旅游护照"，以此带领和推动越来越多的地球公民走上相互交流、相互尊重、相互欣赏、共同分享的"旅游整合世界"之路，为建设一个没有战争，只有旅游的新地球而努力！

谢谢大家！

# Appendix Ⅱ: Writen speech to the General Assembly of the United Nations Correspondents in 2012—— Tourism Integrates the World and Shares Civilization

Dear Secretary – General Ban Ki – Moon, and distinguished guests from all over the world, Ladies and gentlemen:

Good night!

Please accept my grateful thanks to conference organizer for inviting me to the "General Assembly of the United Nations Correspondents" and giving me the opportunity to give this written speech here.

At this moment, I feel very proud to be here with Honorable guests from all around the world, and share my academic achievements in human peace research.

Dear Honorable Guests, Human history is a history of the pursuit of peace. Two thousand years ago, the Chinese philosopher Confucius used "One world" to illustrate the ultimate goal of human politics; in the Old Testament of the Bible in the Book of Isiah, there is a prophecy that one day in the future, people will turn swords into plowshares, spears into pruninghooks. Countries will no longer be hostile to one other, and the world will not learn war any more.

Although the sages pictured a beautiful future for the human race, unfortunately, many politicians, religious leaders with many people have struggled in life with lofty the ideal of human peace. A few thousand years have passed, however conflict still exists on our earth. There could be a disaster for humans if there ever is nuclear war.

Day after day, politicians are still saying: all are done for peaceful.

Year after year, religionists are still saying: we are praying for peace every day.

However, American scholar Samuel Huntington told us in his book "The Clash of Civilizations", that the war world is bound to occur due to differences in civilization.

The pessimists lamented: is human civilization coming to the end in terms of human history?!

In the eyes of optimists, when the veil of history and the truth gradually removing, man finally found: political forces often geographically barriers, the power of religion often leads to the estrangement of the soul, and only travel, can make people from different races, different beliefs and different cultures gather together, and share the fruit of human civilization.

Suddenly, we just realized, tourism goes hand by hand with history in an imperceptible way.

Here, I would like to trace ancient Chinese history——

In China's Spring and Autumn Period, there have been over two hundred countries at the peak, only seven countries left after a long period of annexed war, known as the "Warring States" Later. At that time, there was an intellectual elite called "Shi", they were solicited by these countries because of their professional skills.

During the "world war" period among different vassal countries, the Shi's and their disciples either wrote book, debated conflicts at the academy, or travelled outside countries, so as to address political ideas. Confucius has visited among countries with his students for fourteen years.

In the long-term travel, Confucius was an advocate for the orderly nature, which in turn made him feels that an orderly societies should also be like laws of nature. It, therefore, gradually brought out the "celestial being" Confucianism which has great impact on China and even the whole East.

Another represented person among "Shi" worth identifying is called Zhang Yi. He was a very poor student running around, lobbying kings for few years and yielding no result. Once on his journey, his rich landlord lost a gem, and then he was suspected and arrested, then seriously hurt.

When came back home, Zhang Yi's wife said sadly "if you don't study, don't go to lobby, and no grievance would be heard". But Zhang Yi retorted "does my tongue still help?" His wife answered "Surely your tongue is working." Zhang Yi firmly stated "no need to worry about the future if I hold my tongue".

Finally, during his trip to the vassal countries later, he finally convinced King of Qin kingdom to accept his politics with this silver-tongued, and he became Qin's "foreign minister", helped the King of Qin defeat other six countries, established the largest feudal empire at that time.

After Qin occupied other six countries, it linked the separate defensive walls and made it the Great wall.

Hundreds of thousands of scholars like Confucius and Zhang Yi travelled outside yearly during the time of contending and warring. They were fully exposed to nature, and having the sun and moon partner them, and weathering the storms. But they didn't think it painful, rather than enjoying it and showed a unique spiritual quality.

In retrospect, we would rather to say the Shis are tourists with political ideals, than to say the Shis are politicians to help Kings conquer the world. When war was ruling, even though Shis played a limited role, they showed the great power of tourisms, and Tourism Unifies the World and Embraces Civilization came into being for the very first time.

When Xuanzang was back to China with Indian Buddhist scriptures, when Zhenghe's fleet set out laden with Oriental porcelain seven time, and when footsteps of Marco Polo resounded among European and Asian continent, there are countless examples to prove that Tourism Unifies the World and Embraces Civilization.

Although the world is not yet extinct with the smoke of war until now, world war has been cast aside by human rational. People all over the world generally enhanced sense of exchange, and non-violent is starting to move into the mainstream for resolving disputes.

It is quite clear that there is no activity other than travel on the earth that can draw the different countries so closer, make different ethnic groups exchange so easily. Throughout history, there are two big leaps for mankind tourism:

The first one happened during the industrial revolution. Thanks to the invention of the steam engine, human can get rid of the animal-driven transport for the first time. Travel is no longer the monopoly of the small group. Ordinary white-collar, blue-collar also embarked on a journey, which enter an era of mass tourism.

The second leap was made in eighty, ninety in the last century. With the end of Cold War as well as overall-development of high technique based on information revolution, came into being the "global village". Since "Economic Globalization" brings human unprecedented large-scale exchange; the time is ripe for "global tourism".

While people has not yet be able to predict the exact time of the third leap of human travelling, the human core values identity, could be an important symbol of the third leap, and also the prerequisite for realization of "the global village".

Only the core values identity existing for all mankind, can the traditional political and religious conflicts truly be ended. Then people can maximally add their numerical strengths against limited resources, rather than squandering them on developing weapons for massacre.

However, when the dream come true mainly depends on the "conscious" behavior of all mankind, I strongly concur that the 2012 Nobel Peace Prize goes to European Union. I really appreciate the judges' judgment and their remarkable insight about the trend in human civilization development.

Dear Honorable Guests, let's just imagine, what could happen in the past for Greece under the financial crisis while facing it? Perhaps, it may get from other countries ridicule, schadenfreude, even attack, because those happened more than once in the history.

But this time, the EU members behaved like a very close-knit family and supported their first fallen brother.

Although some disadvantage factors exist within EU, Europeans find out a way for resolving conflict, averting war, sharing economic, boosting cultural prosperity and keeping peace in front of the world people. This is no doubt a useful reference for rest of the world in term of peace and development.

So, I think, the 2012 Nobel Peace Prize is awarded not only to the Europe Union, but also to the future of mankind!

In 1922, when only 28 years old author of "pan-European" Mr. Kurdish Ivanov Caray Wikie wrote in the memories of his childhood, he remarks "we dine together with my mother's Hugarian personal maid, my father's Bavarian private secretary, the chief steward of our Czechs and one Russian teacher. My fathers' Turkish teacher, an Albanian Muslim is also always dining with us".

I believe it will be everywhere to see this cosmopolitan and enjoyable life!

Dear Honorable Guests, the knowledge-based "post-modern society" is blowing to humans. The future world is an era of "cultural hybrid". There is no doubt that the traveler is a "cultural hybrid" pioneer.

There was a saying in ancient China that "read a lot and make trip further". The Great Danish writer Hans Christian Andersen said: "Tourism is the life".

Here, I woiuld like to initiate the establishment of a Global Tourism Peace Organization, alongside friends from the five continents. This organization will advocate and promote a "Travel Passport of the United Nations" for those people who have made significant contributions to human peace or have made a significant contribution to the earth. We would like to offer a global visa-free "United Nations Travel Passport", in order to lead and promote greater integration of tourism in the world, where citizens can make mutual exchanges, show mutual respect, mutual appreciation, and share the road of "Tourism Integrates the World", as part of our best efforts to build a new earth without war, rather only with New Earth Tourism!

Thank you all!

(Translator: Yueqing Tang)

## 附录三：

## 初版自序

当人类迈入 21 世纪门槛时，旅游的浪潮已撞击地球每一个角落。随着科学技术的进步，交通和通讯的发达，人们的生活质量和生活方式，都在发生日新月异的变化。而旅游因其包容的广泛性，往往是这种变化的最重要的标杆之一。旅游业作为 21 世纪最大产业，越来越受到世界各国和地区的重视与推行。

随着全球旅游、全民旅游时代的蓬勃展开，关注人类发展的诸多有识之士，也开始重新对旅游在世界文明进程中的定位作出评估和调整。人们越来越清晰地看到，在世界范围内，各国发展旅游业的目的，不仅仅是对旅游产业本身的提升，而且是促进人类多样文明的交流与共享。

近几年来，笔者借工作之机，有幸与包括各国旅游部长、外交部长和驻华大使在内的 80 余位重量级人物，就旅游的相关话题，进行了交谈。笔者深深感受到，文化全球化使得全球公民不再局限以一个国家或一个地区的狭小范围来考虑问题，而是用一种新的眼光和视角来环顾世界、审视自己的文化。旅游最广泛地促进了不同文明的接触、对话和交流，使全人类能够分享世界文化的资源和人类文明的成果。

正因为此，2005 年 8 月《环球游报》创刊时，笔者就提出了"旅游整合世界 人类共享文明"这一理念。这句话的关键词"整合"，笔者认为主要有两层含义：一是指使原本分散的人或物联系到一起；二是指一个"优化"的过程，"整合世界"自然就是"优化"世界，以达到"共享"的目的。

"旅游整合世界"理念的提出，迅即在产业界和社会上产生的反响，是笔者始料不及的。

中国社会科学院旅游研究中心主任张广瑞先生率先撰文呼应，他在《旅游，从中国到世界》一文中，针对旅游在不同时代的"称呼"如"民间外交"、"创汇产业""无烟工业""无形贸易""先导产业""强势产业""支柱产业""环保产业"

"学习产业""文化产业"和"动力产业"……说明了旅游内涵和影响力的变化;中国著名旅游专家李庚先生认为这一理念"站到了理论的最前沿";《江西日报》高级记者、著名作家朱昌勤先生更是在其所撰《很有思想力的报纸格言》一文中称"这是提升整个旅游行业价值的'地标性'格言"。

2006年4月,"中国最值得外国人去的50个地方"颁奖活动在北京人民大会堂举行,许多参与此盛况的国内外嘉宾、专家学者、产业人士在听完笔者所做"旅游整合世界"的演讲后,非常激动,希望笔者能够尽快"著书立说",让更多的人了解此一思想。津巴布韦驻华大使K.H.穆茨万格瓦先生还特地走到笔者面前说:"你的演讲很精彩!"

2006年9月,中国国庆"黄金周"即将到来,新华社记者曾曦先生来采访笔者,希望笔者阐述这一理念的精髓。专稿发表后,国内外近千家平面、网络媒体予以转载,让笔者感受到一种前所未有的思想震撼。

而每一次参加各种"国际旅博会",与各种肤色的外国朋友就这一理念进行交流时,每当看到他们会心的理解,听到他们首肯的和声,都产生了我写作的冲动。

所以,从某种程度来说,这本书得以迅速出版,本身就是各种力量"整合"的结果。没有国内外朋友的鼓励和支持,此书恐难以面世。

在此,笔者向所有为"旅游整合世界 人类共享文明"这一崇高理念添砖加瓦的国内外友人表示最诚挚的谢意!

为了能让更多外国读者读到拙作和国内大中专院校师生拥有高质量的中英文对照教本,出版社还特邀《中国日报》(*China Daily*)高级编辑晓光先生为此书作了翻译,在此一并表示真挚感谢!

最后,借拙作出版之机,希望有更多有识之士完善和发展这一理念,为共建人类和谐"地球村"出力!

是为序。

伍 飞

2007年10月

于中国首都北京

# Appendix Ⅲ: The first edition preface

As the human kind strode forward into the threshold of the 21$^{st}$ century, the waves of tourism have stricken every corner of the globe. Along with the advance of science and technology, and the progress of transportation and communication, people are seeing daily rapid changes in their life quality and lifestyle. And tourism, due to its all-inclusive embraces, is always one of the most important symbols of these changes. As the largest industry of the 21$^{st}$ century, tourism industry has received more and more attention and promotion in all countries and regions of the world.

Amid the flourishing unfolding of the global travel and mass tourism epoch, many people of insight, who pay attention to the human development, have begun to reappraise and readjust the position of tourism in the process of world civilization. People have come to see more clearly that in the whole world, the purpose of developing tourism by all nations is not only aimed at elevating tourism industry itself, but also promoting the exchanges and sharing of diversified civilization of the human beings.

Starting from this, I put forward a motto that "Tourism Unifies the World and Embraces Civilization" when the Global Travel newspaper was set up in August 2005. The key word of the motto is "unifies", because as long as I understand it, it has two main meanings: For one thing, it means that the previously-separated people or things have been linked with each other. And for the other, it refers to a process of "optimization", Thus the process of unifying the world is naturally a process of "optimizing" the world, so as to make people to "embrace" civilizations.

During the past few years, I have been lucky enough to hold conversations with 80-odd VIPs, including tourism ministers and foreign ministers of foreign countries and China-based diplomatic envoys, on related topics of tourism while doing my beat as an executive editor-in-chief of a newspaper. I deeply felt that the globalization of cultures has made people to use a new eyesight and a new angle to look all around the world and closely examine their own culture while considering problems, instead of being limited by the confined scope of one country or one region. Tourism has promoted the contacts, dialogues and exchanges of different civilization in the maximum degree, and made all the human kind to be able to share the global cultural resources and the achievement of human civilization.

Since it was put forward, the concept that "Tourism Unifies the World" has evoked rapid resounding responses among the tourism circle and the society, running counter to all my expectations.

Mr. Zhang Guangrui, director of the Tourism Research Centre of the Chinese Academy of Social Sciences, first wrote an article to offer his approval of this concept. By touching on the various "names" of tourism in different times, such as "people-to-people diplomacy", "foreign-exchange-earning industry", "smokeless industry", "invisible trade", "forerunning industry", "powerful industry", "pillar industry", "environmental-friendly industry", "learning industry", "cultural industry" and "motivating industry", he explained the changes of the connotation and influences of tourism in his thesis entitled "Tourism: From China to the World".

Mr. Li Geng, a noted Chinese tourism expert, said he thought the motto has "stood in the very forefront of theory".

And Mr. Zhu Changqin, a senior reporter of *Jiangxi Daily* and famous writer, commented in his article "*A Newspaper Motto with Deep Ideological Insight*" that "this is a 'symbolic motto' that has elevated the value of the whole tourism industry".

On April 2006, when the awarding ceremony of "Top 50 Chinese Destinations for Foreigners" was held at the Great Hall of the People in Beijing, many participants — including domestic and overseas dignitaries, scholars and experts and professionals from the tourism industry—were very excited after listening to my keynote speech that "tourism unifies the world" and expressed their hopes that I could "write a book to expound my theory" as soon as possible, in a bid to let more people come to see this concept. Mr. Christopher H. Mutsvangwa, ambassador of Zimbabwe to China, came specially to me, saying "your speech is excellent".

In September 2006, when the annual week-long "golden week" of Chinese National Day holiday was to come, Mr. Zeng Xi — a reporter from the Xinhua News Agency — had an interview with me, saying he also hoped I could elaborate on the essence of this concept. When his news story was published, nearly a thousand media at home and abroad carried his article in their newspaper, TV, radio, magazine and website reports. This made me feel an unprecedented ideological shock.

Every time when I attended various kinds of world tourism fairs and conducted discussions with foreign friends of all colors on this concept, I always had an impulse to write a book after hearing their understanding acknowledgement and approving voices.

Thus, in a certain degree, the quick publishing of this book is in itself a result of "unification" of all forces. I am afraid the book is hard to come out if not for the encouragement and support of friends from home and abroad.

Here, I would like to express my most sincere thanks to all the friends both at home and abroad who have done their efforts on the lofty idea of "tourism unifying the world".

Moreover, in order to let more overseas can read this book, as well as to offer a high qualified bilingual textbook to Chinese universities, colleges, and institutes, the publishing house invited Mr. Xiao Guang, the senior editors of *China Daily* joined the work of translation on this book, for this, here I send to the special thanks to them.

In addition, I also would like to welcome further discussions on this issue and wish more people with widen horizon to come for help perfect and develop this topic, so that to let us make a joint contribution to the goal of a harmonious "global village" of human beings.

This is the reason of my foreword.

Wu Fei,

Writing in the Chinese capital, Beijing,

In October 2007

# 参考文献

1. 谢彦君. 基础旅游学［M］. 北京：中国旅游出版社，2001.
2. 章必功. 中国旅游史［M］. 昆明：云南人民出版社，1992.
3. 王晓云. 中国旅游史话［M］. 合肥：黄山书社，1997.
4. 王永忠. 西方旅游史［M］. 南京：东南大学出版社，2004.
5. 沈祖祥. 旅游与中国文化［M］. 北京：旅游教育出版社，1996.
6. 〔瑞士〕若泽塞依杜. 旅游接待的今天与明天［M］. 北京：旅游教育出版社，1990.
7. 张广瑞，刘德谦等. 中国旅游绿皮书［M］. 北京：社会科学文献出版社，2005、2006、2007.
8. 〔美〕罗伯特·郎卡尔. 旅游及旅行社会学［M］. 北京：旅游教育出版社，1989.
9. 冯乃康. 中国旅游文学论稿［M］. 北京：旅游教育出版社，1995.
10. 陈安泽，卢云亭. 旅游地学概论［M］. 北京：北京大学出版社，1991.
11. 博卡特，梅特利克. 西方旅游业［M］. 上海：同济大学出版社，1990.
12. 田里. 旅游学概论［M］. 天津：南开大学出版社，1998.
13. 章培恒，骆玉明. 中国文学史［M］. 北京：中国社科院出版社，1985.
14. 〔希腊〕普鲁塔克. 希腊罗马名人传［M］. 北京：商务印书馆，1992
15. 杜江. 旅行社管理［M］. 天津：南开大学出版社，1997.
16. 〔美〕杰夫瑞·戈比. 21世纪的休闲与休闲服务［M］. 昆明：云南人民出版社，2000.
17. 〔奥〕茨威格. 归来没有统帅——麦哲伦传［M］. 长沙：湖南文艺出版社，1982.
18. 〔西班牙〕马达里亚加. 哥伦布评传［M］. 北京：中国社会科学出版社，1991.
19. 陆国俊. 中西文化交流先驱——马可波罗［M］. 北京：商务印书馆，1995.
20. 沈福伟. 中西文化交流史［M］. 上海：上海人民出版社，1985.
21. 罗竹风. 宗教通史简编［M］. 上海：华东师范大学出版社，1990.
22. 〔英〕汤因比. 文明经受着考验［M］. 杭州：浙江人民出版社，1988.

23. 〔美〕邓恩. 从利马窦到汤若望——晚明的耶稣会教士［M］. 上海：上海古籍出版社，2003

24. 周春生. 文明史概论［M］. 上海：上海教育出版社，2006.

25. 〔美〕托卡勒. 宗教内部改革刻不容缓［J］. 参考消息，2002.

26. 〔英〕亚·沃尔夫. 18世纪科学、技术和哲学史［M］. 北京：商务印书馆，1991.

27. 〔法〕达特. 十字军东征——以耶路撒冷之名［M］. 上海：上海书店，1998.

28. 〔美〕J.C霍若威. 旅游事业概论［M］. 北京：中国对外经济贸易出版社，1990.

29. 〔德〕格罗塞. 艺术的起源［M］. 北京：商务印书馆，1984.

30. 〔美〕亨廷顿. 文明的冲突与世界秩序的重建［M］. 北京：新华出版社，1999.

31. 裴勇. 文明的整合：开启地球文明的新纪元. 中国博客网 http://column.bokee.com/120582.html.

32. 周民峰. 重新认识世界的文明版图［J］. 深圳特区报，2001.

33. 〔美〕阿尔文·托夫勒. 第三次浪潮［M］. 北京：新华出版社，1996.

34. 〔德〕赫尔穆特·施密特. 全球化与道德重建［M］. 北京：社会科学文献出版社，2001.

35. 费孝通. 创建一个和而不同的全球社会［J］. 新华文摘，2002年第2期.